Communications
in Computer and Information Science   1280

More information about this series at http://www.springer.com/series/7899

Miguel Félix Mata-Rivera ·
Roberto Zagal-Flores ·
Cristian Barria-Huidobro (Eds.)

Telematics and Computing

9th International Congress, WITCOM 2020
Puerto Vallarta, Mexico, November 2–6, 2020
Proceedings

 Springer

Editors
Miguel Félix Mata-Rivera 🆔
Instituto Politécnico Nacional
México, Mexico

Roberto Zagal-Flores 🆔
Instituto Politécnico Nacional
México, Mexico

Cristian Barria-Huidobro 🆔
Universidad Mayor
Santiago de Chile, Chile

ISSN 1865-0929   ISSN 1865-0937 (electronic)
Communications in Computer and Information Science
ISBN 978-3-030-62553-5   ISBN 978-3-030-62554-2 (eBook)
https://doi.org/10.1007/978-3-030-62554-2

This Springer imprint is published by the registered company Springer Nature Switzerland AG
The registered company address is: Gewerbestrasse 11, 6330 Cham, Switzerland

Preface

At the time of writing this volume, the world is facing the COVID-19 pandemic, and the global scientific community is looking for different perspectives and lines of knowledge, to solutions such as vaccines and tools to continue daily life as close to the face-to-face scheme. Nevertheless, research continues to progress, not only in the health contingency (this volume is evidence of this fact), but also in a wide range of knowledge lines such as: deep and machine learning, cybersecurity, wireless networks, computer vision, communications, and of course education applied to different scenarios of study and COVID-19.

The International Congress of Telematics and Computing (WITCOM) conference, as with many events, was developed online and remotely, attracting a large number of students, researchers, and industrialists. The opportunity for meeting and interacting between attendees in a remote way represented challenges, but it was fruitful. These proceedings contain complete research papers. Submissions went through a peer-review process. 79 Research papers were submitted; three members of the Program Committee reviewed each one, and 31 were accepted (an acceptance rate of 40%).

The conference program presented a broad set of session topics that extend beyond the documents contained in these proceedings. The materials for all sessions are available on the conference website at www.witcom.upiita.ipn.mx and www.witcom.org.mx.

It took great effort to review and work in a remote way, and to build all the tracks and workshops of WITCOM 2020 into a consistent program. We want to thank God and all those who contributed to this effort, especially the ANTACOM A.C., who supported the registration fee for all authors, and mainly the students. Of course, thanks go to UPIITA-IPN and the Laboratory of Geospatial Intelligence and Mobile Computing, article authors, session presenters, coordinators, members of the Program Committee, and UPIITA staff and sponsors. Without them, the event would not have been as successful.

November 2020

Miguel Félix Mata-Rivera
Roberto Zagal-Flores
Cristian Barria-Huidobro

Organization

Organizing Committee

General Chair

Miguel Félix Mata-Rivera   UPIITA-IPN, Mexico

Co-chair

Roberto Zagal-Flores   ESCOM-IPN, Mexico

Cybersecurity Track Chair

Cristian Barria-Huidobro   Universidad Mayor, Chile

Local Manager

Jairo Zagal-Flores   UNADM, Mexico

Staff Chair

Sergio Quiroz Almaraz   UNAM and LICEO Pedro de Gante, Mexico

Program Committee (Research Papers)

Christophe Claramunt	Naval Academy Research Institute, France
Cristian Barria	Universidad Mayor, Chile
Lorena Galeazzi	Universidad Mayor, Chile
Claudio Casasolo	Universidad Mayor, Chile
Alejandra Acuña Villalobos	Universidad Mayor, Chile
Clara Burbano	Unicomfacauca, Colombia
Gerardo Rubino	Inria, France
Cesar Viho	IRISA, France
Jose E. Gomez	Université de Grenoble, France
Kenn Arrizabal	Delft University of Technology, The Netherlands
Mario Aldape Perez	CIDETEC-IPN, Mexico
Anzueto Rios Alvaro	UPIITA-IPN, Mexico
Ludovic Moncla	LIUPPA, Université de Pau et des Pays de l'Adour, France
Jose Lopez	Hochschule Furtwangen University, Germany
Shoko Wakamiya	Kyoto Sangyo University, Japan
Patrick Laube	ZAUW, Switzerland
Sergio Ilarri	University of Zaragoza, Spain
Sisi Zlatanova	TU Delft, The Netherlands
Stephan Winter	The University of Melbourne, Australia

Stephen Hirtle	University of Pittsburgh, USA
Steve Liang	University of Calgary, Canada
Tao Cheng	University College, London, UK
Willington Siabato	Universidad Nacional de Colombia, Colombia
Xiang Li	East Normal China University, China
Andrea Ballatore	University of London, UK
Carlos Di Bella	INTA, Argentina
Haosheng Huang	University of Zurich, Switzerland
Hassan Karimi	University of Pittsburgh, USA
Luis Manuel Vilches	CIC-IPN, Mexico
Victor Barrera Figueroa	UPIITA-IPN, Mexico
Blanca Tovar Corona	UPIITA-IPN, Mexico
Thomaz Eduardo Figueiredo Oliveira	CINVESTAV-IPN, Mexico
Hiram Galeana Zapién	Laboratorio de TI, Cinvestav-Tamaulipas, Mexico
Laura Ivoone Garay Jiménez	SEPI-UPIITA, Mexico
Leandro Flórez Aristizábal	UADEO, Mexico
Dulce Loza Pacheco	UNAM, Mexico
Giovanni Guzman Lugo	CIC-IPN, Mexico
Cristian Delgado	UNAM, Mexico
Carlos Hernandez	UPIITA-IPN, Mexico
Itzama Lopez Yañez	CIDETEC-IPN
Mayra Diaz -Sosa	UNAM, Mexico
Jorge Vasconcelos	UNAM, Mexico
Marco Antonio Moreno Ibarra	CIC-IPN, Mexico
Mario H. Ramírez Díaz	CICATA-IPN, Mexico
Mario Eduardo Rivero Ángeles	Communication Networks Laboratory, CIC-IPN, Mexico
Teresa Carrillo	FES Acatlán-UNAM, Mexico
Georgina Eslava	FES Acatlán-UNAM, Mexico
Izlian Orea	UPIITA-IPN, Mexico
Zoraida Palacios	UNIAJC, Mexico
Ingrid Torres	UNAM, Mexico
Miguel Jesus Torres Ruiz	CIC-IPN, Mexico
Rosa Mercado	ESIME UC, Mexico
Blanca Rico	UPIITA-IPN, Mexico
Chadwick Carreto	ESCOM-IPN, Mexico
Ana Herrera	UAQ, Mexico
Hugo Jimenez	CIDESI, Mexico
José-Antonio León-Borges	UQROO, Mexico
Alejandro Molina-Villegas	CENTROGEO, Mexico
Néstor Darío Duque Méndez	UNAL, Colombia
Diego Muñoz	Universidad Mayor, Chile

David Cordero	Universidad Mayor, Chile
Jacobo Gonzalez-Leon	UPIITA-IPN, Mexico
Saul Ortega	Universidad Mayor, Chile
Robinson Osses	Universidad Mayor, Chile
Hugo Lazcano	ECOSUR, Mexico
Daniel Soto	Universidad Mayor, Chile
Gomez-Balderas Jose	GIPSA LAB, France
Carolina Tripp Barba	UAS, Mexico
Iliana Amabely	UPSIN, Mexico
Leonor Espinoza	UAS, Mexico
Diana Castro	ENCB-IPN, Mexico

Sponsors

ANTACOM A.C.
UPIITA-IPN

Collaborators

Alldatum Systems
FES ACATLAN
LICEO Pedro de Gante

Contents

Deep Learning Systems for Automated Segmentation of Brain Tissues
and Tumors in MRIs... 1
Dante Mújica-Vargas, Manuel Matuz-Cruz, Eduardo Ramos-Díaz,
and Jean Marie Vianney Kinani

Tri-Band Log-Periodic Microstrip Antenna Design (2.4, 5.5 and 3.6 GHz
Bands) for Wireless Mobile Devices Application..................... 18
Salvador Ricardo Meneses González
and Rita Trinidad Rodríguez Márquez

Computer Vision Navigation System for an Indoors Unmanned
Aerial Vehicle 30
R. Roman Ibarra, Moisés V. Márquez, Gerardo Martínez,
and Viridiana Hernández

Embedded Human Detection System for Home Security 48
Oscar Arturo González González, Alina Mariana Pérez Soberanes,
Víctor Hugo García Ortega, and Julio César Sosa Savedra

File Restore Automation with Machine Learning.................... 61
Saúl Esquivel-García and Óscar Hernández-Uribe

Open Educational Resource on Responsible, Ethical, Aesthetic
and Functional Learning in Surgery Procedures Requiring Management
of Incisions and Sutures....................................... 73
Margarita Dorado Valencia

On the Computation of Optimized Trading Policies Using Deep
Reinforcement Learning....................................... 83
Uriel Corona-Bermudez, Rolando Menchaca-Mendez,
and Ricardo Menchaca-Mendez

High Data Rate Efficiency Improvement via Variable Length Coding
for LoRaWAN 97
G. A. Yáñez-Casas, I. Medina, J. J. Hernández-Gómez,
M. G. Orozco-del-Castillo, C. Couder-Castañeda,
and R. de-la-Rosa-Rabago

Design of a Watt Mechanism with Crossed Axes 116
Jesus Alvarez-Cedillo, Teodoro Alvarez-Sanchez,
and Mario Aguilar-Fernandez

Learning Analytics in M-learning: Periodontic Education   128
  Diana C. Burbano G. and Jaime Alvarez Soler

Evaluation of a Machine Vision System Applied to Quality Control
in a Liquid Filling, Lid and Labeling Line for Bottles   140
  Julio Eduardo Mejía Manzano, Thalia Alejandra Hoyos Bolaños,
  Miguel Ángel Ortega Muñoz, Victoria Eugenia Patiño Arenas,
  and Helmer Paz Orozco

An Approach for Development and Testing a Reliable Speedometer
Software for Speed Competitions on Motorsport   155
  Luis de Alba González and Óscar Hernández-Uribe

Offline Optimum Tuning of the Proportional Integral Controller for Speed
Regulation of a BLDC Motor Through Bio-inspired Algorithms   169
  Alam Gabriel Rojas-López, Miguel Gabriel Villarreal-Cervantes,
  Alejandro Rodríguez-Molina, and Consuelo Varinia García-Mendoza

Reinforcement Learning Applied to Hexapod Robot Locomotion:
An Overview   185
  Espinosa Jorge, Gorrostieta Efren, Vargas-Soto Emilio,
  and Ramos-Arreguín Juan Manuel

Lockdown or Unlock in COVID-19 Disease? A Reinforcement Learning
Approach   202
  Jacobo Gerardo González León and Miguel Félix Mata Rivera

Cybersecurity Analysis on PACS-DICOM Servers in Chile   215
  David Cordero Vidal and Cristian Barría Huidobro

Experimental Based-Analisis of the Optimal Transmission Thresholds
for WSNs in Noisy Channels   225
  Edgar Romo-Montiel, Mario Eduardo Rivero-Ángeles,
  Ricardo Menchaca-Méndez, Herón Molina-Lozano,
  and Rolando Menchaca-Méndez

A Parallel Rollout Algorithm for Wildfire Suppression   244
  Mauro Montenegro, Roberto López, Rolando Menchaca-Méndez,
  Emanuel Becerra, and Ricardo Menchaca-Méndez

Safety Instructions in a Virtual Machining Process: The Use of Motion
Capture to Develop a VR App for Industrial Safety Purposes   256
  Anna Lucía Díaz Vázquez and Óscar Hernández-Uribe

The Effect of Bilateral Filtering in 3D Reconstruction Using PSP   268
  Luis Arturo Alvarado Escoto, Jesús Carlos Pedraza Ortega,
  Juan Manuel Ramos Arreguin, Efren Gorrostieta Hurtado,
  and Saúl Tovar Arriaga

Regulation of a Van der Pol Oscillator Using Reinforcement Learning   281
  Carlos Emiliano Solórzano-Espíndola, José Ángel Avelar-Barragán,
  and Rolando Menchaca-Mendez

Flow Velocity Estimation by Means Multi-layer Perceptron in a Pipeline. . . .   297
  José Francisco Uribe Vázquez, Héctor Rodríguez Rangel,
  Mario Cesar Maya Rodríguez, René Tolentino Eslava,
  and Eduardo Yudho Montes de Oca

Evolution of COVID-19 Patients in Mexico City Using Markov Chains.   309
  Ricardo C. Villarreal-Calva, Ponciano J. Escamilla-Ambrosio,
  Abraham Rodríguez-Mota, and Juan M. Ramírez-Cortés

Design and Development of Photovoltaic Power Automatic System.   319
  Jaime Vega Pérez, Blanca García, and Nayeli Vega García

Availability Vulnerabilities Evaluation to LoRaWAN   333
  Pamela Beltrán-García, Ponciano Jorge Escamilla-Ambrosio,
  Eleazar Aguirre-Anaya, and Abraham Rodríguez-Mota

LoRa and LoRaWAN Protocol Analysis Using Cupcarbon.   352
  Esau Bermudez Sanchez and Djamel Fawzi Hadj Sadok

Machine Learning Security Assessment Method Based on Adversary
and Attack Methods   377
  Hugo Sebastian Pacheco-Rodríguez, Eleazar Aguirre-Anaya,
  Ricardo Menchaca-Méndez, and Manel Medina-Llinàs

A Novel Approach for Ensemble Feature Selection Using Clustering
with Automatic Threshold   390
  Muhammad Shah Jahan, Anam Amjad, Usman Qamar,
  Muhammad Talha Riaz, and Kashif Ayub

Fuzzy Logic-Based COVID-19 and Other Respiratory Conditions
Pre-clinical Diagnosis System.   402
  M. G. Orozco-del-Castillo, R. A. Novelo-Cruz, J. J. Hernández-Gómez,
  P. A. Mena-Zapata, E. Brito-Borges, A. E. Álvarez-Pacheco,
  A. E. García-Gutiérrez, and G. A. Yáñez-Casas

A Review of the Security Information Controls in Wireless
Networks Wi-Fi   420
  Lorena Galeazzi Ávalos, Cristian Barría Huidobro,
  and Julio Ariel Hurtado

Local Tours Recommendation Applying Machine Learning
in Social Networks   428
   Braulio Medina, Alejandro Pineda, Giovanni Guzmán,
   Laura Ivoone Garay Jimenez, and Miguel Félix Mata Rivera

Author Index   441

Deep Learning Systems for Automated Segmentation of Brain Tissues and Tumors in MRIs

Dante Mújica-Vargas[1]([✉]), Manuel Matuz-Cruz[2], Eduardo Ramos-Díaz[3], and Jean Marie Vianney Kinani[3]

[1] Departamento de Ciencias Computacionales, TecNM/CENIDET, Cuernavaca-Morelos, México
dante.mv@cenidet.tecnm.mx
[2] Departamento de Sistemas Computacionales, TecNM/ITTapachula, Tapachula, Chiapas, México
[3] Instituto Politécnico Nacional-UPIIH, San Agustín Tlaxiaca-Hidalgo, México

Abstract. A pair of fully automatic brain tissue and tumor segmentation frameworks are introduced in current paper, these consist of a parallel and cascade architectures of a specialized convolutional deep neural network designed to develop binary segmentation. The main contributions of this proposal imply their ability to segment Magnetic Resonance Imaging (MRI) of the brain, of different acquisition modes without any parameter, they do not require any preprocessing stage to improve the quality of each slice. Experimental tests were developed considering BraTS 2017 database. The robustness and effectiveness of this proposal is verified by quantitative and qualitative results.

Keywords: Magnetic resonance imaging of the brain · Tissues and tumor segmentation · Convolutional deep neural network

1 Introduction

Magnetic resonance imaging is a medical modality used to guide the diagnosis process and the treatment planning. To do so, it needs to develop the images or slices segmentation, in order to detect and characterize the lesions, as well as to visualize and quantify the pathology severity. Based on their experiences and knowledge, medical specialists make a subjective interpretation of this type of images; in other words, a manual segmentation is performed. This task is long, painstaking and subject to human variability. Brain tumor segmentation is one of the crucial steps for surgery planning and treatment evaluation. Despite the great amount of effort being put to address this challenging problem in the past two decades, segmentation of brain tumor remains to be one of the most challenging tasks in medical image analysis. This is due to both the intrinsic nature of the tumor tissue being heterogeneous and the extrinsic problems with

© Springer Nature Switzerland AG 2020
M. F. Mata-Rivera et al. (Eds.): WITCOM 2020, CCIS 1280, pp. 1–17, 2020.
https://doi.org/10.1007/978-3-030-62554-2_1

unsatisfactory image quality of clinical MRI scans. For example, the tumor mass of a glioma patient, the most common brain tumor, often consists of peritumoral edema, necrotic core, enhancing and non-enhancing tumor core. In addition to the complicated tumor tissue pattern, the MRI images can be further corrupted with a slowly varying bias field and/or motion artifacts, etc. Brain MRIs in most cases do not have well-defined limits between the elements that compose them; in addition, they include non-soft tissues, as well as artifacts that can hinder segmentation. Despite all these inherent conditions, numerous automatic algorithms or techniques have been developed and introduced in state-of-the-art. Among approaches exclusively designed to segment the brain tissues stand out those that are based on the paradigm of fuzzy clustering as well as all its variants [1–4,28]. With the same purpose, hybrid methods based on combinations of different paradigms of machine learning and optimization algorithms have also been presented, e.g. [5–7]. On the other hand, methods designed to segment brain tumors or other abnormalities have also been introduced, among which one can refer to [8–14,29]. For this task it is possible to affirm that in the state-of-the-art the proposals based on Deep Learning are the most novel and have the best results. The majority of these proposals yielded a high performance in the image processing task, specifically when these were brain magnetic resonance images. Nevertheless, after the pertinent analysis it was noted that most methods of them suffer from one or more challenges such as: training need, special handcrafted features (local or global), sensitive to initializations, many parameters that require a tuning, various processing stages, designed to segment just *T1*-weighted brain MRI images, among others. In this research paper, we concentrate on brain tissues and tumors segmentation in magnetic resonance images. For that purpose we introduce a system consisting in a cascade of U-Net models enhanced with a fusion information approach, this proposal can be considered an extension to the one presented in [29], as well as a formalization of theoretical concepts. The introduced proposal has the following special features in contrast with those above-mentioned: 1) it is able to segment RMIs with different relaxation times such as *T1, T2, T1ce* and *Flair*, 2) it is easily adaptable to segment brain tumors, 3) it does not require the initialization of any parameter, such as the number of regions in which the slice will be segmented, 4) it does not require any preprocessing stage to improve the segmentation quality of each slice and 5) it does not need various processing stages to increase its performance. The rest of this paper is organized as follow. A mathematical formulation of U-Net is introduced in detail in Sect. 2. The parallel and cascade architectures of Convolutional Neural Networks are introduced in Sect. 3. Experimental results and a comparative analysis with other current methods in the literature are presented in Sect. 4. In the final section the Conclusions are drawn and future work is outlined.

2   U-Net: Convolutional Networks for Biomedical Image Segmentation

Deep neural networks have shown remarkable success in domains such as image classification [6,15], object detection and localization [17–19], language processing applications [20,21], speech recognition [22], medical image processing [16,23,24], among many others. In the deep learning paradigm, Convolutional Neural Networks (CNNs) outstands as the major architecture, they deploy convolution operations on hidden layers for weight sharing and parameter reduction, in order to extract local information from grid-like input data. In simple words, they process de information by means of hierarchical layers in order to understand representations and features from data in increasing levels of complexity.

For biomedical image segmentation, U-Net is one of the most important architectures that have been introduced in the state of the art [25]. It is a fully convolutional neural network model originally designed to develop a binary segmentation; that is, the main object and the background of the image. This network is divided into two parts, in the first part, the images are subjected to a downward sampling (Contracting Path or Encoder), by means of convolution operations with a kernel of 3×3 each followed by a rectified linear unit (ReLU) and a maximum grouping layer of 2×2. The next part of the model (Expanding Path or Decoder) consists of layers of deconvolution and convolution with 2×2 kernel, finally the output will correspond to a specific class of objects to be segmented. The processing implies nineteen convolutions ($\mathcal{C}$), four subsamplings ($\mathcal{S}$), four upsamplings ($\mathcal{U}$) and four mergings ($\mathcal{M}$). To understand the model variant that we propose to segment brain tumors from BraTS 2017, it can be see Fig. 1.

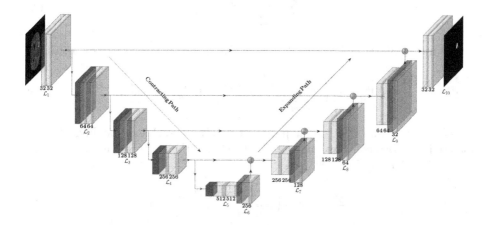

Fig. 1. U-Net model.

In the **Contracting Path**: *Layer 1* is a convolution layer which takes input image X of size 240×240 and convolves it with 32 filters of size 3×3; producing 32 feature maps of 240×240. In order to make the output of linear operation nonlinear, it is advisable to output of convolution operation is passed through a Rectified Linear Units (ReLU) activation function $\sigma(x) = \max(0, x)$, in this way:

$$C1_{i,j}^k = \sigma \left(\sum_{m=0}^{2} \sum_{n=0}^{2} w_{m,n}^k * X_{i+m,j+n} + b^k \right) \tag{1}$$

where $C1^k$ stands for k-th output feature map in $C1$ layer, (m,n) are the indices of the k-th kernel (filter), while that (i,j) are the indices of output. $C1_{i,j}^k$ is convolved with 32 kernels of size 3×3; in the same way, the output is rectified:

$$C2_{i,j}^k = \sigma \left(\sum_{d=0}^{31} \sum_{m=0}^{2} \sum_{n=0}^{2} w_{m,n}^{k,d} * C1_{i+m,j+n}^d + b^k \right) \tag{2}$$

In *Layer 2*, the output of the convolution layer $C2^k$ is fed to max-pooling layer $S1^k = \max \text{Pool} \left(C2^k \right)$. For each feature map in $C2^k$, max-pooling performs the following operation:

$$S1_{i,j}^k = \max \left(\begin{matrix} C2_{2i,2j}^k & C2_{2i+1,2j}^k \\ C2_{2i,2j+1}^k & C2_{2i+1,2j+1}^k \end{matrix} \right) \tag{3}$$

where (i,j) are the indices of k-th feature map of output, and k is the feature map index. The output consists in 32 feature maps with size of 120×120, which implies one-half the size of the input image $(X/2)$. $S1^k$ is convolved with 64 kernels of size 3×3, and the result is rectified:

$$C3_{i,j}^k = \sigma \left(\sum_{d=0}^{63} \sum_{m=0}^{2} \sum_{n=0}^{2} w_{m,n}^{k,d} * S1_{i+m,j+n}^d + b^k \right) \tag{4}$$

By means of 64 3×3 filters $C3^k$ is convolved, and then the results is rectified:

$$C4_{i,j}^k = \sigma \left(\sum_{d=0}^{63} \sum_{m=0}^{2} \sum_{n=0}^{2} w_{m,n}^{k,d} * C3_{i+m,j+n}^d + b^k \right) \tag{5}$$

Layers 3, 4 and *5* a similar process than *Layer 2*. A max-pooling filtering followed that two convolutional stages along with their respective linear rectification. In brief, for *Layer 3*:

$$S2_{i,j}^k = \max \left(\begin{matrix} C4_{2i,2j}^k & C4_{2i+1,2j}^k \\ C4_{2i,2j+1}^k & C4_{2i+1,2j+1}^k \end{matrix} \right) \tag{6}$$

with size $(X/4)$ is convolved with 128×128 kernels with size 3×3 kernel in order to obtain 128×128 feature maps:

$$C5_{i,j}^k = \sigma \left(\sum_{d=0}^{127} \sum_{m=0}^{2} \sum_{n=0}^{2} w_{m,n}^{k,d} * S2_{i+m,j+n}^d + b^k \right) \tag{7}$$

$$\mathcal{C}6_{i,j}^k = \sigma \left(\sum_{d=0}^{127} \sum_{m=0}^{2} \sum_{n=0}^{2} w_{m,n}^{k,d} * \mathcal{C}5_{i+m,j+n}^d + b^k \right) \tag{8}$$

For *Layer 4*, the max-pooling filtering on $\mathcal{C}6^k$ is calculated as:

$$\mathcal{S}3_{i,j}^k = \max \begin{pmatrix} \mathcal{C}6_{2i,2j}^k & \mathcal{C}6_{2i+1,2j}^k \\ \mathcal{C}6_{2i,2j+1}^k & \mathcal{C}6_{2i+1,2j+1}^k \end{pmatrix} \tag{9}$$

The result with size $(X/8)$ is convolved with 3×3 size 256×256 kernels to obtain same number of rectified feature maps:

$$\mathcal{C}7_{i,j}^k = \sigma \left(\sum_{d=0}^{255} \sum_{m=0}^{2} \sum_{n=0}^{2} w_{m,n}^{k,d} * \mathcal{S}3_{i+m,j+n}^d + b^k \right) \tag{10}$$

$$\mathcal{C}8_{i,j}^k = \sigma \left(\sum_{d=0}^{255} \sum_{m=0}^{2} \sum_{n=0}^{2} w_{m,n}^{k,d} * \mathcal{C}7_{i+m,j+n}^d + b^k \right) \tag{11}$$

Last layer in contracting path takes as input $\mathcal{C}8^k$, and performances a downsampling to reduce the feature maps into 15×15 size (i.e. $X/16$), the filter is given as:

$$\mathcal{S}4_{i,j}^k = \max \begin{pmatrix} \mathcal{C}8_{2i,2j}^k & \mathcal{C}8_{2i+1,2j}^k \\ \mathcal{C}8_{2i,2j+1}^k & \mathcal{C}8_{2i+1,2j+1}^k \end{pmatrix} \tag{12}$$

A 3×3 pair of kernels are considered to extract the deepest features, for that purpose $\mathcal{S}4^k$ is convolved with 512 kernels, and the result is once again convolved with other 512 kernels, in both cases it is necessary to consider a linear rectification to avoid negative numbers, these operations are given as:

$$\mathcal{C}9_{i,j}^k = \sigma \left(\sum_{d=0}^{511} \sum_{m=0}^{2} \sum_{n=0}^{2} w_{m,n}^{k,d} * \mathcal{S}4_{i+m,j+n}^d + b^k \right) \tag{13}$$

$$\mathcal{C}10_{i,j}^k = \sigma \left(\sum_{d=0}^{511} \sum_{m=0}^{2} \sum_{n=0}^{2} w_{m,n}^{k,d} * \mathcal{C}9_{i+m,j+n}^d + b^k \right) \tag{14}$$

In the **Expanding Path**: *Layer 6* develops an un-pooling process by means of nearest interpolation with an up-sampling factor of $\uparrow_2$ for rows and columns. In short, it repeats twice each row and column of the k-th feature map:

$$\mathcal{U}1_{i,j}^k = \begin{bmatrix} \mathcal{C}10_{2i,2j}^k & \mathcal{C}10_{2i,2j}^k \\ \mathcal{C}10_{2i,2j}^k & \mathcal{C}10_{2i,2j}^k \end{bmatrix} \tag{15}$$

$\mathcal{U}1^k$ makes that the k-th feature map increase its size to $X/8$. *Layers 6* and *4* are merged such as a concatenation process, i.e.:

$$\mathcal{M}1_{i,j}^k = \begin{bmatrix} \mathcal{U}1_{i,j}^k; & \mathcal{C}8_{i,j}^k \end{bmatrix} \tag{16}$$

$\mathcal{M}1^k$ consists of 768×768 feature maps. In *Layer 7*, $\mathcal{M}1^k$ is in the first instance convolved with 256×256 kernels with a size of 3×3, each of the results is rectified in order to avoid negative numbers:

$$\mathcal{C}11^k_{i,j} = \sigma \left(\sum_{d=0}^{255} \sum_{m=0}^{2} \sum_{n=0}^{2} w^{k,d}_{m,n} * \mathcal{M}1^d_{i+m,j+n} + b^k \right) \tag{17}$$

$$\mathcal{C}12^k_{i,j} = \sigma \left(\sum_{d=0}^{255} \sum_{m=0}^{2} \sum_{n=0}^{2} w^{k,d}_{m,n} * \mathcal{C}11^d_{i+m,j+n} + b^k \right) \tag{18}$$

Afterwards, (18) is up-sampling with a $\uparrow_2$ factor in order to increase the feature maps to an $X/4$ size:

$$\mathcal{U}2^k_{i,j} = \begin{bmatrix} \mathcal{C}12^k_{2i,2j} & \mathcal{C}12^k_{2i,2j} \\ \mathcal{C}12^k_{2i,2j} & \mathcal{C}12^k_{2i,2j} \end{bmatrix} \tag{19}$$

Outflows of *Layers 7* and *3* are concatenated as:

$$\mathcal{M}2^k_{i,j} = [\mathcal{U}2^k_{i,j}; \mathcal{C}6^k_{i,j}] \tag{20}$$

$\mathcal{M}2^k$ consists of 384×384 feature maps. *Layers 8* and *9* follow a similar processing than *Layer 7*; but with a decreasing of feature maps number. In this regard, for *Layer 8*:

$$\mathcal{C}13^k_{i,j} = \sigma \left(\sum_{d=0}^{127} \sum_{m=0}^{2} \sum_{n=0}^{2} w^{k,d}_{m,n} * \mathcal{M}1^d_{i+m,j+n} + b^k \right) \tag{21}$$

$$\mathcal{C}14^k_{i,j} = \sigma \left(\sum_{d=0}^{127} \sum_{m=0}^{2} \sum_{n=0}^{2} w^{k,d}_{m,n} * \mathcal{C}13^d_{i+m,j+n} + b^k \right) \tag{22}$$

$$\mathcal{U}3^k_{i,j} = \begin{bmatrix} \mathcal{C}14^k_{2i,2j} & \mathcal{C}14^k_{2i,2j} \\ \mathcal{C}14^k_{2i,2j} & \mathcal{C}14^k_{2i,2j} \end{bmatrix} \tag{23}$$

$\mathcal{U}3^k$ makes that all feature maps increase their size to $X/2$. $\mathcal{U}3^k$ is concatenated with $\mathcal{C}4^k$, the output implies 192×192 features maps:

$$\mathcal{M}3^k_{i,j} = [\mathcal{U}3^k_{i,j}; \mathcal{C}4^k_{i,j}] \tag{24}$$

For *Layer 9*:

$$\mathcal{C}15^k_{i,j} = \sigma \left(\sum_{d=0}^{63} \sum_{m=0}^{2} \sum_{n=0}^{2} w^{k,d}_{m,n} * \mathcal{M}3^d_{i+m,j+n} + b^k \right) \tag{25}$$

$$\mathcal{C}16^k_{i,j} = \sigma \left(\sum_{d=0}^{63} \sum_{m=0}^{2} \sum_{n=0}^{2} w^{k,d}_{m,n} * \mathcal{C}15^d_{i+m,j+n} + b^k \right) \tag{26}$$

$$\mathcal{U}4_{i,j}^{k} = \begin{bmatrix} \mathcal{C}16_{2i,2j}^{k} & \mathcal{C}16_{2i,2j}^{k} \\ \mathcal{C}16_{2i,2j}^{k} & \mathcal{C}16_{2i,2j}^{k} \end{bmatrix} \tag{27}$$

Last up-sampling process $\mathcal{U}4^{k}$ makes that all feature maps increase their size to X. $\mathcal{U}4^{k}$ is concatenated with $\mathcal{C}2^{k}$:

$$\mathcal{M}4_{i,j}^{k} = [\mathcal{U}4_{i,j}^{k}; \mathcal{C}2_{i,j}^{k}] \tag{28}$$

$\mathcal{M}4^{k}$ implies 96×96 features maps, these are convolved with 32×32 kernels with size 3×3:

$$\mathcal{C}17_{i,j}^{k} = \sigma \left(\sum_{d=0}^{31} \sum_{m=0}^{2} \sum_{n=0}^{2} w_{m,n}^{k,d} * \mathcal{M}4_{i+m,j+n}^{d} + b^{k} \right) \tag{29}$$

$$\mathcal{C}18_{i,j}^{k} = \sigma \left(\sum_{d=0}^{31} \sum_{m=0}^{2} \sum_{n=0}^{2} w_{m,n}^{k,d} * \mathcal{C}17_{i+m,j+n}^{d} + b^{k} \right) \tag{30}$$

Last convolution layer convolves $\mathcal{C}18^{k}$ with 32 kernels of size 1×1, the linear activation function is replaced by a Sigmoid one, $\sigma(x) = \dfrac{1}{1 + \exp^{-x}}$; this function lets to highlight the region of interest (region to be segmented) in the segmented image $\check{X}$, since it squashes to $\mathcal{C}18^{k}$ into the range $[0, 1]$. In this way:

$$\check{X}_{i,j} = \sigma \left(\sum_{d=0}^{31} \sum_{m=0}^{1} \sum_{n=0}^{1} w_{m,n}^{k,d} * \mathcal{C}18_{i+m,j+n}^{d} + b^{k} \right) \tag{31}$$

The segmented image $\check{X}$ has a size 240×240 such as the input image X. Expressions (1) to (31) let us to depict how CNNs follow a hierarchical processing to extract specific features in order to detect and segment specific regions; in this case, brain tumors.

3 Deep Learning Systems for Brain Image Segmentation

3.1 Proposed Parallel System for Brain Tissues Segmentation

Conventionally, it may be assumed that different tissues can be found in a MRI slice: (1) White Matter (WM), (2) Gray Matter (GM), (3) Cerebral Spinal Fluid (CSF) and (4) Abnormalities (ABN). Nevertheless, it should be clarified that depending on the slice, not all regions may be present or the magnitude of their presence will be variant. In order to develop an automatic soft tissues recognition and their segmentation we suggest the system depicted in Fig. 2; it is basically comprised by four U-Nets models trained to work on a specific soft. After each tissue segmentation, it is necessary to perform the joint area representation by means of a method that determines appropriately the target and background region. From following rules [26], it is possible to perform the fusion of the segmented tissues, the background fusion, as well as the fusion of the detected and regions:

1. If R^1 and R^2 do not intersect, two regions are formed in the representation of joint area, that is $R_1^3 = R^1$ and $R_2^3 = R^2$.
2. If R_1 and R_2 are partly intersected, three regions are formed in the representation of joint area, that is $R_1^3 = R^1 \cap R^2$, $R_2^3 = R^1 - R_1^3$, $R_3^3 = R^2 - R_1^3$.
3. If there is an area that is completely include, such as $R^1 \subset R^2$, then two regions are formed in the representation of joint area, that is $R_1^3 = R^2$ and $R_2^3 = R^2 - R_1^3$.

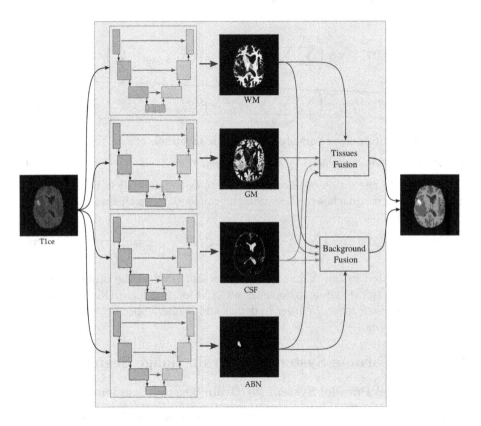

Fig. 2. Parallel deep learning system for tissues segmentation.

The operation of proposed scheme is quite intuitive, in the first instance any slice of a study must be entered into the system, then a binary segmentation is developed by each U-Net model. That is, all of them have to identify the pixels that correspond to the tissue for which it was trained, and therefore must be able to segment it. After that, the binary segmented images are merged in order to obtain the final segmentation. Two remarks must be stated: (1) Depending on the slice number, the different tissues should appear; in this situation, if the input image does not contain certain specific tissue, the U-Net in charge of segmenting it will return the corresponding label to the background of the image as a result. (2) If the study corresponds to a healthy patient, then there will be no abnormality or tumor, in the same way as in the previous remark, the result should be the label of the image background. This adaptive capacity of the proposed scheme allows it to be able to segment all slices of a complete medical study, automatically and without human assistance.

3.2 Proposed Cascade System for Brain Tumors Segmentation

To address the automatic brain tumor segmentation in multimodal MRI of high-grade (HG) glioma patients, a variation of the proposed previous system should be considered, since the information provided by the tissues is not sufficient to detect and segment correctly a brain tumor. In this regard, other modalities T1, T1 contrast-enhanced, T2 and Flair must be taking into account. How it was stated in [27], Enhancing Tumor (ET) structure is visible in T1ce, whereas the Tumor Core (TC) is in T2, and Whole Tumor (WT) by means of FLAIR. In view of this, the proposal to detect an segment these sub-regions is illustrated in Fig. 3.

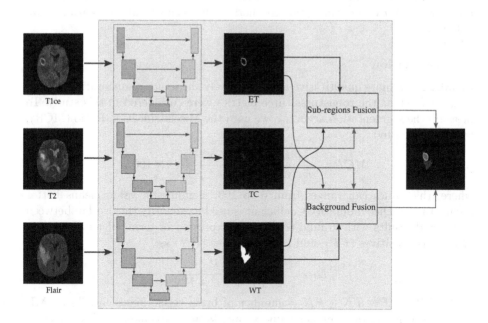

Fig. 3. Cascade deep learning system for tumor segmentation.

As can be seen, these is an U-Net trained for segmenting a specific glioma sub-region; then, the binary outputs are fused to reshape whole brain tumor, based on three rules stated in Subsect. (3.1). It is necessary to point out that although both methods are based on the same deep neural network, they cannot be used alternately, since the first model must be trained to identify and segment the soft tissues of the brain, while the second is trained to detect and segment the sub-regions of the gliomas and therefore reconstruct a brain tumor. As is well known, CNNs from the input information but with a specific objective.

4   Experimental Setup

4.1   Data

In this research paper, it was considered BraTS2017 database. In specific, 210 pre-operative MRI scans of subjects with glioblastoma (GBM/HGG) were used for training and 75 scans of subjects with lower grade glioma (LGG) were used for testing the proposed system. Each study has RMIs in modalities T1, T1ce, T2 and Flair, as well as their respective ground truth images, for each modality there are 155 images of 8-bits with a size of 240×240 pixels.

4.2   Training

In order to obtain the best results in the test phase it is suggested for BraTS2017 database: a) gray-scale of $8-$ bits, b) TIFF image format, c) Adaptive Moment Estimation (ADAM) optimization method, d) 1000 epochs and e) learning rate of 0.001.

4.3   Evaluation

In order to evaluate quantitative and objectively the image segmentation performance as well as the robustness three metrics were considered in this study. To measure the segmentation accuracy, we used the Misclassification Ratio (MCR), which is given by:

$$MCR = \frac{misclassified\ pixels}{overall\ number\ of\ pixels} \times 100 \tag{32}$$

where, the values can ranges from 0 to 100, a minimum value means better segmentation. Dice Similarity Coefficient is used to quantify the overlap between segmented results with ground-truth; it is expressed in terms of true positives (TP), false positives (FP), and false negatives (FN) as:

$$Dice = \frac{2 \cdot TP}{2 \cdot TP + FP + FN} \tag{33}$$

where $TP + FP + TN + FN$ = number of brain tissue pixels in a brain MR image. In this metric a higher value means better agreement with respect to ground-truth. In addition to stated metrics, the Intersection-Over-Union (IOU) metric was also considered. This is defined by:

$$IOU = \frac{TP}{TP + FP + FN} \tag{34}$$

The IOU metric takes values in $[0, 1]$ with a value of 1 indicating a perfect segmentation.

5   Results and Discussion

5.1   Tissues Segmentation

A convincing way to know the true performance of the proposed method is to subject it to the task of tissues segmentation of real brain magnetic resonance images. In this regard, the first experiment is related with the segmentation of images with modalities T1, T1ce, T2 and Flair taken from the BraTS-2017 database; specifically, the Low-grade Gliomas Brats17_TCIA_420_1 study.

The performance of the proposed Parallel and Cascade Deep Learning Systems (for convenience they will be identified as P-DLS and C-DLS, respectively) is compared with other methods designed to segment brain tissues, which were mentioned previously in the introductory section, such as the Chaotic Firefly Integrated Fuzzy C-Means (C-FAFCM) [2], Discrete Cosine Transform Based Local and Nonlocal FCM (DCT-LNLFCM) [4], Generalized Rough Intutionistic Fuzzy C-Means (GRIFCM) [3], Particle Swarm Optimization - Kernelized Fuzzy Entropy Clustering with Spatial Information and Bias Correction (PSO-KFECSB) [7]. All of them were implemented in the MATLAB R2018a environment, while for ours we used CUDA+CuDNN+TensorFlow+ Keras, that is, conventional frameworks and libraries for Deep Learning, as well as a GPU Nvidia Titan X.

The quantitative evaluation was done considering the MCR, Dice and IOU metrics. A summary of these is presented in Table 1. The numerical results reveal a superior performance of the segmentation method proposed in all the metrics considered, as well as all exposition modalities.

Table 1. Average performance on Brats17_TCIA_420_1 study.

Modality	Metric	C-FAFCM	DCT-LNLFCM	GRIFCM	PSO-KFECSB	P-DLS
T1	MCR	8.042	8.991	9.274	10.181	**7.132**
	Dice	0.899	0.892	0.879	0.827	**0.915**
	IOU	0.911	0.905	0.880	0.840	**0.924**
T1ce	MCR	8.937	10.412	10.402	11.698	**7.388**
	Dice	0.891	0.864	0.853	0.814	**0.908**
	IOU	0.895	0.868	0.853	0.818	**0.911**
T2	MCR	9.294	9.500	9.638	10.487	**7.491**
	Dice	0.886	0.846	0.876	0.805	**0.907**
	IOU	0.894	0.855	0.877	0.814	**0.914**
Flair	MCR	9.743	10.797	9.015	11.321	**7.621**
	Dice	0.872	0.800	0.862	0.783	**0.899**
	IOU	0.880	0.809	0.863	0.792	**0.905**

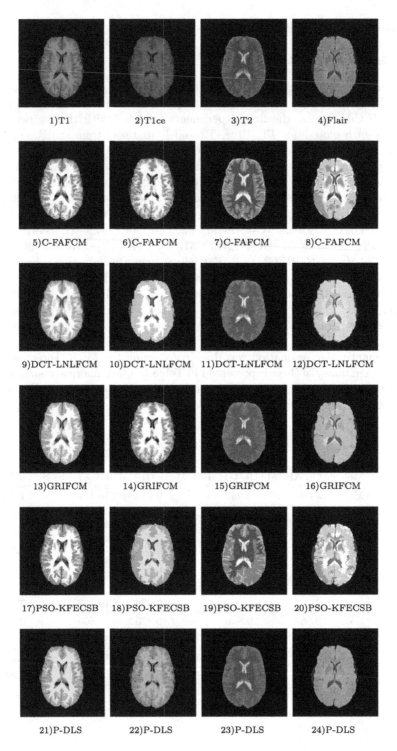

Fig. 4. Tissues segmentation sample results of Brats17_TCIA_420_1 study.

A sample image and the segmentation provided by all algorithms evaluated in this experiment are depicted in Fig. 4, it is possible to see that just the proposed algorithm was able to segment images with different modalities. On the other hand, all the other methods presented problems of loss of information in the segmented regions, and in some cases they were not even able to segment the images in the 4 established regions. In brief, a good segmentation of the images in these modalities can guarantee the identification and segmentation of brain tumors.

5.2 Tumor Segmentation

Second experiment is related with Multimodal Brain Tumor Segmentation, with the aim to detect and segment the sub-regions: ET, WT and TC. In this respect, the proposed cascade system is used (see Fig. 3). In order to make a comparison of system performance, some methods based on deep learning are considered; particularly, Multi-dimensional Gated Recurrent Units for Brain Tumor Segmentation (MD-GRU-BTS) [10], Masked V-Net (MV-N) [11], 3D Deep Detection-Classification Model (3DDD-CM) [12], Ensembles of Multiple Models and Architectures (EMMA) [13] and Deep U-Net (DU-N) [14]. The quantitative evaluation is made from the studies CBICA_ATX_1 and TCIA_639_1 considering the metrics established previously, a summary of the obtained results is given in Table 2 and Table 3, respectively.

Table 2. Average performance on the CBICA_ATX_1 study.

Approach	ET			WT			TC		
	MCR	Dice	IOU	MCR	Dice	IOU	MCR	Dice	IOU
MD-GRU-BTS	10.762	0.833	0.872	12.213	0.797	0.822	10.409	0.841	0.856
MV-N	11.531	0.793	0.811	12.639	0.757	0.774	10.756	0.831	0.834
3DDD-CM	14.028	0.768	0.860	14.657	0.734	0.784	12.687	0.783	0.792
EMMA	15.451	0.709	0.745	15.633	0.675	0.702	13.748	0.732	0.740
DU-N	12.553	0.755	0.816	13.855	0.755	0.767	12.457	0.778	0.790
C-DLS	**10.182**	**0.863**	**0.882**	**11.511**	**0.835**	**0.846**	**9.585**	**0.876**	**0.889**

Table 3. Average performance on the TCIA_639_1 study.

Approach	ET			WT			TC		
	MCR	Dice	IOU	MCR	Dice	IOU	MCR	Dice	IOU
MD-GRU-BTS	11.809	0.810	0.842	12.440	0.768	0.776	12.648	0.826	0.843
MV-N	11.934	0.789	0.830	13.279	0.753	0.765	14.010	0.820	0.846
3DDD-CM	13.183	0.747	0.787	15.404	0.704	0.704	13.141	0.771	0.784
EMMA	12.981	0.689	0.704	14.851	0.654	0.681	11.153	0.772	0.819
DU-N	14.238	0.753	0.784	15.901	0.752	0.756	18.270	0.763	0.774
C-DLS	**10.227**	**0.841**	**0.850**	**11.877**	**0.826**	**0.829**	**10.119**	**0.875**	**0.869**

14   D. Mújica-Vargas et al.

The numerical results reveal a superior performance of the segmentation method proposed in all the metrics considered for three tumor sub-regions. In brief, for CBICA_ATX_1 study the proposed system obtained $9.585 \leq MCR \leq 11.511$, $0.835 \leq Dice \leq 0.876$ and $0.846 \leq IOU \leq 0.889$; whilst for other study results showed a slight change, i.e. $10.119 \leq MCR \leq 11.877$, $0.875 \leq Dice \leq 0.826$ and $0.829 \leq IOU \leq 0.869$. Although all the methods evaluated are based on the use of deep neural networks, the fusion of information that we consider in our proposal helped to increase its performance. To ratify and illustrate the quantitative results obtained, it can be seen in Fig. 5, samples 71 of the first study and 127 of the second study, where a segmentation closer to ground-truth can be seen. It can also be seen that some of the comparative methods could not correctly identify and segment the three sub-regions considered.

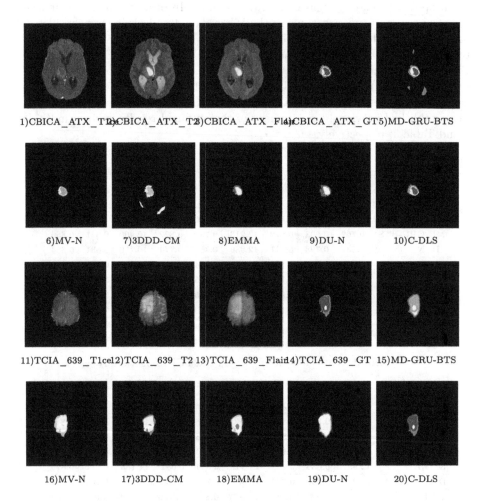

1)CBICA_ATX_T1ce 2)CBICA_ATX_T2 3)CBICA_ATX_Flair 4)CBICA_ATX_GT 5)MD-GRU-BTS

6)MV-N   7)3DDD-CM   8)EMMA   9)DU-N   10)C-DLS

11)TCIA_639_T1ce 12)TCIA_639_T2 13)TCIA_639_Flair 14)TCIA_639_GT 15)MD-GRU-BTS

16)MV-N   17)3DDD-CM   18)EMMA   19)DU-N   20)C-DLS

Fig. 5. Tumor segmentation sample results of CBICA_ATX_1 and TCIA_639_1 studies.

6 Conclusions and Future Improvements

Based on the U-Net CNN, it was introduced a parallel system to detect and segment tissues on RMIs with different modalities; considering the same idea, a cascade version was proposed to detect and segment brain tumors. Both systems were enhanced by means three fusion rules in order to do a better job. The first proposal was able to segment different modalities of real RMI images degraded inherent noise densities. Instead, the second proposal was able to detect and segment the ET, WT and TC sub-regions of a brain tumor, with a superior performance than all comparative methods. As future work, we will consider proposing a deep neural network that can perform both tasks simultaneously.

Acknowledgments. The authors thank to CONACYT, as well as Tecnológico Nacional de México/Centro Nacional de Investigación y Desarrollo Tecnológico for their financial support trough the project so-called "Controlador Difuso para ajuste de coeficientes de rigidez de un modelo deformable para simulación en tiempo real de los tejidos del hígado humano".

References

1. Ganesh, M., Naresh, M., Arvind, C.: MRI brain image segmentation using enhanced adaptive fuzzy K-means algorithm. Intell. Autom. Soft Comput. **23**(2), 325–330 (2017)
2. Ghosh, P., Mali, K., Das, S.K.: Chaotic firefly algorithm-based fuzzy C-means algorithm for segmentation of brain tissues in magnetic resonance images. J. Vis. Commun. Image Represent. **54**, 63–79 (2018)
3. Namburu, A., Samayamantula, S.K., Edara, S.R.: Generalised rough intuitionistic fuzzy c-means for magnetic resonance brain image segmentation. IET Image Proc. **11**(9), 777–785 (2017)
4. Singh, C., Bala, A.: A DCT-based local and non-local fuzzy C-means algorithm for segmentation of brain magnetic resonance images. Appl. Soft Comput. **68**, 447–457 (2018)
5. Narayanan, A., Rajasekaran, M.P., Zhang, Y., Govindaraj, V., Thiyagarajan, A.: Multi-channeled MR brain image segmentation: a novel double optimization approach combined with clustering technique for tumor identification and tissue segmentation. Biocybern. Biomed. Eng. **39**(2), 350–381 (2019)
6. Pham, T.X., Siarry, P., Oulhadj, H.: Integrating fuzzy entropy clustering with an improved PSO for MRI brain image segmentation. Appl. Soft Comput. **65**, 230–242 (2018)
7. Senthilkumar, C., Gnanamurthy, R.K.: A Fuzzy clustering based MRI brain image segmentation using back propagation neural networks. Cluster Comput. **22**(5), 12305–12312 (2018). https://doi.org/10.1007/s10586-017-1613-x
8. Angulakshmi, M., Lakshmi Priya, G.G.: Brain tumour segmentation from MRI using superpixels based spectral clustering. J. King Saud Univ. Comput. Inf. Sci. 1–12 (2018). https://www.sciencedirect.com/science/article/pii/S1319157817303476

9. Charron, O., Lallement, A., Jarnet, D., Noblet, V., Clavier, J.-B., Meyer, P.: Automatic detection and segmentation of brain metastases on multimodal MR images with a deep convolutional neural network. Comput. Biol. Med. **95**, 43–54 (2018)

10. Andermatt, S., Pezold, S., Cattin, P.: Multi-dimensional gated recurrent units for brain tumor segmentation. In: International MICCAI BraTS Challenge. Pre-Conference Proceedings, pp. 15-19 (2017)

11. Marcel, C., et al.: Masked V-Net: an approach to brain tumor segmentation. In: International MICCAI BraTS Challenge. Pre-Conference Proceedings, pp. 42-49 (2017)

12. Hu, Y., Xia, Y.: Automated brain tumor segmentation using a 3D deep detection-classification model, pp. 94–99 (2017)

13. Kamnitsas, K., et al.: Ensembles of multiple models and architectures for robust brain tumour segmentation. In: Crimi, A., Bakas, S., Kuijf, H., Menze, B., Reyes, M. (eds.) BrainLes 2017. LNCS, vol. 10670, pp. 450–462. Springer, Cham (2018). https://doi.org/10.1007/978-3-319-75238-9_38

14. Kim, G.: Brain tumor segmentation using deep u-net. In: International MICCAI BraTS Challenge. Pre-Conference Proceedings, pp. 154–160 (2017)

15. Krizhevsky, A., Sutskever, I., Hinton, G.E.: ImageNet classification with deep convolutional neural networks. Commun. ACM **60**(6), 84–90 (2017)

16. Qi, R., et al.: Pointnet: deep learning on point sets for 3D classification and segmentation. In: Proceedings of the IEEE Conference on Computer Vision and Pattern Recognition, pp. 652-660 (2017)

17. Girshick, R., Donahue, J., Darrell, T., Malik, J.: Region-based convolutional networks for accurate object detection and segmentation. IEEE Trans. Pattern Anal. Mach. Intell. **38**(1), 142–158 (2016)

18. Uijlings, J.R.R., van de Sande, K.E.A., Gevers, T., Smeulders, A.W.M.: Selective search for object recognition. Int. J. Comput. Vis. **104**(2), 154–171 (2013). https://doi.org/10.1007/s11263-013-0620-5

19. Ren, S., He, K., Girshick, R., Sun, J.: Faster R-CNN: towards real-time object detection with region proposal networks. IEEE Trans. Pattern Anal. Mach. Intell. **39**(6), 1137–1149 (2017)

20. Sutskever, I., Vinyals, O., Le, V.: Sequence to sequence learning with neural networks. In: Advances in Neural Information Processing Systems, pp. 3104–3112 (2014)

21. Bahdanau, D., Cho, K., Bengio, Y.: Neural machine translation by jointly learning to align and translate. arXiv preprint arXiv:1409.0473 (2014)

22. Saon G., et al.: English conversational telephone speech recognition by humans and machines. arXiv preprint arXiv:1703.02136 (2014)

23. Tran, P.V.: A fully convolutional neural network for cardiac segmentation in short-axis MRI. arXiv preprint arXiv:1604.00494 (2016)

24. Andermatt, S., Pezold, S., Amann, M., Cattin, P. C.: Multi-dimensional gated recurrent units for automated anatomical landmark localization. arXiv preprint arXiv:1708.02766 (2017)

25. Ronneberger, O., Fischer, P., Brox, T.: U-Net: convolutional networks for biomedical image segmentation. In: Navab, N., Hornegger, J., Wells, W.M., Frangi, A.F. (eds.) MICCAI 2015. LNCS, vol. 9351, pp. 234–241. Springer, Cham (2015). https://doi.org/10.1007/978-3-319-24574-4_28

26. Gong, S., Liu, C., Ji, Y., Zhong, B., Li, Y., Dong, H.: Advanced Image and Video Processing Using MATLAB. MOST, vol. 12. Springer, Cham (2019). https://doi.org/10.1007/978-3-319-77223-3

27. Menze, B.H., et al.: The multimodal brain tumor image segmentation benchmark (BRATS). IEEE Trans. Med. Imaging **34**(10), 1993–2024 (2015)
28. Mújica-Vargas, D.: Redescending intuitionistic fuzzy clustering to brain magnetic resonance image segmentation. J. Intell. Fuzzy Syst. **39**(1), 1097–1108 (2020)
29. Mújica-Vargas, D., Martínez, A., Matuz-Cruz, M., Luna-Alvarez, A., Morales-Xicohtencatl, M.: Non-parametric brain tissues segmentation via a parallel architecture of CNNs. In: Carrasco-Ochoa, J.A., Martínez-Trinidad, J.F., Olvera-López, J.A., Salas, J. (eds.) MCPR 2019. LNCS, vol. 11524, pp. 216–226. Springer, Cham (2019). https://doi.org/10.1007/978-3-030-21077-9_20

Tri-Band Log-Periodic Microstrip Antenna Design (2.4, 5.5 and 3.6 GHz Bands) for Wireless Mobile Devices Application

Salvador Ricardo Meneses González[(✉)] and Rita Trinidad Rodríguez Márquez

Instituto Politécnico Nacional, Escuela Superior de Ingeniería Mecánica Y Eléctrica,
Unidad Zacatenco, C. P. 07738 Cd. de México, Mexico
rmenesesg@ipn.mx

Abstract. This work proposes a microstrip log periodical antenna, new design, different than the commonly used designs for strip antenna, based on log-periodic dipole array geometry, to be installed into smart wireless mobile devices to be applied to 5G band, 3.6 GHz, and two WiFi bands, 2.4 GHz and 5.5 GHz, describing the design, simulation, implementation, measurement and experimental results. Based on these results, the designed antenna meets with small size, volume, bandwidth, impedance, flexibility and functionality in order to be applied to mobile services in the mentioned bands.

Keywords: 5G band · Microstrip antenna · 3.6 GHz band · WiFi 2.4 GHz · WiFi 5.5 GHz

1 Introduction

In contrast to the antenna described in [1], a Slotted Planar Microstrip Patch Antenna, ranging from $3.1 - 4.2$ GHz, covering only 5G Band, the proposed antenna in this work is based on a log periodic structure focused to cover 2.4, 3.6 and 5.5 GHz frequency bands, not only to be applied to 5G technology but also to WiFi technology. It should also be noted that these microstrip antennas belongs to a group of designed antennas to be applied to wireless mobile devices at different frequency bands and telecommunication services [2, 3].

In this way, spectrum decisions and changes are necessary to enable 5G services In January 2019, the European Commission adopted an amending implementing decision to harmonize the radio spectrum in the 3.4-3.8 GHz (or 3.6 GHz) band for the future use with 5G [4, 5]. ACMA (Australian Communications and Media Authority) is working to provide opportunities for Australians in both regional and urban Australia to take early advantage of new broadband services, including 5G [6]. ITU expresses "5G is expected to operate using a combination of different radio-frequency bands. Some of the spectrum for 5G will be in new frequency bands not previously used for mobile broadband services, and some will be in low- and mid-frequency spectrum that is currently used by 2G, 3G and 4G systems" [7], so a number of organizations in the field are working in this

© Springer Nature Switzerland AG 2020
M. F. Mata-Rivera et al. (Eds.): WITCOM 2020, CCIS 1280, pp. 18–29, 2020.
https://doi.org/10.1007/978-3-030-62554-2_2

direction, awaiting and pending the agreements and resolutions that will be adopted in the Shareholders' Meetings by "The World Radiocommunication Conference 2019 (WRC-19)" – that was held in Sharm El-Sheikh, Egypt, the last November, and which outcome of the meeting, [8] addresses the following: COM6/2 Studies on frequency-related matters for the terrestrial component of International Mobile Telecommunications identification in the frequency bands 3300–3400 MHz, 3600–3800 MHz, 6425–7025 MHz, 7025–7125 MHz, and 10.0–10.5 GHz; COM6/3 Studies to consider possible allocation of the frequency band 3600–3800 MHz to the mobile, except aeronautical mobile, service on a primary basis within Region 1. Consequently, this evaluation will be completed in early November 2020 and will be followed by the finalization of the IMT-2020 standards.

In this regard, the mobile devices should be technically able to operate with this technology at this scale, satisfy the customer's needs, becoming smaller, due to usually the given space and volume within the radio device is limited, then a high degree of miniaturization and an efficient wireless link are required, as well as low cost is demanded, so, microstrip antenna design is an important challenge of radio engineering which should satisfy gain, resonance frequency, wideband, impedance and dimensions small enough for be assembled into these kind of mobile devices.

On the other hand, actually the core of users of cellular networks stated that social networks serve are useful purpose in the workplace, and practically everywhere, so, in order to reduce the cost of cell phone service, these ones use Wi-Fi wireless LAN infrastructure to serve mobile voice and data requirements.

In this sense, the smart phones devices will be called up on demand to operate at least on these bands, Wi Fi 2.4 GHz and/or 5.5 GHz Bands and 5G technology, 3.6 GHz Band, for that, it is necessary that these devices have an integrated antenna which cover the three mentioned bands, but reducing the antenna size not only limits bandwidth, the gain and bandwidth are degraded too, so, it is necessary to select and design an antenna structure, which it is able to revert these factors. In such a way, a log periodic fashion has been selected, due to provides not only broad impedance bandwidth but also significantly gain.

To determine the performance of design parameter, as impedance, resonance frequency, radiation pattern, wideband, etc., by means of virtual simulation of its construction, the CST software (Computer Simulation Technology) has been used, as well as anechoic chamber and vectoral network analyzer as experimental equipment.

The paper is organized as follows: Sect. 2 describes a brief antenna design basis, Sect. 3 discusses experimental tests and results, concluding the presently work with conclusions and references.

2 Antenna Design

2.1 Antenna Foundations

As it is known, the log-periodic dipole array geometry (see Fig. 1) is characterized by a geometry constant, spacing factor, and a number of dipole element. The proposed antenna structure is shown in Fig. 1, which dimensions increase in proportion to the distance from the origin, this sense, the lengths and spacings of adjacent elements must

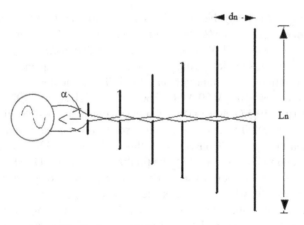

Fig. 1. Log periodic antenna structure.

be related by a constant scale factor τ, which is determined by using the following design expressions [9–12]:

Scale factor τ:

$$\frac{L_n}{L_{n-1}} = \frac{d_n}{d_{n-1}} = \tau \tag{1}$$

where:
L_n, dipole length.
d_n, spacing between dipoles

The longest dipole for the low frequency of the bandwidth, L_1:

$$L_1 = \frac{\lambda_{effmax}}{4} = \frac{c}{4\sqrt{\varepsilon_{reff}}f_{min}} \tag{2}$$

Effective Permittivity:

$$\varepsilon_e = \frac{\varepsilon_r + 1}{2} + \frac{\varepsilon_r - 1}{2}\left(\frac{1}{\sqrt{1 + 12\frac{h}{W}}}\right) \tag{3}$$

where:
ε_r, relative permittivity of the substrate.
h, W, thickness and width of the longest dipole element.

Apex angle α and spacing factor σ:

$$\alpha = arc\,tan\left(\frac{1 - \tau}{4\sigma}\right) \tag{4}$$

Number of dipoles:

$$N = 1 + \frac{ln(BB_{AR})}{ln(\frac{1}{\tau})} \tag{5}$$

where:

B_{AR}, bandwidth of the active región.

B, operating bandwidth.

$$B = \frac{f_{max}}{f_{min}}$$

$$B_{AR} = 1.1 + \frac{7.7(1-\tau)^2}{\tan \alpha} \tag{6}$$

Spacing:

$$S_n = \left[\lambda_n - \lambda_{n-1}\right] * \frac{0.243\tau - 0.051}{1 - \tau} \tag{7}$$

The lower and upper frequency of the bandwidth is determined by the longest dipole and the shortest dipole of the array, respectively.

2.2 Design and Simulation

2.2.1 Design

The designed antenna consists of three dipoles, tuned to the central frequency of each band, 2.4 GHz, 3.6 GHz and 5.5 GHz. Applying the mentioned expressions, being the longest dipole tuned to the lower frequency, the length of the dipole corresponds to both sides, scale factor $\tau = 0.6$, the results are contained in the Table 1.

Table 1. Antenna dimensions.

Frequency (GHz)	Dipole length (mm)	Dipole width (mm)	Spacing (mm)
2.4	44.6	2.93	5.4
3.6	28.7	1.93	7.8
5.5	17.8	1.7	11.2

2.2.2 Simulation

Computer Simulation Technology software [13], CST, has been used to simulate the designed antenna (see Fig. 2). As we know, thick substrates with low permittivity result in antenna designs with high efficiency and large bandwidths, thin substrates with high permittivity lead to small antennas but with a lower bandwidth and high radiation loss [14]; in the simulation stage, a tradeoff between substrate thickness and permittivity for the purpose to define the kind of material has been taken, for that, the prototype has been built using FR-4 substrate, which electric permittivity is $\varepsilon_r = 4.4$ and loss tangent $\delta = 0.0009$, h = 2 mm. On the other hand, the technique to feed the structure is by coaxial feed, which consists of the outermost conductor is connected to the dipole back side (ground surface) and inner conductor is connected to the dipole front side, the feeding line length enables to match impedance antenna with SMA connector. In this way, the antenna dimension is approximately equal to 40 mm × 25 mm, which dimensions comply with volume and space in order to be fit into the radio mobile device.

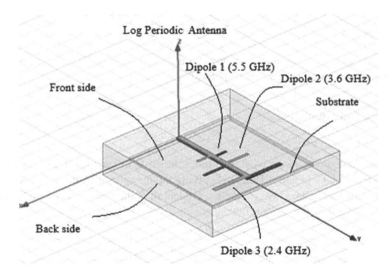

Fig. 2. Simulated antenna.

S_{11} parameter important value that describes the performance antenna, which represents how much power is reflected (ten percent of the radiated energy is reflected from the antenna), and hence is known as the reflection coefficient, -10 dB, (see Fig. 3), S_{11} simulation result graphic, x axe corresponds to Frequency (GHz) and y axe corresponds to Magnitude (dB).

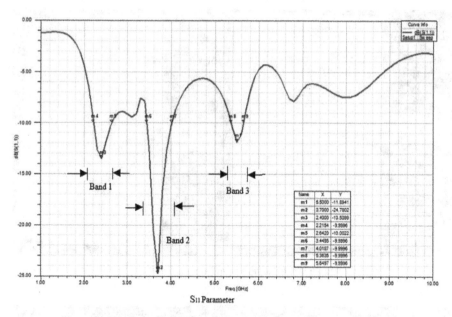

Fig. 3. Magnitude vs. Frequency (simulation).

It is possible to observe three band 1 (2.4–2.6 GHz), band 2 (3.4–4 GHz) and band 3 (5.3–5.7 GHz) and the achieved bandwidth which is approximately equal to 200 MHz in the three cases, enough to cover Wireless Lan Application (Wi-Fi ISM, 2400.– 2483.5 GHz, and 5.5 GHz), in addition the 5G band (3.6 GHz), which antenna efficiency is better.

3 Experimentation

The designed antenna, prototype antenna, is printed on the front and back side of the substrate (see Fig. 4). Exits similarity between the experimental and simulated results, certain construction defects, for instance, bad soldier, bad quality SMA connector due to low cost, or not fit the exact dimensions are the cause of the differences between them.

Vector Network Analyzer ZVB 40 calibrated in the band 500 MHz – 6 GHz, short circuit, opened circuit and matching network has been used to get the S_{11} parameter. Figure 5 shows the result of the S_{11} parameter measurement.

Starting from 1 GHz and ending at 10 GHz, the graphic shows four bands, 2.1 – 3.1 GHz, 3.3.–3.6 GHz, 5.4 –5.6 GHz and a four band 7.8–8 GHz [15], which resonance frequency exceeds the reference value, − 10 dB, even reaches −20 dB, thereby ensuring a favorable antenna performance.

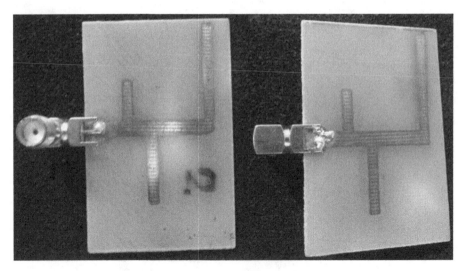

Fig. 4. Prototype antenna.

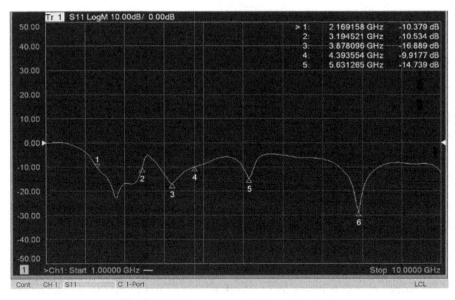

Fig. 5. S11 Parameter graphic (measurement).

In order to measure the radiation pattern, graphical representation of the spatial distribution of radiation, E-Plane (*Evs.θ*, vertical pattern) and H-Plane (*Evs.φ*, horizontal plane) was necessary to install the prototype antenna, acting as receiver antenna, connected to a RF receiver, and a second antenna, whose parameters are known, acting as a transmitter antenna, which is connected to an RF generator transmitting a known power value at certain frequency, distance and height, line of sight, into the anechoic chamber (see Fig. 6 and Fig. 7).

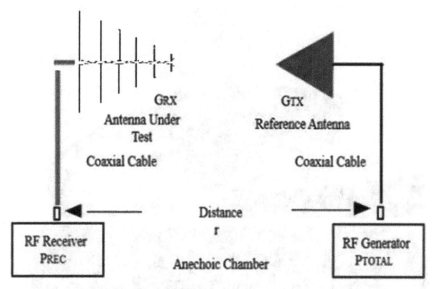

Fig. 6. Radiation pattern measurement standard technique.

Once the data are acquired, the Friis Equation [16–18] is applied (8), resulting the gain antenna value equal approximately to 2.3 dB in the three cases.

$$P_{RX} = P_{TX} G_{TX} G_{RX} \left(\frac{\lambda}{4\pi r} \right)^2 \tag{8}$$

where:
P_{TX}, Transmitted power.
P_{RX}, Received power.
G_{TX}, Transmitter antenna gain.
G_{RX}, Receiver antenna gain.
r, Separation distance between antennas.

Plane E radiation pattern for 2.4 GHz, 3.6 GHz and 5.5 GHz respectively (see Fig. 8) each one is omnidirectional, semi uniform, with no nulls, different respect to a single dipole $\lambda/2$, which radiation pattern shows nulls along the symmetrical axe. Related to the 3.6 GHz, this one shows a better performance, the geometry is closer to a figure circle, which is a great result, because of, this band is assigned to 5G radio mobile devices. The achieved radiation patterns are useful to Wi Fi and for the terrestrial component of International Mobile Telecommunications services (5G) due to the antenna can cover a considerable area.

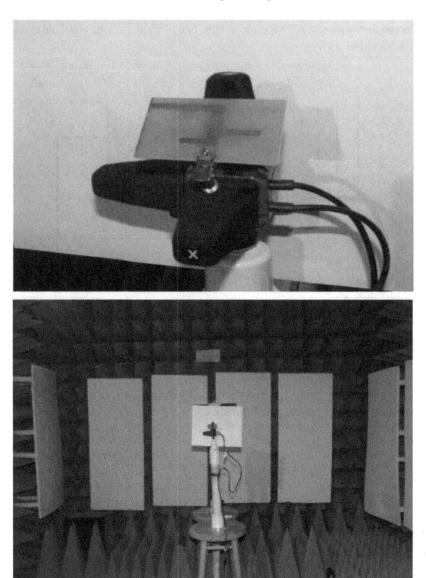

Fig. 7. Prototype antenna under test in the anechoic chamber.

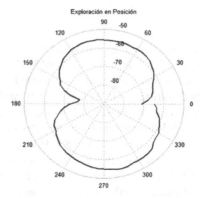

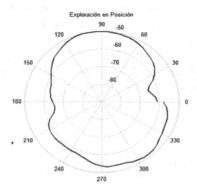

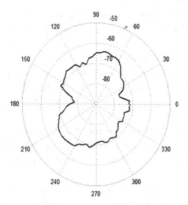

Fig. 8. Result of the radiation pattern measurement, 2.4 GHz, 3.6 GHz and 5.5 GHz respectively.

4 Conclusions

In this paper, we presented a prototype log periodical microstrip antenna in order to be applied to forefront technology, 5G Band (3.6 GHz) and Wi Fi (2.4 and 5.5 GHz). The designed antenna has been simulated, implemented and tested, parameters as resonance frequency, wideband have been verified and the radiation pattern shape has been obtained.

The designed antenna covers a four band too, 7.8–8 GHz band, this one is assigned by the ITU (Recommendation F.386) to Radio-frequency channel arrangements for fixed wireless systems operating in the 8 GHz (7 725 to 8 500 MHz) band.

The prototype antenna meets with small size and low-cost requirements and easily construction. The achieved radiation patterns are omnidirectional, being the 3.6 GHz radiation pattern the best of them, due to the others show semi nulls, the 2.4 GHz shows along 0°–180° semi nulls, and the 5.5 GHz radiation pattern shows a semi-uniform shape. However, the antenna, no matter what operation band, acting as a receiver placed in any desired position to certain distance from the transmitter will receive enough energy to recover the transmitted data.

Finally, we highly recommend this kind of antenna, which comply with small size, volume, bandwidth, impedance, flexibility and functionality in order to be applied to mobile services in the 2.4 GHz, 3.6 GHz and 5.5 GHz bands.

References

1. Ricardo Meneses, S., Rita, G., Rita, G., Rodríguez, M., et al.: Microstrip antenna design for 3.1-4.2 GHz frequency band applied to 5G mobile devices. Euro. J. Eng. Res. Sci. **4**(10), 111–115 (2019)
2. Mungur, D., Durakainan, S.: Microstrip Patch Antenna at 28 GHz for 5G Applications. J. Sci. Technol. Eng. Manage. Adv. Res. Innov. 1(1), (2018)
3. Wang, Q., Mu, N., et al.: 5G MIMO conformal microstrip antenna design. In: Advanced Wireless Communications and Mobile Computing Technologies for the Internet of Things.|Article ID 7616825| p. 11 (2017)
4. www.rfpage.com/what-are-the-challenges-in-5g-technology
5. European Commission/Digital Single Market/News Article/24 Jan 2019
6. ACMA (Australian Communications and Media Authority), "Development of point-to-multipoint apparatus licensing arrangements in the 5.6 GHz band", Discussion paper (2018)
7. Speech by Malcolm Johnson, ITU Deputy Secretary-General, Sixth Wuzhen World Internet Conference - 5G, Opening a new era of digital economy. Wuzhen, China 21 Oct (2019)
8. Key outcomes of the World radiocommunication Conference 2019, ITU News Magazine, No. 6 (2019)
9. Carrel, R.: "Analysis and design of the log periodic dipole antena", Electrical Engineering Research laboratory, Engineering Experimentation Station, University of Illinois. Urbana, Illinois (1961)
10. Alshebeili, S.A., Haraz, O.M., Sebak, A.R.: Low-cost high gain printed log-periodic dipole array antenna with dielectric lenses for V-band applications. IET Microw Antenna Propag **9**, 541–552 (2015)
11. Mazhar, W., Klymyshyn, D.Q.: A Log periodic slot-loaded circular vivaldi antenna for 5-40 GHz UWB applications. Microw. Opt. Technol. Lett. **59**(1), 159–163 (2017)

12. Madhav, B.T.P., et al.: Multiband slot aperture stacked patch antenna for wireless communication applications. Int. J. Comput. Aid. Eng. Technol. **8**(4), 413–423 (2016)
13. https://www.cst.com/Academia/Student-Edition
14. Wheeler, H.A.: fundamental limitations of small antennas. Proc. IRE **35**, 1479–1484 (1947)
15. International Telecommunications Union, ITU_R, Recommendation ITU-R F.386-9, Radio-frequency channel arrangements for fixed wireless systems operating in the 8 GHz (7 725 to 8 500 MHz) (2013)
16. Balanis, C.A.: Antenna Theory, Analysis and Design. John Wiley & Sons Inc (1982)
17. Jordan, E.C., Balmain, K.G.: Electromagnetic Waves and Radiating Systems. Prentice Hall (1968)
18. Wong, K-L.: Compact and Broadband Microstrip Antennas. John Wiley & Sons Inc (2002)

Computer Vision Navigation System for an Indoors Unmanned Aerial Vehicle

R. Roman Ibarra[1]([✉]), Moisés V. Márquez[1], Gerardo Martínez[2], and Viridiana Hernández[1]

[1] Centro de Investigación e Innovación Tecnológica CIITEC-IPN,
Ciudad de México, México
roman.ibarra94@hotmail.com
[2] Centro de Investigación en Ciencia Aplicada y Tecnología Avanzada CICATA-IPN,
Ciudad de México, México
https://www.ciitec.ipn.mx/

Abstract. This paper presents an approach to a navigation system for a UAV that performs indoors tasks. Outdoors UAVs locates itselfs and navigate using GPS that loose effectiveness when physical barriers exist or electrical noise is present. A computer vision system based in artificial markers ArUco is applied in a UAV in a single board computer Jetson nano attached onboard for eliminating communications losses and increase the response time of the system. The markers provide instructions to the aircraft such as turns and displacements and allows pose estimation. Also is presented the model of a cage for UAV tests that is under construction by the time this paper is released.

Keywords: UAV · Computer vision · Indoors · Pose estimation · Navigation

1 Introduction

Mobile robotics is a branch of robotics whose principal concern is developing robots that can move in a determinate environment. One of the main purposes of creating mobile robots is to execute a major spectrum of tasks and also execute them more efficiently, in less time and safer.

This paper focuses on UAVs (Unmanned Aerial Vehicle) which are mobile robots that can fly. This kind of aircrafts have acquired such popularity in the last years because of the versatility they have in accomplishing tasks: they can overfly an area or approach to high structures to acquire data, provide human support in rescue missions, deliver packages, look out for crops health, make topographic surveys, to name a few.

UAVs can manage all these tasks efficiently, safer and in less time with better results in many cases. So, the next step in the development of this technology is making it autonomous. This is a difficult challenge because, in the attempt to give UAVs the ability to take their own decisions about what to do or where

M. F. Mata-Rivera et al. (Eds.): WITCOM 2020, CCIS 1280, pp. 30–47, 2020.
https://doi.org/10.1007/978-3-030-62554-2_3

to go, some limitations need to be considered like battery consumption, weight onboard, computation speed, memory capacity, and safety while operation. Also, another point needs to be considered: Because all the benefits a UAV means, they are starting to be implemented in a very different area: indoors.

If we look at the actual applications of UAVs [1], some of them mentioned above, we will realize that the main part of these are executed outdoors where the UAV have more space to operate, it can be located through GPS and the environment is kind of "clean" from other electric signals.

This paper intends to endow a UAV the ability to locate itself in GPS restricted areas as indoors like warehouses, offices, greenhouses. It is also convenient to remember that in indoors frequently exist another kind of electrical signals such as telephony, wi-fi, magnetic fields, radio signals and other that may interfere in the operation of the UAV if it supports navigation in sensors either active or passive. That is why a computer vision system is proposed.

Computer vision is a branch of computer science that obtains data from digital images by acquiring, processing, segmenting, and interpreting them, emulating the human vision. Computer vision joins digital image processing and artificial intelligence to perform its stages; the same that can be seen in Fig. 1.

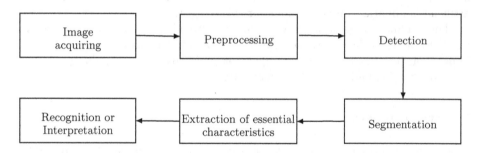

Fig. 1. Computer vision process.

For the first stage a camera is needed. Cameras nowadays are very reliable sensors with relatively low costs that provide images that can be used also for another tasks (most UAV carry a camera for acquiring data, track people, record video or search for cracks in buildings).

The next stages, until the interpretation are performed by the algorithm used using a plethora of methods and techniques available, and the last stage is associated with a decision or action performed majorly by the actuators of the system (the motors in this case). The fact that UAV movements can be controlled through computer vision approaches us one step to the autonomous mobile robots.

2   Motivation

Indoors UAV is not an unexplored area. It has been investigated since a few years ago and recently took impulse due to the availability of a better quality of sensors and the increased computing power and data processing capabilities of new embedded systems and Single Board Computers (SBC), but still exist some problems.

Many systems prefer to do image processing in a ground station because of the robustness of the algorithms (see State of art). This entails problems in communications that may be interfered and data transmission can turn slow because of the size and quantity of data. Because of this, the current paper proposes the use of a SBC that can perform video processing at a constant frame rate, and light enough to be adequated onboard a UAV. Also we propose the use of landmarks.

There are mainly two kinds of landmarks: natural and artificial. The first ones are points in the scene that are selected to perform as references to which the robot measures its displacement. Artificial landmarks are markers intentionally colocated in the environment and specially designed to be detected by a computer vision algorithm. The use of both types is a common solution nowadays in robotics. Although natural landmarks selection, detection, and processing is a task that often consumes more computational resources than artificial landmark detection. Considering that the indoor environment can be manipulated, and image processing is intended to be executed on board the aircraft, the use of artificial landmarks is more suitable for this project.

The landmark may perform two functions: provide relative distance between the UAV and the landmark, and provide a navigation instruction. With this implementation, we face the two important problems for UAV indoors navigation: localization and autonomous navigation.

3   State of Art

Navigation of aerial robots is a field in constant progress due to all the available techniques that provide solutions to problems that navigation carries on such as localization, mapping, pose estimation, stabilize control, and others. Cameras represent a powerful sensor that provides enough data to face some of these problems. In [2] a map is constructed through a monocular camera but some drifting problems occur that force the system to be corrected constantly. Also, this system needs to share data with a ground station for image processing. Other works that also resort to ground stations are [3] and [4] with the difference that the first uses natural landmarks and the second one, artificial landmarks. Interesting works with natural landmarks have been developed such as [5] that design a visual-based guidance system. This system is applied no to navigation but to landing the aircraft. A different approach to UAV localization is given in [6] where a system of fixed multi-cameras capture images for indoors UAV pose estimation and localization. A great survey of all these navigation techniques for UAV based on computer vision can bee seemed in [7].

4   Design. UAV Navigation System Architecture

4.1   Navigation System Description

Navigation requires a reference in the space. This reference can be provided by artificial landmarks. The advantage of this kind of landmarks is that they are easier to detect and require less compute resources to track one single marker instead of tracking a lot of random points in an image as it is usually done. Particularly we use ArUco markers as artificial landmarks [8]. ArUco is a well-supported library with reliable detection and estimating pose algorithms [9,10]. It is composed of dictionaries which are sets of markers with different sizes of the inner grid. An ArUco marker has 4 corners which provide the distance from the marker and the camera and the orientation of the camera respect the marker. Also, an ArUco marker has a particular identifier number (ID). This ID will help us to determine movement instructions afterward.

A UAV has during flight 6 degrees of freedom (DOF) as it can be seen in Fig. 2. Since complete turns in roll and yaw are restricted for this paper, only 4 DOF are considered in which we can order a navigation instruction.

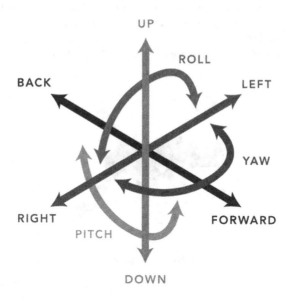

Fig. 2. DOF of a UAV during flight.

A navigation instruction consists in indicating to the UAV a movement around or through an axis (turn or displacement). A set of 8 navigation instructions were defined and every single movement was associated with a specific ArUco marker. This association can be seen in Table 1.

Table 1. Navigation instructions set.

ID marker	Navigation instruction
01	Activation
02	Stand by
03	Ascending
04	Descending
05	Right displacement
06	Left displacement
07	Turn right
08	Turn left

4.2 Hardware Description

The UAV prototype used was built with a class 450 frame, BLDC motors scorpion mt-2205 with 6 in propeller; also a camera Mobius A was used and a CC3D flight controller. All components were powered by a Li-po battery with 3 s and 8000 mAh. The prototype in Fig. 3 achieved a flight time of 25 min with a weight of 1.062 kg. A video of its operation can been seen on https://www.youtube.com/watch?v=mBctdSKAybc.

A typical UAV (RC ones) are connected as shown in Fig. 4.

Fig. 3. RC UAV prototype.

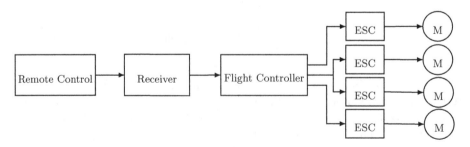

Fig. 4. Scheme of a radio-controlled UAV.

The intention is to remove the first two blocks and replace them with an embedded system capable enough to process images in real-time and send signals that can be interpreted by the flight controller. The embedded system selected for support the algorithm was Jetson Nano Developer Kit from Nvidia. The advantage that this SBC has over other computers like the ones cited in [11] is that Jetson nano has low power consumption at the time it offers high data processing capabilities in a lightweight board with reduced dimensions.

Jetson nano has a 40 pin of signal interface that are predefined with communications protocols such as UART and I2C [12]. PWM output signals are not available unless SoC (System on Chip) is modified, but another alternative exists and is to generate de PWM signal in an external device.

For this, PCA9685 PWM driver with 12 bits resolution and controlled by the I2C protocol was used for creating the corresponding signals. Its 16 PWM outputs available were enough for the requirements. PWM signals are necessary since the CC3D flight controller receives data in that way. So, with these two devices, we are can replace the first two blocks in the Fig. 4 and represent the UAV scheme as shown in Fig. 5.

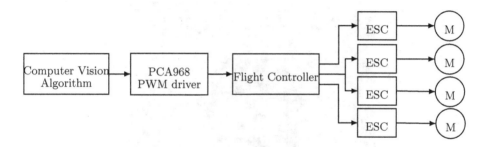

Fig. 5. Scheme of UAV with Jetson nano.

4.3   Software Description

After estimating pose, the camera calibration must be performed. This calibration consists in obtaining the fundamental parameters of the camera such as de distortion coefficients. These distortions are caused by the morphology of the camera lens.

$$x_{distorted} = x(1 + k_1 r^2 + k/2r^4 + k_3 r^6) \tag{1}$$

$$y_{distorted} = y(1 + k_1 r^2 + k_2 r^4 + k_3 r^6) \tag{2}$$

And are represented as:

$$C = (k_1, k_2, p_1, p_2, k_3) \tag{3}$$

These coefficients explain how a 3D point is projected in a 2D plane. So the calibration process should throw the camera matrix that contains the focal length and the optical center of the camera and has the next appearance:

$$camera\,matrix = \begin{bmatrix} f_x & 0 & c_z \\ 0 & f_y & c_y \\ 0 & 0 & 1 \end{bmatrix} \tag{4}$$

The ArUco library was used for marker detection and as a pose estimation tool. It can be seen in Fig. 6 that multiple data is thrown when a marker is presented to the camera. At the center of the ArUco marker is located the origin of the coordinated axis with the x-axis in red, y in green and z in blue. At the top of the image x, y, and z denote the lineal distance in centimeters between the center of the image and the center of the coordinated axis. Below, roll, pitch and yaw denote the inclination in degrees of the marker respect to the camera. By last, besides the origin of the coordinated axis, appears the ID of the marker in blue which, for this example, is the marker number one.

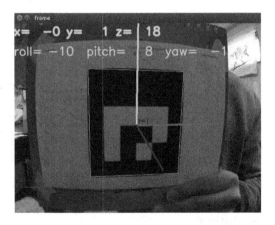

Fig. 6. Pose estimation with ArUco library.

4.4 Selecting Dictionary

Even though we have a calibrated camera [13], the pose estimation algorithm varies from one execution to another in some centimeters and degrees. To select the most appropriate dictionary a characterization was done of 4 different dictionaries (different size of inner grid) and also different physical measurements which were 18 cm, 12 cm, and 6 cm. As can be seen in the graphic of Fig. 7, fewer dimensions of the inner grid combined with larger physical sizes of the marker, provide larger detection distance.

This maximum distance detection was taken by comparing the algorithm estimated distance and the real distance between the marker and the camera. If this error was inferior to 10 cm the measuring was taken. This was made with the purpose to achieve a maximum distance error of 10 cm.

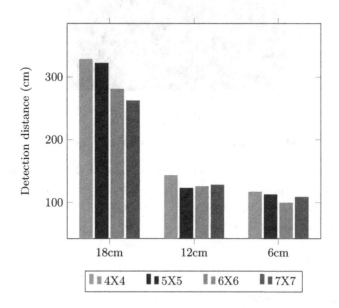

Fig. 7. Maximum distance detection with error inferior to 10cm.

Hence, a 4X4 dictionary was selected and markers size was defined as 18 cm. Markers provide two kinds of information: specify the lineal and angular distance between the marker and the camera, and show its ID. This data will be used in the next section.

Also, illumination tests were executed for knowing the illumination conditions needed for the algorithm to perform adequately. The pose estimation algorithm demonstrated to perform well perceiving around 2.83 luxes, but going under that value, the detection algorithm may start failing. With 1.26 luxes detection is imprecise as Fig. 8 shows. The marker detected appears to be smaller than the real one and therefore, further. Also, Fig. 8 shows a deviation in the roll axis.

However, these mistakes in low conditions can be discarded since illumination conditions indoors usually are above these values. Table 2 shows the recommended luxes values for indoors [14].

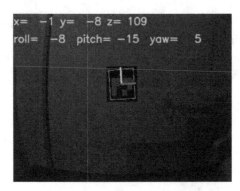

Fig. 8. Illumination test.

Table 2. Luxes values recommended for indoors.

Place	Minimum (lux)	Optimum (lux)	Maximum (lux)
Circulation areas, hallways	50	100	150
Stairs, warehouses, achieve	100	150	200
Classrooms and laboratories	300	400	500
Offices	450	500	750

4.5   General Overview

With markers collocated in the area, the process of the navigation system running can be synthesized in Fig. 9 for a general overview.

The UAV in flight equipped with the camera and connected to the Jetson nano will be recording video. When a marker appears in the image frame the estimating pose algorithm will be executed and the ID marker will be identified. Depending on the instruction, Jetson nano will send the kind of signal that the PCA driver has to create. This order, now traduced in a pulses train, will enter to the CC3D flight controller and then sent to each of the ESC motors to generate de desired movement. These movements will be explained in more detail in the next section. The purpose is that, once this first instruction is executed, the UAV continues its flight and find other markers with different instructions until it finds one that orders landing.

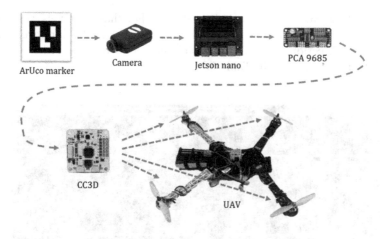

Fig. 9. General process overview.

5 Experimentation

5.1 Instructions Set

To accomplish a navigation instruction, the right width of pulse needs to be applied to the correct DOF. The figure shows how the motors in the UAV are distributed. The F letter denotes the front of the aircraft. If we want to perform a movement to the right or the left, a signal in roll must be indicated. This will produce the acceleration of a pair of motors: M1 and M2 for left, and M3 and M4 for right; meanwhile, if we pretend a movement to the front, yaw channel is the one that needs to be actioned. For ascending, all motors must accelerate and the opposite is required for descending (Fig. 10).

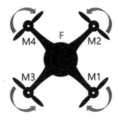

Fig. 10. Motors distribution in the UAV.

The CC3D flight controller [15] receives in its Flex-IO port PWM signals in different channels that are associated with each DOF of the UAV. The operating range for these PWM signals is between 5% and 10% of duty cycle. For the throttle channel, this represents the minimum and the maximum respectively (blue line in Fig. 11 is throttle set at minimum), but this not occurs the same for the rest of the channels (roll, pitch, and yaw). For these channels, the neutral point is set at 7.5% (yellow line in Fig. 11) A decrement in the duty cycle means a turn in one direction (left) and an increment, a turn in the other direction (right). All this is resumed in Table 3.

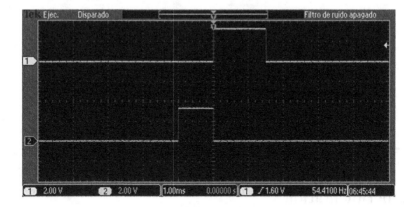

Fig. 11. PWM in throttle and yaw. (Color figure online)

Table 3. Duty cycle for each DOF.

Channel	DOF	Movement	Duty cycle
1	roll	right	10%
1	roll	left	5%
2	pitch	forward	10%
2	pitch	backward	5%
3	throttle	ascend	10%
3	throttle	descend	5%
4	yaw	left	5%
4	yaw	right	10%

5.2 Wiring

A connection diagram between the components is shown in Fig. 12. The computer vision algorithm is running in the jetson nano developer kit and orders a movement through de PCA driver and the CCD3 flight controller.

To achieve the goal of attaching de SBC onboard the UAV, power consumption is an important fact to consider. Jetson nano has two power modes [16]: 10W and 5 W. Using the first mode (10 W) we have:

$$I = \frac{P}{V} = \frac{10\,W}{5\,V} = 2\,A \tag{5}$$

The 2 A as maximum current consumption allows the Jetson nano to be powered by its micro-USB port and, since the Jetson nano will have no peripherals attached, 2A power supply should be enough to get a good performance.

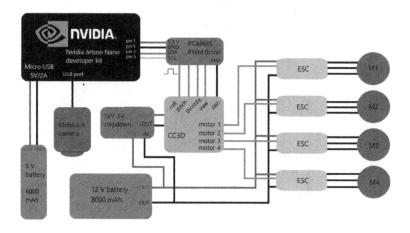

Fig. 12. Wiring diagram.

Using an independent battery for supplying the Jetson nano avoids the faster consumption of the main battery for the motors. Algo gives de SBC a stable energy supply. Experimentally, the battery duration was about 6 h, 15 min.

$$electrical\ device\ consumption = \frac{6000\,mAh}{6.4\,hrs} = 937.5\,mA = 0.937\,A \quad (6)$$

Which is below the energy budget defined despite the addition of a fan in the heatsink. Jetson nano operates well without overheating and with a constant voltage.

5.3 Algorithm

The next flowchart shows the algorithm of the navigation system. For security, an arming sequence is required for starting the UAV, this sequence is an order in yaw to the right for a few seconds. The system is looking for markers in the imagen and, in case of founding one, the algorithm estimates pose (distance and attitude). Cause the marker detection is not perfect, and the code might find a marker that does not correspond to any of the instructions set, even in a single frame, the system falls in an ambiguity. To avoid that, and since the ids of the markers detected are stored in a list. A phase of evaluation is included. The algorithm asks if all the markers in the list are equal. In case this is true, the algorithm proceeds to execute the associated task to that marker and if not, the algorithm ignores the frame and skips to the next.

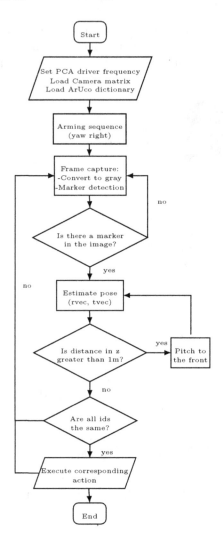

6   Results

The code was developed in Python3 in the Jetson nano developer kit with OS Ubuntu 18.04. The size of the videos used was of 480×640 at 30 fps. Putting together the instruction set and the PWM signals required we can consider the marker as the input of the system and the changes in acceleration of the motor as the output. In Fig. 13 the navigation system has been started up. A monitor has been connected to visualizing the video deployed. Depending on the marker shown (input), the system will accelerate a different pair of motors. These movements are according to Table 4.

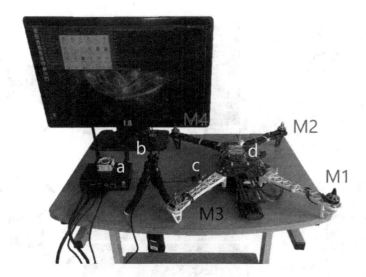

Fig. 13. Navigation system; *a.* Jetson nano; *b.* Mobius A camera; *c.* PCA9685 driver; *d.* CC3D controller; *Mn.* Motor.

Table 4. Inputs and outputs of the system.

Marker	Motors activated	Duty cycle
01	All	6%
02	All	0%
03	ALL	+0.1%
04	ALL	−0.1%
05	M3, M4	10%
06	M1, M2	5%
07	M1, M4	10%
08	M2, M3	10%

Figure 14 exemplifies the functioning. When a marker is founded in the image, for example, marker with ID 5 in Fig. 14d, which is associated with right displacement (see Table 1), the PCA driver output read in the oscilloscope is the one in Fig. 14e with a duty cycle of 10%, which increase the duty cycle of the motors colored in green in Fig. 14f through the flight controller. Something similar occurs for left turn. Marker with ID 8, the one in Fig. 14g produces the PWM output with duty cycle of 5% (Fig. 14h) and opposite motors are accelerated (Fig. 14i). For the algorithm, the average response time measured between de marker detection and the generation of the PWM signal output was 6.686 ms.

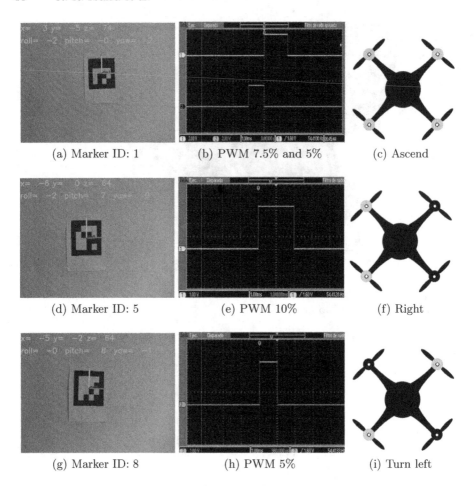

(a) Marker ID: 1   (b) PWM 7.5% and 5%   (c) Ascend

(d) Marker ID: 5   (e) PWM 10%   (f) Right

(g) Marker ID: 8   (h) PWM 5%   (i) Turn left

Fig. 14. Inputs, actions and outputs in the navigation system.

The next test phase consisted in joining hardware and software onboard the UAV and put on propellers, power the Jetson nano with the 5V battery no peripherals attached, and manage it through SSH in a local wi-fi network. The assembled prototype is the one that follows in Fig. 15. A video of the UAV operation can be seen at https://www.youtube.com/watch?v=PYX7cdg5R0g.

Further tests are in progression at the time this paper is written. The next step is testing the system with propellers on but in a cage that restricts the lineal displacements of the UAV but allowing turns and motor acceleration. This cage has been developed first in a model in Solidworks software that can be seen in Fig. 16.

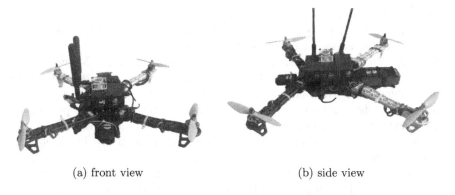

(a) front view   (b) side view

Fig. 15. Final prototype.

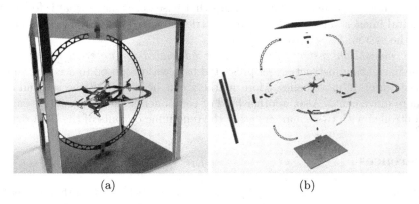

(a)   (b)

Fig. 16. UAV cage for tests.

7   Conclusions

- *The algorithm performs effectively*: The computer vision algorithm proved to perform in real-time (6.686 ms average response time) at a reasonable frame rate (30 fps). While marker distributions do not pass 3.2 m, we can have the certainty that the estimation pose error will be inferior to 10 cm. To achieve larger distances, increase the size of the marker is recommended.
- *Computer Vision can explode the use of cameras in mobile robots*: Cameras are reliable and effective sensors. Taking advantage of cameras is a powerful alternative since most UAVs carry them for data acquisition either or real-time and recording video. Computer vision can explode this resource by providing scalable solutions referring to detection, recognizing, tracking, and learning from images.
- *Autonomous aerial robots with robust embedded systems onboard for data processing are viable*: Data transmission for processing on capable computers has been one of the problems of computer vision in mobile robots, even more for aerial robots. Since new technologies focused on these kinds of applications

have arisen with low power consumption and lightweight, mobile robots can perform effectively carrying these computers avoiding data transmission, loss of information, and allowing a faster reaction time.

- *Since localization is relative, no refreshing needs to be done*: Many systems that are based in maps, SLAM, odometry, and visual reconstruction, face the problem that, eventually, these techniques tend to accumulate error. This not occurs when using relative location. Markers have a defined position in the environment and location is obtained from the data provided from the marker at the moment of detection, so there is no map drifting or system reset needed.
- *Mistakes in markers detection must be considered*: Despite fiducial markers are effective tools with powerful algorithms of error correction, detection may fail at one point, even for a single frame giving false positives. These possible errors must be considered in programs that base decisions in what it founds in digital images. Thus, padlocks and restrictions are necessary to avoid errors in the system for security reasons.
- *The navigation instruction set can be adequated for different applications*: the navigation instruction set presented here was proposed to accomplish the basic aircraft movements. More markers can be added to the set and also more movements. Also, another kind of components like servo motors can be controlled with these markers using the remaining outputs of the PCA driver.

References

1. Mazur, M., Wisniewski, A., McMillan, J.: PWC global report on the commercial applications of drone technology. PricewaterhouseCoopers, Technical report (2016)
2. Blösch, M., Weiss, S., Scaramuzza, D., Siegwart, R.: Vision based MAV navigation in unknown and unstructured environments. In: 2010 IEEE International Conference on Robotics and Automation, pp. 21–28. IEEE (2010)
3. Carrillo, L.R.G., López, A.E.D., Lozano, R., Pégard, C.: Combining stereo vision and inertial navigation system for a quad-rotor UAV. J. Intell. Robot. Syst. **65**(1–4), 373–387 (2012)
4. Apvrille, L., Dugelay, J.L., Ranft, B.: Indoor autonomous navigation of low-cost MAVs using landmarks and 3D perception. In: Proceedings Ocean and Coastal Observation, Sensors and Observing Systems (2013)
5. Cesetti, A., Frontoni, E., Mancini, A., Zingaretti, P., Longhi, S.: A vision-based guidance system for UAV navigation and safe landing using natural landmarks. J. Intell. Robot. Syst. **57**(1–4), 233 (2010)
6. Oh, H., Won, D.Y., Huh, S.S., Shim, D.H., Tahk, M.J., Tsourdos, A.: Indoor UAV control using multi-camera visual feedback. J. Intell. Robot. Syst. **61**(1–4), 57–84 (2011)
7. Kanellakis, C., Nikolakopoulos, G.: Survey on computer vision for UAVs: current developments and trends. J. Intell. Robot. Syst. **87**(1), 141–168 (2017)
8. Garrido-Jurado, S., Muñoz-Salinas, R., Madrid-Cuevas, F.J., Marín-Jiménez, M.J.: Automatic generation and detection of highly reliable fiducial markers under occlusion. Pattern Recogn. **47**(6), 2280–2292 (2014)

9. Garrido-Jurado, S., Muñoz-Salinas, R., Madrid-Cuevas, F., Medina-Carnicer, R.: Generation of fiducial marker dictionaries using mixed integer linear programming. Pattern Recognit. **51**, 481–491 (2015)
10. Romero-Ramirez, F., Muñoz-Salinas, R., Medina-Carnicer, R.: Speeded up detection of squared fiducial markers. Image Vis. Comput. **76**, 38–47 (2018)
11. Hulens, D., Verbeke, J., Goedemé, T.: Choosing the best embedded processing platform for on-board UAV image processing. In: Braz, J., Pettré, J., Richard, P., Kerren, A., Linsen, L., Battiato, S., Imai, F. (eds.) VISIGRAPP 2015. CCIS, vol. 598, pp. 455–472. Springer, Cham (2016). https://doi.org/10.1007/978-3-319-29971-6_24
12. JetsonHacks: Nvidia jetson nano J41 header pinout (2019). https://www.jetsonhacks.com/nvidia-jetson-nano-j41-header-pinout/
13. OpenCV: Camera calibration and 3D reconstruction (2019). https://docs.opencv.org/3.4/d9/d0c/group__calib3d.html
14. Sánchez, M.: Luminotecnia. IC Editorial (2010)
15. LibrePilot: Coptercontrol/cc3d/atom hardware setup (2015). https://opwiki.readthedocs.io/en/latest/user_manual/cc3d/cc3d.html
16. Lawrence, P.: Jetson Nano Developer Kit. User Guide. Nvidia, March 2019

Embedded Human Detection
System for Home Security

Oscar Arturo González González[1]([✉]), Alina Mariana Pérez Soberanes[1],
Víctor Hugo García Ortega[1], and Julio César Sosa Savedra[2]

[1] Instituto Politécnico Nacional, ESCOM, Ciudad de México, Mexico
oscar.ar-56@hotmail.com, vgarciao@ipn.mx
[2] Instituto Politécnico Nacional, CICATA, Querétaro, Mexico
jcsosa@ipn.mx

Abstract. This paper presents the development of an embedded system
prototype that performs the home security monitoring, through image
processing and classification algorithms to detect human form. If human
presence is detected, the system will send an alert message to the user.
The embedded system is implemented on a Raspberry Pi 3 B, supported
by a Pyroelectric Infrared Radial (PIR) motion sensor and a Raspberry
Pi Camera V2. The algorithms are implemented in C language and were
designed to take advantage of the hardware resources of the platform,
through High Performance Computing (HPC) techniques. The selected
classifier is a multilayer perceptron. This classifier obtained an accuracy
of 96%, approximately.

Keywords: Image processing · Embedded system · Multilayer
perceptron · HPC · Raspberry Pi

1 Introduction

Statistics from the nonprofit organization *Observatorio Nacional Ciudadano* in
Mexico indicates that only in the period March - April 2019, there was an
increase of burglary investigation processes from 6,734 to 7,017 [1], that is an
increase of 4.20%, in the number of investigation processes from March to April
2019. The situation of burglary in Mexico generates the need for people to keep
their home safe. A possible solution to this problem is to develop new technologies that allow home automation. These technologies focus on the automation
of processes within a building. This improves the quality of life and comfort,
inside the home. It also allows constant monitoring of the place, through the
Internet and the use of alarms, sensors or surveillance cameras. This domotics
development has driven the creation of security systems such as those that are
installed and monitored by private companies, which usually have a monthly
cost per service, or commercial devices that can be installed and configured by
the user. Some of these alternatives tend to be inefficient, and some others are
often expensive or cannot be obtained by the majority of the population.

M. F. Mata-Rivera et al. (Eds.): WITCOM 2020, CCIS 1280, pp. 48–60, 2020.
https://doi.org/10.1007/978-3-030-62554-2_4

There are some papers proposed related to the home security monitoring and human detection. The applications that will be described next are developed in a Raspberry Pi platform and are supported by a camera and by sensors. The first paper *A New IoT Combined Body Detection of People by Using Computer Vision for Security Application* [2] presents a system developed on the Raspberry Pi platform with sensor elements: Raspberry Pi camera and a Pyroelectric Infrared Radial (PIR) sensor, which is used for motion detection. Once the image is obtained, the algorithm of the Histogram of Oriented Gradients (HOG) extracts the object's features and a Support Vector Machine (SVM) is used for the classification and learning of the human form. If a human presence is detected, the image is sent to a smartphone over the Internet, using the Telegram application. The artificial vision tool used for the development of this system is OpenCV. Regarding the results of the proposed method, it is presented that it was obtained a detection rate of 93.89 ±5.3%.

The paper *Human Detector and Counter Using Raspberry Pi Microcontroller* [3] presents a system that identifies humans entering a room through a door. The system performs digital image processing using HOG as a feature extraction algorithm and a SVM for the classification, based on the OpenCV tool and developed in the Python programming language. It is specified that it is supported on a Raspberry Pi and uses a Raspberry Pi Camera, other sensors are a pair of PIR sensors, to indicate to the system the capture of input or output images; and a Bluetooth module (HC-05) to send the required data to another system through serial communication. It is has an efficiency of 83%. In addition, it is mentioned that the use of Raspberry Pi platform avoided the use of desktop CPU and as a result it was reduced the system power consumption and the cost.

In this paper it is proposed an embedded system for home security monitoring, which is implemented in a Raspberry Pi 3 B platform using HPC techniques, that unlike the described papers, this allows the system to take advantage of the hardware and software resources of the platform. To keep the home safe through the remote monitoring, the system detects the human presence and sends an alert message to the user. For this, the system uses a motion sensor to perform the motion detection and the images are obtained from a Raspberry Pi Camera V2. Also the system implements image processing and classification algorithms. This feature allows the system to improve its robustness and to perform a reliable detection of human presence inside the enclosure. Additionally, the system is considered to be scalable as a security module of a robust home automation system. This system can include the control of doors, windows, temperature, among other possible modules. The general diagram of the proposed system is presented in Fig. 1.

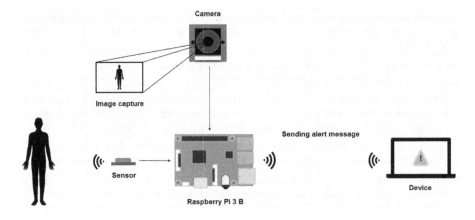

Fig. 1. Proposed system.

2 Metodology

Raspberry Pi is a suitable platform for home automation systems. This is the selected platform for the implementation of the system. In [4] is mentioned that Raspberry Pi is a platform that supports a large number of input and output peripherals. Raspberry Pi is also suitable for interacting with different devices, allowing its use in a wide range of applications. On the other hand, the ability to access the Internet makes the Raspberry Pi suitable for home automation related applications.

The system is composed of four main modules:

1. **Motion detection module**: In this module the embedded system through the AS312 PIR sensor detects movement and the Raspberry Pi Camera Module V2 perform the acquisition of images.
2. **Image processing module**: In this module the image subtraction for motion detection is performed. Then the algorithms for the image segmentation and the image feature extraction are performed.
3. **Classification module**: In this module the descriptor vectors obtained from the image feature extraction are analysed by the classification algorithm.
4. **Communication module**: This module sends a notification to the user's device to notify the possible human presence.

Each of the previous modules will be described in the following sections.

2.1 Motion Detection Module

For the motion detection it was implemented a circuit for the AS312 sensor, which is powered with 3.3 V. The circuit output depends on the activation of the AS312 sensor, if the sensor detects movement the output will be high (3.3 V), otherwise the output will be low (0 V). The sensor has a detection distance of

4 m and a viewing angle of 60° approximately. The reading of the circuit output is performed through the General Purpose Terminals (GPIO) of the Raspberry Pi. This reading allows to send the signal to the system indicating if movement was detected or not. This signal is read through the WiringPi library, which is a GPIO access library written in C language for the BCM2835, BCM2836 and BCM2837 System on Chip (SoC) devices used in all Raspberry Pi platforms [6]. If movement is detected the system will capture an image that will be processed by the next system module. This image capture is performed through the Raspberry Pi Camera Module V2, which is connected to the Raspberry Pi platform through the Camera Serial Interface (CSI) and is controlled by the *raspistill* commands of the operating system of the Raspberry Pi (Raspbian Stretch).

2.2 Image Processing Module

This module is divided into 4 submodules.

A. Image Acquisition, Grayscale Conversion and Noise Filter Application. The image obtained by the Raspberry Pi camera V2 is in BMP format -Bitmap-, which is a bitmap file, these kind of files are uncompressed and have 24 bits per pixel, also this kind of image do not have any type of processing of data, or alteration, so the original data is preserved [5]. Once the BMP image is obtained a grayscale conversion, and then a Gaussian filter is applied to the image. This filter allows to attenuate the noise and has a better frequency response. For its implementation, a convolution operation is performed with a mask, with a window size of 3×3 (2). Equation (1) is used to obtain the mask and the value of σ is 1.0.

$$G(x, y) = \frac{1}{2\pi\sigma^2} e^{-\frac{x^2 + y^2}{2\sigma^2}}. \tag{1}$$

$$G = \begin{pmatrix} 0.0751 & 0.1238 & 0.0751 \\ 0.1238 & 0.2042 & 0.1238 \\ 0.0751 & 0.1238 & 0.0751 \end{pmatrix}. \tag{2}$$

To avoid using the floating point unit by the Raspberry Pi processor, an approximation of (2) is obtained in (3).

$$G = \frac{1}{16} \begin{pmatrix} 1 & 2 & 1 \\ 2 & 4 & 2 \\ 1 & 2 & 1 \end{pmatrix}. \tag{3}$$

This mask or kernel is multiplied by each pixel and its neighbors, in order to homogenize the colors of nearby neighbors. This achieve the elimination of white dots or white noise in an image, because the noise usually takes different pixel values from those in a neighborhood of pixels. The Broadcom BCM2837 processor of the Raspberry Pi 3 B card has four cores, so the processing can be divided into four processing blocks. The Gaussian filter is implemented by dividing the processing in parallel into four processes working on the same image (data parallelism). This allows to take advantage of the resources provided by the platform. The implementation of this Gaussian filter and all the algorithms that will be presented in the next sections are built in C language, which is a programming language that allows the compiler to generate the assembly code directly from the processor.

B. Motion Detection in an Image. Once the processing of the previous modules was applied to a base image - which is captured at the first process of the execution of the system -, this image is set as a background. Then if motion is detected by the sensor movement a subsequent image will be captured. The motion detection in the image is performed through implementing the background subtraction method, which is performed with the subtraction operation between the two images, with this operation is obtained the pixel differences between two images and thus be able to identify if there are differences between one scenario and another. Mathematically, the subtraction can be represented as $f = x - y$, where x and y are images respectively.

The simplest case to perform the subtraction and not to obtain negative values is to apply the absolute value function (4).

$$f_a = |x - -y|. \tag{4}$$

Considering that the subtraction has the property of being commutative. The result of the subtraction between the two images must be a positive value. For this the value obtained is verified, if it is negative, the result of the subtraction will be replaced by the value of 0, otherwise the value obtained from the subtraction is assigned.

C. Image Segmentation. This submodule is dedicated to the subdivision and analysis of image regions for segmentation. The region corresponding to the object of interest is represented with a pixel value of 255, while the region belonging to the background of the image adopts a pixel value of 0. First, the Otsu segmentation algorithm is performed to obtain an automatic global threshold depending on the analysis of the image pixels, it requires three parameters: the image obtained from the motion detection module, its width and height. With this operation the threshold is obtained and then it will be used in the image thresholding. The Otsu method requires the values of the image histogram, and are used to perform the consequent operations to get the maximum value. The Otsu method allows segmentation of an image through discriminant analysis, separating the image into two classes C_0 and C_1 this classes correspond to object and background. This method automatically finds the threshold of an image using its gray segmentation levels [7]. Class values take values $C_0 = \{0, 1, ..., u\}$ where u is the gray level and $C_1 = \{u+1, u+2, ..., L-1\}$ where L is the number of gray levels. To obtain the probability of occurrence of a gray level P_i in a digital image the following expression is used, where N is the number of pixels in gray level of the image and f_i is the number of frequency of pixels with the same gray level (5).

$$P_i = \frac{f_i}{N}.$$

(5)

The classes C_0 and C_1 are given by (6) and (7).

$$C_0 : \frac{P_1}{\omega_0(u)}, ..., \frac{P_u}{\omega_0(u)}.$$

(6)

$$C_1 : \frac{P_{u+1}}{\omega_1(u)}, ..., \frac{P_L}{\omega_1(u)}.$$

(7)

Equations (8) and (9) define ω_0 and ω_1.

$$\omega_0(u) = \sum_{i=u+1}^{L} P_i.$$

(8)

$$\omega_1(u) = \sum_{i=u+1}^{L} P_i.$$

(9)

Subsequently, the average for each class is obtained, given by μ_0 and μ_1 (10) (11).

$$\mu_0 = \sum_{i=1}^{u} \frac{i * P_i}{\omega_0(u)}.$$

(10)

$$\mu_1 = \sum_{i=u+1}^{L} \frac{i * P_i}{\omega_1(u)}.$$

(11)

Once the means of the classes are obtained, the variance is obtained (12).

$$\sigma_B^2 = \omega_0 * (\mu_1 - \mu_T)^2 + \omega_1 * (\mu_2 - \mu_T)^2.$$

(12)

Where μ_T is the average obtained from the total pixels of the image in gray levels. The threshold t^* is selected by maximising the separation of classes from the image and the coefficient between the variance between classes is maximised. The greater the variance between classes and the smaller the variance within them, the discrimination will be better between the groups (13).

$$t^* = MAX(\sigma_B^2(u)) \quad 1 \leq u \leq L. \tag{13}$$

Subsequently, the thresholding of the image is performed using the threshold value obtained with the Otsu method. To do this, we proceed to verify if the value of the pixel of the image to be thresholded is greater or less than the desired threshold and depending on this, modify its value in 0 or 255 (14).

$$f(i,j) = \begin{cases} 255 & l > u, \\ 0 & l < u, \end{cases} \tag{14}$$

To perform the image threshold, it is required to define a threshold value u. If the gray level value l of an image $f(i,j)$ is greater than the threshold u.

After the Otsu threshold, the image is partitioned into subimages of specific size. In this subimages the pixel values are ordered and if the neighborhood is adequate, the area is dilated. The pixel values of the subimage are saved, considering the binarized image obtained with the Otsu method and once the values are sorted, a value of 0 or 255 is assigned to the analyzed pixel depending on the relationship that it has with the neighbor pixels, related with the pixel average. This processing of the white pixels allows to obtain a better image of the section that belongs to the object. This operations require further processing, thus operations are divided by four processes to take advantage of the hardware and software resources.

Finally, the Sauvola method is used to complete thicken regions in the image in addition to correcting shadows that are not related to the object. This method is used to reduce light intensities in an image. This method uses the average intensity of the values of a given region of pixels and their standard deviation. This region is defined within a bxb neighborhood or matrix, with a k parameter which varies between 0.2 and 0.5. This is implemented in the Eq. (15) obtained from [8].

$$T(x,y) = m(x,y)\left[1 + k\left(\frac{\sigma(x,y)}{R} - 1\right)\right]. \tag{15}$$

Where:

- $\sigma(x,y)$: Is the standard deviation of the neighborhood.
- R: Is maximum value of the standard deviation, $R = 128$ with the maximum intensity being 255 in a neighborhood with $b = 15$.

- k: A value between 0.2 and 0.5.
- $m(x,y)$: Arithmetic mean of the neighborhood.
- $T(x,y)$: Value of the threshold in the neighborhood.

The processing result images of image subtraction and the image segmentation submodule are presented in the following Fig. 2.

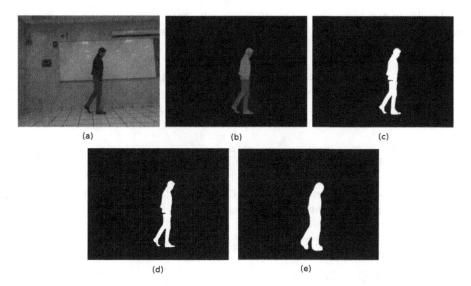

Fig. 2. Original image (a), substraction image (b), Otsu image (c), local threshold image (d), Sauvola image (e).

D. Feature Extraction. This submodule obtains the descriptors of the segmented object. The invariant descriptors selected for this submodule are the Hu moments which are descriptors that extract invariant features to translations, rotations, changes of scale and illumination. These invariant moments are obtained from the geometric moments [7].

For the discrete case of an image $f(i,j)$ the standard geometric moments are obtained in (16).

$$M_{pq} = \sum_i \sum_j i^p j^q f(i,j) \quad \forall \quad p,q = 0,1,2,\ldots \tag{16}$$

To obtain the central moments of the object (17).

$$\mu_{pq} = \sum_i \sum_j (i - \bar{x})^p (j - \bar{y})^q f(i,j) \quad \forall\, p,q = 0,1,\ldots \tag{17}$$

Where $\bar{x}$ and $\bar{y}$ correspond to the coordinates of the center of gravity of the analysed object, which are obtained from the geometric moments of order 10, 01 and 00 (18).

$$\bar{x} = \frac{m_{10}}{m_{00}} \quad \bar{y} = \frac{m_{01}}{m_{00}}. \tag{18}$$

To obtain the invariants to changes of scale, each moment must be divided by a normalization factor (19) that cancels the scaling effect [7].

$$\gamma = \frac{p+q}{2} + 1 \quad \text{for } p+q = 2, 3, ... \tag{19}$$

Equation (20) is used to calculate the normalized central moments.

$$\eta_{pq} = \frac{\mu_{pq}}{\mu_{00}^{\gamma}}. \tag{20}$$

Once obtained the normalized central moments with (20), it can be calculated the seven invariant moments –Hu moments– (21).

$$
\begin{aligned}
\phi_1 &= \eta_{20} + \eta_{02} \\
\phi_2 &= (\eta_{20} - \eta_{02})^2 + 4\eta_{11}^2 \\
\phi_3 &= (\eta_{30} - 3\eta_{12})^2 + (3\eta_{21} - \eta_{03})^2 \\
\phi_4 &= (\eta_{30} + \eta_{12})^2 + (\eta_{21} + \eta_{03})^2 \\
\phi_5 &= (\eta_{30} - 3\eta_{12})(\eta_{30} + \eta_{12})\left[(\eta_{30} + \eta_{12})^2 - 3(\eta_{21} + \eta_{03})^2\right] \\
&\quad + (3\eta_{21} - \eta_{03})(\eta_{21} + \eta_{03})\left[3(\eta_{30} + \eta_{12})^2 - (\eta_{21} + \eta_{03})^2\right] \\
\phi_6 &= (\eta_{20} - \eta_{02})\left[(\eta_{30} + \eta_{12})^2 - (\eta_{21} + \eta_{03})^2\right] + 4\eta_{11}(\eta_{30} + \eta_{12})(\eta_{21} + \eta_{03}) \\
\phi_7 &= (3\eta_{21} - \eta_{30})(\eta_{30} + \eta_{12})\left[(\eta_{30} + \eta_{12})^2 - 3(\eta_{21} + \eta_{03})^2\right] \\
&\quad + (3\eta_{12} - \eta_{30})(\eta_{21} + \eta_{03})\left[3(\eta_{30} + \eta_{12})^2 - (\eta_{21} + \eta_{03})^2\right].
\end{aligned}
\tag{21}
$$

2.3   Classification Module

Once the Hu moments have been obtained from (21), they must be processed by the classification module to determine if the shape obtained from the image corresponds to a human form. For this, a classifier is required, in this case the multilayer perceptron was chosen, because it allows the classification of linearly non-separable patterns and it is adequate to solve biclass classification problems [7]. The *backpropagation* algorithm is used for multilayer perceptron training. The training of the network requires training patterns, which correspond to a group of feature vectors obtained from segmented objects of a set of training images, which were processed with the algorithms of the previous modules. The number of elements of the training set is 182, divided into 91 elements that correspond to human form and the remaining 91 are non-human forms.

The 91 human forms were obtained from 6 volunteers, each person was photographed in different positions resembling the walking position of a person –Fig. 3–. On the other hand, the 91 images of non-human form are images of ordinary objects that are commonly found in a house, such as pets, balls, lamps. In both sets, the images were obtained in an ideal scenario with controlled light conditions and an ideal background color.

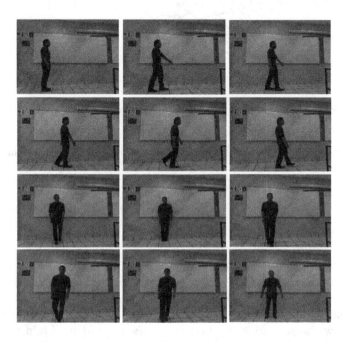

Fig. 3. Sample of human form images obtained from the set of 91 training elements.

The final architecture of the neural network, after performing several tests, is presented in Fig. 4, which shows an architecture of 7 inputs, 5 neurons were required in the hidden layer and only one neuron in the output layer. The 7 inputs correspond to the 7 elements of the feature vector obtained from Hu moments (21), these are the image descriptors. The activation function of the hidden layer neurons is the *hyperbolic tangent*, which allowed the backpropagation algorithm to train faster. For the output layer it is assigned the *sigmoid function*, because of the output of the network is between 0 and 1 (1 correspond to human form and 0 correspond to non-human form).

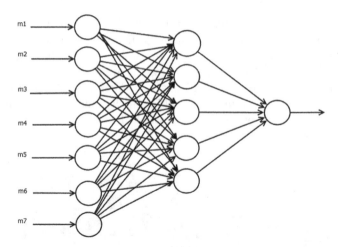

Fig. 4. Final architecture used for the classification module.

Before training, the feature vectors of the set of 182 images were normalized with (22) obtained from [9].

$$
x'_j = \frac{1 - \exp^{-\left(\frac{x_j - \mu_j}{\sigma_j}\right)}}{1 + \exp^{-\left(\frac{x_j - \mu_j}{\sigma_j}\right)}}. \tag{22}
$$

Where x'_j corresponds to the normalized value, x_j is the value to be normalized, μ_j is the average of the corresponding dimension and σ_j is the standard deviation of the corresponding dimension. This normalization allows to obtain a set of normalized data within the range of -1 to $+1$, which is the range of values that allow the activation function *hyperbolic tangent* to obtain appropriate activation values and to avoid values that can saturate the function.

Once the values of the normalized dataset are obtained these are labeled with the value of 0 and 1 (human form: 1 and non-human form: 0). This dataset is processed by the *backpropagation* training algorithm. The training parameters were an $\alpha = 0.5$ and a $\eta = 0.25$. The algorithm converges when the error between the target and the multilayer perceptron output is as small as possible, updating in each iteration the set of weights and bias of each layer connection.

2.4   Communication Module

The communication is a simple client-server architecture, in which the image processing and classification server is implemented on the Raspberry Pi platform. The communication is implemented using a socket. The client is implemented on a computer with a Linux distribution, such as Ubuntu, which receives the status of the home monitoring performed by the server, through port 5000. The server and the client are developed under the TCP/IP protocol stack in C language.

3   Results

The performance of the classification model can be analyzed in a confusion matrix in Table 1. This matrix is a table of NxN –where N is the number of classes– that summarizes the level of success of the predictions of a classification model. In the case of the multilayer perceptron designed and implemented, the number of classes is equal to 2, because of the problem of recognizing a human form, in this case, is a binary classification problem.

The confusion matrix obtained is a matrix of 2×2. And the results were obtained using a test set of 46 elements. The dataset of 228 images is divided in 182 training set images and 46 test set images.

Table 1. Confusion matrix of the classification model.

	Human form	No human form
Human form	22	1
No human form	1	22

The confusion matrix in Table 1 describes that the 23 images containing human form were correctly classified 22 and incorrectly classified 1 image. And the other 23 images that do not contain human form were correctly classified 22 and 1 incorrectly classified. Of the total of the 46 elements of the test set, 95.65% were classified by the model correctly, while 4.34% were incorrectly classified. The execution time in which the Raspberry Pi platform performs the image processing, from the image acquisition module to the classifier module, is approximately of 21 seconds per image. This was measured considering the execution of the algorithms sequentially. Because of these results it was decided to apply HPC techniques, based in data parallelism. These techniques improved the performance, obtaining only 7 s of image processing, approximately. The Raspberry Pi Camera V2 obtains an image in an amount of time of approximately 1 s, this execution time was obtained due to the reduction of the configuration time of the camera to only 500 ms, which is the minimum required for the camera. As a result the total execution time is approximately of 7 to 8 seconds per image. Also the PIR sensor reading is configured to perform a sampling time of 0.5 s.

4   Conclusions

The development of the system on a SoC-based platform and the use of HPC techniques allowed to take advantage of the available software and hardware resources of the Raspberry Pi 3 B, which improved the computational performance of the system.

About the image processing algorithms, the lighting changes on the test scenario generated noise in the sample images. To avoid this it was necessary to implement global and local thresholds in the image regions, in addition to the

Sauvola algorithm. This algorithms of the segmentation module obtained an image without white noise or lighting changes, this result improved the robustness of the system, because of the avoiding of inaccuracies. Also obtaining the characteristic features of an object in an image through the Hu moments allowed to avoid the problem of translations, rotations, changes of scale and illumination.

The classification module required the soft-max normalization algorithm to improve the separation of the descriptor vectors of each object detected in an image. This normalization also improved the execution of the backpropagation algorithm. The result of the classifier was satisfactory. It was obtained an accuracy of approximately 96%. This result allows to place the system as a reliable and robust application for home automation. In comparison with the development presented by Othman and Aydin in [2], it has an accuracy of 93%, approximately. And Mathur et al. in [3] presents a development with an accuracy of only 83%. As well, unlike this projects, the development presented in this paper is implemented taking advantage of the available resources of the Raspberry Pi platform, through HPC techniques.

Acknowledgements. The authors thank the support of Instituto Politécnico Nacional (IPN). SIP-IPN contributed to the development of this work through 20180341 project.

References

1. Reporte sobre delitos de alto impacto. Observatorio Nacional Ciudadano, April 2019. http://onc.org.mx/wp-content/uploads/2019/06/mensual-abril.pdf. Accessed 11 June 2019
2. Othman, N.A., Aydin, I.: A new IoT combined body detection of people by using computer vision for security application. In: 9th International Conference on Computational Intelligence and Communication Networks (CICN), pp. 108–112, September 2017
3. Mathur, S., Subramanian, B., Jain, S., Choudhary, K., Prabha, D.R.: Human detector and counter using Raspberry Pi microcontroller. In: 2017 Innovations in Power and Advanced Computing Technologies (i-PACT), pp. 1–7, April 2017
4. Maksimovic, M. , Vujovic, V., Davidovi, N., Milosevic, V., Perisic, B.: Raspberry Pi as internet of things hardware: performances and constraints. In: IcETRAN 2014, Vrnjacka Banja, Serbia, June 2014
5. Villagómez, C.: El formato BMP, CCM, 24 July 2017. https://es.ccm.net/contents/719-el-formato-bmp. Accessed 21 Jan 2019
6. Wiring Pi. GPIO Interface library for the Raspberry Pi. Wiring Pi. http://wiringpi.com/. Accessed 20 Mar 2019
7. Rodríguez, R., Sossa, J.H.: Procesamiento y Análisis Digital de Imágenes, 1st edn, pp. 180–230, 250–290, 297–350. Alfaomega Grupo Editor, México (2012)
8. Cortés, J., Chaves, J., Mendoza, J.: Comparación cualitativa y cuantitativa de las técnicas básicas de umbralización local para el procesamiento digital de imágenes. Scientia et Technica, vol. 2, no. 51, pp. 236–241, August 2012. https://revistas.utp.edu.co/index.php/revistaciencia/article/view/7561/4707. Accessed 11 Dec 2018
9. Kevin, P., Priddy, L.: Artificial Neural Networks: An Introduction, pp. 16–17. SPIE, Washington (2005)

File Restore Automation with Machine Learning

Saúl Esquivel-García$^{(\boxtimes)}$ (ID) and Óscar Hernández-Uribe (ID)

CIATEQ, A.C. Centro de Tecnología Avanzada, Av. del Retablo 150, Col.
Constituyentes-Fovissste, Querétaro 76150, Mexico
eg.saul@gmail.com, oscar.hernandez@ciateq.mx

Abstract. IT storage enterprise infrastructure management and support is becoming more and more complicated. Engineers have to face everyday with technical challenges to ensure the availability and performance of the data for users and virtual instances. In addition, storage requirements are different for every single business unit and storage support teams have to deal with multivendor storage systems. Certain storage support group used to receive on their ticket queue numerous restore tasks from end users which wrongly deleted important files or folders. The high repetitiveness of restore tasks can be dangerous for the storage engineer because several restores involves larges files and folders with similar names (business naming convention), and the tediousness may lead the engineer to lower the focus and increase human error. An intelligent automation based on machine learning, capable to analyze text and perform repetitive large time consuming restore tasks has been developed to alleviate the workload of the storage support group.

Keywords: Network Attached Storage · Distributed File System · Machine learning · Automation

1 Introduction

Enterprise IT infrastructure (composed of servers, network switches, applications, etc.) support is a primary success key for any company. Supporting storage technology is one of the most important services on IT industry, data must be available for the users keeping all the time its integrity and confidentiality. Furthermore, technical complexity is added to storage support group as IT environments used to run multivendor storage array systems for different purposes as block storage, file storage, and backup depending on the business unit supported.

Keeping IT storage systems healthy is committed by technical engineering experts providing the best professional service to the company. Storage engineers are involved on daily challenging key infrastructure activities (e.g. storage array capacity planning, data migration & business continuity planning for disaster recovery, administer storage fiber channel switch connectivity).

In order to keep a track on daily activities, incidents, changes and problems in IT infrastructure, companies have been deploying and implementing during the last two decades a service ticket system tool. Additionally to activity tracking support, service

M. F. Mata-Rivera et al. (Eds.): WITCOM 2020, CCIS 1280, pp. 61–72, 2020.
https://doi.org/10.1007/978-3-030-62554-2_5

ticket system gives an insight on service time and contractual Service Level Agreements (SLAs) compliance to service management executives.

Certain storage support group is receiving daily, on their ticket tool queue, work order tickets to recover files and folders deleted accidentally by end users under personal and shared drives. This specific storage is provided to end users via Network Attached Storage (NAS) arrays. Snapshot copies is one of the backup protection methods preferred on NAS arrays because they use a minimal capacity on the volume, there is no performance cost and data can be restored quickly from one of the latest snapshot copies. The completion of file and folder restore is a service key for storage support team as it has a high impact on end users business continuity. From storage support team, this has been the restore' process executed by the engineer:

1. From ticket tool system, validate if missing file or folder share path provided by the end user is correct (no typos).
2. Extract from share path the Distributed File System (DFS) folder and its physical volume location.
3. Physical volumes live in NAS array, login to the proper array and locate the volume.
4. Select the volume and proper historic snapshot based on the requested "Restore date" provided by the end user on the ticket, in the snapshot with the requested date the missing file is supposed to live before the deletion occurred.
5. Navigate inside the snapshot folders and locate the requested file or folder, execute the "restore" command.
6. Validate the existence of the file after restore job is completed. Notify end user via email and close the ticket.

If end user has submitted correctly the share path and requested restore date in the ticket form, the process above takes storage engineer around 12 min to be completed. If inconsistences are detected in the ticket, the restore execution time will be longer.

Storage support team work order ticket queue used to receive at least 4 restore tasks per day, in a high workload day 12 tasks are received. This means that for a normal day, storage engineer is focused on restore activities at least 40 min. This time can be used by the engineer on different high impact storage infrastructure activities or taking useful trainings.

The high repetitiveness of the restore tasks can be dangerous for the engineer as several file restores tasks involves numerous files and folders with similar names, this is because of business naming convention, and the tediousness may lead the engineer lower the focus and increase human error.

This article presents an intelligent automation programmed in Python language which connects to ticket tool system, extracts storage support group active restore tickets, text ticket is processed and classified by an Artificial Neural Network (ANN) and finally a restore command and an email notification algorithm is executed by the automation.

2   Related Works

According to [3], the increasing volume of documents in the internet has turned document indexing and searching more complex. This issue leaded the development of several researches in the text classification area. The model proposed deals with stages of feature extraction, classification, labeling and indexing of documents for searching purposes. The extraction is the key part contributing to this work.

On [4], challenges on neural network text classification are presented, one is high dimensional feature spaces. There are big amount of stand-by features when do feature extraction. A group of 100 of training texts may generate 10 times candidate features. The classification is based on Reuter-21578 text collection focused on Natural Language.

Quinteiro-Gonzaléz on [5] separates every single word (tokenize) and then the words are stemmed on its root word to generate a bag of words which will work as "corpus" on natural language processing. Stemmed words are not important on DFS path analysis, however tokenization technique, similar to compilers, will extract keywords on DFS path.

From [6], some experiments are carried out for multiclass text classification using Back Propagation Neural Network (BPNN). The adaptation of the combined method achieved the improvement of accuracy for the multi-class text classification task. This article is helpful on accuracy of ANN, as performance is not constrain on our IT infrastructure environment.

On [7], classification is applied on a ticket tool system, Convolutional Neural Network (CNN) is proposed because has attracted much in text mining due its effectiveness in automatic feature extraction. The author is considering ticket titles for classification, comparison between traditional and deep learning approaches for automatic categorization of IT tickets in a real world production ticketing system is concluded in author´s paper.

Kandkumar on [8], text classification project addresses a real life business challenge of IT Service Management. Almost 30–40% of incident tickets are not routed to the right team and the tickets keep roaming around and around and by the time it reaches the right team. This is one of the known challenges in IT industry where a lot of time is wasted.

3   Automation

3.1   Distributed File System Namespace

Access and file location used to be a problem for big companies, Distributed File System (DFS) is a solution provided by Microsoft to unify multiple file server and NAS file systems into a logical access point (Fig. 1).

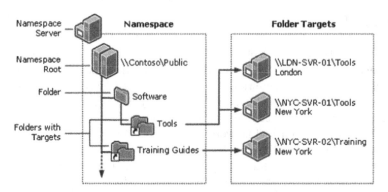

Fig. 1. DFS Namespace structure [1].

- Namespace server - A namespace server hosts a namespace. The namespace server can be a member server or a domain controller.
- Namespace root - The namespace root is the starting point of the namespace. In previous figure, the name of the root is Public, and namespace path is \\Contoso\Public
- Folder - When users browse a folder that has folder targets in the namespace, the client computer receives a referral that transparently redirects the client computer to one of the folder targets.
- Folder targets - A folder target is the Universal Naming Convention (UNC) path of a shared folder or another namespace that is associated with a folder in a namespace. The folder target is where data and content is stored. A user who browses to \\Contoso\Public\Software\Tools is transparently redirected to the shared folder \\LDN-SVR-01\Tools or \\NYC-SVR-01\Tools, depending on which site the user is currently located in [1].

End users provide in ticket system the DFS path of the folder where they are missing a file or folder.

3.2 Neural Network for Text Classification

Artificial Neural Network is the main actor in this automation system, from software design stage has been established as central instance because it interacts with most of the actors based on the decision taken by the classification. ANN has one direct association with the active restore task ticket and three independent dependencies (Fig. 2). Dependencies are detailed explained in next sections.

In order to validate DFS path provided by the end user, an Artificial Neural Network (ANN) has been selected for classifying the path provided by the end user as Multinomial Naïve Bayes algorithm has several disadvantages:

- The algorithm produces a score rather than a probability. We want a probability to ignore predictions below some threshold [2].

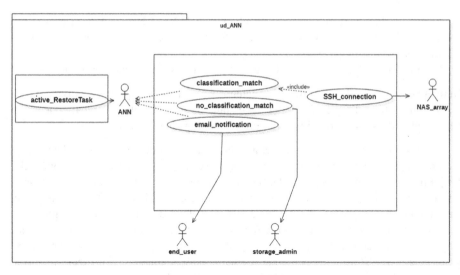

Fig. 2. UML ANN use case diagram.

• The algorithm 'learns' from examples of what is in a class, but not what isn't. This learning of patterns of what does not belong to a class is often very important [2].

Neural networks are a biologically inspired paradigm (imitating the functioning of the mammalian brain) that enables a computer to learn human faculties from observational data. They currently provide solutions to many problems: image recognition, handwriting recognition, speech recognition, speech analysis [9].

The first stage of the automatic classification model is composed of the preprocessing and feature extraction, which provide subsidies for the classification start up [3]. From ticket information, DFS initial structure is extracted and the first four folders in the path are identified with Microsoft DFS Namespace structure (Table 1 Category column). Folder names are temporarily stored in our Python program as local string variables (Table 1 Local variable column).

Table 1. Sample DFS path divided.

Category	Local variable	Sample DFS path divided
Namespace	namespace	company.domain.com
DFS Folder	DFS_folder	business_unit
DFS Subfolder	DFS_subfolder	Marketing
Share	share	folder 1

These variables are consecutively classified by the ANN. Classification success relies on ANN training data set, which has been filled with partial folders from DFS server information for testing purposes.

Sample DFS path: "\\company.domain.com\business_unit\marketing\folder 1\"

Neural Network Training Data. Text categorization is the key process to divide information into different topics for better understanding [4]. The observational concept in neural network is transformed in this work as training data feature.

As with all supervised learning algorithms, an appropriately labeled data set is required to design and train an algorithm capable of classifying information appropriately [10]. Information from production DFS management server has been extracted towards our training data, four classes have been created based in Microsoft DFS Namespace structure [1]: namespace_c, dfs_folder_c, dfs_subfolder_c, share_c. Every single class is filled with its folders contained. For inner class "share_c", PowerShell cmdlet "Get-ChildItem" resulted useful as plain text output was easily exported to Python ANN program. (e.g. "Get-ChildItems \\company.domain.com\test\marketing"). Figure 3 shows some encoding parameters added into the data training classes.

```
training_data.append({"class":"namespace_c", "sentence":"company.domain.com"})
training_data.append({"class":"namespace_c", "sentence":"company"})

training_data.append({"class":"dfs_folder_c", "sentence":"production"})
training_data.append({"class":"dfs_folder_c", "sentence":"test_environment"})
training_data.append({"class":"dfs_folder_c", "sentence":"read-only"})
training_data.append({"class":"dfs_folder_c", "sentence":"qos"})

training_data.append({"class":"dfs_subfolder_c", "sentence":"marketing"})
training_data.append({"class":"dfs_subfolder_c", "sentence":"human_resources"})
training_data.append({"class":"dfs_subfolder_c", "sentence":"accounting"})
training_data.append({"class":"dfs_subfolder_c", "sentence":"logistics"})
training_data.append({"class":"dfs_subfolder_c", "sentence":"invoices"})
training_data.append({"class":"dfs_subfolder_c", "sentence":"communications"})
training_data.append({"class":"dfs_subfolder_c", "sentence":"test"})

training_data.append({"class":"share_c", "sentence":"plans_2019"})
training_data.append({"class":"share_c", "sentence":"project01"})
training_data.append({"class":"share_c", "sentence":"FY2020"})
training_data.append({"class":"share_c", "sentence":"Automation_Test"})
```

Fig. 3. ANN training data.

The tokenized training data is transformed into a matrix or "array". The NumPy package provides functions to create and manipulate arrays. An array is a collection of uniform data types such as vector, matrix, or tensor, in addition NumPy commands have a tremendous speed advantage because of its computational optimization [11].

Training matrix is processed by a single layer perceptron (Fig. 4), the weighted linear combination of input values enter into the active node, where it will be transformed by a so called activation function [12]. Activation function is used to make the output fall within a desired range, thereby preventing the paralysis of the network. Additionally to the nonlinearity, the continuous differentiability of these functions helps in preventing the inhibition of the training [9].

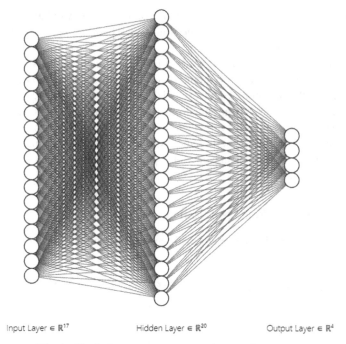

Input Layer $\in \mathbb{R}^{17}$ Hidden Layer $\in \mathbb{R}^{20}$ Output Layer $\in \mathbb{R}^{4}$

Fig. 4. Single-layer perceptron neural network structure.

3.3 Ticket Information, Path Validation and Physical Volume Extraction

Ticket tool system incorporates a REST API (Representational State Transfer Application Programming Interface), which enables interaction with external services. HTTP verb GET is used by the automation to access a resource in a read-only mode [13]. Using this verb, ticket task metadata information is extracted which includes requestor name, DFS path, file name, required restore date.

DFS path information is analyzed by trained ANN, if four first items in DFS path matches with an established category with a prediction rate above 97%, it means the user submitted correctly the first characters of the path. As after fourth element on a path is not part of training data because of complicated production tree folder structure, now full DFS path existence needs to be validated. End users may perform type errors in any of inner folders names. Next code is executed to validate folder existence:

```
import os                    #Import OS module
def path_existence(path):    #Validation function
  isdir = os.path.isdir(path) #isdir var path validation
  if (isdir == True):        #Is path True?
    extract_volume(path)     #Yes, function is called
  else:                      #else
    error(3)                 #error function is called
```

Python code above validates directory path existence, if path validation is successful, program flow continues to "extract_volume" function. If path validation is not succeeded, an error code is sent to by the automation.

Function extract_volume() incorporates a PowerShell subroutine. PowerShell provides a great acquisition engine for obtaining a vast array of information from live systems, servers, peripherals, mobile devices, and data-driven applications. PowerShell has traditionally been used by system administrators, IT teams, incident response groups, and forensic investigators to gain access to operational information regarding the infrastructures they manage [14]. PowerShell cmdlet "Get-DfsnFolder" is submitted to retrieve to automation physical path, which includes physical volume name and NAS array identifier.

3.4 Restore Script and Email Notification

A restore script command is generated with the information gathered and validated in previous steps:

1. NAS array identifier.
2. Physical volume.
3. Data path.
4. Restore date.

The script is submitted to NAS array through SSH (Secure Shell). SSH is a network protocol that allows data to be exchanged using a secure channel between two networked devices. Used primarily on Linux- and Unix-based systems to access shell accounts, SSH was designed as a replacement for Telnet and other insecure remote shells, which send information, notably passwords, in plaintext, rendering them susceptible to packet analysis [15].

An email notification is sent to end user notifying the success of file or folder restore. Email message contains the name of the file/folder restored and its DFS path. In case classification is not succeeded, message includes the error found. Both email templates include storage support group contact information.

Email dependence has been configured in automation using a local SMTP (Simple Mail Transfer Protocol) server. SMTP instances transfer mail between domains and also connect with the users of the email in a client/server relationship [16]. Finally, HTTP verb POST is used to update a given resource [13], tickets are closed using POST verb with file information once the restore is finished.

4 Results and Discussion

Automation has been deployed and implemented in a test environment not compromising business production data. From test NAS array a new 10 GB volume "Automation_Test" was created and added as share in DFS test subfolder.

New path: \\company.domain.com\test_environment\test\Automation_Test\

Inside new share, inner folders and .txt dummy files were created for testing purposes. The new share path added a new input in the training data, resulting in next ANN architecture:

- Input layer: 17 neurons.
- Hidden layer: 20 neurons.
- Output layer: 4 neurons.

After 10,000 iterations, delta error is reduced from 0.542089 to 0.007707 (Fig. 5). Synaptic weights are stored in a local file, which are going to be used as reference when automation runs in production environment.

```
17 sentences in training data
Training with 20 neurons
Input matrix: 17x17     Output matrix: 1x4
delta after 0 iterations:0.5420895905494633
delta after 100 iterations:0.2382688479544547
delta after 200 iterations:0.144468569242975
delta after 300 iterations:0.0928095904576039
delta after 400 iterations:0.0689422790522891
delta after 500 iterations:0.05601156593698377
delta after 600 iterations:0.04787363996016239
delta after 700 iterations:0.042232564950937725
delta after 800 iterations:0.03806090691965077
delta after 900 iterations:0.034831145367980876
delta after 1000 iterations:0.03224012502477756
delta after 2000 iterations:0.02014911772129237
delta after 3000 iterations:0.015626632945500925
delta after 4000 iterations:0.013128065667839002
delta after 5000 iterations:0.011499802521268648
delta after 6000 iterations:0.01035683079261845
delta after 7000 iterations:0.00945232818999067
delta after 8000 iterations:0.008753571644000003
delta after 9000 iterations:0.008183615903329135
delta after 10000 iterations:0.007707625564381474
```

Fig. 5. ANN iterations.

Test restore ticket was raised with correct DFS information. Automation query to ticket tool REST API worked smoothly with no interruptions nor delays. Ticket metadata was extracted and DFS path analyzed by trained ANN which showed a classification certainty rate above 0.99 which is almost 100% certainty (Fig. 6).

On the other hand, test restore tickets were raised with wrong DFS information and classification rates resulted in score around 0.12, which does not meet classification criteria. Some wrong folders were not even classified (Fig. 7). More classification tests are planned, which will include a validation subset instead train/test split data set.

Manual file restore tasks has been a monotonous activity which storage engineer has to spent large valuable time. These large time monotonous work may cause problems with attention, and may lead to low arousal, lack of alertness and more accidents

```
company.domain.com
  classification: [['namespace_c', 0.9957933042434507]]
test_environment
  classification: [['dfs_folder_c', 0.9964677963593462]]
test
  classification: [['dfs_subfolder_c', 0.9755158583362045]]
Automation_Test
  classification: [['share_c', 0.9967755478884792]]
```

Fig. 6. Test restore ticket with correct DFS information.

```
wrong.domain.com
  classification: []
unexistent_folder
  classification: []
badsubfolder
  classification: []
nothing
  classification: []
```

Fig. 7. Test restore ticket with wrong DFS information.

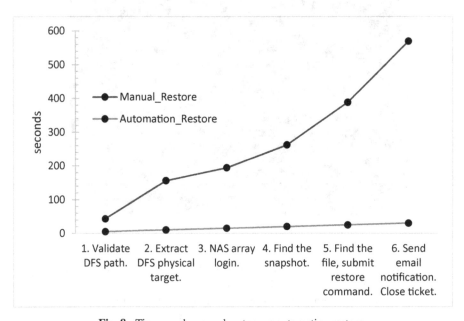

Fig. 8. Time graph manual restore vs automation restore.

[17]. Previous researches has accorded a central place to repetitive work tasks on the inhibition of cortical activity through habituation to monotonous tasks [18]. In addition,

task monotony affects attention, the assumption is that when there is a necessity to perform a repetitive task, it will be perceived as boring or uninteresting, attention will be deteriorated and this will be expressed as lower performance [19].

A manual restore has been implemented in order to record the time per executed stage and compare it with total automation restore time. This manual restore has been executed in an ideal environment prepared with web browser with ticket tool & NAS array management open tabs. Manual restore execution took storage engineer 572 s (9.5 min). Automation restore execution took 38 s. Figure 8 shows the huge time difference as automation saves time up to 1500% against the manual process.

5   Conclusions and Future Work

Automation implementation minimum involves storage team in restore activities. Storage experts are only involved when ANN is not able to classify properly the ticket due type errors or lack of words on text entered by end user. Thus, restore activities are no longer a monotonous repetitive activity, now it is a basic end user support providing guidance and feedback to user, which will avoid these kind of errors in future restore tickets.

During testing stage, automation demonstrated its fast performance execution saving up to 10 min per task against manual restore process executed by storage engineer. Automation helps storage support teams alleviating the workload and allowing them focus on high impact tickets, responding to service interruption, problem and incident with appropriate approach, investigating to determine the root cause of the problem and providing quick resolution. Furthermore, allowing storage experts focusing as well on high key infrastructure activities as:

– Storage system capacity planning, data migration, management and support.
– Business continuity analysis and planning. Reports.
– Proactive health checks, capacity & performance management.
– Ensure the availability, reliability, scalability and manageability of the storage environment.

During automation validation, REST API ticket extraction was performed manually for behavior analysis and testing purposes, for future work execution of an algorithm to check recurrently active tickets will be required during approved maintenance window.

Additionally, in order to deploy automation in production environment, a file-folder size restrictor is required. Miscommunication inside collaboration group may lead to distracted end user to raise a restore ticket for existing large file or folder which entire team has been working in last days. 800 MB size is tentatively proposed for restrictor threshold.

References

1. Docs, Overview of DFS Namespaces. https://docs.microsoft.com/en-us/previous-versions/windows/it-pro/windows-server-2008-R2-and-2008/cc730736(v=ws.11)?redirectedfrom=MSDN. Accessed 3 Apr 2020

2. Kassabgi, G.: machinelearnings.co. https://machinelearnings.co/text-classification-using-neu ral-networks-f5cd7b8765c6. Accessed 7 Apr 2020
3. Fernandes de Mello, R.: Automatic text classification using an artificial neural network. Universidade de Sao Paulo, Sao Paulo (n.d.)
4. Chen, J., Pan, H., Ao, Q.: Study a text classification method based on neural network model. In: Jin, D., Lin, S. (eds.) Advances in Multimedia, Software Engineering and Computing Vol. 1, pp. 471–475. Springer, Heidelberg (2011). https://doi.org/10.1007/978-3-642-25989-0_76
5. Quinteiro-González, J.M.: Clasificación de textos en lenguaje natural usando la Wikipedia. Revista Ibérica de Sistemas e Tecnologias de Informação (2011)
6. Zhang, W., Tang, X., Yoshida, T.: Text classification with support vector machine and back propagation neural network. In: Shi, Y., van Albada, G.D., Dongarra, J., Sloot, P.M.A. (eds.) ICCS 2007. LNCS, vol. 4490, pp. 150–157. Springer, Heidelberg (2007). https://doi.org/10. 1007/978-3-540-72590-9_21
7. Han, J.: Vertical domain text classification: towards understanding IT tickets using deep neural networks. In: The Thirty-Second AAAI Conference on Artificial Intelligence, pp. 8202–8203 (2018)
8. Kandakumar, K.: medium.com. https://medium.com/@karthikkumar_57917/it-support-ticket-classification-using-machine-learning-and-ml-model-deployment-ba694c01e416. Accessed 3 Mar 2020
9. Goyal, P.: Deep Learning for Natural Language Processing (2018)
10. Arellano-Verdejo, J.: Moderate resolution imaging spectroradiometer products classification using deep learning. In: Mata-Rivera, M.F., Zagal-Flores, R., Barría-Huidobro, C. (eds.) WITCOM 2019. CCIS, vol. 1053, pp. 61–70. Springer, Cham (2019). https://doi.org/10. 1007/978-3-030-33229-7_6
11. Lindblad, T.: Image Processing Using Pulse-Coupled Neural Networks. Springer, Heidelberg (2013)
12. Awange, J. (ed.): Hybrid Imaging and Visualization. CCIS. Springer, Cham (2020). https:// doi.org/10.1007/978-3-030-26153-5_5
13. Doglio, F.: REST API Development with Node.js. Apress, Uruguay (2018)
14. Hosmer, C.: PowerShell and Python Together (2019)
15. Tilborg, H.C.: Encyclopedia of Cryptography and Security. Springer, Heidelberg (2005)
16. Howser, G.: Simple mail transfer protocol: email. In: Howser, G. (ed.) Computer Networks and the Internet, pp. 385–417. Springer, Cham (2020). https://doi.org/10.1007/978-3-030-34496-2_22
17. McBain in Loukidou, E.: Boredom in the workplace: more than monotonous tasks. Int. J. Manag. Rev. 381–405 (2009)
18. O'Hanlon in Loukidou, E.: Boredom in the workplace: more than monotonous tasks. Int. J. Manag. Rev. 381–405 (2009)
19. Loukidou, E.: Boredom in the workplace: more than monotonous tasks. Int. J. Manag. Rev. 381–405 (2009)

Open Educational Resource on Responsible, Ethical, Aesthetic and Functional Learning in Surgery Procedures Requiring Management of Incisions and Sutures

Margarita Dorado Valencia(⊠)

Universidad Santiago de Cali –Valle, Cali, Colombia
margarita.dorado00@usc.edu.co

Abstract. Open educational resources (OER) facilitate the availability of up-to-date and relevant information according to the contexts and disciplines in which learning takes place autonomously on the basis of prior knowledge. This document describes the ADDIE method, the Analysis, Design, Development, application and evaluation of an open educational resource, designed to complement training in the management of soft tissue incisions and sutures, in third-year dental students. The OER is composed of three modules that present the information sequential manner, taking into account the inclusion of the knowledge of the discipline: know how to do, know how to be and know how to be. During the phases of construction of the resource, surveys were applied to the students, in order to offer them content that would allow them to interact according to the different contexts.

Keywords: ICT · Open educational resource · OER · Sutures

1 Introduction

Open Educational Resource (OER) are free educational materials, which are used as a basis for learning, training or as a complement to formal education. They are offered with freely available licenses for their production, distribution and use on the web and are made of materials such as audio, text, video, software tools and multimedia, among others; which means that they can be freely used, copied, studied, modified and redistributed by anyone who obtains a copy. Its objective is to generate knowledge, promoting the participation of teachers and students in specific fields of knowledge to collectively seek the transformation from global thinking to local action.

The REA prepared as a complement in the management of incisions and sutures of soft tissues, is presented as a complement to the course of Oral Surgery for students who are in the third and fourth year of Dentistry before their clinical practices. Its construction, design, implementation and evaluation required the participation of a multidisciplinary team that responds to the process of incorporating technologies in education, as a "consequence of variables of political-educational, economic and infrastructure, cultural, curricular and organizational nature" [1]. With this innovative resource, the policies to

M. F. Mata-Rivera et al. (Eds.): WITCOM 2020, CCIS 1280, pp. 73–82, 2020.
https://doi.org/10.1007/978-3-030-62554-2_6

promote the production of open educational material proposed by the Ministry of Education for the use and appropriation of ICT are fulfilled, contributing to flexibility and interactivity as essential elements in the educational process.

2 Population and Sample

This research had in the initial phase the Context Analysis, the final phase, of Implementation and Evaluation with the collaboration and participation of the students of the faculty of Dentistry of the University of the Valle who are studying 3 and 4 years, distributed in two groups of Approximately 19 students.

For the design and development of the OER in its pedagogical, instrumental, editing and exeLearning management aspect, the teaching group linked to the DINTEV of the University of the Valle was counted as a contribution to achieve the expected achievement. The edition of contents, information, graphics and videos by the author of this project.

3 Methodological Design

This research is a case study, which was designed with a qualitative methodological approach, according to Sampieri and was born from the need felt by students regarding the appropriate concepts and techniques in the management of incisions and sutures in the Oral surgery module of undergraduate students of Dentistry at the University of the Valle, and in turn, to facilitate its application in different contexts. In order to solve this problem, the research objective is to achieve a better performance and development of skills in oral surgery by students.

4 Methodological Support

For the analysis of the context prior to the design of the resource, a questionnaire was prepared and filled in using the google form, as a tool to gather key information on the use of educational resources on the web, knowledge and application management in their educational activities and finally complemented by a physical survey that was coded to maintain confidentiality which the students' knowledge on the handling of soft tissue incisions and sutures was addressed.

This work incorporates two phases for its development: the first aimed to identify the theoretical basis of the proposal and the second in the development of the resources.

The opening of the OER (Open Educational resources) is associated to severe dimensions: legal, economic, technical and in particulary pedagogical and transformative, which refers to the roles of teachers and students during learning and the interpretation of practices and work proposals adapting them to the application contexts (learning situation). The development of content in ITC is carried out by "layers" [12], which allows the degree of interrelationship of the dimensions of content and pedagogy to be differentiated and accounted for. When interacting with the resource, knowledge is generated in the student, that, when validated, allows it to be used in similar or different contexts [9].

The ITC have renewed the methodologies that make it possible to adapt the contents to the different learning styles of the students. The use of multimedia programs implies innumerable advantages for students with different learning styles, compared to the methodologies used in traditional teaching [4].

5   Results

According to the answers, the use of ICT in education should be used as a complement, which facilitates learning and can be gradually implemented in the institution at all levels: teacher training, improvement of networks and internet connection, so that virtual education has the importance and relevance it deserves.

Students interact and collaborate with their peers, demonstrating that technology is the opportunity to share and communicate information as indicated [8].

The Table 1 shows that 50% of students use digital tools a lot to obtain information from other sources. Confirming these data with the problems of Herrera, who manifests the great possibility of access to technology that facilitates the search for information.

The fundamental role that ICT play in the development of any professional activity is relevant. The use of ICT to organize activities, solve problems and carry out projects. [5]. students share experiences [15], generating collaborative work and exchange of information. In addition to interaction, appropriation and communication Herrera, 2009. However, it is necessary to reduce the digital gap that still remains at a low percentage.

By involving technology, the student has the opportunity to learn independently and with other sources, thus generating the active construction of knowledge; In addition to training them in skills that induce autonomous learning for life [14].

It has been demonstrated that ICT are building a global society that cuts across the fields of communication [18].

Students need to be motivated to work in teams, as they learn more when they work with others than when they work alone, with the guidance of teachers. [10]. According to the survey, see Table 1, the educational resource designed presents a greater emphasis on the visual through videos and graphics that support the theme. It is agile, practical, easy to share and responds to the learning needs of students in the area of health.

The design of the OER: see Table 2: is based on these premises: the responsibility with the supervision of the incisions by which those who accept the management must have a specific prior knowledge of the tissues to be affected and the disposition of the affected skin folds at the source; The ethics to understand that a seriously affected incision affects the function and the aesthetics of the tissues involved, generating emotional, psychosocial alterations and of projection of the individual in his context; concepts that are considered in the OER where, from the formulation of the problem and the objectives, it establishes the knowledge and establishes the knowledge, the knowledge and the being that give rise to the protocols of management. When we relate the ethical, aesthetic and functional aspects in a transversal way in the design of the Resource, we establish how, what and why they work and what they are used for.

Table 1. Results: Diagnostic Survey (Students) (Source:Ramírez, S. 2012)

Diagnostic survey	Results Soft tissue management when performing incisions and sutures	
1. Do you remember the histological structures that form the epithelia?	Yes	16 – 80%
	No	4 – 20%
2. Sutures have the sole purpose of confronting wounds	F	12 – 60%
	T	8 – 40%
3. To make incisions on the skin, the most frequently used scalpel blade is	11	4 – 20%
	12	2 – 10%
	15	14 – 70%
4. The suture material that guarantees better skin healing corresponds to:	S-4	8 – 40%
	N-4	6 – 30%
	C-4	6 – 30%
5. To achieve a "symmetrical" tension when approaching the mucous edges in a bone remodeling, you would recommend.	PS	3 – 15%
	CC	15 – 75%
	CV	2 – 10%
6. In sutures where resorbable material is used, it must be removed.	V	5 – 25%
	H	1 – 5%
	V Y H	14 – 70%
7. In sutures where resorbable material is used, it must be removed.	SI	2 – 10%
	NO	18 – 90%
8. Briefly explain how a suture is performed in two stages	Comments: 1. "I don't know. Insert the needle through one of the ends, take it out and return it to Meter through the other end." 2. "Gripping the needle passes the needle and then grabs the other edge with the clamp" 3. "Laced in 2 steps to avoid tearing" 4. "The needle is passed first on one side of the incision and then on the other side.	

Table 2. Design of the OER (Source: Chiappe,2012)

Result Open Educational Resource as a complement to responsible, ethical, aesthetic and functional learning of durable procedures that require management of incisions and sutures	
ABSTRACT: Open Educational Resource as a complement to the learning of "Incisions and sutures in soft tissues" that promotes a responsible, ethical, aesthetic and functional management in the module of Oral Surgery, of the undergraduate students of Dentistry of the university of Valle	
Public Object – User	Dental students of IV year-Health Area
General objetives	Design an open educational resource REA, which contributes to the learning of soft tissue incisions and sutures, promoting a responsible, ethical, aesthetic and functional management in the oral surgery module of undergraduate students od Dentistry
Keywords	Incisions - Sutures – Healing – Skin Wounds – Mucosal Wounds – Tissue repair
Knowledge area	Oral Surgery – Therapeutics - Health
Skills and Knowledge	Previus Knowledge in anatomy, histology, physiology and semiology Required skills: Instrumentals, Cognitive and Conceptual
Competition	Recognizes soft tissues: skin and mucosa, its alterations and healing mechanisms, the design of incisions, materials and suturing techniques

KNOWLEDGE: for the development of the activities included in the three modules that make up the educational resource it is necessary that the student in his autonomous learning process, keep in mind the implicit knowledge in his formative process: the know-how (cognitive), the know-how (practical) and know-how (personal). This knowledge is discriminated against and associated with the module that is being worked on, interrelated at the end of the exercise.

	Know to know (KK)		know to do (KD)		know how to be (KB)
KK1	Structure of the skin and mucosa	KD1	Separates (dissects) the skin and mucous components	KB1	Protects the integrity and function of soft tissues.
KK2	Factors that alter healing	KD2	Prepare the tissues for suture	KB2	Promotes the aesthetics and function of the tissue to be repaired
		KD3	Locate areas where the incision does not injure nerves		
KK3	Tissue Repair Mechanisms	KD4	Review patient factors that may alter tissue repair	KB3	Evaluate management alternatives to offer the best ethical, aesthetic and functional result to the patient

(*continued*)

Table 2. (*continued*)

K K 4	Folds and tissue traction vectors	K D 5	Locate the sites where you can make the incision safely	
K K 5	Suture materials to use according to the type of tissue	K D 6	Recognize the type of material you should use and how you should do it	

Module I: TISUUE STRUCTURE

Learning objectives	Differentiate the components that give the structure to skin and mucosa, their alterations and tissue repair mechanisms
Themes	Tissue structure: skin and mucosa 2. General: Factors that alter the repair
Associated knowledge	KK1 – KK3 – KD1 - KD3 – KD4 – KB1
Activity	Evaluation heading

Module II: INCISIONS

Learning objectives	Apply knowledge about the contents of the tissue structure in order to draw incisions
Themes	1. General: Incisions 2. Techniques: characteristics and designs
Associated knowledge	KK1 - KK4 - KK6 - KD3 - KD5 - KD2 - KB3 -kB5
Activity	Evaluation heading

(*continued*)

Table 2. (*continued*)

Module III: SUTURES	
Learning objectives	Repair tissues by locating and holding firm the edges of a wound in order to promote healing and optimal repair
Themes	1. General: Sutures 2. Techniques: characteristics and designs
Associated knowledge	KK1 - KK4 - KK6 - KD3 - KD5 - KB2 - KB3 -KB5
Activity	Evaluation heading

In terms of the teachers' appreciation, see Table 3, there was total acceptance of using the OER as a pedagogical tool in their classes, they agreed that the OER contributes to the strengthening of their own teaching, planning and evaluation by building on the needs from their own context.

The achievement of significant learning in students is recognized through activities based on real problems posed in the OER, where they must be solved through alternative treatments.

As can be seen in the table, only 25% of respondents [2] are not aware of the OER, nor do they know of the existence of the free Creative Commons license.

Although 75% of the teachers claim to be aware of the open educational resources and their advantages, 25% respond that there is not participation in the construction of these OER in their disciplinary areas.

Those who responded positively accept the low level of ownership and use of OER in their own teaching practice.

The fact that 100% consider the use of technology for better learning and the use of OER as a pedagogical tool is surprising. However, the lack of institutional incentives, the formation of interdisciplinary teams for design and implementation, as well as the problems of technological infrastructure and Internet connection, have been found to be limitations for its creation [11].

Table 3. Evaluation of the use of the Open Educational Resource (OER) Teachers Ramírez, S. [2012]

1	Considers that when using the OER, as support for education, knowledge, skills and attitudes are generated in the students	YES – 100%	
2	The OER used shows content and application elements congruent to the context	YES – 100%	
3	The OER used managed to arouse their interest to use it as an educational tool	YES – 100%	
4	The OER used handles language appropriate to the context	YES – 100%	
5	The OER used is current and updated in the contents and elements that integrate it	YES – 100%	
6	The OER allows the teacher to identify areas of opportunity for the strengthening of their teaching	YES– 100%	
7	The REA allows the teacher to strengthen the areas of educational planning and evaluation	YES – 100%	
8	The OER presents a clear organization	YES– 100%	
9	I would visit this resource again	YES – 100%	
10	Would you recommend this OER to other people interested in the subject that IS	YES – 100%	
11	Did you know what Open Educational Resources (OER) are, and what they consist	YES – 75%	NO 25%
12	Considers that the real problems and the combination of Technology help to obtain a better learning	YES – 100%	

6 Conclusions

With the construction of the open educational resource, which is in ICESI's virtual object repository, (ftp://icesi.edu.co/tgrado/mlrodriguez_rea/index.html) under a Creative Commons Attribution Share Alike 4.0 license; the resource was worked on in exeLearning 2.1, complying with the characteristics of open resources: accessibility, reuse, interoperability, sustainability and metadata [17]. The needs of the students were identified [3] to relate theory with practice, to solve problems based on reality, since in training programs there is a tendency to separate theory from practice thinking not of the student but of the teacher. In accordance with the above, the OER made it possible to link theory and practice to the real context, which was reflected in the activities proposed in the resource at the end of each Module. As the OER can be modified, clinical cases can continue to be presented which students apply the basic concepts learned previously, with new ones to solve problems, supported by real experiences that are presented in daily practice and for which they must propose alternative solutions.

Regarding its design and application as a pedagogical strategy, the OER allows for constant renewal and enrichment, by incorporating new concepts according to the context of application, thus avoiding the loss of its initial attractiveness without altering the proposed objective. moreover, the work experience using the OER as a complement to the classes, inplies a multidisciplinary team, which must be willing with its dedication to put at the service of its technical, scientific and administrative knowledge to achieve new products that promote and satisfy the training needs in the digital age. By evaluating the resource with students and teachers from different disciplines, it was possible to encourage the use of the OER as a pedagogical strategy, which allows constant renewal and enrichment, incorporating new concepts according to the disciplinary area.

The OER for the Management of incisions and sutures in soft tissues, seeks to complement preclinical practices and for this to be plausible it will be necessary to test it in different institutional and social contexts. This resource is one more opportunity to renew traditional didactics, used in the health area, taking advantage of the use of technology, redesigning the forms of learning, expanding its possibilities through ICT. The OER that was built for the management of incisions and sutures in soft tissues, allows to be revised, updated and improved as evidence and scientific advances reaffirm or not, the postulates described here.

Finally, answering the research question, it was possible to motivate the students for the development of learning, improving the skills that allowed them to strengthen the autonomous work through the activities proposed in the resource, based on clinical cases that placed them in a real context, applying the method of the turned classroom. In addition, the OER supports, from the formative evaluation, through the feedback of their work, finding meaning to that feedback because they could contrast it with what they had done before, achieving an active learning. According to Zamora, active learning is achieved when the student is motivated and committed, the student asks interesting questions because he or she has a conceptual appropriation, takes into account learning styles, (Integrates videos, graphics, sounds).

Students come to class more prepared, more knowledge application activities can be done because the OER has allowed them to appropriate the conceptual bases, so they come to class to apply that knowledge in practical exercises, with activities that make the student act not only on a theoretical level but also to apply it to real situations that he or she will face when he or she is professional, making the learning deep, that he or she learns from what he or she will find in real life.

References

1. Area, M.: Las tecnologías de la información y comunicación en el sistema escolar. Una revisión de las líneas de investigación (2004)
2. Chiappe, L., et al.: Prácticas educativas abiertas como factor de innovación educativa (2012)
3. Coll, C., Sánchez, E.: Presentación. El análisis de la interacción alumnoprofesor: líneas de investigación Presentation. the analysis of the pupilteacher interaction: researching lines. Revista de educación **346**, 15–32 (2008)
4. Collis, D., Montgomery, C.: Competing on resources: strategy in the 1990s. Knowl. Strat. **73**(4), 25–40 (1995)

5. Figueira, M., Rivas, M.: Las TIC en manos de los estudiantes universitarios. Revista Latinoamericana de Tecnología Educativa-RELATEC **5**(2), 165–176 (2006)
6. González, J.: El aprendizaje activo y la formación universitaria. Universidad Icesi (2010)
7. Hernández-Sampieri, R.; Torres, C., Mendoza, P.: Metodología de la investigación. México D.F. McGraw-Hill Interamericana
8. Kozma, R.: Comparative analysis of policies for ICT in education. In: International handbook of information technology in primary and secondary education. p. 1083–1096, Springer, Boston, MA (2008)
9. Mcloughlin, C., Lee, M.: Social software and participatory learning: Pedagogical choices with technology affordances in the Web 2.0 era. (2007)
10. Martínez-Olvera, W., Esquivel-Gámez, I., Martínez Castillo, J.: Aula invertida o modelo invertido de aprendizaje: Origen, sustento e implicaciones. Los Modelos Tecno-Educativos, revolucionando el aprendizaje del siglo XXI, p. 143–160 (2014)
11. Michael, J.: Where's the evidence that active learning works? Advances in physiology education (2006)
12. Mora-Rivera, S., Coto-Chotto, M., Villalobos-Murillo, J.: Participación de las mujeres en la carrera de Ingeniería Informática de la Universidad National y su desempeño en los cursos de programación. Revista Electrónica Educare **21**(1), 221–242 (2017)
13. Mulder, F.: Towards national strategies for OER HE. En Communication at the EADTU OER-HE Stakeholder Workshop, Leuven. http://mc/www2.arts.kuleuven.be/info/bestanden-div/EADTU%20OER-HE%20Stakeholder%20Workshop%20KU%20Leuven.ppt (2011)
14. Ramírez, M.: Modelos y estrategias de enseñanza para ambientes innovadores. Monterrey, México: Editorial Digital del Tecnológico de Monterrey, p. 47 (2012)
15. Romiszowski, A.: The development of physical skills: Instruction in the psychomotor domain. Instructional-design theories and models: A new paradigm of instructional theory, p. 457–481 (1999)
16. Torres, C., Alcántar, M.: Uso de las redes sociales como estrategias de aprendizaje.? Transformación educativa? Apertura, 3(2) (2011)
17. Torres, L.: Estrategias de aprendizaje en estudiantes universitarios. Un aporte a la construcción del Espacio Europeo de Educación Superior. Educación y educadores **12**(3), 75–98 (2009)
18. Varlamis, I., Apostolakis, I.: The present and future of standards for e-learning technologies. Int. J. E-Learn. Learn. Objects **2**(1), 59–76 (2006)
19. Vidal Ledo, M., Gómez Martínez, F., Ruiz Piedraz, A.M.: Software educativos. Educación Médica Superior **24**(1), 97–110 (2010)

On the Computation of Optimized Trading Policies Using Deep Reinforcement Learning

Uriel Corona-Bermudez$^{(\boxtimes)}$ ⓘ, Rolando Menchaca-Mendez ⓘ,
and Ricardo Menchaca-Mendez ⓘ

Centro de Investigación en Computación,
Av. Juan de Dios Bátiz S/N, Nueva Industrial Vallejo, Gustavo A. Madero,
07738 Ciudad de México, CDMX, Mexico
b160630@sagitario.cic.ipn.mx, {rmen,ric}@cic.ipn.mx

Abstract. In this paper we present a deep reinforcement learning-based methodology for computing optimized trading policies. During the first stage of the methodology, we employ Gated Recurrent Units (GRUs) to predict the immediate future behaviour of the time series that describe the temporal dynamics of the value of a set of assets. Then, we employ a Deep Q-Learning Architecture to compute optimized trading policies that describe, at every point in time, which assets have to be bought and which have to be sold in order to maximize profit. Our experimental results, which are based on trading cryptocurrencies, show that the proposed algorithm effectively computes trading policies that achieve incremental profits from an initial budget.

Keywords: Reinforcement learning · Machine learning for trading · Cryptocurrencies

Investing and trading have been a way to keep safe our money or increase its future value, depending on the risk of our investments. Many investment instruments have become available, like saving accounts, certificates of deposits, stocks, mutual funds, among others. Many of these instruments are available for almost every person via their bank entities and online brokers.

A particularly dynamic and attractive market is based on cryptocurrencies. With the born of bitcoin, in 2009, a new industry emerged and many interested people with it. Hundreds of cryptocurrencies have been developed, many of them fall trying [1], and others have persisted until the point that they are used in many markets for transactions as real money [2].

The main problem with trading is that we can't predict how instruments are going to move. This means that we can't decide when to make an offer or when we should withdraw one. Experts have developed many observation-based techniques, but learning them is time-consuming and requires a complete dedication to it. That is why automated methods are popular and widely used.

© Springer Nature Switzerland AG 2020
M. F. Mata-Rivera et al. (Eds.): WITCOM 2020, CCIS 1280, pp. 83–96, 2020.
https://doi.org/10.1007/978-3-030-62554-2_7

A naive machine learning approach involves using time-series for predicting how the price of an asset will be move in the future, and then, make decisions based on it. On the other hand, we could use reinforcement learning techniques, where we construct a decision-maker instead of a predictor. Reinforcement learning is a better approach since the agent can learn how to treat the inversion risk and can distribute the available budget to maximize profit maintaining later constraints. Our posterior results show the improvement done when using a reinforcement learning approach instead of a supervised learning one.

Up-to-date, there have been many proposals for solving the autonomous trading problem which include using straightforward versions of classic reinforcement learning algorithms like Q-learning or time differences [3,4], heuristic methods like genetic programming [5,6], and trading-tools based on recurrent reinforcement learning [7–11]. The major disadvantages are that inputs require technical indicators, which sometimes don't contain full information or generalized information. Other approaches test over zero-cost transactions being unreal or impractical.

The rest of this paper is organized as follows. In Sect. 1, we present a sample of previous work. Then, in Sects. 2 and 3, we formally formulate the problem of computing optimized trading policies, and present our proposed solution, respectively. In Sect. 3.1, we discuss the main properties of the proposed solution, and Sect. 4 we present the results of a series of experiments that characterize the performance of the proposed solution. Lastly, in Sect. 5 we present the conclusions derived from this work as well as future work.

1   Related Work

As our revisions of the related work reveals, reinforcement learning is an adequate alternative to solve smart-trading problems. In this section we present a representative sample of such proposals.

In [3] Temporal-Difference (TD) and Q-learning were used for selecting stocks and optimizing trading parameters, respectively. Multiple Q-learning agents were used to integrate global trend prediction with local trading strategy efficiently by sharing training episodes and learned policies while keeping the overall scheme of conventional Q-learning. Also, they achieved better performance than supervised learning systems on risk management. Multiple Q-learning agents also were used in [4], allowing them to divide and conquer the stock trading problem by defining roles for cooperatively carrying out stock pricing and selection decisions. Later, in [12], a reinforcement learning framework called meta policy was proposed. Meta policy introduces a dynamic asset al.location, designed to utilize the temporal information from stock recommendations and the ratio of the stock fund over the assets.

An extended approach was taken in [13], by mixing deep and reinforcement learning. While the deep learning component automatically senses the dynamic market condition for informative feature learning, the reinforcement learning module interacts with deep representations making trading decisions to accumulate the ultimate rewards in an unknown environment. Another similar framework was using Long short-term memories (LSTMs) with reinforcement learning for generating agents that accomplish the same level of performance and generality like a human trader by learning for themselves to create successful strategies that lead to the human-level long-term rewards agents [14].

An alternative approach used reinforcement learning techniques and genetic programming ones by defining trading rules on stocks using technical indicators [5,6].

A particularly interesting technique is recurrent reinforcement learning[7]. The first approaches using recurrent reinforcement learning for trading systems involved solutions that don't require forecasting methods; instead, they try to solve the trading task by optimizing objective functions that directly measure trading and investment performance [7,8]. Recurrent reinforcement learning was the base used in many articles later as in adaptive reinforcement learning [9], which allows for a risk-return trade-off to be made by the user within the system. Adaptive reinforcement learning outperforms genetic programming methods with frequent data [10] and improves trading and investment performance when it is mixed with genetic programming [11].

2   Problem Formulation

The problem of optimized trading can be formulated in terms of a set of instruments and an initial budget. More specifically, given k time-series describing the behavior in the past of the k assets, and given an initial budget, we want to determine an optimal trading policy for these k instruments that maximizes profit (minimizes loss) during a finite horizon of T time slots.

Now, in order to formulate a reinforcement learning solution, we can define state and action spaces that naturally fits with the way in which human traders analyze the environment and take decisions.

Following the previous rationale, the state of the environment will be determined by the three components:

- k time-series, one per each instrument, that describe the past behaviour of the instruments.
- The current amount of money invested on each asset.
- The current amount of money in the account.

It is important to note that we assume that the environment evolves in discrete steps, and that the agent gets information about the price of the assets at the begging and the end of a day.

The actions space is composed by all the ways in which the current budget can be invested the assets under consideration, plus the percent of money left in the personal fund. In total, they must sum to 100% of the available money. Since the size of the action space is infinite, we will use a discretization technique to keep the complexity of our solution tractable.

From the previous discussion, we can formally define state space as:

$$x_t = (S_t, I_t, A_t) \in \mathcal{R}^{k \times l} \times \mathcal{R}^{k+1} \times \mathcal{R} \tag{1}$$

where S_t is a matrix where each row is a time-series of length l for k-th assets, I_t are the invested amounts for each of k assets plus the money left in the account, such that $\sum_{i_t \in I_t} i_t = A_{t-1}$ and A_t is the amount in the account.

And the action space can be defined as:

$$u_t = (u_t^1, u_t^2, ..., u_t^k, u_t^{k+1}) \in [0,1]^{k+1} \text{ s.t. } \sum_{i=1}^{k+1} u_t^i = 1 \tag{2}$$

In this model, the loss in a transaction will be measured by Q-values defined in Bellman's equation, particularly in deep Q-learning (DQN)

Let $Q_t(x_t, u_t)$ be the trading movement cost (money lost) in the day t, $g_t(x_t, u_t)$ be the immediate cost (fees and money lost due to the transaction) in the day t and $f_t(x_t, u_t)$ be the next state function (next time-series, invested amounts per asset and final funds). The DQN optimization is defined by:

$$Q_t = Q_t + \alpha \left[g_t + \gamma \min_{u_{t+1} \in U_{t+1}} Q_{t+1}(f_t, u_{t+1}) - Q_t \right] \tag{3}$$

where α is the learning rate and γ is the discount factor.

In the following section, we will present our proposed experiments and the proposed solution. We will introduce all considered constraints and some technical information related to the solution.

3   Proposed Solution

To tackle the problem described in the previous chapter, we propose a decision-maker based on the DQN algorithm [15]. We consider a single agent which is change of taking decisions over trading transactions involving all the assets. The discretization scheme used in this work consist on using either the 100%, 50% or 25% of money for trading on each asset.

The considered fees are always the 1% of the invested amount on each asset. For instance, if we are trading 100 dollars, the commission will be 1 dollar.

Since Q-factors are unknown for us, we propose a neural network architecture that is fed with the state x, and the outputs will represent the Q-values for each control. When selecting the minimum value in neural network outputs, we will choose the action with the smallest cost. Figure 1 shows the proposed architecture.

The proposed architecture considers the evaluation of three assets. In our tests, we evaluate three cryptocurrencies: bitcoin [16], litecoin [17], and ethereum [18]. The architecture processes the time-series of each asset using a GRU for each one, and the last linear input processes the invested amounts extracted from the state in the current step t. The final neural network layer has $|U|$ (actions space size) outputs, representing the Q-values for each of them, and it

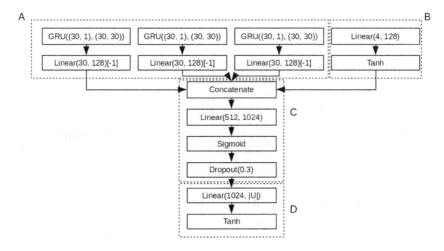

Fig. 1. Proposed architecture for Q-values prediction using three assets.

varies depending on the granularity of the discretization scheme. Additionally, we implement an epsilon greedy policy, using the start probability in 0.9, finishing in 0.4 for increasing exploration in 300 steps. This policy applies to all tests.

It is important to note that the solved problem is an aggregated problem for real trading problems because we aren't considering volume, multi-days, or bear-market transactions.

3.1   Discussion

In this section we describe the rationale behind each of the components of the proposed architecture.

Replay Memory. We decide to use a replay memory given that episodes are not so long and, as is well known, to avoid the neural network to forget previous experiences [19]. By sampling from memory at random, the transitions that build up a batch are de-correlated which has been shown that significantly stabilizes and improves the DQN training procedure [19,20].

Deep Q-Learning Algorithm. Usually, Q-learning uses a table to select the best action, but in deep Q-learning, we replace this table with a neural network which gives us the Q-values for all possible controls. Our objective is to train a policy that tries to minimize the discounted, cumulative cost, described in Eq. 3.

The main idea is to have a function $f : X_t \times U_t \to \mathcal{R}$ that tells us which is the cost incurred by each action (also referred as controls). Then, by minimizing overall possible controls we can construct a sub-optimal policy.

$$\pi^*(s_t) = \arg\min_{u_t \in U_t} Q(s_t, u_t) \tag{4}$$

For the training update rule, we use the fact that every Q-function for some policy obeys the Bellman equation:

$$Q^\pi(s_t, u_t) = g(x_t, u_t) + \gamma Q^\pi(f(x_t, u_t), \pi(f(x_t, u_t))) \tag{5}$$

Moreover, Q-function converges given that it is a contraction map [21].

From the difference between both sides of Eq. 5, we can compute a temporal difference error δ that can be minimized using regression.

3.2   Computational Complexity

For the proposed architecture in Fig. 1. we will determine the asymptotic complexity.

3.3   Part A

Considering k assets, for each of them, a GRU is required for time-series processing. Each time-series slot (each piece of time-series) is processed in $O(1)$ considering hidden state vector dimension as a constant, and then each GRU will process the time-series in $O(l)$. Since there are k processors of time-series, the information of all assets will be available in $O(lk)$. Each subsequent layer stacked in each GRU will take $O(1)$, but they are dependent on the number of assets, adding the complexity of $O(k)$.

3.4   Part B

The last linear input layer will depend on the number of assets k. Since network hidden dimensions are constants, the final linear input layer will be processed in $O(k)$. The same applies to its activation function (Tanh).

3.5   Part C

Since concatenation is done over GRU outputs, then it will take $O(k)$ because we will have GRU units as much as assets analyzed. The next linear layer depends on the size of the concatenation output, which depends on the assets number, adding $O(k)$ time for processing considering the activation function.

3.6   Part D

The last part depends on the selected discretization. If the discretization takes large percents, then fewer actions will be available. If the discretization percents are small more controls are possible. With the same argument as before (constant size in hidden layers), it will take $O(|U|)$ steps for processing, including the activation function.

In general, the architecture complexity is $O(lk + k + |U|)$.

4   Performance Evaluation

As mentioned before, our experiments consider three assets, specifically, three cryptocurrencies: bitcoin, litecoin, and ethereum. We selected these instruments because they are in ten the most popular cryptocurrencies based on their market capitalization [22], and also, the historical pricing data is available on the internet.

All time-series were transformed by dividing the close asset price by the open asset price; with this, we will get the growth ratio along the day and avoid significant variations. Code and data are available in the next GitHub URL: https://github.com/cobu93/optimized-policies-rl-dqn.

4.1   Supervised Learning Approach

For comparison propose, we develop a supervised learning approach with a greedy policy. The supervised learning part consists of fed the time-series into stacked GRUs for trying to predict the next price. We developed a predictor for each cryptocurrency, and the greedy policy chose that asset with the highest predicted increment.

The only experiment uses a discretization considering fractions of 100% on the higher predicted earnings. All predictors used architecture in Fig. 2, and Table 1 shows all technical indicators for the training phase.

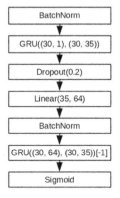

Fig. 2. Proposed architecture for predicting prices on cryptocurrencies.

We train the neural network as a classification problem, where target labels are increasing or decreasing since regression problem results weren't good enough. The considered metric for evaluation was accuracy, and the greedy policy evaluates outputs and selects the increasing one with the highest value considering the value as the security on the label.

The accuracies for bitcoin, ethereum, and litecoin were 0.747, 0.744, and 0.735, respectively. Following the greedy policy, at the end of the simulation, we

Table 1. Technical supervised training specifications.

Specification	Value
Sequences length	30
Dropout	0.2
Batch size	3
Learning rate	0.000005
Epochs	50
Optimizer	Adam
Error function	Cross entropy

get a loss of 963.608 dollars. Figure 3 shows how was the behavior on earnings ans losses using this approach.

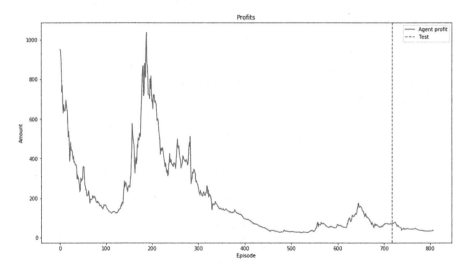

Fig. 3. Profits during training and testing. At the end of the experiment 963.608 dollars were lost.

4.2   Reinforcement Learning Approach

The discretization used in these experiments considers fractions of 100% (experiment A), 50% (experiment B), and 25% (experiment C) of the available funds. Table 2 shows all the technical details used when training the agent.

We use the following metrics during our evaluation process:

– Mean squared error (MSE) as a regression error function for the task. By reducing the temporal difference error on each step, the algorithm approximates better the Q-values.

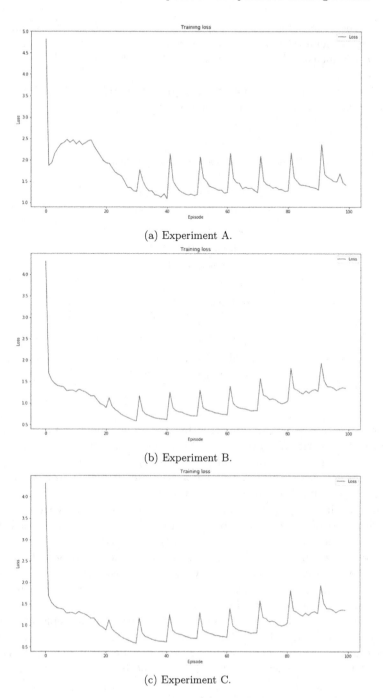

(a) Experiment A.

(b) Experiment B.

(c) Experiment C.

Fig. 4. Loss incurred at each episode. (a) Loss for experiment A. (b) Loss for experiment B. (c) Loss for experiment C. The loss at the end of 100 episodes were 1.4169 for experiment A, 1.3591 for experiment B and 1.1699.

- Cost is the crucial metric; the expected behavior is a cost decreasing while training. It means that the agent is selecting the best action at each episode. The cost is measured as the decreasing ratio in the future value, while lower will be better.
- The last used metric is profit at the end of the training. It will give us an idea the how well is our trading decision-maker.

Table 2. Technical training specifications.

Specification	Value
Replay memory	10000
Batch size	128
Gamma	0.999
Learning rate	0.001
Episodes	100
Optimizer	Adam
Epsilon start	0.9
Epsilon end	0.4
Epsilon decay	300
Error function	MSE

First, we compare the loss incurred by the three experiments. The propose is to show the algorithm convergence and the error minimization through time, moreover, the consistency and stability of training. From Fig. 4, we can observe the behavior of tests. While Fig. 4a shows a slight increase through time after reaching a minimum, Fig. 4b and 4c shows a higher increase of MSE, but moreover, the loss in experiment B and C are lower than that of experiment A. Although the MSE is a general error measure, what we are looking for is maximizing the profit which is the same as reducing the cost.

Figure 5 shows how costs decreases with time. The behavior of both experiments is very similar. Moreover, the value in the last episode is close among three tests. While in experiment A the cost is -7.1, the cost in experiment B is -7.1561 and the cost in C is -7.0126.

Once we have trained our proposed agent for 100 training episodes consisting of 808 steps, and with an initial fund of 1000 dollars, we measured the profit attained by the agent. In Fig. 6, we can see the profit behavior using the training data and then with test the data. In the figure, the dotted green line indicates the beginning of the test phase. In experiment A, the profit, including initial funds, was 277,738,582,033.48 dollars while in experiment B is almost twice with 5,154,558,339,28.41 dollars and almost half in experiment C with 125,599,154,982.00 dollars. Even though these results could look impressive, it

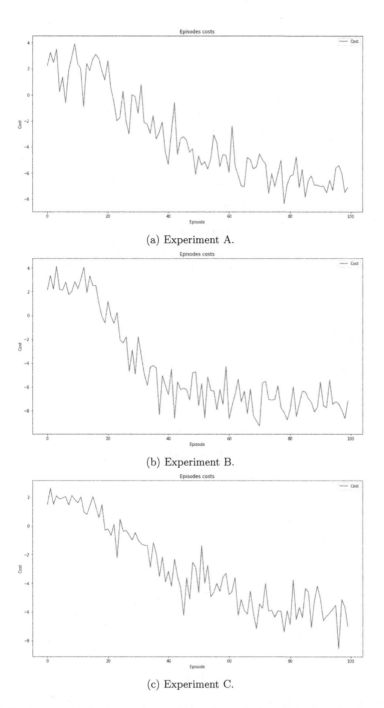

(a) Experiment A.

(b) Experiment B.

(c) Experiment C.

Fig. 5. Costs incurred during training. The cost at the last episode for experiment A was −7.1, for experiment B was −7.1561 and for experiment C was −7.0126.

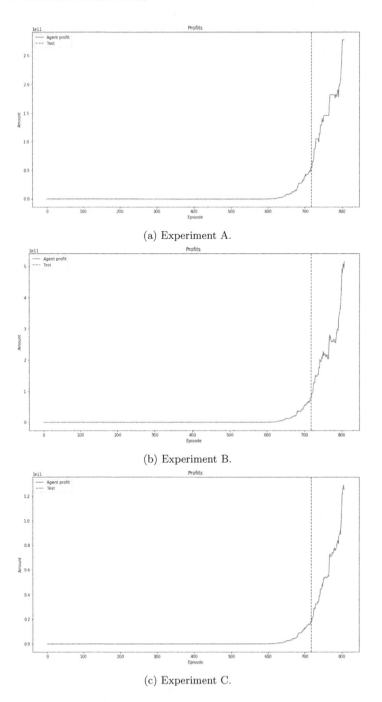

(a) Experiment A.

(b) Experiment B.

(c) Experiment C.

Fig. 6. Profits during training and testing. For experiment A, at the last episode step, the gain, including original funds, was 277738582033.483 dollars. For experiment B, it was 515455833928.4102. For experiment C, it was 125599154982.008.

is because we reinvest all earned money, which allow us to archive exponential gains. It is also important to point out that the optimal reachable profit is 1,349,833,832,226,382.2 dollars, which is much larger than our results.

5 Conclusions and Future Work

In this paper we presented an architecture based on Gated Recurrent Units and Deep Q-Learning for computing optimized trading policies. Our experimental results, based on time-series describing the behaviour of a set of cryptocurrencies, show that the resulting trading agent is capable of optimize profit. This is true, even in situations where the forecasts obtained from the Gated Recurrent Units are not highly accurate. From this results we can conclude that the trading algorithm actually learns to overcome the intrinsic limitation of predicting the behaviour of the cost of a cryptocurrency. It is also interesting to note, that the trading agent achieves good performance even with a coarse granularity in the discretization scheme, and with just 100 episodes of training.

For future work, we are planning to use more sophisticated analytical tools and to incorporate feature based on trading indicators. The objective is to take advantage of the knowledge of human experts to develop general strategies for any market. We want to test how well an artificial agent can produce trading policies under more complicated scenarios.

References

1. More than 1,000 cryptocurrencies have already failed - here's what will affect successes in the future. https://finance.yahoo.com/news/more-1-000-cryptocurrencies-already-144541916.html. Accessed 03 Jun 2020
2. Crypto payments processor coinpayments partners with shopify. https://ibsintelligence.com/ibs-journal/ibs-news/crypto-payments-processor-coinpayments-partners-with-shopify/. Accessed 03 Jun 2020
3. Lee, J.W., Kim, S.D., Lee, J.: An intelligent stock trading system based on reinforcement learning. IEICE Trans. Inf. Syst. **86**(20), 296–305 (2003)
4. Lee, J.W., Park, J., Jangmin, O., Lee, J., Hong, E.: A multiagent approach to q-learning for daily stock trading. IEEE Trans. Syst. Man Cybern. Part A Syst. Hum. **37**(6), 864–877 (2007)
5. Dempster, M.A.H., Payne, T.W., Romahi, Y., Thompson, G.W.P.: Computational learning techniques for intraday FX trading using popular technical indicators. IEEE Trans. Neural Netw. **12**(4), 744–754 (2001)
6. Chen, Y., Mabu, S., Hirasawa, K., Hu, J.: Trading rules on stock markets using genetic network programming with sarsa learning. In: Proceedings of the 9th Annual Conference on Genetic and Evolutionary Computation, GECCO 2007, New York, NY, USA, p. 1503. Association for Computing Machinery (2007)
7. Moody, J., Saffell, M.: Learning to trade via direct reinforcement. IEEE Trans. Neural Netw. **12**(4), 875–889 (2001)
8. Moody, J., Wu, L.: Optimization of trading systems and portfolios. In: Proceedings of the IEEE/IAFE 1997 Computational Intelligence for Financial Engineering (CIFEr), pp. 300–307 (1997)

9. Dempster, M.A.H., Leemans, V.: An automated FX trading system using adaptive reinforcement learning. Expert Syst. Appl. **30**(3), 543–552 (2006). Intelligent Information Systems for Financial Engineering
10. Gorse, D.: Application of stochastic recurrent reinforcement learning to index trading. In: ESANN 2011: European Symposium on Artificial Neural Networks, Computational Intelligence and Machine Learning (2011)
11. Zhang, J., Maringer, D.: Using a genetic algorithm to improve recurrent reinforcement learning for equity trading. Comput. Econ. **47**(4), 551–567 (2016). https://doi.org/10.1007/s10614-015-9490-y
12. Jangmin, O., Lee, J., Lee, J.W., Zhang, B.T.: Adaptive stock trading with dynamic asset allocation using reinforcement learning. Inf. Sci. **176**(15), 2121–2147 (2006)
13. Deng, Y., Bao, F., Kong, Y., Ren, Z., Dai, Q.: Deep direct reinforcement learning for financial signal representation and trading. IEEE Trans. Neural Netw. Learn. Syst. **28**(3), 653–664 (2017)
14. David, W.L.: Agent inspired trading using recurrent reinforcement learning and LSTM neural networks (2017)
15. Mnih, V.: Playing atari with deep reinforcement learning. 2013. cite arxiv:1312.5602Comment. NIPS Deep Learning Workshop (2013)
16. Get started with bitcoin. https://bitcoin.org/en/. Accessed: 2020–06-04
17. What is litecoin? https://litecoin.org/. Accessed 04 Jun 2020
18. What is ethereum? https://ethereum.org/what-is-ethereum/. Accessed 04 Jun 2020
19. Lin, L.J.: Reinforcement learning for robots using neural networks. Ph.D. thesis, USA (1992)
20. Liu, R., Zou, J: The effects of memory replay in reinforcement learning, October 2017
21. Bertsekas, D.P.: Reinforcement learning and optimal control. In: Bertsekas, D., Nedić, A., Ozdaglar, A.E. (eds.) Athena Scientific Optimization and Computation Series. Athena Scientific, Belmont (2019)
22. Top 100 cryptocurrencies by market capitalization. https://coinmarketcap.com/. Accessed 04 Jun 2020

High Data Rate Efficiency Improvement via Variable Length Coding for LoRaWAN

G. A. Yáñez-Casas[1,2], I. Medina[2], J. J. Hernández-Gómez[2,4(✉)],
M. G. Orozco-del-Castillo[3,4], C. Couder-Castañeda[2],
and R. de-la-Rosa-Rabago[2]

[1] Instituto Politécnico Nacional, Escuela Superior de Ingeniería Mecánica y Eléctrica
Unidad Zacatenco, Sección de Estudios de Posgrado e Investigación,
Mexico City, Mexico
[2] Instituto Politécnico Nacional, Centro de Desarrollo Aeroespacial,
Mexico City, Mexico
jjhernandezgo@ipn.mx
[3] Tecnológico Nacional de México/ IT de Mérida, Departamento de Sistemas y
Computación, Yucatán, Mexico
[4] AAAI Student Chapter at Yucatán, México (AAAIMX), Association for the
Advancement of Artificial Intelligence, Mérida, Mexico

Abstract. Low-cost options to provide local transactional network coverage are LPWAN (Low Power Wide Area Network), which are simpler to implement and to manage. The emerging technology known as LoRaWAN represents a promising LPWAN option due to its relative long range, as well as the technological development opportunities given its recent introduction and unfinished standard. The main LoRaWAN protocol consists of frames with fixed length encoded data from end-devices, no matter the length of such data; this choice is to simplify coding, transmission and decoding, in order to keep the low-power consumption of the network. In this work we present a modification of the LoRaWAN communications protocol in which payload data are encoded within customised frames which respect the nature and length of such data. The methodology is exemplified considering low-power end-devices (sensors) which generate 9 position, orientation and meteorological variables, and it is carefully implemented in order to simplify the decoding stage in the receiver as well as to optimise the manageability of the network traffic. The main outcome of this frame encoding of variable length technique is a considerable improvement of transmission data rates (with a factor of ∼50× for the chosen sensing modules) as the payload field is never filled with zeros up to the fixed size of the corresponding frame (according to original LoRaWAN standard). As the obtained frames are way smaller for this kind of sensors, the maximum number of end-devices supported by the network before its saturation point also increases substantially. This proposal is aimed to represent a viable and inexpensive option to cover the increasing demand in network coverage for end-devices as those used in Internet of Things and smart cities.

© Springer Nature Switzerland AG 2020
M. F. Mata-Rivera et al. (Eds.): WITCOM 2020, CCIS 1280, pp. 97–115, 2020.
https://doi.org/10.1007/978-3-030-62554-2_8

Keywords: LoRaWAN Standard · Low power wide area network ·
LPWAN · Communications protocol · Variable length codification ·
Encoding · Data rate transmission · Optimization

1   Introduction

One sector that nowadays suffers a vertiginous evolving is that of telecommunications, due to the highly increasing number of end users demanding mainly wireless connectivity services to keep several devices connected in real time. This fact implies new needs and new challenges that constantly arise, involving innovation and the search for new ways of transmitting information for higher data rates and signal fidelity [1].

Although it is an imperious necessity for all networks to evolve, wireless communication networks represent an important sector of telecommunications infrastructure [2]. Thus, networks such as satellite, microwave, Wi-Fi, among other standards, make up a large part of all the communication links currently available, even for underwater applications and research [3]. Nevertheless, such wireless networks have some drawbacks because they are composed by a complex structure. Their operation is under strict company and governmental regulations, their components and construction represent high costs, and their management is sometimes difficult and it is, in many times, very restricted for manipulation. These facts have often resulted in low-cost alternatives for these technologies [4–6].

A solution to complement and to allow further exploration in the field of wireless communications arises from the so-called Low Power Wide Area Networks or LPWAN [7]. These networks represent a type of technology that is developed under various independent standards that constitute less expensive and more versatile options. LPWAN operation is much more manipulable than a traditional technology based networks.

The LPWAN operation is based on power consumption efficiency of its components, yielding to a the relative low-cost of implementation. In this sense, the main applications of these networks focus on the construction of sensor networks [8], which is deeply involved in the concept of the Internet of Things (IoT) [9–11] and smart cities [10–12], where commonly used devices are connected through a network and can be manipulated by end users.

Technologies such as those based on the Zigbee or Bluetooth protocols belong to the category of LPWAN networks, as well as the emerging standards LoRaWAN , SigFox and IQRF [13]. The main difference is that protocols like Zigbee or Bluetooth constitute short-range networks (some meters of coverage), while LoRaWAN , SigFox and IQRF are long-range technologies. This work is based on the LoRaWAN standard.

LoRaWAN is a specification of wireless LPWAN whose coverage can be local (hundreds of km^2), regional or global, and it is designed to optimise and maximise features such as battery lifetime, cost, long range coverage and capacities of the network and devices [14,15]. The suggested topology and LoRaWAN protocol are managed by LoRa Alliance, who establish the common operating frequency in the ISM band (~800–900 MHz). The specific bandwidth range depends on the geographic region [14].

Precisely, the topology and the protocol are the most important features of LoRaWAN , and its operation depends on the use of each of them [14]. Then, the operation of this technology is simpler and it consists typically in a star topology composed by the end-devices [16], which can be sensors or any low consumption devices. Data are received by one or multiple gateways which shall forward the received packet to a server where the data processing is done.

The communication protocol is very important because it is the element which determines how data shall be sent, and within this part is where data are coded and modulated before transmission. LoRaWAN protocol is prepared to be used in a bidirectional link, commonly respecting a fixed data frame size [14]. Data rate and transmission time are established for the communication with the purpose of maintaining a low consumption level, while the modulation purpose is to carry the data frames to the gateway. LoRaWAN typically implements a Chirp Spread Spectrum modulation [17], but in some cases or applications a Frequency Shift Keying (FSK) modulation [18] can be implemented. These modulation techniques allow to maintain the standard communication and adaptive features according to the communications link.

LoRaWAN can be used in multiple applications, which can be implemented through one of the three types of LoRaWAN modes, named classes A, B and C [14]. This work focuses on class A, since it refers to applications types where data traffic is mostly sent from end-devices to gateways and data are transmitted by uplink data frames followed by two short downlink time receive windows so the server must wait to receive any other uplink data frame [14].

In this paper, we implement a version of LoRaWAN protocol based on class A mode, by modifying the fixed length coding of standard protocol and present a variable length coding for frames with the purpose of improving the data rate efficiency according to different sensor scenarios. This work is organised as follows: in Sect. 2 we present the main characteristics of LoRaWAN technology by geographic region, as well as the main structure of LoRaWAN protocol. In Sect. 3 we present the features of end-devices and the architecture used for this application, while in Sect. 4 we show a strategy to encode data from different sensors, yielding to a payload frame structure derived from the nature of the data acquired. The obtained results and their discussion are featured in Sect. 5, while finally in Sect. 6 and 7 we present the final remarks as well as future work, respectively.

2 LoRaWAN Technology

2.1 LoRaWAN Coverage

LoRaWAN technology has been studied, developed and regulated by LoRa Alliance, a private association aimed to promote technologies based on IoT and their standardisation and expansion around the world [19]. In this sense,

LoRa Alliance aims to collaborate with an increasing number of countries and to improve the technical specification of the protocol until it becomes a global standard.

Attending the national telecommunications regulatory bodies across the world as well as local/global companies, nowadays LoRaWAN possesses eight main regional standards for their operation. Such regional standards, vary mainly in the accessible portion of bandwidth *per* region [20], as well as approved data rates and the total bits per LoRaWAN frame. Table 1 presents the main ISM bandwidth in each regional standard, where we assign a unique Region's ID which shall be used along the manuscript. For further details of additional assigned bands per country, we refer the reader to [21]. The data rates and total frame bits *per* region can be consulted in other tables further on.

Table 1. Main ISM bandwidth for each LoRaWAN regional standard [21].

Region's ID	Region's name	Bandwidth (MHz)	Region's ID	Region's name	Bandwidth (MHz)
EU	Europe	863–870	AS	Asia	923
US	United States	902–928	KR	Korea	920–923
CN	China	779–787	IN	India	865–867
AU	Australia	915–928	RU	Russia	864–870

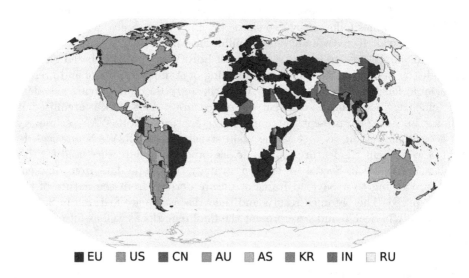

Fig. 1. Schematic map showing the potential coverage of LoRaWAN as well as the global distribution of regional LoRaWAN standards [21].

Nowadays, the coverage of LoRaWAN extends to 192 countries throughout the world [21], which means that LoRaWAN has a potential coverage of 93.3468%

without considering the Antarctic territory, and of 84.3197% (considering the Antartic). However, the coverage *per* country is not always of 100% of its earth territory. A schematic figure of the global coverage of LoRaWAN is given in Fig. 1, where it can be observed that many countries comply with more than one regional LoRaWAN standard. For further details by country, please refer to [21]. Moreover, this regional division is aimed to ease the introduction of new countries to the LoRaWAN technology, by adapting their own radio infrastructure, lowering costs.

2.2   LoRaWAN Communications Protocol Structure for Class A

The LoRaWAN standard communications protocol is designed to optimise the battery life of devices on the network. Currently, the standard provides three operation modes with slight changes on the protocol's structure depending on the interaction between end-devices and the LoRaWAN receptor [14]. While class A only allows uplinks from end-devices to the receptor (which in turn optimises even more the power consumption of devices), class B allows bidirectional links with programmed transmission (through time windows). Finally, LoRaWAN class C provides bidirectional continuous links, which demands more energy and a better synchronisation [14]. Hereafter we use (fixed) sensors as end-devices continuously sending information to the gateway, so without loss of generality, we focus in the LoRaWAN class A specification. Nevertheless, as the differences between different classes protocols are slight, the presented structure can be straightforwardly extrapolated to class B and C.

The main structure of LoRaWAN uplink frame protocol in class A can be observed in Fig. 2, which features the size in bits of each of the five parts of the main frame, which encompasses the important aspects for uplink transmission. The description of each of such five fields is:

- **Preamble.** Contains an specific synchronisation word which is useful to assign a classification to the frame type, to be decoded in the receiver. For class A, it defines that frame is of uplink type.
- **PHDR (Physical Header).** It includes information about payload length in bytes and it specifies if LoRaWAN includes a forward error correction technique (and which one). For LoRaWAN standard protocol, the commonly used error correction technique is a bits sequence based on CRC (Cyclic Redundancy Check) [22].
- **PHDR CRC (Physical Header CRC).** Features a CRC bits sequence based in field PHDR.

Field name	Preamble	PHDR	PHDR CRC	PHYPayload	CRC
Size (bits)	8	8	4	R	16

Fig. 2. Principal LoRa Frame uplink.

- **PHYPayload (Physical Payload).** This field contains data generated by end-devices. Its size R (see Fig. 2) depends on the capabilities of the network and the regulations corresponding to each region. This field has a structure composed by three fields which shall be explained in what follows.
- **CRC (Cyclic Redundancy Check).** It includes a CRC bits sequence to ensure the integrity of data, which is based on PHYPayload field.

It can be considered that PHYPayload and CRC are the most important fields of LoRaWAN protocol because they include data from end-devices and they are in charge of giving security and integrity to the transmission, respectively. As previously mentioned, beside transporting data application, PHYPayload contains extra information about data to be transmitted. Particularly, PHYPayload field is composed by a MAC layer, which includes information about channel and the network [23]. In this way, PHYPayload is divided into three subframes which are observed in Fig. 3. The description of such subframes is:

- **MHDR (MAC Header).** It contains information about the type of message sent as well as the LoRaWAN protocol version used.
- **MACPayload.** It is a part of MAC layer where data application are inserted. Its length N depends on the regional LoRaWAN standard. Details about its structure are explained in what follows.
- **MIC (Message Integrity Code).** It contains an encrypted bits sequence based on the main LoRaWAN frame.

Field name	MHDR	MACPayload	MIC
Size (bits)	8	M	32

Fig. 3. PHYPayload field of LoRa frame uplink.

The subframe MACPayload carries, beside data application, an identifier of the end-device(s), data rate and MAC commands. In this sense, it has an internal structure which consists in three fields. The fields of such structure, which can be observed in Fig. 4, has the following descriptions:

- **FHDR (Frame Header).** It contains an unique identifier for each end-device on the network, as well as a group of commands called MAC commands, a bits sequence that contains information for network administration. If no data application are present, the frame transports only MAC commands, in order to let the receiver know about the status of the network, of an end-device, or simply to let the receiver know that the transmission is ready to start.
- **FPORT (Frame Port).** It is a mandatory field that indicates whether there are data application to be sent or not. If FPORT is missing or contains a zeros sequence, there are no data application.
- **FRMPayload (Frame Payload).** Finally, the FRMPayload field contains data application from end-devices. Its length N depends on the regional standard.

Field name	FHDR	FPort	FRMPayload
Size (bits)	56···184	8	N

Fig. 4. MACPayload field of LoRa frame uplink.

The values of the lengths of FRMPayload, MACPayload and PHYPayload, M, N and R respectively, can be observed for the different LoRaWAN regional standards in Table 2.

Table 2. Values of M, N and R lengths for each LoRaWAN regional standard [14,21].

ID	M bits	N bits	R bits	ID	M bits	N bits	R bits
EU	1,840	1,776	1,880	AS	1,840	1,840	1,880
US	1,840	1,776	1,880	KR	1,840	1,776	1,880
CN	1,840	1,776	1,880	IN	1,840	1,776	1,880
AU	1,840	1,776	1,880	RU	1,840	1,776	1,880

3 Data Acquisition

As previously mentioned, in order to implement our proposal of variable length encoding for data application, in this work we use a dataset generated by sensing modules. Such data acquisition devices were selected due to their adequate power characteristics in order for them to be incorporated in a LPWAN network as LoRaWAN. Details of the used modules as well as the acquired variables are summarised in Table 3.

Table 3. Characteristics and specifications of used the sensors (end-devices).

Module ID	Power features (V, mA)	Variable(s)
GPS6MV2 [24]	5.0–6.0, 10.00	Longitude, Latitude, Date, Hour
BMP180 [25]	3.3–5.0, 1.00	Atmospheric Pressure
DHT11 [26]	3.3–5.0, 2.50	Temperature and Humidity
MPU6050 [27]	2.3–3.4, 0.14	Acceleration and Orientation

As can be observed from Table 3, the variables acquired from sensors can be considered of two types: physical positioning parameters and meteorological variables. The idea behind the election of such sensors, is to be able to light-weight and low power mobile meteorological stations that Authors require for a project related to climate change. These end-devices have common features, similar supply voltage, low current consumption, protection and conditioning included in the module circuit, digital data output and are compatible with various microcontroller architectures' for processing acquired data.

Positioning data are acquired by the GPS6MV2 and MPU6050 modules. GPS6MV2 is able to obtain position data in complete GPS format [24]. Nevertheless, we used a short version of the GPS protocol (lat, long, date and hour)[1]. Furthermore, the MPU6050 module produces both acceleration and attitude data in vector form, i.e. it produces three scalars *per* measurement (x, y and z components). On the other hand, meteorological variables are obtained from the BMP180 and the DHT11 modules. The BMP180 module allows to obtain atmospheric pressure in real time [25], while the DHT11 module is used for measurements of environment temperature and humidity [26].

In order to maintain a low power consumption operation network, data processing ought to be carried out on devices meeting these features. For this prototype, Arduino electronic development platform is suitable [28]. Besides its simplicity, accessibility and compatibility with the used end-devices (Table 3), it aligns with the main purpose of LoRaWAN technology of providing low-power and low-cost infrastructure by using commercial off the shelf (COTS) components.

Finally, it must be remarked that the selection of GPS6MV2, DHT11 and MPU6050 modules as end-devices allows the acquisition of multiple variables within the same sensor, providing more data application within the same electrical circuitry, aiding to reduce the power consumption and interconnections between end-devices instead of introducing one sensor *per* acquired variable.

4   Codification of Variable Length Frames for Payload Data

In this work we propose a different codification than the standard one of LoRaWAN, which fixes the length of the payload frames by fixing the values of M, N and R (see Table 2). The introduction of fixed length frames in the original LoRaWAN protocol has several purposes: it simplifies the codification of frames and it allows to simply determine in the receiver if bits were lost or if they collided. This is due to the fact that, for a class A LoRaWAN network, the protocol to channel access is similar to the ALOHA one, where end-devices send their data application through an uplink and receive no downlink from the receiver. Furthermore, fixed length frames do not require further processing, complying with the low-power characteristics of the standard.

As the LoRaWAN communications protocol is of general purpose, the (fixed) lengths of payload data are designed to fit as many data applications as possible, considering that LoRaWAN is a LPWAN network (i.e. unsuitable for transmitting large data as image and video). Nevertheless, when data application is very

---

[1] The bits related to the operation of the GPS module and network are omitted for the sake of simplicity, but they can be systematically included with the methodology of Sect. 4.

short with respect to the length of frames, fixed by the LoRaWAN protocol, the uplink transmits inefficiently data application, as the rest of the FRMPayload is filled with zeros up to N (see Table 2).

This is the case of networks of sensors, particularly with end-devices such as those in Table 3. In this case, notwithstanding the length of each payload data (which shall be described in what follows), one simultaneous record obtained by the four end-devices can take up to 17,244 bits in the worst case (to put each variable in Table 3 in different main LoRaWAN uplink frames), which in turn shall reduce drastically the data transmission rate of effective data application.

The core of this proposal is to improve the data transmission rate of effective payload data by customising the length of data application frames in order for them to exactly fit into frames, eliminating extra zeros to fill frames up to a fixed length. This proposal is ideal for end-devices producing very short data application because, within the same data structure, information of different origin and type is inserted.

4.1   Structure of the Data Application

In order to perform codification, the acquaintance of the structure of variables generated by each sensor is fundamental. Of particular interest is if the variable is or not signed, as well as its measurement interval. The highest possible recordable value shall determine the maximum size X (in bits) of the data application in the corresponding FRMPayload of the frame structure. This generic structure for each variable generated by end-devices can be observed in Fig. 5.

Field name	Sign	Data Application
Size (bits)	1	$0 \cdots X$

Fig. 5. Internal frame proposed for each variable acquired from sensors.

In Fig. 5, the **Sign** field consists of a single bit which takes the values 0 or 1 to represent positive or negative data, respectively. The **Data Application** field has the absolute value of the data generated by end-devices.

Furthermore, in this work we build one data frame per end-device, so following the sensors in Table 3, we have four main frames. This choice is intended to ease the decoding in the receiver; however, further details on this choice can be found in Sect. 5. In this sense, all variables acquired by the same end-device are included in the same data frame. In what follows, the description of each of the four main frames built in this work can be found.

Figure 6 shows the structure of the frame for GPS6MV2 module, where the acquired variables (see Table 5) can be observed. Respecting the format of the variables provided by the sensor, only latitude and longitude feature the Sign field.

Field name	Sign	Latitude	Sign	Longitude	Date	Hour
# bit	58	51···57	50	41···49	23···41	0···23

Fig. 6. Data application structure for variables acquired by GPS6MV2 module [24].

Figure 7 shows the structure of the frame for DHT11 module frame, and it includes temperature and humidity data. Since this sensor acquires only positive records for the variables, no Sign fields are required.

Field name	Temperature	Humidity
# bit	6···12	0···5

Fig. 7. Data application structure for variables acquired by DHT11 module [26].

As the BMP180 module only acquires atmospheric pressure, which is always positive, in Fig. 8 there is only a field reserved the atmospheric pressure value.

Field name	Atmospheric Pressure
# bit	0···10

Fig. 8. Data application structure for variables acquired by BMP180 module [25].

Finally, as the MPU650 module acquires two vector variables, there are six signed scalars to be placed in the data frame, which can be observed in Fig. 9, three acceleration and three attitude variables, each on a different cartesian axis.

Field name	Sign	A_x	Sign	A_y	Sign	A_z	Sign	G_x	Sign	G_y	Sign	G_z
# bit	56	44···55	43	31···42	30	18···29	17	12···16	11	6···10	5	0···4

Fig. 9. Data application structure for variables acquired by the MPU650 module [27].

4.2 Main LoRaWAN Frame Structure of Variable Length Coding

In order to generate the main LoRaWAN frame for this proposal, we respect the 5 subframes structure of the original LoRaWAN uplink protocol (see Fig. 2), but with modified sizes in bits, which are shown in Fig. 10. It is important to remark that the drastically reduced field, PHYPayload, contains the data of the 9 variables acquired by the 4 end-devices.

Field name	Preamble	PHDR	PHDR CRC	PHYPayload	CRC
Size (bits)	6	8	4	r	4

Fig. 10. Main structure for variable length LoRaWAN frame.

From Fig. 10, the only unchanged field with respect to the original LoRaWAN main frame is PHDR. **Preamble** is reduced by selecting a 6 bit frame synchronisation word. In the case of the **CRC** field, although the standard allows 16 bits as its maximum length, we have chosen a CRC of 4 bits, mainly because data from sensors are considerably shorter than the original LoRaWAN frame length. Finally, as **PHYPayload** carries the data application, this field suffered the greater reduction in its length. The structure of this field is observed in Fig. 11. As expected, in this case, the reduction in length impacted the **MACPayload**, while both **MHDR** and **MIC** fields retain their original sizes.

Field name	MHDR	MACPayload	MIC
Size (bits)	8	m	32

Fig. 11. PHYPayload field of LoRa frame uplink.

Figure 12 shows the structure of MACPayload field. **FHDR** is of 90 bits due to the reduction of different information, particularly of the identifier of the end-device, which uses a sequence of only 2 bits. **FPORT** remains unchanged, while **FRMPayload** is adjusted to the data application of each sensor, and its length can be observed in Table 4. It is important to note that the construction of FRMPayload does not include encryption in this work as the coded variables do not require further security.

Field name	FHDR	FPort	FRMPayload
Size (bits)	90	8	n

Fig. 12. MACPayload field of LoRa frame uplink.

Table 4. FRMPayload length n (bits) for each considered sensor.

End-device	GPS6MV2	DHT11	BM180	MPU650
n (bits)	59	13	11	59

5 Results and Discussion

In what follows we compare the performance of this proposal of variable length coding of data application against the original (of fixed length) in the LoRaWAN standard protocol. For this purpose, it is important to remember that we decided to build four main LoRaWAN frames, one *per* end-device. Thus, the comparison is between the construction of two frames *per* sensor, one with fixed and the other with variable length coding.

Although this work does not tackle the decoding phase in the receiver, the choice of building one frame *per* sensor is motivated by the fact that the decoding of each frame shall be simpler and more ordered than if all variables are placed in a unique frame (requiring a more complex, slow and power-demanding algorithm). It also reduces synchronisation errors, which are more feasible in long frames. This choice also aids in the monitoring of the functioning of each sensor and of the network, as if the receiver does not receive frames coming from one end-device, it is straightforward to know the origin of the lost frames. In this sense, one frame with all variables hinders the identification of faulty end-devices, whose data may be taken as correct. A further advantage is that this choice simplifies the management of the channel traffic, as smaller frames keep the traffic manageable without saturating the channel.

Table 5 shows the sum of the values of the FRMPayload fields of the frames built for the four sensors, for both fixed and variable length codings, considering the eight regional LoRaWAN standards. The column Frame with Fixed Length Codification (FFLC) length column features data from Table 2, while in the column Frame with Variable Length Codification (FVLC), data from Table 4.

Table 5. FRMPayload Frame with Fixed Length Codification (FFLC) and Frame with Variable Length Codification (FVLC) for each LoRaWAN region.

ID	FFLC	FVLC	ID	FFLC	FVLC
	$4N$ (bits)	$4n$ (bits)		$4N$ (bits)	$4n$ (bits)
EU	7,104	142	AS	7,360	142
US	7,104	142	KR	7,104	142
CN	7,104	142	IN	7,104	142
AU	7,104	142	RU	7,104	142

Table 6 shows a comparison of the transmission data rate based on the size of FRMPayload Frame with Fixed Length Codification (FFLC) and Frame with Variable Length Codification (FVLC). FFLC transmission data rate is given by LoRaWAN regional standards [21]. FVLC data rate is computed as

$$\text{FVLC data rate} = (\text{FFLC data rate})\frac{4N}{\sum_{i=1}^{4} n_i} \, , \tag{1}$$

where N depends on the region (see Table 2).

Table 6. Transmission data rate (bps) for FRMPayload Frame with Fixed Length Codification (FFLC) and Frame with Variable Length Codification (FVLC) for each LoRaWAN region.

ID	FFLC data rate (bps)	FVLC data rate (bps)	ID	FFLC data rate (bps)	FVLC data rate (bps)
EU	50,000 [21]	2,501,408	AS	50,000 [21]	2,591,549
US	21,900 [21]	1,095,616	KR	5,470 [21]	273,654
CN	50,000 [21]	2,501,408	IN	5,470 [21]	273,654
AU	21,900 [21]	1,095,616	RU	50,000 [21]	2,501,408

As it can be observed, a very important increase in the data rate of $\sim 50\times$ is obtained with this proposal, surpassing conventional LoRaWAN rates up to Mbps. This increment can be graphically observed in Fig. 13, where LoRaWAN regions have been reordered in an increasing data rate order.

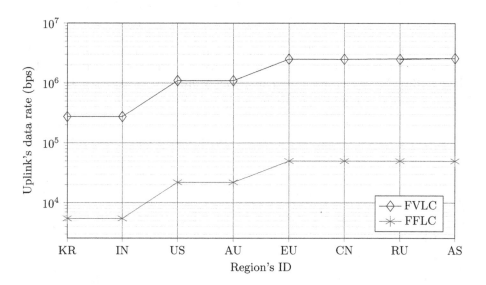

Fig. 13. Transmission data rate (bps) for FRMPayload Frame with Fixed Length Codification (FFLC) and Frame with Variable Length Codification (FVLC) for each LoRaWAN region.

Furthermore, Table 7 shows an estimate of the total number of supported end-devices considering data transmission rates in Table 6. The number of sensors in FFLC is obtained with the quotient between the data rate and the FRM-Payload length (N) *per* LoRaWAN region, while the number of sensors in FVLC is obtained through Eq. (2), which is

$$\text{No. FVLC Sensors} = 4\frac{\text{FFLC data rate}}{n}. \tag{2}$$

Table 7. Result values for number of sensors network for each region.

ID	No. FFLC Sensors	No. FVLC Sensors	ID	No. FFLC Sensors	No. FVLC Sensors
EU	28	1,408	AS	27	1,408
US	12	617	KR	3	154
CN	28	1,408	IN	3	154
AU	12	617	RU	28	1,408

As it can be observed, the amount of sensors that support the network increases by a factor of ~51×. This comparison can be better observed in Fig. 14, where LoRaWAN regions have been increasingly ordered. As expected, the number of supported sensors is directly proportional to the data rate transmission.

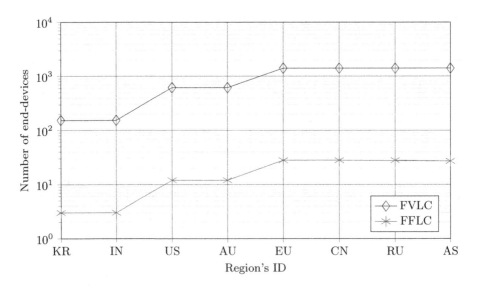

Fig. 14. Maximum number of supported end-devices for FRMPayload Frame with Fixed Length Codification (FFLC) and Frame with Variable Length Codification (FVLC) for each LoRaWAN region.

Finally, it is well known that one of the most important facets of a LPWAN is the energy consumption of the elements that compose the network, which ought to maintain a low energy profile in order to preserve battery life for long time periods. In what follows we present an insight of data rate (bps) and current consumption of a system as a function of the number of sensors connected to the system.

As the reference devices taken for the development of the protocol are based in the Arduino® architecture (see Table 3), the commercial versions of such development platform (Nano®, Micro®, Mini®, Zero®, Uno®, Leonardo®, Mega®and Due®) in order to determine the platform providing the largest support for sets of such four end-devices (see Table 3) while requiring the lowest possible power consumption. The maximum number of connected sets of sensors (considering available pins) as well as the current and the total LoRaWAN frame bits of such development platform along with the connected sensors were determined.

In order to determine the current consumption, for each Arduino® development platform, the equivalent circuit of the Arduino board, the maximum number of supported sensors per board and a generic transceptor able to radiate in the LoRaWAN band (model CC1101, operation current 30 mA) [29].

From this exercises, we determined that Arduino Mega® development platform provided a support for 144 sensors (36 sets of the four sensors featured in Table 3) with the lowest consumption (4.77 A). To determine the data rate provided by this system, we considered a global frequency 5 Hz for all the sensors in Table 3. This is actually the frequency of the digital module GPS6MV2 [24], and despite BMP180 [25] and MPU6050 [27] are digital modules with higher frequencies, we established the lowest frequency as the parameter to provide consistent data frames. Furthermore, the module DHT11 is analogical so it is sampled with 5 Hz ADC.

With this methodology, the system with the Arduino Mega® board provides a data rate of 5,112 bps. The interconnection between each system is done through I2C (Inter-Integrated Circuits) protocol. With this arrange, we require 9.78, 4.28 and 1.12 systems to reach the maximum nominal data rate of LoRaWAN for {EU, CN, AS, RU}, {US, AU} and {KR, IN} regions, respectively (see Table 6). In this sense, they support 1,324, 616 and 161 sensors for each LoRaWAN region, respectively. These upper bounds for each region case, are shown in Fig. 15.

Figure 15 shows the relationship of the power consumption and the data rate (bps) as functions of the number of possible connected end-devices, considering the required Arduino Mega® boards to perform such interconnection. As it can be observed, the relation is essentially linear, representing the points in the graph, systems of board + sensors, as well as one transceptor. Please note that the current consumption supports a very large number of sensors because module GPS6MV2 [24] constrained us with a very low ADC frequency, which is a cost inherent when using low cost COTS components. Nevertheless, with faster ADC technologies, the possibility of increasing the data rate with lower consumption than those shown in Fig. 15 are possible.

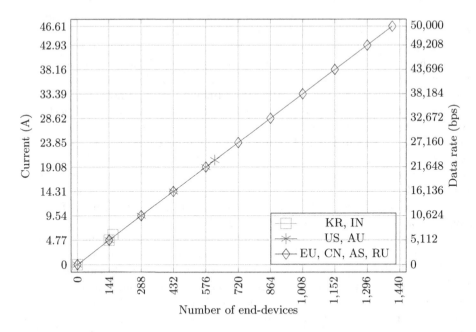

Fig. 15. FVLC data rate (bps) and current consumption (A) as a function of the number of sensors (sampling 5 Hz) up to the maximum LoRaWAN nominal bandwidth *per* region (see Table 6). Each point considers the current consumption of an Arduino Mega® development card to interconnect the number of devices shown in the abscissa's axis.

6   Conclusions

Nowadays, LoRaWAN is a technological proposal with vast development opportunities that keeps growing. It is applicable to several environments, and it also is flexible enough to incorporate different data acquisition and processing devices, and its elements are generally inexpensive [15]. The recent introduction of LoRaWAN standard, its relatively short operation time, as well as its unfinished standard, are factors that allow detailed analysis of the communications protocol to introduce several improvements even within the operating limits of the standard [30].

The coding format proposed to carry out the reduction of number of elements used to build data application field of LoRaWAN frame allows a more adequate design for the application to be implemented. Frames are customized according to the used acquisition end-devices, making it possible to create frames that fit to the number of elements necessary to represent each data that comes from the sensors. Thus, variable length coding makes possible to take advantage of the space in FRMPayload field and therefore include more information in the uplink for the case of class A LoRaWAN networks.

Although at first sight it might seem that customising LoRaWAN frames for each application is a hard task, it is required to be done only when planning the network links. Moreover, the benefits of variable length coding are evident, and they are summarised in Table 8. With this proposal, transmission data rates as well as the number of supported end-devices increases by factors of ~50× and ~51× respectively, increasing noticeably the data application to be transmitted.

Table 8. Comparison between data rate versus number of sensors in network with variable length codification frames.

ID	FVLC data rate (bps)	No. FVLC Sensors	ID	FVLC data rate (bps)	No. FVLC Sensors
EU	2,501,408	1,408	AS	2,591,549	1,408
US	1,095,616	617	KR	273,654	154
CN	2,501,408	1,408	IN	273,654	154
AU	1,095,616	617	RU	2,501,408	1,408

The choice of building a main LoRaWAN frame *per* end-device notwithstanding how many variables it is able to record, follows from several considerations regarding with advantages in the decoding phase as well as in the manageability of the channel traffic. Thus, the construction method of FRMPayload field takes into account the type of data and the type of sensor so to adequately encode data to be transmitted. With the chosen end-devices for this work, we showed how to build FRMPayload field even for sensing modules that generate simultaneously several variables to be encoded.

It is to be noted that, although LoRaWAN incorporates security in its frames, encryption was not used in this work. Moreover, CRC field was reduced. These sacrifices provided superior data rates and number of supported sensors, and were based on the nature of the data application and the sensing modules. Nevertheless, for further applications, security requirements must be evaluated before deciding whether to make or not to make such sacrifices as well as their scope.

A drawback of the increase in data transmission and number of supported sensors arise when reaching the saturation point of the network. The probability of collision of frames also increases considerably, but the network performance is expected to be good before reaching such saturation point. The later fact occurs because the probability of collisions within the channel is sensibly reduced with the FVLC strategy. Although the number of sensors and therefore the number of frames increases, since the sizes of the frames generated by each sensor are different, the traffic on the network shall be highly manageable. Further experiments on the collision probability in a saturated LoRaWAN network are required to state concluding remarks, but they are out of the scope of this work.

7   Future Work

Three research directions are possible for this work:

1. To develop a complete prototype under the same physical architecture and considering FVLC used in this work, constituted with a noticeable larger sensor network of similar devices, in order to achieve the uplink process of Class A LoRaWAN standard, also by including the process of reception and decoding of the frames.
2. To estimate the collisions probability of the frames in a LoRaWAN network when reaching its saturation point, in order to determine the quality of the information managed by the network.
3. To extend this proposal to Class B and Class C LoRaWAN links.

Acknowledgements. The authors acknowledge partial economical support by projects 20202014, 20200378, 20200259 and 20201040, as well as EDI grant, provided by SIP/IPN. Authors also acknowledge Tecnológico Nacional de México/IT de Mérida, as well as AAAI and the AAAI student chapter at Yucatan, México (AAAIMX), for the support provided to perform this work.

References

1. Arnon, S.: Optimization of urban optical wireless communication systems. IEEE Trans. Wireless Commun. **2**(4), 626–629 (2003)
2. Wang, C.X., et al.: Cellular architecture and key technologies for 5G wireless communication networks. IEEE Commun. Mag. **52**(2), 122–130 (2014)
3. Jaruwatanadilok, S.: Underwater wireless optical communication channel modeling and performance evaluation using vector radiative transfer theory. IEEE J. Sel. Areas Commun. **26**(9), 1620–1627 (2008)
4. Haider, A., Chatterjee, A.: Low-cost alternate EVM test for wireless receiver systems. In: VTS, pp. 255–260 (2005)
5. Zhao, Y., Ye, Z.: A low-cost GSM/GPRS based wireless home security system. IEEE Trans. Consum. Electron. **54**(2), 567–572 (2008)
6. Kildal, P.S., Glazunov, A.A., Carlsson, J., Majidzadeh, A.: Cost-effective measurement setups for testing wireless communication to vehicles in reverberation chambers and anechoic chambers. In: 2014 IEEE Conference on Antenna Measurements & Applications (CAMA), pp. 1–4. IEEE (2014)
7. International Telecommunication Union: Technical and operational aspects of Low Power Wide Area Networks for machine-type communication and the Internet of Things in frequency ranges harmonised for SRD operation. Technical Report 1, International Telecommunication Union, Ginebra, Switzerland (2018)
8. Kim, D.Y., Jung, M.: Data transmission and network architecture in long range low power sensor networks for IoT. Wireless Pers. Commun. **93**(1), 119–129 (2017)
9. Rizzi, M., Ferrari, P., Flammini, A., Sisinni, E.: Evaluation of the IoT LoRaWAN solution for distributed measurement applications. IEEE Trans. Instrum. Meas. **66**(12), 3340–3349 (2017)
10. Mikhaylov, K., et al.: Multi-RAT LPWAN in smart cities: trial of LoRaWAN and NB-IoT integration. In: 2018 IEEE International Conference on Communications (ICC), vol. 2018, May 2018

11. Duangsuwan, S., Takarn, A., Nujankaew, R., Jamjareegulgarn, P.: A study of air pollution smart sensors LPWAN via NB-IoT for Thailand smart cities 4.0. In: 2018 10th International Conference on Knowledge and Smart Technology (KST), pp. 206–209 (2018)
12. Guibene, W., Nowack, J., Chalikias, N., Fitzgibbon, K., Kelly, M., Prendergast, D.: Evaluation of LPWAN technologies for smart cities: river monitoring use-case. In: 2017 IEEE Wireless Communications and Networking Conference Workshops (WCNCW) (2017)
13. Ismail, D., Rahman, M., Saifullah, A.: Low power wide area networks: opportunities, challenges, and directions. In: Proceedings of the Workshop Program of the 19th International Conference on Distributed Computing and Networking, pp. 1–6 (2018)
14. LoRa Alliance Corporate Bylaws: LoRaWAN Specification. Technical report 2, LoRa Alliance, Fermont, California, United States (1 2017)
15. LoRa Alliance Corporate Bylaws: A technical overview of LoRa and LoRaWAN. Technical report 1, LoRa Alliance, Fermont, California, United States (2015)
16. Ochoa, M., Guizar, A., Maman, M., Duda, A.: Evaluating LoRa energy efficiency for adaptive networks: From star to mesh topologies. In: 2017 IEEE 13th International Conference on Wireless and Mobile Computing, Networking and Communications (WiMob), vol. 2017-October (2017)
17. Nguyen, T.T., Nguyen, H.H., Barton, R., Grossetete, P.: Efficient design of chirp spread spectrum modulation for low power wide area networks. IEEE Internet of Things J. 6(6), 9503–9515 (2019)
18. Xiong, F.: Digital modulation techniques. Artech house, inc. (2006)
19. LoRa Alliance: About LoRa Alliance (2020). https://lora-alliance.org. Accessed 15 April 2020
20. International Telecommunication Union : Spectrum Management Overview. Technical report, International Telecommunication Union, Ginebra, Switzerland (2010)
21. LoRa Alliance Corporate Bylaws: LoRaWAN Regional Parameters. Technical report 2, LoRa Alliance, Fermont, California, United States, November 2019
22. Sheinwald, D., Satran, J., Thaler, P., Cavanna, V.: Agilent: Internet Protocol Small Computer System Interface (ISCSI) Cyclic Redundancy Check (CRC)/Checksum Considerations. Technical report, Network Working Group, Fermont, California, United States (2002)
23. Tanenbaum, A., Wetherall, D.: Computer Networks. Pearson Custom Library, Pearson (2013)
24. U-blox: GPS Neo-6 GPS modules. U-blox, Thalwil, Switzerland, 1 edn. (2011)
25. Bosch: BMP180 Digital Pressure Sensor. Bosch, Gerlingen, Germany, 2 edn., April 2013
26. Mouser Electronics: DHT11 Humidity and Temperature Sensor. MouserElectronics, Mansfield, Texas, United States, 1 edn. (2019)
27. IvenSense Inc.: MPU-6000 and MPU-6050 Product Specification. IvenSense Inc., Sunnyvale, California, United States, 3 edn. (2013)
28. Arduino: About Arduino (2020). urlhttps://www.arduino.cc/en/Main/AboutUs. Accessed 20 May 2020
29. Chipcon Products.: Low-Cost Low-Power Sub-1GHz RF Transceiver. Texas Instrument., Texas, United States, 6 edn. (2015)
30. Adelantado, F., Vilajosana, X., Tuset-Peiro, P., Martinez, B., Melia-Segui, J., Watteyne, T.: Understanding the limits of LoRaWAN. IEEE Commun. Mag. 55(9), 34–40 (2017)

Design of a Watt Mechanism with Crossed Axes

Jesus Alvarez-Cedillo[1]([✉]), Teodoro Alvarez-Sanchez[2], and Mario Aguilar-Fernandez[1]

[1] Instituto Politécnico Nacional, UPIICSA, Av. Te 950 Iztacalco, CDMX, Mexico
`jaalvarez@ipn.mx`
[2] Instituto Politécnico Nacional, CITEDI, Av. IPN s/n, Tijuana, BC, Mexico

Abstract. The Watt mechanism was invented by James Watt and consisted of a central point of the system that is configured to move as close as possible to a straight line. At one time this Mechanism was used in automobile suspensions as a lateral guiding mechanism, and in the field of robotics, it is used for various robots and in different applications. This article deals with the design and state of the art of new Watt mechanisms, their classification and analysis, their crossed kinematics are analyzed, these efforts represent a first moment to modify the movements of parallel delta-type robots and will allow to increase their precision.

Keywords: Analysis · Mechanical parallel robot mechanism parallel cross workspace · Pressure angle · Uniqueness · Delta robots

1 Introduction

One of the problems that occupied the engineers of the late 18th century and much of the 19th century consisted in finding a mechanism capable of guaranteeing that the forces suffered by the piston rod of steam engines when entering or leaving the cylinder were perfectly parallel to your direction of motion.

Watt's mechanism (also known as the parallel linkage) is a type of mechanical linkage invented by James Watt (January 19, 1736 to August 25, 1819) in which the central moving point of the linkage is constrained from traveling on an approximation to a straight line. It was described in Watt's 1784 patent for the Watt steam engine. It is also used in automobile suspensions, allowing the axle of a vehicle to travel vertically while preventing side movement.

Watt's mechanism consists of a chain of three bars, two of greater length and equal at the outer ends of the chain, connected by a short rod in the middle. The outer end points of the long bars are fixed in place relative to each other, and otherwise the three bars are free to pivot around the joints where they meet. Therefore, counting the fixed-length connection between the outer end points as another bar, watt's mechanism is an example of a four-bar joint.

During the industrial revolution, the mechanisms for converting rotary to linear motion were widely adopted in industrial and mining machinery, locomotives, and measuring devices. Such devices had to combine engineering simplicity with a high degree of precision, and the ability to operate at speed for long periods. For many purposes approximate linear motion is an acceptable substitute for exact linear motion.

M. F. Mata-Rivera et al. (Eds.): WITCOM 2020, CCIS 1280, pp. 116–127, 2020.
https://doi.org/10.1007/978-3-030-62554-2_9

The theory of machines and mechanisms is in this moment, an applied science that deals with the relationships between the geometry and the movement of the elements of a machine or a mechanism, the forces that intervene in these movements and the energy associated with their operation.

Knowledge of mechanics forms the basis for the study of mechanisms and machines.

In the field of machine and mechanism theory, the analysis and synthesis of mechanisms differ. The analysis consists of studying the kinematics and dynamics of a mechanism according to the characteristics of the elements that constitute it. Therefore, the analysis of a mechanism will allow, for example, to determine the trajectory of a point of a bar or a relation of speeds between two members.

Conversely, the synthesis consists of choosing and sizing a mechanism that meets or tends to meet, with a certain degree of approximation, given design requirements. Thus, for example, a design will have to undertake the determination of a mechanism - synthesis - that allows guiding a solid to move from one configuration to another.

It is well known in the literature that the working space of parallel manipulators is less than that of serial manipulators due to limitation and interference caused by linkages of the kinematic chains or caused by singularities [1–4].

The Watt mechanism contains a large number of kinematic chains, so the construction of the base or the mobile platform is not a trivial task due to the characterization of the kinematic links that interconnect the kinematic chains with the base and with the platform.

One of the solutions to this problem is to locate two or more actuators in several kinematic chains so that the number of these chains is less than six, which requires a sophisticated design for the architecture of the kinematic chains that contain several actuators.

In this article, we develop another solution for design, using parallel crossed mechanisms, that is, mechanisms in which some crossed kinematic chains are located between parallel kinematic chains [7].

The classification of these mechanisms and their analysis are shown and are compared based on their singularities and pressure angles [9, 10].

2   Taxonomy of Parallel Cross Mechanisms

In this section, structures known in the literature will be classified with a degree of freedom between one to six, with at least one link interconnected to two others. Degrees of freedom (G) is defined as the minimum number of parameters so that the position of a mechanism is wholly defined.

The number of degrees of freedom defines the number of inputs. That is, the number of motors and actuators that must be placed in the Mechanism to provide movement. See Fig. 1.

Grübler's criterion is used to determine the number of degrees of freedom of a mechanism. The criterion for the case of flat mechanisms is shown in Eq. 1:

$$G = 3(N - 1) - 2P_I - P_{II} \tag{1}$$

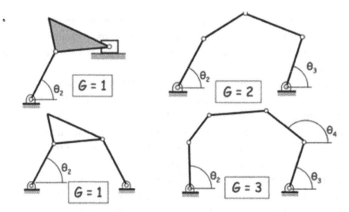

Fig. 1. Example of a Delta robot mechanism with G degrees of freedom.

Where N: number of elements, PI: number of class I pairs and PII: number of class II pairs.

The I Class pairs allow movement in one degree of freedom and restrict it in two degrees of freedom. Class II pairs restrict movement by one degree of freedom.

Grübler's criterion is used to determine the number of degrees of freedom of a mechanism.

The criterion for the case of flat mechanisms is as follows: In the proposed taxonomy, each link can be made up of a maximum of six joints, considering that one link is likely to be interconnected with six more and must have at least one torque driven. See Table 1.

3 Proposal Development

Our proposal is for a mechanism with six degrees of freedom. It is possible to use two cases based on the position of the actuators: the actuators are located on the base (Fig. 2); the actuators are located under the base (Fig. 3).

Both manipulators are composed of a fixed base formed by the notation $A_1A_2A_3$ and a mobile platform $B_1B_2B_3$.

The platform is attached to the base by using three connecting elements, each of which is composed of a spherical at point A_i, a powered prismatic pair A_iB_i, and a spherical joint B_i.

Each link is joined to three other links composed of a ball joint C_i, a prismatic pair C_iD_j and a ball joint D_j where $j = i + 1$ for $i = 1, 2$ and $j = 1$ for $i = 3$.

The Mechanism contains internal mobility limited by the Cardan joints. See Fig. 4.

The Grübler formula can give the number of degrees of freedom m of the Mechanism:

$$m = 6n - 5p_5 - 4p_4 - 3p_3 = 6 \tag{2}$$

Where: n corresponds to the body number without the base (n = 13); p5 corresponds to the number of pairs with only one degree of mobility ($p_5 = 6$ prismatic joints); p4 corresponds to the number of pairs with two degrees of mobility ($p_4 = 6$ gimbal joints); p3 corresponds to the number of pairs with three degrees of mobility ($p_3 = 6$ ball joints).

Table 1. Grübler taxonomy.

Mechanism	Grübler.	Structure type
	G <0	Hyperstatic structure
	G = 0	Isostatic structure
	G = 1	Desmodromic mechanism: given the position of one element the position of all other elements is known
	G = 2	Differential mechanism
	G> 2	Mechanism with n degrees of freedom.

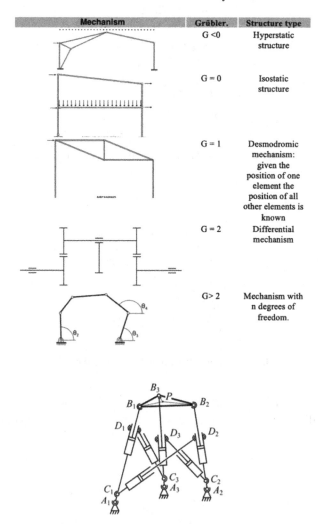

Fig. 2. The actuators are located on the base.

The simultaneous displacements of the activated joints allow the Mechanism to have three translating and three rotating DOFs. We denote: the lengths of the prismatic pairs A_iB_i as ρi, (i = 1 to 3); the lengths of the prismatic pairs C_iD_j as $\rho i +3$, (j = i + 1 for i = 1, 2, j = 1 for i = 3). Triangles $A_1A_2A_3$ and $B_1B_2B_3$ are considered equilateral. We consider the controlled point to be point P, located in the centre of triangle $B_1B_2B_3$.

The position of P is expressed by the vector $[x, y, z]^T$. The base frame is centred at point O located in the centre of triangle $A_1A_2A_3$. So x_0 goes a long line A_1A_2, y_0 along line OA_3.

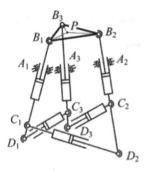

Fig. 3. The actuators are located below the base.

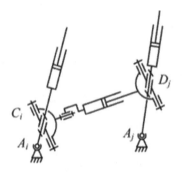

Fig. 4. Internal mobility limited by the Cardan joints

The rotations of the platform are denoted as α, β, γ, which can be obtained by expressing the directional cosines in terms of $z_0 - x_1 - y_2$ Euler angles α, β, γ. See Fig. 5.

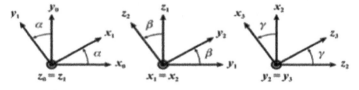

Fig. 5. Description of Euler's chosen angles.

Let us consider inverse geometric analysis. The positions of the points A_i, B_i, C_i, D_i of the manipulators which would be as $i = 1, 2, 3$:

$$OA_I = ROT(\delta, z_a)[R_b\ 0\ 0]^T \tag{3}$$

$$OB_I = [x\ and\ z] + ROT(\alpha, z_0)ROT(\beta, z_1)ROT(\gamma, z_2)\left[R_{pi}\ cos\ cos\ \delta_i\ R_{pi}\ sin\ sin\ \delta_i\ 0\right] \tag{4}$$

$$OC_I = OA_I + \frac{l_1}{\rho_I} A_I B_I \tag{5}$$

$$OD_I = OA_I + \frac{l_2}{\rho_I} A_I B_I \tag{6}$$

with $R_b = OAi$, $R_{pl} = PBi$, $\delta = \left[-5\pi/6, -\pi/6, -\pi/2\right]$ $(i = 1, 2, 3)$, $l_1 = \overline{A_i C_i}$, $l_2 = \overline{A_i D_i}$, and $\mathbf{Rot}(\zeta, w)$ the matrix representing the rotation of the angle ζ $(\zeta = \alpha, \beta$ and $\gamma)$ around the axis of the intermediate frame $(w = z_0, x_1$ and $and_2)$.

Therefore, the expressions of the joint coordinates are given by:

$$\rho_i = \sqrt{(A_i B_i)} \text{ for } i = 1, 2, 3 \tag{7}$$

$$\rho_i = \sqrt{(C_i D_i)}^T + \sqrt{(C_i D_i)}^T, \ (j = i + 1 \text{ for } i = 1, 2, j = 1 \text{ for } i = 3) \tag{8}$$

Consider the kinematic analysis. The closing equations are represented by the expressions:

$$f_i = 0 = \rho_i^2 - (A_i B_i)^T (A_i B_i) \text{ for } i = 1, 2, 3 \tag{9}$$

$$f_{i+3} = 0 = \rho_{i+3}^2 - (C_i D_i)^T (C_i D_i), \ (j = i + 1 \text{ for } i = 1, 2, j = 1 \text{ for } i = 3) \tag{10}$$

By differentiating the closing equations concerning time, the following expression can be obtained (Gosselin and Angeles [5]):

$$Av + Bq = 0 \tag{11}$$

where:

$$A = \left[\frac{\partial f_i}{\partial \rho_i}\right], \quad B = \left[\frac{\partial f_i}{\partial \rho_i}\right], X_i = (x, y, z, \alpha, \beta, \gamma) \tag{12}$$

The vector v can be related to the torsion t of the platform expressed in the base frame using a transformation matrix $\mathbf{D}$ (Merlet [4]):

$$t = Dv \text{ with } D = [I_{3x3} \ 0_{3x3} \ 0_{3x3} \ L] \text{ where}$$
$$L = [0 \ cos \ cos \ \alpha - without \ \alpha \ cos\beta \ 0 \ sin \ \alpha cos \ cos\alpha \ cos\beta \ one \ 0 \ sin\beta] \tag{13}$$

$I_{3.3}$ and $0_{3.3}$ correspond to identity and zero matrices of dimensions 3·3 respectively.

However, the Jacobian matrix $\mathbf{J}$ that relates the rotation t of the platform to the speeds of the actuators is given by the relation:

$$J = -DA^{-1}B \tag{14}$$

The elements of matrices $\mathbf{A}$ and $\mathbf{B}$ depend on the parameters of the mechanisms and the position of the mobile platform.

4   Comparative Analysis of the Yields

In order to measure the performance of the proposed Mechanism, it was compared with two other manipulators widely studied in the literature and used by some manufacturers, which have a six-pair drive system.

1. The Gough platform: The F robot is used $-200iB$ ($Rpl = 0.2$ m and $Rb = 0.3$ m; maximum actuator stroke equal to 0.65 m. See Fig. 6.

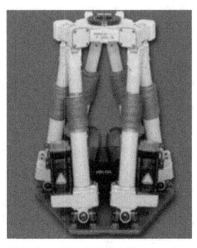

Fig. 6. The F-200iB is a parallel robot of six degrees of freedom for applications in manufacturing and assembly processes in the automotive industry (courtesy of Fanuc Robotics America Inc.) (Fanuc, 2005).

2. The Stewart platform:

We can consider in our comparison the actuator arrangements that will lead to the most significant space of work taking into account: the stroke of the actuators, the displacement of the spherical torques and the interferences between the elements; The quality of the transmission of the effort in the Mechanism (Fig. 7).

Let us consider the analysis of the workspace, taking into account the geometric limitations. The corresponding procedure is straightforward. First, we discretize the Cartesian space at n points and the orientation space at p configurations. The pitch for the Cartesian space is equal to 0.05 m and for the orientation space at $10°$ for angles between $-60°$ and $+60°$ for each angle α, β and γ. For a point Q to belong to the workspace of the considered manipulator, it must have at least one of the p settings of the orientation space that validates the geometric limitations. Therefore, this workspace is defined as the maximum workspace (Merlet [4]).

The geometric limitations under study are, for each manipulator:

1. The maximum actuator stroke must be identical and equal to 0.65 m;

Fig. 7. An account with six same actuators di positions symmetrically. Each of these arms consists of two pieces joined by a prismatic connection.

2. To avoid interference between the different elements of the manipulators, the minimum distance between non-secant links must be equal to 0.1 m, and we consider that the minimum angle between two secant links is equal to 15°. For example, in Fig. 3c, the angle between the AiDi and CiDi links cannot be less than 15°;
3. The rotation interval for ball joints must be between −60° and +60°.

The geometric parameters for the Gough platform are already fixed. For the other manipulators, we chose the geometric parameters that are as close as possible to the parameters of the Gough platform.

For the Stewart platform: points C1, C2 and C3 coincide with A2, A3 and A1 respectively, and AiDi = 0.2 m;

1. proposed new manipulator, case one (actuators on base): $l1 = 0.15, l2 = 0.65$;
2. proposed new manipulator, case two (actuators below base): $l1 = −0.3, l2 = −0.75$.

Figure 8 presents the workspaces obtained for the Gough platform and the Stewart Platform;

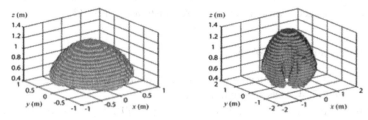

Fig. 8. Workspaces for the Gough and Stewart platform

In our proposed case, the obtained values are shown, which are shown in Fig. 9.

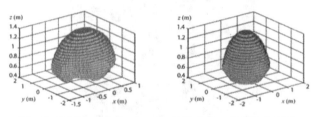

Fig. 9. Workspaces for the proposed design (1,959; 2,168).

4.1 Displacement in the Z-Axis

For this case, because the movement did not imply displacement in z, the actuators must present an identical behaviour to each other. This behaviour corresponds to an increase in the final length of the actuators as the distance displaced on the z-axis increases. When the values are: $D = 2d$, $\Phi A = 30°$, $\Phi B = 60°$; The actuators follow the behaviour shown in Fig. 10.

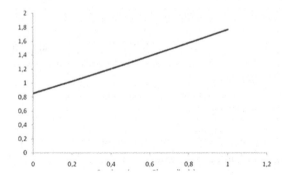

Fig. 10. The behavior of the actuators with z displacement.

Once the variation in the length of the actuators was verified, the data was obtained with various parameter values. The results are illustrated in Fig. 11.

4.2 Rotation Around the Z-Axis

For this case, as already explained above, the actuators must change length in groups of three (1, 3, 5) and (2, 4, 6) as shown in Fig. 12.

When the values are: $D = 2d$, $\Phi A = 30°$, $\Phi B = 60°$; The actuators followed the behaviour shown in Fig. 13.

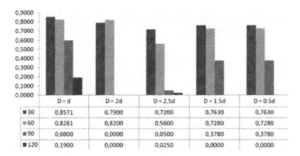

Fig. 11. Displacement in the z-axis (normalized), Results.

	D = d	D = 2d	D = 2.5d	D = 1.5d	D = 0.5d
■ 30	0,8571	0,7900	0,7200	0,7630	0,7630
▩ 60	0,8261	0,8200	0,5600	0,7280	0,7280
■ 90	0,6000	0,0000	0,0500	0,3780	0,3780
■ 120	0,1900	0,0000	0,0250	0,0000	0,0000

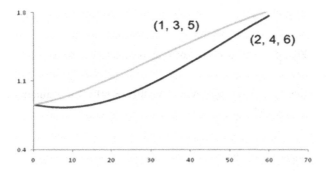

Fig. 12. The behavior of actuators with rotation around the z-axis

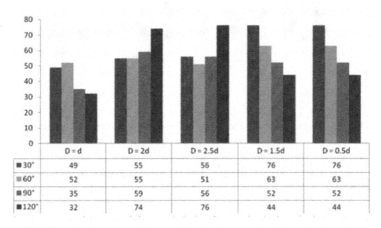

	D = d	D = 2d	D = 2.5d	D = 1.5d	D = 0.5d
■ 30°	49	55	56	76	76
▩ 60°	52	55	51	63	63
■ 90°	35	59	56	52	52
■ 120°	32	74	76	44	44

Fig. 13. Rotation around the z-axis in h min, results (values in degrees)

4.3 Positive Displacement in the X-Axis

In this case, the movement of the actuators seems not to be obvious or trivial. However, if Fig. 14 is taken into account, it will be understood how it works. The actuators will move in pairs, i.e. (1, 2), (3, 6) and (4, 5). D = 2d, ΦA = 30°, ΦB = 60°; The actuators followed the behavior shown in Fig. 14.

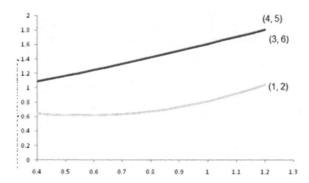

Fig. 14. Actuators behavior with rotation around the x-axis

When the values are: D = 2d, ΦA = 30°, ΦB = 60°; The actuators followed the behaviour shown in Fig. 15.

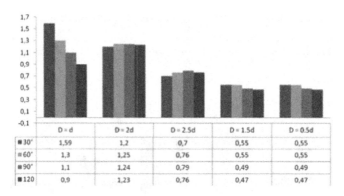

	D = d	D = 2d	D = 2.5d	D = 1.5d	D = 0.5d
■ 30'	1,59	1,2	0,7	0,55	0,55
■ 60'	1,3	1,25	0,76	0,55	0,55
■ 90'	1,1	1,24	0,79	0,49	0,49
■ 120	0,9	1,23	0,76	0,47	0,47

Fig. 15. Rotation around the x-axis in h min, results (values in degrees)

5   Conclusion

In this article, we present a new design based on Watt mechanisms to assist non-experts without advanced knowledge in the design of kinetic mechanisms.

The implications of the developments and implementations indicated that the results obtained show a robust design. At the beginning the design process involved a lot of effort due to the trial and error approach y is not a trivial process, in which many adjustments must be made; however, the best values obtained are shown.

Parallel cross manipulators are represented, as well as their classification. The comparison analysis performed for the new manipulators and known parallel manipulators, taking into account the geometric limitations and the possible pressure angles, leads to the conclusion that the working space of the new manipulators is not less than that of the known parallel manipulators.

Acknowledgements. We appreciate the facilities granted to carry out this work to the "Instituto Politécnico Nacional" through the Secretariat of Research and Postgraduate with the SIP 20180023 project. To the Interdisciplinary Unit of Engineering and Social and Administrative Sciences, Center for Technological Innovation and Development in Computing and Digital Technologies Research and Development Center. Likewise, to the Program of Stimulus to the Performance of the Researchers (EDI) and the Program of Stimulus COFAA and SIBE.

References

1. Gough, V.E.: Contribution to the discussion of papers on research on automobile stability and control and tire performance by Cornell staff. In: Proceedings of Automobile Division Institute Mechanical Engineering, 1956/57, pp. 392–396 (1956)
2. Stewart, D.A.: Platform with six degrees of freedom. In: Proceedings of the Institution of Mechanical Engineers, London, vol. 180, Part 1, no. 15, pp. 371–386 (1965)
3. Hunt, K.: Structural kinematics of parallel actuated robot arms. ASME J. Mech. Transmiss. Autom Des. **105**(4), 705–712 (1983)
4. Merlet, J.P.: Parallel Robots, 372 p. Kluwer Academic Publishers, Dordrecht (2000)
5. Gosselin, C.M., Ángeles, J.: Singularity analysis of closed-loop kinematic chains. IEEE Trans. Robot. Autom. **6**(3), 281–290 (1990)
6. Parenti-Castelli, V., Innocenti, C.: Direct displacement analysis for some kinds of parallel spatial mechanisms, procedures. In: VIII CISM-IFToMM Symposium on Theory and Practice of Robots and Manipulators, Krakow, Poland, pp. 123–130 (1990)
7. Glazunov, V.A., Briot, S., Arakelyan, V., Gruntovich, M.M., Thanh, N.M.: Development of manipulators with a parallel cross-structure. J. Mach. Manuf. Reliab. **2**, 85–91 (2008)
8. Sutherland, G., Roth, B.: A transmission index for spatial mechanisms. ASME Trans. Ind. Eng. Mag. **95**, 589–597 (1973)
9. Lin, C.-C., Chang, W.-T.: The force transmissivity index of planar bond mechanisms. Mech. Mach. Theor. **37**, 1465–1485 (2002)
10. Arakelian, V., Briot, S., Glazunov, V.: Increase of singularity-free zones in the workspace of parallel manipulators using mechanisms of variable structure. Mech. Mach. Theor. **43**(9), 1129–1140 (2008)

Learning Analytics in M-learning: Periodontic Education

Diana C. Burbano G.[1]([✉]) [iD] and Jaime Alvarez Soler[2]([✉]) [iD]

[1] Universidad Santiago de Cali-Valle, Cali, Colombia
diana.burbano02@usc.edu.co
[2] Universidad Cauca-Popayan, Popayán, Colombia
jalvarezs@unicauca.edu.co

Abstract. This study aims to understand the transformation of educational and training systems from the perspective of the ubiquitous learning experience of medical and dental students in the period 2019 and 2020 A. The configuration of the learning environment integrates digital ecosystems, monitoring of the actual temporal experience that guides learning outcomes. The training of dental students (clinical periodontology), motivated the design and implementation of teaching strategies with interactive and collaborative activities, which can be carried out in real time with intelligent learning systems; which requires new forms of learning and teaching, with mobile applications that make collaboration networks possible. The development of a didactic sequence that supports collaborative learning with the use of the application, improves the meta-cognitive knowledge of medical and dental students. The analysis plan was carried out with the SPPS 21 software, the T Students test, Crombach alpha test, levene test. The complementary research methodology, the design is descriptive transectional or transversal; the technological mediation is the mHealth application. The results obtained, in real time (data 16 weeks) reveal that the application was used in its entirety 574 h and 19 min, showing a great interest in the developing collaborative learning.

Keywords: Liquid generation · Learning analytics · Ubiquitous learning

1 Introduction

Higher education in today's learning society is no stranger to the various ups and downs that have shaped the evolution of technological mediations, and through this evolution of humanity, determining needs are being generated; actions are being promoted or decisions justified that extend, limit or question the function and purposes of higher education, both from the diachronic point of view and at a given historical moment [1]. The place of cyberculture changes when technological mediation goes from being merely instrumental to becoming structural; Technology today refers, not to the novelty of devices, but to new forms of multisite thinking, modes of perception and language, new sensibilities and writing, to transformations of culture that involve the educommunicative association that turns knowledge into a direct productive force. In this context, the need arises to confront the unique thinking that legitimizes the idea that current technology

© Springer Nature Switzerland AG 2020
M. F. Mata-Rivera et al. (Eds.): WITCOM 2020, CCIS 1280, pp. 128–139, 2020.
https://doi.org/10.1007/978-3-030-62554-2_10

transforms societies. These revolutions draw new coordinates in all areas of human activity that particularly impact the institutions that deal with the training of students in biomedical sciences - (clinical dental specialties) to facilitate their insertion in a changing, technologically complex and highly competitive world in which it is necessary to know and speak new discourses in order not to suffer the exclusion gaps that have emerged or have been consolidated in the heterogeneous and unequal society

Any look highlights the realities of the university that going through multiple problems, involves evaluating its system of operation and governance, reconsidering its structure, reviewing its contributions, identifying the expectations that the achievements and learning experiences in the current generation T (tactile) of our students. In short, revealing the features that are part of the current academic scenarios make university a bastion of culture, knowledge and science; despite the successive questions it has received and the profound challenges it faces; perhaps more than ever, they set in motion its principles, processes and results.

This article reveals how technological mediation in learning is generated, from a trans and interdisciplinary perspective, by establishing relations between knowledge. Learning is vitalized by interaction as a generator of knowledge through the promotion of study networks. However, this problem usually opens the spectrum of the fourth technological revolution, which has undoubtedly contributed significantly to today's society, education, health, and business around the world.

2   Related Work

The expansion of the use of information and communication technologies, in particular the internet and more recently web 2.0 applications, has promoted an unusual circulation of information, which is also created and shared autonomously and openly, generating a leading role and providing the means for consumers or producers, to transit, express their positions and confront their imposition of hegemonic thinking and behavior. Therefore, revolutions draw new coordinates in all spheres of human activity that particularly impact on institutions, especially those that deal with the education and training of citizens to facilitate their insertion in a changing, technologically complex and highly competitive world, in which it is necessary to know and manage the new discourses to minimize the exclusion gap that has emerged or has been consolidated in a heterogeneous and unequal society. Although some authors tend to review the literature in the theoretical categories (Table 1), we agree that to carry out the search chains when considering the methodological design of the research.

2.1   Learn Connected

Castell [2] indicates in the prologue of his trilogy on the information society [3], that our current society is organized through networks (interconnected nodes), which disrupts a change in our social morphology. These nodes interact with each other, generate new structures, exchange information, and determine a dynamic and flexible social structure, which is constantly moving and, therefore, constantly changing. Analyses of the past are less and less useful in explaining how we are, what we do, how we learn, how our

Table 1. Methodological phases with the application and methodological desingn

Phase I: Preprocessing	Phase II: Process	Phase III: Post process
Planning	Didactic sequence (student)	Formative assessment
Didactic sequence	Intergroup cooperation	Closing of activities
ADDI model	Monitor interface	Peer dialogue
Execution of activities	Feedback	Learning outcome (Rubrics)
Thread diagram: App and design of augmented reality Feedback Tracking student		
	Student discussion	

institutions are organized and what purpose they serve. Change, although not always easily accepted, is the thread of a way of life that finds in the interaction between nodes the models of analysis and development of our society.

The technological system centred on ICT has allowed the emergence of a new economy, a new form of management, a new media system, a new culture and new forms of organization and political and administrative participation. It is Siemens [4] that first suggested that, although until recently behaviorism, cognitivism and constructivism were the main theories that tried to respond to how learning take place, the social change resulting from globalization and the information and knowledge society makes these theories insufficient.

Connectivism in Siemens' words is based on the following principles: a. learning is a process of connecting nodes or sources of information, b. learning can reside in non-human devices. c. power and maintenance of connections is necessary to facilitate continuous learning.

Learning can take place in different enviroments, so "describes learning as a process of creating a personal knowledge network, an idea consistent with the way people teach and learn on the web [5].

Siemens [6] goes on to indicate that learning is related to creation of connections between information nodes and patterns recognition. Nodes are external entities that can be used to form a network. As Garcia Aretio [7] points out, the good thing about any learning is to be able to dispose, the ability to know how to locate the sources where we are and connect with them is nowadays a vital skill.

2.2 Collaborative Learning: A Look from the Research Experience

The most important contribution from the perspective of the research process in the field of M-teaching and learning is based on experience, as part of the context of building a Smilearning application. This constitutes a pedagogical tool, from the subject of oral pathological anatomy, and therefore is the first characteristic that structures an educational epistemology, that is, a new educational knowledge, related to the design and structuring of a didactic sequence, as part of the context of teaching the specialization in periodontology.

The design of the didactic sequence includes opening, development and closing activities. Each of these activities received input from different active sub-themes such as students, teachers and external experts, who entered, interrogated and interacted to solve the different cases of clinical problems, with different themes within the application. This generated an integrative, interdisciplinary and transdisciplinary knowledge, with theoretical and practical components that generated motivations, feedback, personalization and internalization of the contents in the students, making them accessible at any time, that is, it breaks with temporal synchrony and becomes a ubiquitous type of learning.

The analysis and structuring of the design of the Smilearning application design is a complex and interdisciplinary teamwork process that requires the development in the Ionic language and the ideation of the programming sequence by system engineers, graphic designers and experts in specific topics in the development of applications, who have the contributions and knowledge of the discipline in periodontology and dentistry. To achieve this, it was necessary to monitor in real time, the learning activities of students, this is an activity that escapes the observation and human monitoring, so it requires the use of artificial intelligence for future studies.

From this perspective of ubiquity, the monitoring of students allows us to conclude that the time of use and interaction generates a habit or strategy of using multiple channels, that is, when students enter the application they need and are eager for more information. through various channels, with a tendency to look for different ways, to obtain the information they want, assuming multiple simultaneous tasks. In this sense, we can state that information and communication technologies promote this type of contact with learning content in order to make it meaningful or situated.

The present research puts in special emphasis on the fact that students had up to three computers to connect, such as: cell phones, tablets, among others, with multiple records, that is, they downloaded the application to several computers, in order to achieve the greatest possible multi-situation or ubiquity, this generated a greater appropriation and fostered competitiveness, generated by the reliefs and stimuli they received in each lesson as a prize and qualification, this is not a bias, but reflects the dependence of human beings on technologies and also the conditioned learning that is very useful for these non-contact strategies.

2.3 Learning Environments and Their Mediations

Mediation applied in the educational field is valid as long as the student appropriates its content and puts it into practice in the classroom; educational mediation should have an impact in such a way that the individual is able to solve problems in different disciplinary fields. It is important to emphasize that the teaching-learning processes, the types of scaffolding implemented in an educational mediation must be taken as means and as ends in the teaching processes generated in the different practice scenarios. All educational practice must be accompanied by a wide knowledge of the theory of mediation on the part of the teacher, it must be supported by elements that promote the emotionality of the students, so that the external representations used in their independent work were a fundamental artefact Due to the curiosity that I generate, the versatility in its use, the application of the concepts to the environment, fundamental aspects in the success of the teaching task.

In the documentary review carried out on pedagogical mediation, it is important to mention the research carried out by Renne Rickenmann (University of Geneva, Switzerland) "The role of the cultural artefact in the structure and management of the teaching-learning sequences", where some elements that constitute the didactics in education sciences and their use in effective learning practices are addressed. the applications as instrumental mediation in the development of the topic of oral journalism through a categorization of its structure with models of augmented reality are basic elements in the disruptive trends of journalistic practices of the three-dimensional relationship of space.

2.4 Virtual Learning Environments PLE (Personal Learning Environments)

The concept of PLE (personal learning environment) is defined, from a pedagogical perspective, as the set of all the tools, materials and human resources that a person knows and uses to learn throughout his/her life [1]. Among the functions taken into account in this work, indicated by [2], are: information management (related to personal knowledge management), content creation and connection with others (what is known as learning or personal network knowledge).

The PLE makes the student, either alone or in collaboration with others, gradually and procedurally build their own digital spaces in which they integrate those resources, portals, websites, tools, applications or networks that are usually used to learn-communicate or perform some training activity both formal and informal. This powerful concept is linked to an e-portfolio (electronic portfolio) understood as a kind of compilation or repository of the subject's own digital productions, such as: his multimedia presentations, his essays, his videos, his concept maps, among others.

Collaboration as a learning strategy is based on working in groups of several people but with similar levels of knowledge to achieve common objectives and carry out activities together, with a positive interdependence between them [3]. In collaborative activities there is not only one right answer, but different ways to reach the result, and for that, students must share and come to agreements, which helps them to be more autonomous and socially and intellectually. The information must be fed back and stimulated by the student; furthermore, you must have a self-regulation of knowledge, you must learn to learn, hence the key for the student to really learn with these new learning methodologies.

3   Research Design

The methodological design is mixed or complementary; the type of research is non-experimental, transactional or transversal (descriptive). Table 1, presents the planning activities of the methodological design.

3.1 Techniques and Instruments for Information Gathering

In this research, the instruments used to collect the information were: technique: real-time, the instrument (Smilernig app - phase 2 designs augmented reality in oral periodontics and special pathology, pre-concept, pre-test and post-test questionnaire technique and the instrument is the mobile application (Available on hybrid mobile and web platforms with software registration, Ministry of the Interior, number 13-79-326, May 28, 2020, Colombia.

3.2 Population and Sample

For the purposes of this study, the population and the sample were established as follows: following the qualitative approach of the research, the study group was formed by a purposive or convenience sampling procedure. The target population is heterogeneous and consists of the academic program specialized in periodontology. The sample was composed of students enrolled between semesters 4 and 6.

Convenience or intentional sampling, through this method, the researcher is in charge of choosing the subjects that will be part of the sample according to his/her criteria or scope. The participants were selected based on the following criteria: they must be graduate students of journalism who are taking the subject of oral journalism. The total was: 10 medical students from Universidad Unicauca; and 28 residents of the postgraduate course in periodontology at Universidad USC, Cali in the period 2019-2020 A.

The present research, in the methodological design is phase II, and the publication of phase I was published last year in witcom 2019 [4], of which I am the main author.

3.3 Consent to Participate in the Study

In accordance with internationally accepted standards to ensure the ethical treatment of persons participating in scientific research, an informed consent form was developed, explaining to the persons participating in the study, its purpose, possible benefits as well as their right not to participate or to discontinue their participation at any time, without prejudice to the study. The investigator provided each person with a copy of this document, which was signed by both the participant and the investigator.

4 Experimental Design and Interpretation of Statistical Tests

By conducting an analysis of the impact generated in students of IV and VI semester of the subject of periodontology, a class of strategies and instruments was proposed to evaluate the progress of the participants from the beginning to the end of the course. Subsequently, the data collected was stored and statistically analyzed to verify the significant improvement in the knowledge obtained and the collaborative learning developed, through the program SPSS version 21, Excel, Power point, M-Learning Smilearning, Google Form and Visual Studio code, using the necessary techniques in each program.

Two tests were used in the knowledge test: pre-test and post-test to evaluate the knowledge obtained through the didactic sequence.

Pre-test: after carrying out the activities with the students, a test was made with the Google Form tool to evaluate the knowledge of the students through an element called "assements rubrics" that corresponds to a series of multiple answers questions where each option has a score indicates: the best answer (5 points), the regular answer (3 points) and the incorrect answer (1 point).

Post-test: after carrying out the corresponding activities with the selected population and the participation in the proposed forums, a test was carried out through the Google form tool with which the knowledge is evaluated through a score in the evaluation headings, in order to demonstrate the knowledge obtained through the Smilearning application.

4.1 Validation of the Instrument

Validation of the data in the SPSS program with Crombach's alpha was necessary to verify how reliable the data are for conducting any study. Oviedo and Campo (2005) recommend that the alpha coefficient should be between 0.7 and 0.9 to be accepted.

In this statistic the error is associated to the calculation of the parameters to all the statistical tests (they must have a degree of error and a degree of reliability), the degree of reliability is expected to be above 90%, the error obtained in the normality test of the alpha Crombach have an error of 5%, are not associated to the sampling that was made, it is associated to the applied tests.

The group is so small that, if applied to these groups separately, the results would not be significant, and the teacher is the same. An initial test was applied, to find out their knowledge about the subject of APB topic and then contrast it with the learning obtained through the designed App resource. The design of the research is non-experimental, transactional or transversal.

In the present investigation cronbach's alpha was, 7 acceptable

4.2 Processes for Data Analysis

The methodology used is complementary (quantitative and qualitative), and the analysis of the data obtained was carried out according to their nature (Gibbs, 2012). For the processing and analysis of the quantitative data, the statistical software SPSS (Statistical Package for the Social Science), version 21 for Windows, was used. As recommended by several authors such as López Morán (2016), the first thing that was done was descriptive statistics, including frequencies, calculation of central tendency measures (mean) and dispersion (standard deviation). Group differences were analyzed (normalization, student's t-test for independent samples and analysis unidirectional variance) and the degree of association or relationship between the variables (Pearson's correlation coefficient and chi-square tests).

The preparation of the quantitative data includes:

- Preparation of the students at the beginning of the didactic sequence, obtaining the previous results with the participants.
- Planning of the proposed activities with the programmatic content of the periodontology subject.

- Use of the Smilearning application, when assigning events and tasks of thematic development.
- Measurement of the times used by students during the 16 weeks of classes in the first period of 2019.
- Orientation of the students in dental cases to perform a theoretical-practical evaluation of the knowledge generating collaborative learning.
- Carrying out the corresponding evaluation to assess the knowledge obtained at the end of the teaching sequence.

5 Analysis of Quantitative Data

5.1 Interpretation of Results

During the research process, the use and performance of the application was analyzed with the students of the first academic period 2019 B-2020 A; taking the data collected by the TIMONEL platform that allows the analysis of certain characteristics of the students: academic grades, academic history, enrollment, registration. In the development of this research project, two groups of four people were voluntarily selected (four from group A and four from group B) who were studying the "Specialization in Periodontology " and who were studying the subject "Oral pathology" using the M-Health Smilearning tool. In addition, information was collected by means of a knowledge test to identify the bases obtained from the selected unit.

To follow up with the students in the development of the activities and the time spent, a record of multiple sheets of the students was made to calculate the handling times and some important characteristics of access to the Smilearning application, this process was carried out in the first months of 2019 until the end of the semester, being used during 574 h: 19 m hours by eight students.

During the development of the activities proposed in the didactic sequence, a control was carried out to record the time used in the Smilearning platform when carrying out each of the activities and challenges proposed to reinforce the knowledge of the subject. In addition, it was observed that the periodontics graduate students of the Cooperative University, Bogotá headquarters use IOS or Android mobile devices with internet access, to work at any time.

The Smilearning system records the activities carried out by the students, specifies the duration and the process carried out detailing each of the proposed activities, including the participation of students in the tool's discussion forum.

Activities analyzed with the Smilearning tool

- Proposed themes subcategorized
- Search terms
- Study of clinical cases
- Reinforcement with multimedia elements
- Discussion forums
- Events and planned activities (Fig. 2)

Once the course was completed, the data revealed that the entire application was used for 574 h and 19 min, showing a great interest on the part of the participants in developing collaborative learning between the teacher and the students.

By obtaining the collected information, the time used by the students in each of the subcategories was calculated, resulting in Fig. 1, which shows the support in knowledge and the development of collaborative learning. For example, we used the subcategory od discussion forum at 153 h: 10 m, an important means of communication between students and teachers; Then we have the proposed topics for the subject that are used in a range of 93 h to 41 h and finally the access to extra tools such as the presentation of clinical cases and video tutorials (Fig. 3).

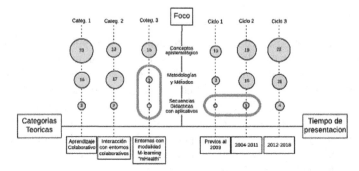

Fig. 1. Bubble diagram - systematic mapping (Note: own elaboration).

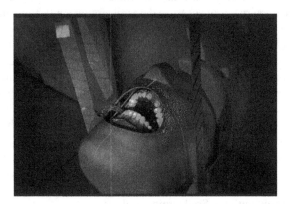

Fig. 2. Augmented reality from the first shot in the oral cavity. Smilearning app.

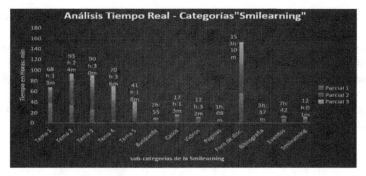

Fig. 3. Real Time Analysis - Smilearning Categories (**Note:** own elaboration)

5.2 Pedagogical Usability Test

Obtaining the usability heuristics: From the examination of different types of usability principles and recommendations for general purpose mobile applications, a set of heuristics was obtained to guide the process of designing and building web applications.

According to Burriel, by referring exclusively to the set of usability criteria associated with each of the 7 heuristics described in Sect. 4. All these relationships are structured and evaluated in a range of 0 to 5, with 0 being the absence of the criterion in the application and 5 the maximum compliance with the criteria within the application. It is then within this analysis that the criteria of the web or mobile application in question can be observed, the tool offers the evaluator the possibility of choosing the option (N/A). Therefore, within these relationships at the design level, the tool is based on tabs, each of which includes a heuristic and its associated criteria.

Fig. 4. Results

Figure 4 shows the results obtained for each use criterion, indicating the heuristics levels used, where H5 and H3 meet the highest level of the criteria assessed. The options taken for the application are defined below:

- Content: it represents a space to complement the thematic development with the students.

- Personalization: it represents an illustrative environment that generates an environment on the topic "Oral pariodontic anatomy".
- Social interaction: a space is designed in which students can communicate with their classmates and with the teacher in charge.
- Multimedia: within the application, a category is generated obtaining a list of videos and a link that reinforces the knowledge of the topic.
- Activities and tasks: finally, a set of tasks was selected to complement the knowledge received by the application.

6 Conclusions

The investigation provided elements of judgment by deducing that the application with augmented reality in the subject of oral periodontics when used was employed as didactic mediation. For this, it is necessary to know the T generation (corresponding to the current generation) that leads this mediation, taking into account the thematic contents are developed with suitability.

Based on this research with a descriptive-quantitative design, and after the analyzing the results, it is concluded from the research experience of phase II in this period called by the WHO covid 19 pandemic, this type of effective mediation is of great importance to improve learning outcomes, which is supported by higher education institutions.

The design of the activities in the didactic sequence of oral pathology topic, generates motivation in M-Learning and provides a real-time supervision of intellectual learning systems in the Smilearning application; these are factors that influence collaborative learning and the interaction between students and teachers.

The mHealth application in the subject of oral pathology is useful for mobile application learning activities (M-Learning), since it facilitates the creation of content, interaction and offers possibilities for personalization. Some of the outstanding advantages are: flexibility, personalization with multimedia, collaborative work and accessibility.

The new forms of interaction and the different actors that coexist in the network suggest new forms of collaborative learning in virtual communities, taking into account the various existing actors: subjects, objects, agents, mobile applications. Therefore, it is important to continue with the analysis of interactions, roles, profiles and behaviors in virtual communities. Without losing sight of the observation towards the real and offline. The effects, relationships and social and cultural changes that are created.

In this way, the Smilearning application improved learning outcomes in the student's academic activities. The teacher can define criteria or attributes to evaluate and monitor the collaboration process, following up in real time; necessary in the desitions making about how and when to intervene, when determining the degree of learning achieved by each student in each stage of the collaboration activity. It provides students with the necessary information on participant-content collaboration and their level of knowledge. The use of applications in M-Learning learning provides quick information to the teacher or the student, in the decision making in each collaborative activity. Although it is difficult to monitor the work of two groups at the same time, this work was done with the help of the Survey monkey program. This allows the teacher to monitor all groups during the collaborative activities. In this way, students and teachers are provided with adequate mechanisms to improve collaborative activities.

The analysis of the results suggests that the strategies in the group work adopted by each member are related to a successful process of individual construction of the cognitive context and the experience shared by the group members. Therefore, it is important to improve the development of strategies and facilitate their implementation; This was generated in the didactic sequence, making the language somewhat homogeneous, clear and unequivocal when referring to the common characteristics of the problem. The main contribution of this research is the approach of three elements directly related to the positive perception of pedagogical presence by students, namely: feedback, academy, and socialization. In general, both students and teachers consider that the contribution of peer interaction makes learning important.

References

1. Castañeda, L., Book, A.J.: Entornos personales de aprendizaje: claves para el ecosistema educativo en red., Alcoy: Marfi. (2013)
2. Weller, M.: A pedagogy of abundance. Revista española de Pedagogia., pp. 223–236 (2011)
3. Dillenburg, P.: What do you mean by collaboartive learning? En P Dillenburg (Ed) Collaborative learning: cognitive and computational approaches. Ed. Elseiver. Collaborative learning., pp. 1–19 (1999)
4. Burbano, D.: Intelligent learning ecosystem in m-learning systems. Telematics and Computing. (2019)
5. Li, Z., Bouazizi, I.: Light Weight Content Fingerprinting for Video Playback Verification in MPEG DASH, Samsung Research America (2013)
6. Muller, C., Lederer, S., Rainer, B., Waltl, M., Grafl, M., Timmerer. C.: Open source column: dynamic adaptive streaming over HTTP toolset. In: ACM SIGMM Records, vol. 16, no. 9 (2013)
7. Timmerer, C., Griwodz, C.: Dynamic Adaptive Streaming over HTTP: From Content Creation to Consumption. In: MM 2012, 2 Noviembre (2012)
8. Siemens, G.: Conectivismo: una teoria de aprendizaje para la era digital, Nuevas tecnologias y metodologias en Educacion Superior (2000)
9. Gibbs, B.R. (ed.): Thinking about Higher Education. Springer, Cham (2014). https://doi.org/10.1007/978-3-319-03254-2_9
10. Castell, M.: Sociedad del Conocimiento. Como cambia el mundo ante nuestros ojos., Barcelona: Edinouc.: Prologo en Tubella, I. Vilesca, J. (Eds.) (2005)
11. Tubella, J.: Sociedad del conocimiento. Como cambia el mundo ante nuestros ojos, Barcelona.: Ediuoc (2005)
12. Siemens, G.: Conectivism: a learning theory for the digital age. International Journal of Instruccinal technology and distance learning (2004)
13. Sobrino, A.: Proceso de enseñanza aprendizaje y web 2.0: valoracion del conectivismo como teoria de aprendizaje post – constructivista. Estudios sobre educacion 20, pp. 117–14 (2011)
14. Siemens, G.: Knowing Knowledge. Lulu Pres (2006)
15. Aretio, G.: Sociedad del conocimeinto y educacion. Madrid: UNED (2012)

Evaluation of a Machine Vision System Applied to Quality Control in a Liquid Filling, Lid and Labeling Line for Bottles

Julio Eduardo Mejía Manzano$^{(\boxtimes)}$, Thalia Alejandra Hoyos Bolaños$^{(\boxtimes)}$, Miguel Ángel Ortega Muñoz$^{(\boxtimes)}$, Victoria Eugenia Patiño Arenas$^{(\boxtimes)}$, and Helmer Paz Orozco$^{(\boxtimes)}$

Corporación Universitaria Comfacauca - Unicomfacauca, Cauca, Popayán, Colombia
{jmejia,thaliahoyos,miguelortega,vpatino,
hpaz}@unicomfacauca.edu.co

Abstract. This paper deals with the development of a low-cost machine vision system for the analysis of dosing, screwing and labeling variables in processes developed on industrial production lines. The algorithm for the evaluation of the variables is developed in Matlab ® software making use of the image processing toolbox, in addition to the use of electro-pneumatic actuators for the detection and ejection of bottles through a programmable logic controller, PLC, finally The simulation of the machine vision system is performed through the use of the simulation software FlexSim®, to analyze the feasibility in the implementation of industrial lines, tests are carried out on each of the variables, obtaining percentages of correct classification of 95% for the level of filling, 91.25% for the state of the cap and 97% for the analysis of the label, showing great complexity in the classification of the bottles in the study line.

Keywords: Automation · Control · Supervision · Industrial processes · Machine vision

1 Introduction

In companies, industrial automation is considered as a way to improve processes and productivity, making use of control mechanisms that are capable of making decisions in real time, incorporating automated control systems, aided by computer systems for the autonomous execution of the processes.

Traditional quality control procedures carried out by humans generate high response times and high variability in decisions, adapt special automated machines that allow information to be processed more efficiently by implementing mathematical models that allow machines understand human analytical and regulatory activity, allow the improvement of production lines [1, 2].

© Springer Nature Switzerland AG 2020
M. F. Mata-Rivera et al. (Eds.): WITCOM 2020, CCIS 1280, pp. 140–154, 2020.
https://doi.org/10.1007/978-3-030-62554-2_11

Artificial Intelligence is a technology that has been developing in order to imitate the dynamics of human thought, currently it seeks to solve engineering problems by providing greater processing speed and less variability in industrial-type processes [3, 4].

The application of artificial intelligence in industrial processes has been widely accepted in recent years, specifically computer vision or artificial vision inspection systems, since it is assured that the system is reliable compared to sit. human, which may fail to verify a final product [5].

Artificial vision systems employ cameras for industrial solutions [6, 7], this can be used to perform a visual inspection and meet industrial and factory performance, thus improving the results of product quality control. The inspection system must adapt to a scenario that has a wide variety of product characteristics and high production speed assembly lines as well as complex environment variables from the perspective of machine vision [8].

In this paper, we present a machine vision system for monitoring the filling level, the state of the cover and labeling in an industrial line. The algorithm model was validated by conducting in-line experiments, and simulations of the system's behavior were carried out using the FlexSim® software to understand its operation over time. The system was implemented using electro-pneumatic elements and a programmable logic controller (PLC), which is responsible for eliminating products that do not meet the characteristics on the production line.

2   Description Workspace

The development of this work was carried out by the Mechatronic engineering program in the manufacturing process laboratory of the Industrial Engineering program of the Comfacauca University Corporation, where the analysis of the characteristics of the line of filling, screwing and labeling, allowing to know the working space available for the implementation of an image processing system in charge of verifying the level of filling in the bottles, the proper screwing of the bottles and the correct positioning of the label.

The industrial line of study is a predesigned system to which structural modifications could not be made, for this reason the designed system had to be adaptable and flexible to its predetermined conditions. The designed system has a chamber with controlled lighting for image processing and an electro-pneumatic actuator system that is connected to a programmable logic device (PLC), in charge of developing the control actions configured in the code. of processing, in Fig. 1, the filling and labeling lines in the manufacturing process laboratory are observed.

3   Methodology

3.1   Mechatronic Design Methodology

In Mechatronic design, design ideas and control systems are conceptualized, for the production of parts in a short period of time in order to meet the necessary requirements, thus Mechatronic design takes the foundations of basic and advanced design, taking into account the knowledge and information necessary to achieve the manufacture of

Fig. 1. Filling, lid and labeling lines.

precise parts, optimizing each parameter in each of the design phases, and obtaining a quality product in a short cycle; Likewise, it is possible to combine the design and production phases of products in a special way. Using the principles of Mechatronic engineering as a guide, the designed product is likely to meet the basic requirements: high quality, robustness, low cost, customer satisfaction, and time investment. Therefore, it is important to know the process of Mechatronic Design, as evidenced in Fig. 2 [9].

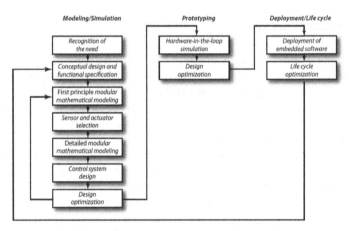

Fig. 2. Mechatronic design methodology [9].

In the sections, each of the steps carried out using the Mechatronic design methodology shown above is observed.

3.2 Modeling and Simulation

Recognition of Needs: Unicomfacauca manufacturing process laboratory has a three-station production line, which does not have a system capable of recognizing and taking action for defects or anomalies in its production, generating losses and reducing quality.

of the line. The design of a system for image acquisition was proposed, capable of classifying three variables such as the level of capping and labeling of the bottles and thus eliminating bottled that do not meet quality standards.

Conceptual design and functional specifications: For the development of the capture system, it was necessary to build a system to isolate the ambient light and to be able to acquire images with better controlled lighting by using an external source. Design sketches were made for the image acquisition system, as shown in Fig. 3.

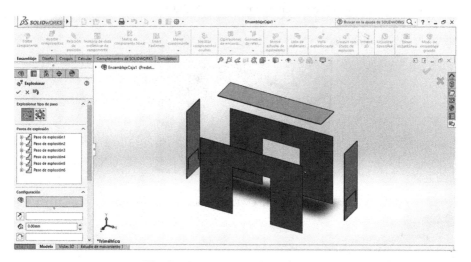

Fig. 3. Sketch of acquisition chamber.

Selection of Sensors and Actuators: In the development of the project, one of the most important parameters to take into account is the constant movement of the belt, varying in its speeds, so it is necessary to implement a system that is capable of stopping the bottles for a short time to proceed with the digital processing of the information, that is why two electro-pneumatic actuators were implemented that will be in charge of controlling the passage of analysis products to the acquisition chamber of the image where there is a 2 megapixel Jeway brand VGA camera with image resolution of 640 × 480 connected through the USB port.

The system allows the continuity of work in the production line, it is necessary to have another electro-pneumatic actuator in charge of expelling the product that does not comply with the requirements initially configured by the operator, it should be noted that its implementation, it must not cause damage to the line, it must work as a modular system that is assembled on the original line. It was also necessary to use pneumatic 5-way/2-position DC valves at 24 V, in charge of the pneumatic actuation of the pistons.

In relation to the sensors, I use a distance infrared with IR reference FC-51, which is part of the Arduino modules as well as being a low-cost and easily accessible sensor on the electronic market, among its characteristics is that they are powered at 3.3 V at 5 V, its design is built with an infrared emitting LED and a receiving photodiode that is sensitive to the intensity of the light emitted by the LED, among its characteristics it is appreciated that it captures the distance of some object in the ranges of 2 to 80 cm with a detection angle of 35 degrees.

A mechanical limit switch or contact sensor was also used, which detects the position of the object by means of a mechanical drive. Internally they are built with normally open (NA), normally closed (NC) switches and a common state.

Optimize Design: The initial sketches made on paper are taken, each of the pieces was made in CAD-type software (Solid Works version 2018-2019 of educational license by Unicomfacauca) in Fig. 4 the chamber prepared in Solid Works.

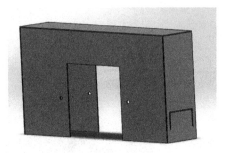

Fig. 4. CAD chamber.

3.3 Prototyping

Hardware Design: Once the final design was obtained in CAD, the parts were manufactured to make the cuts using the CNC laser printer, allowing to obtain precise parts for the assembly of the acquisition chamber, the elements were built using material MDF and steel in order to obtain a robust prototype structure.

Project Life Cycle: Once the modeling and prototyping stages have been carried out, the control processes carried out with Matlab® in charge of processing and obtaining information from the images are validated, with which the first results of the algorithm operation could be obtained and store the data obtained, to study the behavior of the production line, with the image processing station. This information allowed feedback to the development of the project, improving the efficiency of the algorithm.

4 Image Processing

The processing of the image captured from the bottles on the production line was carried out in three phases: the first, the construction of a chamber with controlled lighting, the second, the development of the code for the classification of the level, the state of the lid and the of the bottle label and finally the development of the graphical interface that allows better use of the built program. Each of the stages developed for the development of the project is shown below.

4.1 Lighting System

The lighting has a direct impact on the way in which the analysis image is captured, the range of visibility can be increased with artificial lighting, but some dispersion and absorption effects related to the sources used must be considered, on the other hand, the sources tend to illuminate the scene unevenly, producing a bright spot in the center of the image. with a poorly lit area surrounding it [10].

For the development of the classification system, a lighting bedroom was designed, where the study of the different types of lighting that are handled within the digital image processing was carried out, which are; lateral or directional lighting, back lighting, oblique lighting, structured lighting, coaxial lighting, dark field lighting and diffuse lighting [11]. For the development of the system, it was obtained that the best lighting model for the image acquisition chamber was the type of backlight lighting, since with this type of lighting they make a better contrast with the bottle, allowing to better highlight edges and shapes eliminating shadows produced by external lighting; so that the elements to be analyzed in it (level, screw-in and labeling) are precise, along with this a white background is also managed that makes the lighting diffuse more over the entire acquisition system, in Fig. 5 it can be seen the inside of the bedroom.

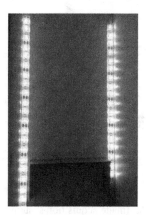

Fig. 5. Lighting assembly

4.2 Development of the Processing Algorithm

The elaboration of the image processing algorithm developed in Matlab® follows the structure shown in the flow diagram of Fig. 6, in important to clarify that S1 is related to a limit switch sensor that detects the passage of the bottle and generates a pulse It is processed by an Arduino programming card that allows that when the mechanical switch is activated, the state of the camera will turn on and will capture the object that is in front of it, then we will proceed to work the image giving way to the processes of image segmentation making use of the image histogram equalization [12], application of opening and closing morphological operations [13], and subsequent decision-making related to level, capping and labeling characteristics defined by the line, this procedure is performed through the graphical interface where you can put the values considered by the operator in which for him a bottle is in optimal conditions. Depending on the conditions, the different states in which the bottle can be found are evaluated, either with the level and the cap in optimal conditions or that both level and cap are rejected or combining a good cap and a bad level or bad cap and good level, in the latter case if the bottle is in the rejected state, the bottle will activate the electro-pneumatic system that will take the bottle out of the production line.

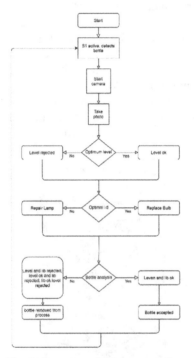

Fig. 6. Image acquisition system flow

In relation to the labeling process, where you will receive the product in compliance with the dosing and screwing standards, in order to later be able to adhere the label to the bottle, for this procedure it is guaranteed that the bottles that have met the characteristics with an adequate level of filling and an optimal state of the lid, are analyzed in relation to the labeling procedure. In Fig. 7, the flow chart for the operation of the processing program for the labeling line is observed.

The development of the graphical user interface makes the system much more flexible since it allows the line operator to configure the fill level parameter, which may depend in some cases on the manufacturing conditions of the desired product on the line in the Fig. 8 some elements of the interface are shown where the operator can also perform the geometric calibration procedure of the camera important for the good operation of the

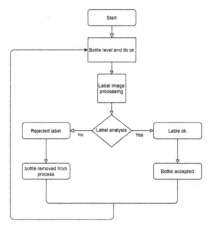

Fig. 7. Label flow diagram.

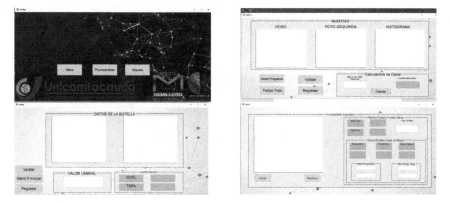

Fig. 8. Main image acquisition interface.

image processing [14], additionally it allows to estimate the values of the thresholding manually that allows to obtain an adequate segmentation of the image.

The communication system between the algorithm and the electro-pneumatic actuators of the system were carried out using a reference 1214 PLC. The algorithm was developed in the TIA Portal environment using the programming language called KOP which is based on the circuit diagram, ladder or ladder, this language makes use of Boolean logic by means of electrical contacts in series and in parallel, Table 1 shows the characteristics of the PLC used.

The characteristics of the PLC are important since they allow to establish the structure of implementation of the system, from them the program is developed to control the actions of the PLC that allowed the control of the electro-pneumatic actuators that carried out the process of retain the bottle within the acquisition chamber and also the objective of rejecting the bottle in case of any anomaly, for this it is important to make a logical structure of the code to be implemented, known as development in GRAFCET

Table 1. PLC 1214 AC/DC/RLY characteristics

Features	Reference
Setting	AC/DC/RLY
Reference	6ES7 214-1BE30-0XB0
Versión firmware	V2.2
Integrated digital I/O	14 In/10 Out
Integrated analog I/O	2 In
Load memory	4 Mb
Programming package	STIP 7V13 SP1 o Superior
Interface type	PROFINET
Physical standard	Ethernet

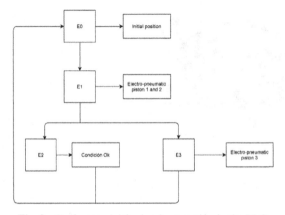

Fig. 9. Grafcet model for implementation in the PLC.

the which is a functional diagram that is used to describe the processes that you want to automate elaborated through stages sequentially, through the development of actions or transitions, in Fig. 9 the diagram in GRAFCET of the system is observed implemented.

5   Results

Once the prototype of the image processing chamber was made and with the algorithm developed, the implementation and validation of the system proceeded, in which bottles were sent to the filling, screwing and labeling line, in which the chamber would analyze the level, the positioning of the cover and the status of the label, to validate the implemented system, the random sampling methodology was used to avoid subjectivities and provide better results, in order to know the behavior of the system in real conditions of work.

The results collected for the level variable and the behavior of the processing algorithm in the classification according to the characteristics of the shipped bottles are shown below, as shown in Table 2, where the number of repetitions performed is observed, which for the analysis was 8 for 10 bottles sent to the production line, as it is observed a total of 80 bottles were sent during the experiment of which 7 of them corresponding to 8.75% are bottles with an incorrect level and 91.25% corresponds to bottles with the correct level.

Table 2. List of internal parameters

Analysis	Units of bottles shipped with level condition									
1	1	2	3	4	5	6	7	8	9	10
2	1	2	3	4	5	6	7	8	9	10
3	1	2	3	4	5	6	7	8	9	10
4	1	2	3	4	5	6	7	8	9	10
5	1	2	3	4	5	6	7	8	9	10
6	1	2	3	4	5	6	7	8	9	10
7	1	2	3	4	5	6	7	8	9	10
8	1	2	3	4	5	6	7	8	9	10

Bottles sent with correct level
Bottles sent with the wrong level
Level reading error

The information obtained from Table 2 was plotted to determine the percentage of error in the identification of the system, in Fig. 10 a detection error of 5% is shown, equivalent to 4 bottles that were classified incorrectly by the system, it is important note that the bottles misclassified by the algorithm correspond to bottles with a correct level.

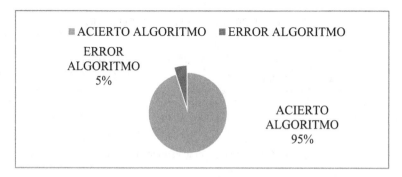

Fig. 10. Circular diagram for bottle level.

In the same way, the same analysis is performed for the lid variable. Table 3 shows the data collected with the corresponding colored labels for the results obtained, together with the validation with the processing algorithm. As can be seen, a total of 80 bottles were shipped during the experiment, of which 10 of them corresponding to 12.5% are bottles with incorrectly capped and 87.5% correspond to bottles with correct lid.

Table 3. List of internal parameters

Analysis	Units of bottles shipped with lib condition									
1	1	2	3	4	5	6	7	8	9	10
2	1	2	3	4	5	6	7	8	9	10
3	1	2	3	4	5	6	7	8	9	10
4	1	2	3	4	5	6	7	8	9	10
5	1	2	3	4	5	6	7	8	9	10
6	1	2	3	4	5	6	7	8	9	10
7	1	2	3	4	5	6	7	8	9	10
8	1	2	3	4	5	6	7	8	9	10

Bottles sent with correct lid
Bottles shipped with incorrect lid
Lid reading error

The data obtained from Table 3 were plotted to determine the percentage of error in the identification of the system. Figure 11 shows a detection error of 8.75% equivalent to 7 bottles that were incorrectly classified by the system. It is important to highlight that the bottles misclassified by the algorithm in this case 4 of the bottles were classified as correctly capped when this was not the case and 3 correctly capped bottles were evaluated as incorrectly capped.

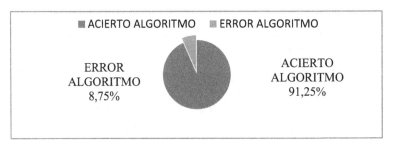

Fig. 11. Circular diagram to estimate the cover

Finally, the labeling section is evaluated, in which for the bottle to reach this station, the level and cap variables must be accepted, for this reason the bottles are only evaluated in relation to the state of the label, in this procedure. 5 repetitions were carried out with a total of 50 bottles, of which 18 were found to have errors in the labeling process equivalent to 36% and the remaining 64% had a correct label.

The data obtained from Table 4 was graphed to determine the percentage of error in the identification of the system. Figure 12 shows a detection error of 3% equivalent to 2 bottles that were incorrectly classified by the system, it is important note that the bottles misclassified by the algorithm in this case 2 were mislabelled bottles that were correctly labeled.

Table 4. List of internal parameters

I	Units of bottles shipped label analysis									
1	1	2	3	4	5	6	7	8	9	10
2	1	2	3	4	5	6	7	8	9	10
3	1	2	3	4	5	6	7	8	9	10
4	1	2	3	4	5	6	7	8	9	10
5	1	2	3	4	5	6	7	8	9	10

Bottles sent with correct label
Bottles shipped with incorrect label
Level reading error

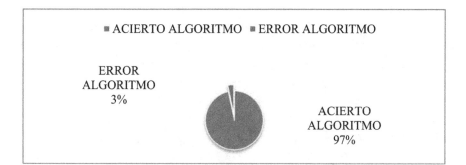

Fig. 12. Circular diagram analysis of label states.

Flexsim simulation

Additionally, a feasibility study of the project was carried out using FlexSim® software, which is an interactive platform dedicated to industrial environments, with which it is possible to simulate full-time production, the number of bottles processed, production time in hours, the efficiency of the stations. In industrial environments, this type of program makes it possible to make the simulation process of industrial facilities more robust, taking into account the exact physical distances of the model elements, and in addition to this, it is possible to carry out data analysis of multiple scenarios. with full domain of variables.

To analyze the feasibility of the implementation of this machine vision system in industrial environments, enhance the time measurement of each station to observe the incidence of the implementation of the chamber and how it can influence the production line, for this It was necessary to take the times of each station to later take these data to the simulation software, as seen in Table 5.

Table 5. Time stations

Filling time (s)	Covered time (s)	Torque meter time (s)	Processed time (s)
38.08	8	4.37	2

These data were obtained by measuring the speed of the band and putting a bottle at the beginning and with the help of a stopwatch, the approximate time it took for each bottle to arrive and work at each station was measured. Once this information is obtained, the data is stored within FlexSim®, in Fig. 13, it shows the simulation of the production line and its workstations, with the values stored within the simulation platform, we proceed to simulate the operation of the production line together with the machine vision system in an 8-hour workday, Table 6 shows the data collected in this period of time.

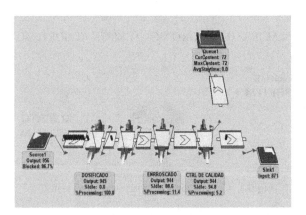

Fig. 13. Flexsim® simulation diagram.

Table 6. Analysis of bottles

Amount processed	Accepted bottles	Rejected bottles
956	884	72

From the information collected it is seen that in an 8-hour day, 956 bottles passed through the line, which the algorithm detected 884 good bottles and a margin of 72 bottles with some defect, these data allow us to calculate the losses that can be save with the implementation of automated systems that guarantee the quality of the manufactured services, additionally the system does not show any necks or accumulation in the image processing stations, which validates the viability of the system in an industrial environment where production lines must work continuously in the manufacture of products.

6 Conclusions

Illumination is a very important parameter that allowed a better analysis of the characteristics of the object of study, for this reason it was important to know its various techniques, thus obtaining precise and detailed information on the element, to proceed with the processing of pictures.

When implementing the classification algorithm, a precision margin of 95% and a margin of error of 5% were obtained on the filling and screwing line, while at the labeling station a success of 97% was obtained and a margin of error of 3%, these values were analyzed with the interactive Flexsim® platform, which allowed simulating the performance of the production line working with the image acquisition prototype at different times and comparing it with the actual production line. This allows complementing industrial and mechatronic simulations to obtain adequate statistical analyzes regarding any type of industrial process that is desired to be carried out.

Using the mechatronic design methodology, it was possible to study and analyze the necessary processes to achieve a product that meets the engineering standards required for industrial process. Taking this methodology into account, the prototype of the image acquisition chamber was made, in materials that allowed it to give robustness and symmetry within the measurement parameters of the production line, allowing stability and fixation, for capture and analysis. of the bottles.

The development of automated systems at low costs allows small and medium-sized companies to open up to new markets with the advancement of intelligent systems capable of supervising production, allowing the manufacture of quality goods and services, promoting technological growth in the region.

As part of future work, it is necessary to improve the development of the algorithm to comply with the standards within the industrial sector to be able to develop a technology transfer model for research development. About to the development of the prototype structure, it is necessary to carry out an optimization process of the materials about the process of industrial use.

References

1. Louw, L., Droomer, M.: Development of a low cost machine vision based quality control system for a learning factory. Proc. Manuf. **31**, 264–269 (2019). https://doi.org/10.1016/j.promfg.2019.03.042w

2. Erol, S., Jäger, A., Hold, P., Ott, K., Sihn, W.: Tangible industry 4.0: a scenario-based approach to learning for the future of production. Proc. CiRp **54**(1), 13–18 (2016)
3. Nandini, V., Vishal, R.D., Prakash, C.A., Aishwarya, S.: A review on applications of machine vision systems in industries. Indian J. Sci. Technol. **9**(48), 1–5 (2016)
4. Golnabi, H., Asadpour, A.: Design and application of industrial machine vision systems. Robot. Comput. Integr. Manuf. **23**(6), 630–637 (2007). https://doi.org/10.1016/j.rcim.2007.02.005
5. Labudzki, R., Legutko, S., Raos, P.: The essence and applications of machine vision. Tehnicki Vjesnik **21**(4), 903–909 (2014)
6. Silva, R.L., Rudek, M., Szejka, A.L., Junior, O.C.: Machine vision systems for industrial quality control inspections. In: Chiabert, P., Bouras, A., Noël, F., Ríos, J. (eds.) PLM 2018. IAICT, vol. 540, pp. 631–641. Springer, Cham (2018). https://doi.org/10.1007/978-3-030-01614-2_58
7. Agin, G.J., Duda, R.O.: SRI vision research for advanced industrial automation. In: Proceedings 2nd USA-Japan Computer Conference, pp. 113–117 (1975)
8. Rosen C.A.: Machine vision and robotics: industrial requirements. In: Dodd G.G., Rossol L. (eds.) Computer Vision and Sensor-Based Robots. Springer, Boston (1979). https://doi.org/10.1007/978-1-4613-3027-1_1
9. Devdas, S., Kolk, R.: Mechatronics System Design 2nd. edn., CL-Engineering, Stamford (2010)
10. Schettini, R., Corchs, S.: Underwater image processing: state of the art of restoration and image enhancement methods. EURASIP J. Adv. Signal Process. **2010**(1), 1–14 (2010). https://doi.org/10.1155/2010/746052
11. Yu, S., Zhu, H.: Algoritmo de mejora de imagen de baja iluminación basado en un modelo de iluminación física. IEEE Trans. Circ. Syst. Video Technol. **29**(1), 28–37. (2019). enero de. https://doi.org/10.1109/TCSVT.2017.2763180
12. Kwak, H.-J., Park, G.-T.: Image contrast enhancement for intelligent surveillance systems using multi-local histogram transformation. J. Intell. Manuf. **25**(2), 303–318 (2012). https://doi.org/10.1007/s10845-012-0663-4
13. Thanki R.M., Kothari A.M. Morphological image processing. In: Thanki, R.M., Kothari, A.M. (eds.) Digital Image Processing using SCILAB. Springer, Cham (2019). https://doi.org/10.1007/978-3-319-89533-8_5
14. Li, W., Tong, X.-J., Gan, H.-T.: A nonlinear camera calibration method based on area. In: Zhu, R., Zhang, Y., Liu, B., Liu, C. (eds.) ICICA 2010. CCIS, vol. 105, pp. 185–192. Springer, Heidelberg (2010). https://doi.org/10.1007/978-3-642-16336-4_25

An Approach for Development and Testing a Reliable Speedometer Software for Speed Competitions on Motorsport

Luis de Alba González[1]([✉]) [iD] and Óscar Hernández-Uribe[2] [iD]

[1] Continental Automotive Occidente, Santa María Tequepexpan, 45601 Jalisco, Mexico
`luis.dealba@continental.com`
[2] CIATEQ AC, Av. del Retablo 150, Col. Constituyentes-Fovissste, 76150 Querétaro, Mexico
`oscar.hernandez@ciateq.mx`

Abstract. Since invention of motor vehicles, the desire to know which machine is the fastest, more powerful and easy to use has been inherent to humans. This competitive nature created the need to develop instruments to measure the capabilities of vehicles through speed, distance and time to have a good comparison between competitors, especially on a rally, which are races with special requirements that need to be met, such as complete a route between control points on a specific time. This work focus on speed and distance measurement through a sensor connected to the wheel, counting each turn and calculating them according the time elapsed. It is an embedded software for ARM devices with 5 inches touch screen and a user-friendly interface making easier to get information for co-pilot and give proper instructions to the driver, who is under high temperatures for 3 to 4 h leading to great stress during speed races. The software is validated following use cases where the test steps are described, these are explained in a general way in this work and the results are explained. The failures are corrected and explained, and a final test is done on a real car with a correct measure of distance and speed.

Keywords: Embedded software · Trip computer · Speedometer

1 Introduction

According to Mexican Sport Racing Federation (FEMADEC, by its Spanish meaning), the competition desire is inherent to humans [1]. Since its origin, competition has been part of our nature, which has allowed us to establish statistics, times and other measurements to recognize who is the fastest, most accurate or simply the best competitor. This created the need to establish rules to avoid anarchy and, without these, the growth of any activity would be weakened. Man has always had the need to control everything around him and the best way to achieve this is by measuring it, because only what is measured can be improved.

The odometer, due to its Greek etymology, means "measure traveled distances" and that is, mainly, the use that has been given to it since ancient times. The operation of this artifact is based on a wheel with a small edge, which is attached to a base that has a

M. F. Mata-Rivera et al. (Eds.): WITCOM 2020, CCIS 1280, pp. 155–168, 2020.
https://doi.org/10.1007/978-3-030-62554-2_12

wedge or tongue such that, when it makes a complete turn, the edge hits the tongue and a click sound is produced. Thus, knowing the size of the circumference of the wheel and the number of clicks heard along a certain route, we can know the distance traveled [2].

The history of instrumentation in motorsport dates to November 7, 1902, when a young German inventor named Otto Schulze patented the first speedometer in history in Berlin [3]. It was an ingenious "eddy current" device that used a flexible shaft and magnets to transmit the speed of rotation of the wheel to a needle-like indicator [Fig. 1]. That's how the automotive instrumentation was born. The speedometer is coupled to the operation of the odometer and we know speed is the distance traveled by an object per unit of time. However, the speedometer of a car does not measure the time it took to go from one point to another. Generally, it measures the rotation of the secondary axis of the gearbox or the tire of the car and the speed is extrapolated using a mathematical formula [4].

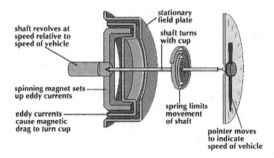

Fig. 1. Eddy Current device showing how the rotation of wheel is transmitted to a distance indicator. (Source: https://www.britannica.com/technology/speedometer)

Since then, the dashboard of cars, where the instruments and indicators are located, has been changing according to technology, fashion and aesthetic trends of each era. In the 1950's many drivers complained that they could not see all the information on the dashboard. Methodologies have been developed to ensure that the pilot can obtain the most important information on these indicators in the least amount of time possible [5]. A good design will clearly inform key information necessary to make decisions fast and effectively [6].

With advances in technology, the first display in an automobile was added in 1978, displacing the classic analogue gauges. However, these were withdrawn from the market in the 1990's. They were difficult to see clearly with sunlight and were also more expensive. The sense of continue acceleration, that is present on analogue gauge, was lost [7] and was a bigger distraction to driver, who took longer to process the information displayed in digits [8].

Over time, the automotive industry became more focused on safety. For this reason, dashboards were made in a way the information provided to the pilot was easier to read and understand with just a glance, knowing the speed and acceleration of vehicle while continuing to focus on the road. In a rally this becomes critical, due to the speed and concentration required. The pilot only focuses on driving and delegates specific functions to the co-pilot or navigator such as speed, distance and time monitoring [9].

This led to the need of the co-driver to have access to the info the pilot has on the dashboard. This was possible with the creation of the trip meters, which are devices that display the speed, distance and time of the vehicle.

Figure 2 shows different devices on the market to measure and display these elements. They can be classified with sensor, GPS or in a mobile device or smartphone.

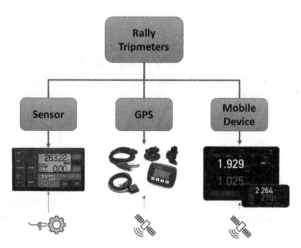

Fig. 2. Different type of tripmeters

- With Sensor: They work with a magnetic sensor connected to a toothed gear that rotates along with one of the wheels and induces electromagnetic pulses used to make the distance measurement [10]. The main disadvantage of these models is the need to install the sensor physically and connect it to the device through a cable. The precision depends on the configuration of the wheel diameter in relation to the pulses obtained by the sensor.
- GPS: They use global position satellite system to determine its position. The main advantage is that it is not invasive. Its precision is around ± 1 m with an update of 4 times per second reaching an accuracy of 0.36 km/ h. The main disadvantage is that passing through a tunnel or silent zones, the satellite signal can be lost, and it will no longer show distance and speed [11].
- Application for Mobile Device: They use the GPS of the device. Its form of operation is the same as the previous one, with the main disadvantage that the precision varies with each manufacturer and are usually less accurate than dedicated devices with same disadvantages, plus the fact that it is not a device for measuring distance and speed which could put in risk the safety of the car occupants. Most official rallies do not allow the use of these devices [12].

2   Proposal

What is intended to be done is a software capable of validate the correct functionality of the module. It will run on ARM devices, mainly low-cost single boards such as the raspberry pi, giving the user the opportunity to adjust the hardware to their needs [13]. It will be intuitive and user friendly, using appropriate colors and fonts [14]. This work will be based on the use of an electromechanical sensor connected to a car's axle and capable of being manually calibrated.

2.1   Purpose

The purpose of this work is to develop a software with friendly user interface. It will be able to be adapted to other embedded systems. Will also be capable of adding input peripherals, such as sensors, to give greater precision to the calculation of speed and distance than that given by the vehicle's instruments.

3   Methods

A rally is two persons motorized sport, the pilot and the co-pilot, also called navigator. In a precision rally, the navigator calculates optimal speeds, times and distances to reach checkpoint in a specified time, they have to get informed the pilot the speed, distance and time needed to get from one point to another no earlier or later than the marked time, the pilot is in charge of maintaining these speeds and following the route according to the co-pilot's instructions. When a precision rally starts, the route book [15] is given to the co-pilot, this book contains the appropriate indications of distances and times that need to be met on the race, as well as graphics that indicate the route to be followed by the crew throughout the rally route.

   To participate in a rally, the navigator will need a calculator to make certain calculations, such as the conversion of hours, minutes and seconds into fractions of an hour, distance, time and speed necessary to travel from the starting point to the ending point. This would take precious time from the co-pilot, and in addition to this, the pilots of these sporting events are subjected to a high temperature that can reach 50 °C during a period of 3 to 4 h [16], which leads to great stress for the pilot. The cardiovascular response often causes the heart to beat at a rate between 142 and 152 beats per minute [17]. Therefore, it will be of great help to have a module with more detailed information. Will be faster to calculate the needed metrics to avoid distractions and have a better response when change in speed is needed, the navigator just tells the driver if he or she needs to go faster or slower to reach the marked time on the book.

3.1   Speed Calculation

To explain this calculation, let's assume that we are measuring the rotation of one of the wheels. When the wheels rotate, they travel a certain space with each turn, this space is, assuming there is no slippage or deformation due to weight, the distance (d). It is the product of the diameter of the wheel (D) by the mathematical constant Π (pi), whose bounded value is 3.1416. It is as shown in Eq. 1.

$$d = D\pi \tag{1}$$

This way, in example, if the wheel of the car has a diameter of 0.96 m, on each round it will travel 3.01 m (Eq. 2).

$$d = 0.93\,\text{m}\,3.1416 = 3.01\,\text{m} \tag{2}$$

This will be rounded to 3 m to ease the calculations. Now, let's assume the wheel rotates during the car displacement at 100 RPM, this will travel at a speed (V) 300 meters per minute (Eq. 3).

$$V = 3\,\text{m} \times 100\,\text{RPM} = 300\,\text{m}\,\text{min} \tag{3}$$

And an hour has 60 min, the travel each hour will be 18 km/h (Eq. 4).

$$V = 300\,\text{m}\,\text{min} \times 60\,\text{min} = 18000\,\text{mh} = 18\,\text{kmh} \tag{4}$$

From this simple calculation we can say that, if we measure the rotation speed of the wheels, or some other axis that rotates proportionally, with a tachometer and, if we know the diameter of the tire, we can calibrate the tachometer directly to show the speed as km/ h, resulting in a speedometer [18].

3.2 Safety and Reliability

This system obtains the data from physical objects that are independent to it. It depends on sensors attached to the vehicle that are always sending the signal of the wheel, making calculations on the moment and displaying this information to the co-pilot and this in turn to the driver. This is what is known as a real-time system, it produces an output almost at the moment it receives an input [19]. Thus, the pilot will have the information needed to react at the right moment.

Now let's imagine what would happen if the co-driver was late in receiving the speed or distance traveled data, he might think that it is missing a certain distance to get to the next checkpoint and tell the pilot to accelerate when they are actually closer than they believe resulting in a negative real time when reaching the next point. This is unfavorable for these races and can be caused by a high processing load on the system or a mismanagement of the available resources, such as RAM, therefore special care must be taken in the way that the calculations are programmed, since it must be simple and efficient.

It also depends on external elements; these can fail resulting in erratic measurements or even not delivering any measurement. At these difficulties, the program must be prepared to indicate the user that there are problems with connection or the sensors so that they can take necessary actions.

3.3 Software and Tools

The main tool used is QT Creator software, which is an object-oriented multiplatform work environment used to develop applications that use a graphical user interface [20].

Through this program, we will use what is called "cross – compiling". This method consists of compiling the SW specifically for the Raspberry pi board outside the board itself, in this case on a Linux PC. This in order to use the tremendous resources of the PC, which are better than those of the board, which will result in a faster compilation [21].

Testing the Software. The need of testing is important because a software that does not work correctly can lead to many problems, including losing a race, injury or even death [22]. Main functional components of the system will be tested such as suitability; ensure the software provides all functions as required and work as specified. Also, accuracy will be tested, to check that measurements are correct.

To ensure that the tests are done correctly according to the requirements, use cases will be applied. Each use case will have an identifier to easily now what the test is about. A description to let the tester know what is exactly to be tested. The steps to make the test so, no matter who makes the test, it can be reproduced the same way every time. The expected results, to know what the correct behavior is. And finally, actual results, to let evidence of what happened when the test was done. In case that actual result is different from expected, it will be considered a failure. Each failure will be analyzed and corrected on a future software release and then it will be tested again to ensure that failure is no longer present

3.4 System Architecture

Figure 3 shows a block diagram that describes the module in a general way. It shows it is powered by 5v through a USB cable, internally the Raspberry Pi has a voltage converter to 3.3v, which is the operating voltage of the processor [23]. It could be connected to the 12v car socket using a cell phone adapter.

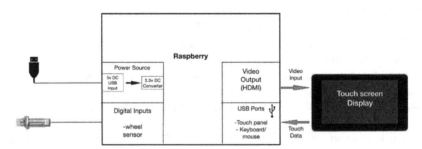

Fig. 3. Block diagram

The sensor that is installed on the car wheel is connected to pin 11 of the GPIO port of the raspberry board which corresponds to GPIO17 input, one of the general-purpose inputs [24]. The display is connected via HDMI cable. This is where the application's user interface will be displayed. This screen in turn connects with a USB cable to the Raspberry Pi to be powered and sends the touch panel input information. The operative system manages the video output, there is no need to make any programming for this.

The base Software on which the module will operate is Raspbian version 9 called Stretch. This system is a distribution of the GNU/Linux operating system and therefore free based on Debian and is designed for the Raspberry Pi board [25].

4   Measurements

The application will be capable of being calibrated at one unit. The number of pulses sent by the tire sensor will be counted and this will be considered a unit of measurement, it could be a kilometer, a mile, or any other reference as needed in the race. These references are given in the road book and must be done before the event begins, normally, marks are placed on the road where the calibration should start and another where it ends. Calibration therefore ensures that our trip meter correctly indicates distances during testing [26]. Calibration of the unit will be done with a button that will start recording the number of pulses detected by the sensor and will end when the button is pressed again.

The calibration will have an offset that can be modified manually at each stage, this is to avoid changing the distance calibration on each phase if the section to be traveled needs to be adjusted.

It will have two routes or "trips" that will be called "Main" and "Book trip", the first will only show the information of the current route and the second the information of the entire race.

There will be a button where only the section distance can be restarted, the total distance traveled must not be restarted. The stopwatch can be restarted at each stage, but there will be a general one that will only be restarted when starting a new race. This should be visible on all screens and should not be obstructed by any image or other object on the screen.

As for the layout of the graphical interface, there will be three different screens, the main screen, the book trip screen and the options screen. The first will show the stopwatch, partial distance, average speed and current speed. In the second, the stopwatch and the general distance will be displayed. On the third screen, the stopwatch will continue to be displayed, as well as three configuration buttons, which are "Calibrate standard", "Units" and "Standard offset". When pressing "Calibrate standard", a new layer with a "start" button will appear, when selected, it will change to "Finish" and the pulses detected by the sensor must be counted between them. The "Units" button will be used to select between kilometers (Km), miles (Mi), meters (m) or feet (ft) and will be used to show the distances. When "Pattern Offset" is selected, two buttons will appear to increase or decrease the calibrated distance, starting at the unit and increasing by hundredths.

To carry out the tests, a test bench is used, this in order to locate the most common errors quickly and easily without having to do the installation in the field, that is, without having to install the sensor in the car.

Figure 4 shows the installation of a simple test bench. We have the computer, where changes can be made to the source code of the application and quickly reload it to the card. A small protoboard is connected to the Raspberry to make quick interconnections.

Fig. 4. Test Bench

A wave generator is connected to the GPIO17 input. The wave generator is a Pico Scope 2000 series, which is an oscilloscope with wave generator option, it gives us the option of simulating the wheel sensor by applying a square signal and varying the frequency, resulting in an accurate pulse count (Fig. 5).

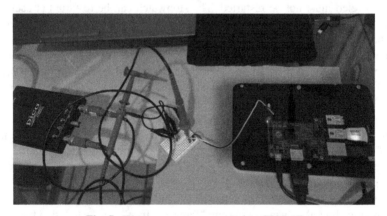

Fig. 5. Wave generator connected to GPIO 17

5 Results and Discussion

On this chapter, the results of the tests are shown. These were made according the use cases for each test. To put the information on an easy way to understand, the procedure and results are written on a more readable way.

First test made is the standard calibration, which mentions that it must be possible to calibrate the distance counting the number of steps. We start at the configuration menu, select "Calibrate standard" and then another window appears with the option to start calibration.

When "Start" button is pressed, the color changes from green to red and the label now says "Stop". The step count starts and is shown in screen. This change of color is a warm color that keep the user focused on this spot, saving time on searching the way to stop the counter [14]. After pressing the button again, the counter stops, and button returns to previous color and label. Back button is pressed, the layer disappears, and we are back to the options menu (Fig. 6).

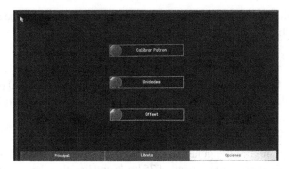

Fig. 6. Options menu

The next test is the "Offset", which means that distance can be manually calibrated, this is because a mark between one kilometer and the next could actually measure 1.2 km or 950 m, this is due to variations in physical measurements that are put on the roads. Selecting "Offset" from the menu will lead to another layer with two buttons, one to increase ("+") and the other to decrease ("−") the base distance (Fig. 6).

We press the " + " button expecting the offset to increase by 0.01, however, the first error appears, when increasing the offset, this change to 101 instead of 1.01, it seems that the decimal disappeared. This failure is documented on the use case list and after analyzing it is corrected, the mistake was on the type of variable, an integer was used instead of a float (Fig. 7).

Next is the test of speed measurement using the pulses, we proceed to start the test on the main screen, we will use the function generator at a frequency of 10 Hz and, taking into account Eq. (1) With a 0.65 m wheel, each turn of the wheel will have a distance of 2.04 m for each turn of the rim.

$$0.65\,\mathrm{m}\,3.1416 = 2.04\,\mathrm{m} \tag{5}$$

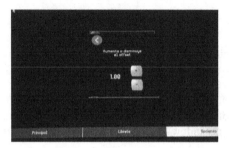 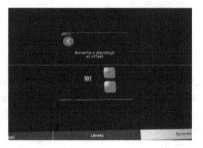

Fig. 7. Offset error due to variable type

To configure the wave generator at the necessary frequency to make the speed measurement, we will assume that a speed of 50 km/ h is required, we will express this in terms of meters/ minute to calculate the RPM, in Eq. (6) we will find this conversion.

$$V = 50 \, \text{kmh} \, 1000 \, \text{m} * h \, 60 \, \text{km} * \text{min} = 833.33 \, \text{m} \, \text{min} \tag{6}$$

To calculate the revolution per minute (RPM) we will divide the speed (V) with the distance traveled by the tire calculated on Eq. (5).

$$PM = 833.33 \, \text{m} \, \text{min} \, 2.04 \, \text{m} = 408.08 \, \text{RPM} \tag{7}$$

Knowing that 1 Hz is equivalent to 60 revolutions per minute, or 60 pulses from the sensor, we can calculate the necessary frequency from this data in the following way

$$Freq = 408.08 \, \text{RPM} \, 60 \, \text{s} = 6.8 \, \text{Hz} \tag{8}$$

Now we will configure the generator at 6.8 Hz to simulate a speed of 50 km/h. We also do the same calculations for a speed of 75 km/h and find that the necessary frequency is 10.2 Hz.

On Fig. 8 can be seen the measurement is correct for both 50 and 75 km/h. When the generator is stopped, the speed shows 0 km/h, which is the expected behavior.

 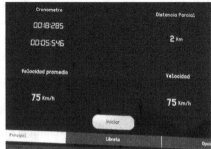

Fig. 8. Speed measurement

Another test is to check the "Start" test, this makes the measurements begin. It also changes from green to red color, and the label changes to "Stop". We also have both stop watches, one for the entire race and the other is for the partial time, this is only for the actual rout. The stop watches can be seen on the main screen and on the book screen, but not on the options screen, this could lead to some issues since, if the co-pilot needs to change some options, will lose visibility of the time. This behavior was analyzed whether is necessary or not, and the stopwatch was added on the menu to always be visible to the navigator.

On the options menu, we check the "Units". This will allow us to change between Kilometers, meters, miles or feet. After selecting each option, the units were correctly set and showed on the main screen. For the meters and feet, only the distance is shown in these units, the speed is shown in Km/h and Mi/h respectively.

Now that main functions are tested and works as expected, the module is tested on a real car. Is a Toyota Yaris 2014 model, this does not change the result of the test, any car model is fine. The Raspberry Pi is powered through a cellphone adapter connected to the 12v connector of the car to get the 5v needed. The turn of the wheel is measured with an inductive PNP sensor working at 12v. To avoid damage to the module a voltage divider made with a 27 kΩ and 10 kΩ resistor is used, obtaining 3.2v of the signal from the wheel. On Fig. 9 can be seen the configuration. A little test board is used for the voltage divider, connected to the sensor, the one with the green tip. The yellow cable is used to power the inductive sensor with 12v.

Fig. 9. Connection to vehicle

On this test, another button was added to main screen, the *Reset* button. This is to make it easier to restart the timers and the distance between routes. The sensor was installed on to the front right wheel for the ease access from the co-pilot's seat. On Fig. 10 is shown the measure directly from the sensor, the speed is very accurate compared with the one that is shown on the vehicle's dashboard.

The distance is also the same as the one measured with the odometer of the car. This means the measurements are correct and can be used for a rally.

Fig. 10. Distance and speed measured from sensor.

6 Conclusions

The results show that the software works on a raspberry Pi. There were some failures that were found on testing, but these were corrected on the next release of software. If more changes were to be made, the same tests described here would be repeated to ensure that new features do not affect the ones that are already working.

One detail that could be found was that software had functionalities that were not asked for on requirements, they cannot be considered failures because they do not affect the functionality, but it is not part of what was requested. This is important because it could lead to rework and changes that could be avoided since the requirements were defined.

Some of the tests were validated at the same time, this helps saving time on the validation, but could lead to misunderstanding of the test, because the use case could become very extensive and, if you want to check what the failure was, it would be necessary to check the full test case, and would be very difficult to understand for development team.

The result of this work is a software that can be integrated with ARM devices. We also get a set of use cases ready to test the application if it is recompiled on a new hardware, or simply if minor changes are made to software. This way will be easier to detect if there is something that is not working and identify the cause. This work can serve as an evaluation method for future platforms.

An advantage of using ARM devices such as Raspberry Pi, is that are low cost, some can have a considerable saving compared with the trip meters that are available on the market, it can be as much as 40% to 60% depending on the customization made by the user, which also makes it a better solution to suit to the required needs. The main disadvantage is that programing skills and cross compiling knowledge is needed to use it and modify this software on different devices.

References

1. FEMADAC: Federación Mexicana de Automovilismo Deportivo A.C. FEMADAC. FEMADAC. https://ww2.femadac.org.mx/index.php. Accessed 06 Oct 2018
2. ¿Qué es un odómetro o topómetro? De Máquinas y herramientas, 21 December 2012. http://www.demaquinasyherramientas.com/herramientas-de-medicion/odometro-tipos-y-usos. Accessed 28 Dec 2017
3. World, Ward's auto. 100 years–and counting. Ward's Auto World **38**(12), 15 (2002)
4. ¿Por qué el velocímetro del GPS no coincide con el del coche? Circula Seguro. http://www.circulaseguro.com/velocimetro-gps-no-coincide-coche/. Accessed 28 Dec 2017
5. James, B.: Rethinking design of car dashboards. The New York Times, 07 Mar 1985. https://www.nytimes.com/1985/03/07/garden/rethinking-design-of-car-dashboards.html. Accessed 07 Mar 2019
6. Richard, B., Michael, P.: Dashboard design: why design is important. DM Rev. Online **85** 1011285–1011291 (2004)
7. Barney, C.: Information technology for energy managers. https://books.google.com/books?id=F2XH3A-n2cEC&pg=PA176&dq=%22digital+speedometer%22&lr=&as_brr=3&ie=ISO-8859-1&output=html. Accessed 08 Mar 2019
8. Andy, G.: Eyes on the road: Digital instrument clusters give drivers more information in less time for added driving safety. Mach. Des.Com **8**, 49 (2009)
9. México, Comisión Nacional de Rallies. ¿Qué es un Rally? Comisión Nacional de Rallies México. https://web.archive.org/web/20121127170340/http://www.cnrm.com.mx/nuevo/queesunrally.php. Accessed 14 Jun 2019
10. Shreejit, C.: How does the odometer work? torque, 16 Dec 2014. https://www.torque.com.sg/features/how-does-the-odometer-work/. Accessed 17 Mar 2019
11. CFIT: Review: gps tripmeter. rally sport magazine, 20 May 2010. https://rallysportmag.com/review-gps-tripmeter/. Accessed 17 Mar 2019
12. New to regularity runs? Blackpalfrey motor club of kent. http://www.blackpalfrey.co.uk/index.php/rally-tripmeters/10-regularity-runs. Accessed 17 Mar 2019
13. Ivković, J., Radulović, B., The advantages of using Raspberry Pi 3 compared to Raspberry Pi 2 SoC computers for sensor system support. Faculty of information and communication technologies Bitola (2016)
14. Deodhar, S.: Effective use of colors in HMI design. J. Eng. Res. Appl. **4**, 384–387 (2014)
15. Manero, N.: La web del copiloto de rallies. CopiRally. https://www.copirally.com/. Accessed 01 Nov 2017
16. Carlson, L., Ferguson, D., Kenefick, R.: Physiological strain of stock car drivers during competitive racing. J. Thermal Biol. **44**, 20–26 (2014)
17. Ebben, W.: Strength and conditioning for stock car racing. NSCA **32**(5), 16–27 (2010). ISBN: 1524-1602
18. Velocímetro del automóvil. Sabelotodo. http://www.sabelotodo.org/automovil/velocimetro.html. Accessed 10 Jun 2018
19. Kopetz, H.: Design Principles for Distributed Embedded Applications. Springer, Wien (2011). https://doi.org/10.1007/978-1-4419-8237-7
20. Company, The QT. What is QT. https://www.qt.io/. Accessed 06 May 2019
21. Warren, Gay.: Cross-Compiling the Kernel. Apress, Berkeley (2018). 978-1-4842-3948-3
22. Müller, T., Debra, F.: Certified tester foundation level syllabus. Int. Softw. Test. Qualifications Board **36**, 11 (2011)
23. Foundation, raspberry Pi. Raspberry Pi documentation. Raspberry Pi. https://www.raspberrypi.org/documentation/. Accessed 10 May 2019

24. Adams, J.: Raspberry Pi documentation. Raspberry Pi, 16 Nov 2016. https://www.raspbe rrypi.org/documentation/hardware/raspberrypi/schematics/rpi_SCH_2b_1p2_reduced.pdf. Accessed 01 Jun 2020
25. Foundation, raspberry Pi. raspbian. Raspberry Pi. https://www.raspberrypi.org/downloads/ raspbian/. Accessed 10 May 2019
26. Rally, R.: Rabbit rally. http://rabbitrally.com/es/calibracion/. Accessed 20 Jun 2020

Offline Optimum Tuning
of the Proportional Integral Controller
for Speed Regulation of a BLDC Motor
Through Bio-inspired Algorithms

Alam Gabriel Rojas-López[1] , Miguel Gabriel Villarreal-Cervantes[1] ,
Alejandro Rodríguez-Molina[2] , and Consuelo Varinia García-Mendoza[3]([⊠])

[1] CIDETEC, Posgraduate Department, OMD Laboratory, Instituto Politécnico
Nacional, 07700 Mexico City, Mexico
`alamrola@gmail.com, mvillarrealc@ipn.mx`
[2] Research and Postgraduate Division, Tecnológico Nacional de México/IT de
Tlalnepantla, 54070 Tlalnepantla, Edo. de México, Mexico
`alejandro.rm@tlalnepantla.tecnm.mx`
[3] Instituto Politécnico Nacional, ESCOM, 07738 Mexico City, Mexico
`consuelo.varinia@gmail.com`

Abstract. In this work, a comparative study among different bio-inspired algorithms for offline optimum tuning of a Proportional Integral Controller (PIC) is presented. The PIC regulates the speed of a Brushless Direct Current (BLDC) Motor. The optimum tuning is proposed as a multi-objective optimization problem transformed into a mono-objective problem through a weighted product approach. The performance functions are the Integrated Absolute Error (IAE) and the Average Power. The first one aims to reduce the speed error within the dynamic and the second one aims to reduce energy consumption. The algorithms used to solve the optimization problem are Differential Evolution (DE), Particle Swarm Optimization (PSO), and Firefly Algorithm (FA). The results present a descriptive statistic comparison and the one which has the best behavior among them is presented. Also, a comparison of convergence and execution speed is discussed. The obtained gains found by using the proposed controller tuning present a suitable trade-off in both performance functions even, with dynamic loads with respect to a trial and error tuning procedure.

Keywords: Brushless motor · Offline tuning · Optimization ·
Bio-inspired approach · Differential evolution · Particle swarm
optimization · Firefly algorithm

The authors acknowledge the support of the Secretaría de Investigación y Posgrado (SIP) of the Instituto Politécnico Nacional under Grant SIP-20200150 and of the Mexican Consejo Nacional de Ciencia y Tecnología (CONACyT).

M. F. Mata-Rivera et al. (Eds.): WITCOM 2020, CCIS 1280, pp. 169–184, 2020.
https://doi.org/10.1007/978-3-030-62554-2_13

1   Introduction

Brushless Direct Current (BLDC) motors have been widely used in the last decades in high-speed industrial applications because they present higher efficiency and reliability, less noise operation, and weight and require less maintenance than brushed motors.

One important issue is the efficient regulation of the BLDC motor speed controller, and several advanced control techniques have been incorporated [2, 3, 7]. Linear controllers such as the Proportional and Integral (PI) controller [17] are still being used in the industry due to the simple structure and the easy of understand the effect of each control parameter. The PI controller behavior depends on the setup of its parameters. Hence, the uncertainties of the BLDC motor due to load or in the set of speed variations make the PI controller tuning a hard task.

Recently, the use of intelligent control methodologies [12] in the control tuning problem has increased due to there exist evidence that those methodologies can provide a better control performance in spite of having different control design requirements. Among controller tuning methodologies [19], one of the most promising methodologies is the optimization method. This is because the optimum gains are found offline through the numerical solution of a mathematical programming problem (MPP) and can be employed in a real scenario [13]. Hence, these gains can be easily set in an industrial controller. The solution of the MPP can be obtained by using gradient-based techniques or bio-inspired algorithms. The latter is inspired by the behavior of natural systems and has been more frequently used in the last decade due to they find solutions near the global one in non-convex and discontinuous design space and do not require specific problem characteristics such as the continuity in the performance functions and constraints. Some of the researches related to the optimization method for the speed controller tuning of the BLDC motor by using bio-inspired algorithms have been proposed in [4, 9, 14, 16]. In [9], the particle swarm optimization, cuckoo search, and bat algorithms are implemented in the fuzzy proportional derivative integral controller for the minimization of four control performance indexes. In [16], the parameters of the adaptive neuro-fuzzy inference system-based controller are optimized by employing the Bacterial Foraging Optimization Algorithm for the minimization of one control performance index and four response characteristics. Genetic algorithms have been also applied for the minimization of two response characteristics in [4], where an artificial neural network is used instead of the dynamic model. Simulated annealing algorithm outperforms the Particle Swarm Optimization (PSO) and the Ziegler-Nichols tuning approaches considering three response characteristics in [14].

In all previous works, the energy consumption is not considered into the control tuning problem of the BLDC motor. Then, in this work, the energy consumption and the regulation velocity error are simultaneously considered as a weighted product method. Three different and well-known bio-inspired search approaches (Differential Evolution, Particle Swarm Optimization, and Firefly algorithm) are studied to find the most suitable control gains that provide a better synergy between both performance functions.

The rest of the paper is organized as follows: Section 2 described the BLDC motor dynamics. The formal optimization problem statement for the PI controller tuning is detailed in Sect. 3. The comparative analysis among the use of different algorithms in the controller tuning of the BLDC motor is discussed in Sect. 4. Finally, in Sect. 5 the conclusions are drawn.

2 Dynamic Model

A BLDC Motor is similar to a Permanent Magnet Synchronous Motor (PMSM). Both motors have magnets in their rotors and a three-phase winding circuit in the stators. The main difference between a PMSM and a BLDC Motor is that the first one is powered by a three-phase sinusoidal current from an Alternating Current (AC) source, while the BLDC motor the three-phase sinusoidal current is generated by an inverter that converts a Direct Current (DC) source to a quasi- sinusoidal current [7].

Considering this, a BLDC motor can be divided into two main sections [18], as shown in Fig. 1.

– Physical Structure: A Three-phase PMSM usually in Star Topology [5].
– Commutation Logic: In which the source signal of the motor is generated and it is composed of two elements [20].
  • Position Sensor: Usually 3 Hall effect sensors, placed 120° from each other. They are activated when a magnet set in the rotor passes in front of them.
  • Inverter: Powered by a DC source converting it to a three-phase AC signal where each phase is dephased 120° from the previous one.

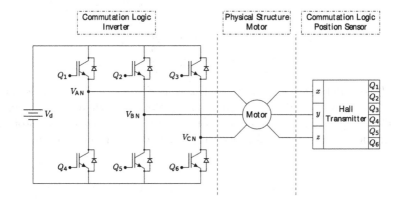

Fig. 1. BLDC motor diagram.

As mentioned before the BLDC motor can be represented as a three-phase motor as shown in Fig. 2. Each phase is conformed for a resistor R, an inductance L and a back electromagnetic force (back-emf) $e_\gamma \ \forall \ \gamma \in \{A, B, C\}$. The magnetic field, the product of the current that runs through the phases, generates an electromagnetic torque that generates rotary movement capable of moving a load.

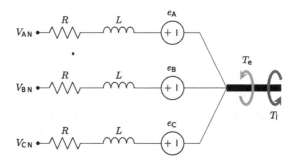

Fig. 2. Three phase motor diagram.

The Eq. (1) defines the electric part the model. In which $V_{\gamma N}$ is the phase voltage, i_γ is the phase current, R is the phase resistance, L is the phase inductance minus mutual inductance and e_γ is the phase back-emf that is defined by the position of the rotor (2) where k_e is the back-emf constant of the motor.

$$\begin{bmatrix} v_{AN} \\ v_{BN} \\ v_{CN} \end{bmatrix} = \begin{bmatrix} R & 0 & 0 \\ 0 & R & 0 \\ 0 & 0 & R \end{bmatrix} \begin{bmatrix} i_A \\ i_B \\ i_C \end{bmatrix} + \begin{bmatrix} L & 0 & 0 \\ 0 & L & 0 \\ 0 & 0 & L \end{bmatrix} \begin{bmatrix} \frac{di_A}{dt} \\ \frac{di_B}{dt} \\ \frac{di_C}{dt} \end{bmatrix} + \begin{bmatrix} e_A \\ e_B \\ e_C \end{bmatrix} \tag{1}$$

$$\begin{bmatrix} e_A \\ e_B \\ e_C \end{bmatrix} = \frac{k_e}{2} \cdot w \cdot \begin{bmatrix} f_A(\theta) \\ f_B(\theta) \\ f_C(\theta) \end{bmatrix} \tag{2}$$

The Eq. (3) define the electromagnetic torque where k_t is the torque constant. Finally Eqs. (4) and (5) define the rotary movement [1]. Where w is the angular speed, θ is the position, T_l is the load of the rotor, J is inertia of the rotor, B is the magnetic friction coefficient between rotor and stator and P is the number of poles pairs.

$$T_e = \frac{k_t}{2} \left(i_A \cdot f_A(\theta) + i_B \cdot f_B(\theta) + i_C \cdot f_C(\theta) \right) \tag{3}$$

$$T_e - T_l = J \cdot \frac{d\omega}{dt} + B \cdot \omega \tag{4}$$

$$\frac{d\theta}{dt} = \frac{P}{2}\omega \tag{5}$$

The system in the state space $[\tilde{x}_1, \tilde{x}_2, \tilde{x}_3, \tilde{x}_4, \tilde{x}_5]^T = [i_A, i_B, i_C, \omega, \theta]^T$ is presented in (6), where

$$A = [A_1, A_2, A_3, A_4, A_5, A_6, A_7]^T = \left[\frac{R}{L}, \frac{k_e}{2L}, \frac{k_t}{2J}, \frac{B}{J}, \frac{1}{2L}, \frac{1}{J}, \frac{P}{2}\right]^T \text{ and } u = V_d \text{ is}$$

the control signal that will be supplied to the inverter. It is important to mention that when each phase voltage $V_{\gamma N}$ is activated its magnitude is only half of the Voltage u supplied to the inverter. Table 1 shows the back-emf functions $f_\gamma(\theta)$ and the phase voltage functions $f_{V\gamma}(\theta)$.

$$\dot{\tilde{x}} = \tilde{A}\tilde{x} + \tilde{B}\left[u\ T_l\right]^T \tag{6}$$

where

$$\tilde{A} = \begin{bmatrix} -A_1 & 0 & 0 & -A_2 f_A(\theta) & 0 \\ 0 & -A_1 & 0 & -A_2 f_B(\theta) & 0 \\ 0 & 0 & -A_1 & -A_2 f_C(\theta) & 0 \\ A_3 f_A(\theta) & A_3 f_B(\theta) & A_3 f_C(\theta) & -A_4 & 0 \\ 0 & 0 & 0 & A_7 & 0 \end{bmatrix}$$

$$\tilde{B} = \begin{bmatrix} A_5 f_{VA}(\theta) & 0 \\ A_5 f_{VB}(\theta) & 0 \\ A_5 f_{VC}(\theta) & 0 \\ 0 & -A_6 \\ 0 & 0 \end{bmatrix}$$

Table 1. Back-emf and voltage functions.

Angular position	$f_A(\theta)$	$f_B(\theta)$	$f_C(\theta)$	$f_{VA}(\theta)$	$f_{VB}(\theta)$	$f_{VC}(\theta)$
$0 \leq \theta < \frac{\pi}{3}$	1	-1	$1 - \frac{6\cdot\theta}{\pi}$	1	-1	0
$\frac{\pi}{3} \leq \theta < \frac{2\pi}{3}$	1	$-3 + \frac{6\cdot\theta}{\pi}$	-1	1	0	-1
$\frac{2\pi}{3} \leq \theta < \pi$	$5 - \frac{6\cdot\theta}{\pi}$	1	-1	0	1	-1
$\pi \leq \theta < \frac{4\pi}{3}$	-1	1	$-7 + \frac{6\cdot\theta}{\pi}$	-1	1	0
$\frac{4\pi}{3} \leq \theta < \frac{5\pi}{3}$	-1	$9 - \frac{6\cdot\theta}{\pi}$	1	-1	0	1
$\frac{5\pi}{3} \leq \theta < 2\pi$	$-11 + \frac{6\cdot\theta}{\pi}$	-1	1	0	-1	1

In order to implement the PIC it is necessary to determine the control signal $u = V_d$ (7) where k_p and k_i are the proportional and integral constant gains respectively and e (8) is the error produced between the desired angular speed ($\omega_d = \bar{x}_4$) and the measured one ($\omega = x_4$). Adding the error integral as a new state (x_6), the BLDC motor dynamics represented in the state space $x = [i_A, i_B, i_C, \omega, \theta, \int e]^T$, results in (9). The terms related are set as: $C_1 = -A_2 f_A(\theta) - k_p A_5 f_{VA}(\theta)$, $C_2 = -A_2 f_B(\theta) - k_p A_5 f_{VB}(\theta)$ and $C_3 = -A_2 f_C(\theta) - k_p A_5 f_{VC}(\theta)$.

$$u = k_p e + ki \int e\, dt = k_p(\bar{x}_4 - x_4) + kix_6 dt \tag{7}$$

$$e = \bar{x}_4 - x_4 \tag{8}$$

$$\dot{x} = Ax + B\left[\bar{x}_4\ T_l\right]^T \tag{9}$$

where

$$A = \begin{bmatrix} -A_1 & 0 & 0 & C_1 & 0 & k_i A_5 f_{VA}(\theta) \\ 0 & -A_1 & 0 & C_2 & 0 & k_i A_5 f_{VB}(\theta) \\ 0 & 0 & -A_1 & C_3 & 0 & k_i A_5 f_{VC}(\theta) \\ A_3 f_A(\theta) & A_3 f_B(\theta) & A_3 f_C(\theta) & -A_4 & 0 & 0 \\ 0 & 0 & 0 & A_7 & 0 & 0 \\ 0 & 0 & 0 & -1 & 0 & 0 \end{bmatrix}$$

$$B = \begin{bmatrix} k_p A_5 f_{VA}(\theta) & 0 \\ k_p A_5 f_{VA}(\theta) & 0 \\ k_p A_5 f_{VA}(\theta) & 0 \\ 0 & -A_6 \\ 0 & 0 \\ 1 & 0 \end{bmatrix}$$

3   Optimization Approach in the Controller Tuning of BLDC Motors

One of the control tuning objectives is to reduce the error in the regulation of the angular speed. In this work the Integrated Absolute Error (IAE) (10) is implemented to reduce such error and also to avoid great oscillations [15]. In (10), t_0 and t_f are the initial and the final time of the dynamic simulation, respectively.

$$J_1 = \int_{t_0}^{t_f} |e|\, dt \tag{10}$$

Other important control tuning criterium is related to the energy consumption. Hence, the Average Power (11) is considered as the second criterium to be minimized, where $P(t) = u(t)\|\, [x_1(t), x_2(t), x_3(t)]^T\,\|$ [11].

$$J_2 = \frac{1}{t_f - t_0} \int_{t_0}^{t_f} P(t)\, dt \tag{11}$$

Algorithm 1: DE pseudo-code

Create initial population;
Set Number of generations (Gmax);
Set Population Size (NP) ;
for *g=1:Gmax* **do**
    for *j=1:NP* **do**
        Create child trough Mutation and Crossover;
        Compare Parent vs Child;
        The best passes to next generation;
    end
end

A mono-objective optimization problem is stated through the Weighted Product Method (WPM) in (12) and (13), where the design variable vector involves the Proportional and Integral controller gains. The WPM has the benefit of setting the weights in a range between 0 and 1 in problems whose products have a great difference of range values [8].

$$\min_{[k_p,k_i]} \quad \prod_{i=1}^{n} J_i^{w_i} \tag{12}$$

Subject to:

$$\dot{x} = f(x, \bar{x}_4); \tag{13}$$

To solve the optimization problem three bio-inspired algorithms are implemented. The first one is Differential Evolution (DE) (Algorithm 1) in its variant Best/1/bin. This is based on the process of natural evolution where the mutation on each generation is based on the information of the best individual [10]. The second algorithm tested in this work is Particle Swarm Optimization (PSO) (Algorithm 2) which is based on a collaborative behavior considering social and individual behaviors [6]. The last algorithm implemented in this work is Firefly Algorithm (FA) (Algorithm 3), which is also based on population behavior, that simulates how fireflies approach each other considering their luminescence (based on the value of the objective function) [21].

4   Description and Discussion of the Simulation Results

This section has two objectives, initially, a comparison of the performance of the implemented algorithms is discussed, then a comparison of the obtained tuning values is presented. The data information of the motor used for the simulation were taken from a motor 607327 model EC 90 flat Maxon Motor whose values are shown in Table 2. The numerical results are implemented with Euler's integration method within an interval from 0 to 0.05 s with a $\Delta t = 5e^{-5}s$. In Table 3 the parameters used to find the optimum solution is shown. The limits for each design variable were $k_p = [1, 100]$ and $k_i = [10, 200]$, and the weights for the

Algorithm 2: PSO pseudo-code

Create initial population;
Set Number of generations (Gmax);
Set Population Size (NP) ;
Set Best-own position ;
Set Best-swarm position ;
for *g=1:Gmax* do
    for *j=1:NP* do
        Calculate new particle velocity;
        Calculate new particle position;
        Update best-own position;
    end
    Update best-swarm position;
end

Algorithm 3: FA pseudo-code

Create initial population;
Set Number of generations (Gmax);
Set Population Size (NP) ;
for *g=1:Gmax* do
    for *j=1:NP* do
        for *i=1:NP* do
            if *FA(i) is better than FA(j)* then
                Calculate distance and attraction FA(j)→FA(i);
                Move FA(j) towards FA(i)
            end
        end
    end
end

weighted product method were $w_1 = 0.775$ and $w_2 = 0.225$. Those parameters were selected by trial and error procedure. The trial and error procedure consisted in setting the limits of the design variables in a wide range (from zero to one thousand for both design variables) and selecting the weight giving the priority to the IAE performance function J_1 i.e., setting $w_1 = 1$ in J_1 and $w_2 = 0$ in J_2 (average power). Such weights produce the largest power consumption. Then, the weight of the Average Power J_2 was increased until both performance functions present a suitable trade-off. Once achieved the weights, the limits of the design variables were systematically reduced. Each bio-inspired algorithm was executed 30 times , where each execution considered as stop criteria 2500 evaluations of the objective function. The program used to solve the simulation was created in C code in Code::Blocks®in a computer with a processor of 2.8 GHz.

The convergence of the performance function trough generations of a random individual of each algorithm is presented in Fig. 3. Remarkably, DE is the most

Table 2. Information of motor 607327 model EC 90 flat Maxon Motor.

Parameter	Value
R	0.422 Ω
L	0.000535 H
k_e	0.207 Vs/rad
k_t	0.231 Nm/A
B	0.000181437 Nms
J	0.000506 kgm^2
P	11
T_l	0 Nm
ω_d	40 rad/s

Table 3. Algorithms parameters.

Algorithm	Parameters
Best/1/bin	$G_{max} = 50$, $NP = 50$, $F = [0.3, 0.9]$, $CR = 0.6$
PSO	$G_{max} = 50$, $NP = 50$, $C_1 = C_2 = 2$,
	$\omega = V_{max} - \frac{g}{G_{max}}(V_{max} - V_{min})$, $V_{max} = \frac{1}{x_{max}}$, $V_{min} = 0$
FA	$G_{max} = 50$, $NP = 50$, $\beta_{min} = 0$, $\omega = 1 - \frac{g}{G_{max}}$,
	$\gamma = 1 - g/G_{max}$

stable after reach the optimum value in spite that needs more generations to reach it. On the other hand FA is the fastest to converge to the optimum value, this is attributed to the fact that an individual in FA has more movements (number of the objective function evaluations) per generation, however once the algorithm reach the optimum value starts to oscillate around it. Finally in terms of speed, PSO can be found in the middle of both algorithm. It is almost as fast as FA, however it presents greater oscillations than FA. Furthermore it is important to mention that each algorithm presents different execution times. PSO presents the fastest execution time taking an average of 0.102 s per execution. DE was the second one taking an average of 0.109 s per execution. This result is due to DE has to find 2 random individuals different from the best so the algorithm waste time finding those individuals. FA is the slowest algorithm with an average of 0.219 s per execution. This is attributed that FA implements exponential operations which requires more computational time.

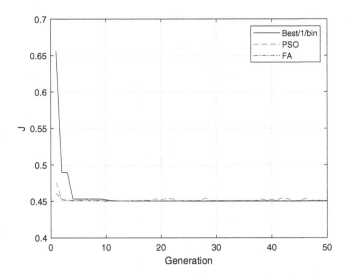

Fig. 3. Convergence of the performance function of the bio-inspired algorithms. In the first generation the obtained solution is not feasible and so, the performance function value is not shown.

To have a comparative reference for the optimum results, an additional control gains obtained by Trial and Error Tuning Procedure (TETP) was included. Such procedure consisted on finding gains that guarantee to reach the steady state within the first 0.05 s of the simulation, and provide a suitable power consumption at the start of the motor. This task is not an easy task and requieres of several trials to get an appropriate performance in both objectives. This is because the velocity error and the power consumption conflict, i.e., to reduce one performance criterium results in the deterioration of the other one. The constant gains obtained by the bio-inspired algorithms and the TETP are presented in Table 4.

Table 4. Controller constant gains obtained through bio-inspired algorithms and the TETP.

	k_p	k_i
Best/1/bin	1.14435	112.63057
PSO	1.14459	112.61539
FA	1.15841	112.25348
TETP	2	200

The comparison of the descriptive statistic among the bio-inspired algorithms is shown in Table 5, where J_{avg} is the average of the 30 executions, J_{max} is the maximum (worst) value obtained, J_{min} is the minimum (best) value obtained and σ is the standard deviation, also the best results of each criteria are written in bold. Before starting to describe the results of Table 5, it is important to mention that the criteria J_{avg}, J_{min} and J_{max} of TETP are the same, due to TETP is not based in a stochastic method so its standard deviation is 0. As is seen, all optimization algorithms present better results than the TETP. Notably, PSO has the best minimum value and the best average convergence. On the other hand, Best/1/bin has the better standard deviation, which increase its probability of give better convergence results. Despite of FA is not better than the other optimization algorithms, it also reaches similar results, so it can be said that all the optimization algorithms are capable of solve the problem of tuning the PIC of a BLDC motor which aims to reduce and find the most suitable trade-off between IAE and the Average Power.

Table 5. Results comparison

	J_{avg}	J_{max}	J_{min}	σ
Best/1/bin	0.45014606	**0.45022646**	0.45012368	**2.1504E-05**
PSO	**0.45014539**	0.45023845	**0.45011844**	3.2548E-05
FA	0.45064774	0.45163619	0.45023896	2.915E-04
TETP	0.49420628	0.49420628	0.49420628	0

A comparison of the speed regulation is presented in Fig. 4, where due to the similarity in gains, the results of Best/1/bin, PSO, and FA are similar. Figure 4 also shows that the results obtained through bio-inspired algorithms have less and shorter oscillations during the transient state response than the result obtained trough TETP, which reaches faster the steady-state. On the other hand, all results have similar oscillations (± 0.22 rad/seg) once they reach the steady-state. Also, a comparison of the average power is presented in Fig. 5, where is important to notice that TETP presents larger oscillations during the transient state than the results obtained through bio-inspired algorithms. Also, TETP presents a more stable average power once it reaches the steady-state. The oscillations in both results show the presence of a trade-off between speed regulation and average power. Finally, it is remarkable to show how a small increase of the speed overshoot of the TETP against the bio-inspired algorithms, generates a considerable difference in power overshot during the start of the BLDC motor. Even when in the TETP and the bio-inspired algorithms aimed to give a suitable power consumption, it is remarkable to point out that the bio-inspired algorithms were more successful for this task.

Finally, to observe the performance function of the obtained gains under parametric uncertainties, a second simulation was performed. Such an experiment considers a variable load, where the load T_l change its value during the whole simulation. The load change is represented by $T_l = 0.964 \sin(500\pi t)$, where

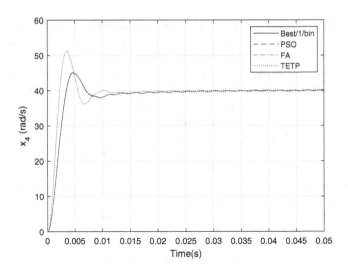

Fig. 4. Speed regulation behavior with the obtained control gains.

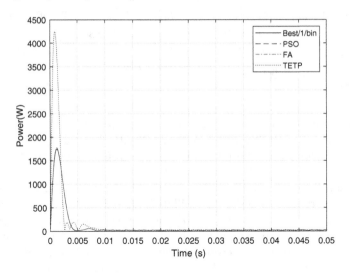

Fig. 5. Average power behavior with the obtained control gains.

$0.964Nm$ is the maximum load for the motor. The performance function of the closed-loop system with such variations are shown in Table 6. It is important to observe that all results obtained through bio-inspired algorithms are better than TETP. On the other hand under the variable load, the gains of FA were the best. Also, it is observed in Fig. 6 that all bio-inspired algorithms present a minor overshoot than TETP. Remarkably, the oscillations in steady-state are around ± 2 rad/s, which implies that under parametric uncertainties (not considered in the offline optimization problem) the results can get ten-time worst. This is confirmed in Fig. 7 where the oscillations of the power consumption during the simulation are twice bigger than the simulation without variable load. This indicates that despite the offline controller tuning does not include uncertainties, the obtained optimum gains provide competitive performance concerning the TETP.

Table 6. Results comparison considering variable load

	J
Best/1/bin	0.605520781
PSO	0.605515091
FA	**0.605490992**
TETP	0.683286914

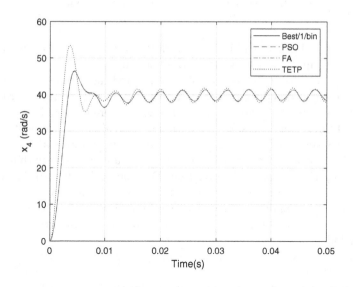

Fig. 6. Speed regulation behavior with variable load.

5 Conclusions

The presented work compares three different bio-inspired algorithms to find the optimum constant gains for a PIC that regulates the angular speed of a BLDC motor. The optimization problem was presented as a mono-objective problem through the weighted product method. The aim of the optimization problem

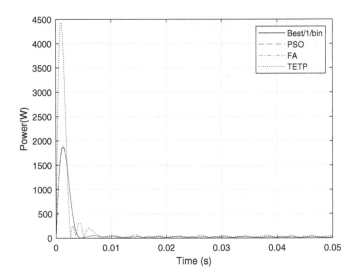

Fig. 7. Average power behavior with variable load.

was to minimize both the IAE and Average power. DE, PSO, and FA were implemented to find the most suitable control gains.

Simulation results indicate that all bio-inspired algorithms present similar results in the regulation error behavior and those present a better control system behavior than a tuning approach where the gains were obtained by a trial and error procedure. Nevertheless, the execution of each algorithm presents different characteristics such as convergence speed, reliability, and execution time which can be useful in future works in online controller tuning. It is shown that PSO has a considerably faster time execution than DE due to DE has to find different random individuals which is a waste of time. In addition, the performance of the optimum gains under parametric uncertainties provide better closed-loop performance with respect to the TETP, in spite that parametric uncertainties are not included in the optimization problem.

Future works involve the online optimum tuning where computational speed is important to be reduced, such approach will be suitable to give better results under parametric uncertainties. Additionally, the compromise between the speed regulation and the average power must be studied as a multi-objective optimization problem.

References

1. Baldursson, S.: BLDC motor modelling and control-a matlab®/simulink® implementation. Master's thesis (2005)
2. Chiasson, J.: Modeling and High-Performance Control of Electric Machines. Wiley, Hoboken (2005)
3. Choi, J., Nam, K., Bobtsov, A.A., Pyrkin, A.A., Ortega, R.: Robust adaptive sensorless control for permanent-magnet synchronous motors. IEEE Trans. Power Electron. **32**, 3989–3997 (2017)
4. Demirtas, M.: Off-line tuning of a PI speed controller for a permanent magnet brushless DC motor using DSP. Energy Convers. Manag. **52**(1), 264–273 (2011)
5. Jethwani, A., Aseri, D., Singh, T.S., Jain, A.K.: A simpler approach to the modelling of permanent magnet brushless DC machine in MATLAB environment. In: 2016 IEEE 6th International Conference on Power Systems (ICPS), pp. 1–6. IEEE (2016)
6. Kennedy, J., Eberhart, R.: Particle swarm optimization. In: 1995 IEEE International Conference on Neural Networks Proceedings, vol. 1, p. 6. IEEE (1948)
7. Krishnan, R.: Electric Motor Drives: Modeling, Analysis and Control, vol. 626. Prentice Hall, New Jersey (2001)
8. Marler, R.T., Arora, J.S.: Survey of multi-objective optimization methods for engineering. Struct. Multi. Optim. **26**(6), 369–395 (2004). https://doi.org/10.1007/s00158-003-0368-6
9. Premkumar, K., Manikandan, B.: Bat algorithm optimized fuzzy PD based speed controller for brushless direct current motor. Eng. Sci. Technol. Int. J. **19**(2), 818–840 (2016)
10. Price, K., Storn, R.M., Lampinen, J.A.: Differential Evolution: a Practical Approach to Global Optimization. Springer, Heidelberg (2006). https://doi.org/10.1007/3-540-31306-0
11. Rashid, M.H.: Power Electronics Handbook. Butterworth-Heinemann, Oxford (2017)
12. Ruano, A.E.: Intelligent control - the road ahead. In: European Control Conference (ECC), pp. 4442–4443 (2007)
13. Serrano-Pérez, O., Villarreal-Cervantes, M.G., González-Robles, J.C., Rodríguez-Molina, A.: Meta-heuristic algorithms for the control tuning of omnidirectional mobile robots. Eng. Optim. **52**(2), 325–342 (2020)
14. Shatnawi, M., Bayoumi, E.: Brushless dc motor controller optimization using simulated annealing. In: 2019 International Conference on Electrical Drives Power Electronics (EDPE), pp. 292–297, September 2019. https://doi.org/10.1109/EDPE.2019.8883924
15. Shinners, S.M.: Modern Control System Theory and Design. Wiley, Hoboken (1998)
16. Sivarani, T., Joseph Jawhar, S., Agees Kumar, C., Premkumar, K.: Novel bacterial foraging-based ANFIS for speed control of matrix converter-fed industrial BLDC motors operated under low speed and high torque. Neural Comput. Appl. **29**, 1411–1434 (2018). https://doi.org/10.1007/s00521-016-2652-6
17. Tariq, M., Bhattacharya, T., Varshney, N., Rajapan, D.: Fast response antiwindup PI speed controller of brushless DC motor drive: Modeling, simulation and implementation on DSP. J. Electr. Syst. Inf. Technol. **3**(1), 1–13 (2016)
18. Tsai, M.F., Quy, T.P., Wu, B.F., Tseng, C.S.: Model construction and verification of a BLDC motor using MATLAB/SIMULINK and FPGA control. In: 2011 6th IEEE Conference on Industrial Electronics and Applications, pp. 1797–1802. IEEE (2011)

19. Villarreal-Cervantes, M.G., Alvarez-Gallegos, J.: Off-line PID control tuning for a planar parallel robot using DE variants. Expert Syst. Appl. **64**, 444–454 (2016)

20. Xia, C.L.: Permanent Magnet Brushless DC Motor Drives and Controls. Wiley, Hoboken (2012)

21. Yang, X.-S.: Firefly algorithms for multimodal optimization. In: Watanabe, O., Zeugmann, T. (eds.) SAGA 2009. LNCS, vol. 5792, pp. 169–178. Springer, Heidelberg (2009). https://doi.org/10.1007/978-3-642-04944-6_14

Reinforcement Learning Applied to Hexapod Robot Locomotion: An Overview

Espinosa Jorge$^{(\boxtimes)}$ ⓘ, Gorrostieta Efren ⓘ, Vargas-Soto Emilio ⓘ,
and Ramos-Arreguín Juan Manuel ⓘ

Universidad Autónoma de Querétaro, Querétaro, Mexico
jorge.luis_espinosa@hotmail.com, efrengorrostieta@gmail.com,
emilio@mecatronica.net, jsistdig@yahoo.com.mx

Abstract. Six-legged robots are very useful in environments with obstacles of a size comparable to its own. However, the locomotion problem of hexapod robots is complex to solve due to the number of degrees of freedom and unknown environments. Nevertheless, the problem definition of Reinforcement Learning fits naturally for solving the robot locomotion problem. Reinforcement Learning has acquired great relevance in the last decade since it has achieved human-level control for specific tasks. This article presents an overview of Reinforcement Learning methods that have been successfully applied to the six-legged robot locomotion problem. First, a description and some achievements of reinforcement learning will be introduced, followed by examples of hexapod robots throughout history focusing on their locomotion systems. Secondly, the locomotion problem for a six-legged hexapod robot will be defined, with special attention to both, the gait and leg motion planning. Thirdly, the classical framework of reinforcement learning will be introduced and the Q-learning algorithm, which is one of the most used Reinforcement Learning algorithms in this context, will be revised. Finally, reinforcement learning methods applied to six-legged robot locomotion will be extensively discussed followed by open questions.

Keywords: Six-legged robot locomotion problem · Hexapod robot locomotion · Applied reinforcement learning in hexapod robots

1 Introduction

Throughout the history of development of mobile robots, it has been discussed that walking robots have some advantages against wheeled robots since the discrete contact with the ground enables them to overcome small obstacles that may be present in the environment. Nevertheless, the analysis of their locomotion and their control systems become more complex when several degrees of freedom are present and it is necessary to generate a coordinated gait pattern that guarantees stability as well as a leg trajectory controller to drive each of the joint movements for each leg [1, 2]. Artificial Intelligence (AI) has acquired strength in the last few years. The integration between AI and the robotics research field has permitted to address the locomotion problem of hexapod robots from another perspective by integrating intelligent controllers where the robots

© Springer Nature Switzerland AG 2020
M. F. Mata-Rivera et al. (Eds.): WITCOM 2020, CCIS 1280, pp. 185–201, 2020.
https://doi.org/10.1007/978-3-030-62554-2_14

can learn their own walking patterns, adapting quickly to changes and operating even if a leg is damaged [3, 4].

1.1 Reinforcement Learning

Reinforcement learning is an artificial intelligence branch that allows an agent to learn through experience. The origins of reinforcement learning are based on different works from several areas of knowledge such as: Informatics, statistics, psychology, neuroscience and computer sciences [5]. It consists of learning through the interaction with the environment. Every action taken under a specific situation will provide a numeric reward as a feedback to the learning agent, indicating how positive the action taken in that moment was. It is possible to make the analogy with how a pet is trained. A positive reward is given to the pet for every "good" action, otherwise it receives a penalization [5, 6]. Even though there are more artificial intelligence branches, reinforcement learning can be adapted naturally to the walking learning process since it consists on interacting with the environment, looking to maximize the stability on a trial an error scheme [7].

Sutton and Barto [5] describe Reinforcement Learning as a problem and, every method that solves it is considered a Reinforcement Learning method. Several algorithms with different pros and cons are available in current literature. A classical set of reinforcement learning algorithms is discussed in Sect. 3. But, one of the first algorithms developed was Q-Learning as proposed by Watkins [6, 8]. This algorithm is of special interest for this article because it is widely implemented in the algorithms discussed in Sect. 4.

Finally, Reinforcement learning methods in combination with deep learning have proven their value by achieving a super-human control level in playing Atari and Go [9–11]. Those two events where groundbreaking for the artificial intelligence field and are motives for further research.

1.2 Hexapod Robots

It is natural to think that hexapod robots were inspired by some arthropods. The study of the movement and the morphology of some insects have contributed to the development of walking algorithms [12–14]. For example, in [15] a hexapod with morphology derived from an ant was proposed (see Fig. 1.). To execute its locomotion, an algorithm using fuzzy logic was designed. From there, a parabolic step trajectory was generated based on similar leg trajectories present in some animals. This trajectory is part of the leg motion controller that generates the movement of a specific leg. Another example is the TUM Walking machine [13] which is a six-legged robot inspired by the *Carausius Morosus*. The coordination of legs in locomotion uses two gaits, one gait pattern called tetrapod gait which is used for low speeds and a tripod gait used for high speeds, just like the biological model does [13]. The differences between the gait patterns are informally defined by how many legs are in contact with the ground simultaneously and how many are executing a swing. Therefore, the swing is the result of executing the trajectory generation algorithm. These gait patterns will be further discussed in Sect. 2.

Fig. 1. Proposed hexapod in [15] with "ant" morphology.

Another interesting robot design is the "Biobot" [12], a six-legged robot inspired by the American Cockroach *Perhiplaneta Americana*. Its locomotion algorithm is the result of a behavioral study of the insect. By videotaping the cockroaches walking over flat surfaces and digitalizing the images it was possible to analyze and mirror their walking pattern. For the trajectory generation of each leg, a PID controller was implemented to ensure the accuracy of each leg movement [12]. Figure 2 shows a simulated hexapod executing a trajectory movement for one leg.

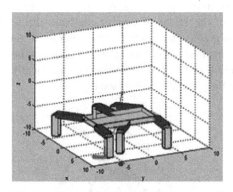

Fig. 2. Simulated hexapod robot with 18 degrees of freedom.

Legged robots are commonly designed for difficult terrains, for example the COMET II and COMET III are robots created for mine detection [16]. This implies that they must adapt themselves properly to the environment in order to achieve their purpose. Thus, the hard coding of a specific gait pattern is not enough to solve the locomotion problem. An unknown environment could contain obstacles that the robot cannot avoid. A human controlling the robot reduces the complexity of designing a path planning algorithm [17]. But, if full autonomy needs to be achieved, sensors may be incorporated to support path planning and obstacle evasion [18, 19]. This has helped to generate better locomotion patterns, but it is impossible to anticipate all the possible configurations that an unknown environment will contain. This has motivated research from an artificial intelligence perspective.

2   Locomotion of Hexapod Robots

2.1   Problem Definition

The problem of locomotion for a six-legged robot can be broken down into three abstraction layers: Path planning, gait planning and leg motion planning [17]. The path planning layer receives the highest level of information such as the desired position of the robot, the desired velocity or acceleration. It is in charge of producing the direction vector that the robot must follow given the current state. The gait planning layer receives the information from the path planning layer and coordinates a sequence of steps given the current position of the joints, the center of gravity and the orientation, amongst other measurable variables. The final layer receives commands from the gait planning layer to generate the desired leg trajectory to move the leg from the current to the desired position [15, 17].

The stability of the robot is an important factor that needs to be under control for a successful locomotion algorithm. There are two types of stability: statically stable locomotion and dynamic locomotion. The dynamic locomotion is needed when the vertical projection of the center of gravity is outside the support polygon, usually when executing tasks such as running or jumping. A statically stable locomotion ensures that the vertical projection of the center of gravity is always inside the support polygon. Whenever the center of gravity is outside or at the border of the support polygon the robot will fall unless force is applied with the legs to correct the position of the center of gravity. The support polygon will be determined geometrically by the number of legs that are in contact with the ground [15, 17] (see Fig. 3.).

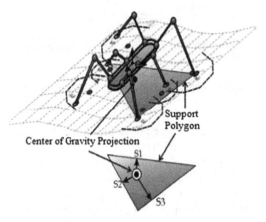

Fig. 3. Support polygon [15].

2.2   Gait Planning

There are several pre-defined walking patterns for hexapod robots. The selection of one option over the other will depend mainly on the application and terrain. A walking pattern is described by its ipsilateral phase, contralateral phase and duty factor [13]. A regular gait happens when each leg has the same duty factor, this means that each leg spends the same amount of time on the ground. A wave gait has a duty factor greater than 0.5 for all the legs. This gait is commonly found in stick insects and they ensure a statically stable motion at a wide range of speed [17].

The tripod gait is one of the most exploited hexapod gaits. It consists of moving the front and back leg of one side and the middle leg of the opposite side at the same time (see Fig. 4). This gait is statically and dynamically stable and works for high speeds over flat ground.

Free gaits are not regular gaits; they are not attached to any rule [17]. Some learning algorithms may generate these gaits during the training process.

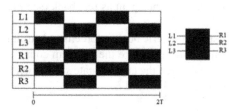

Fig. 4. Two period sequence of tripod gait pattern [17].

2.3 Leg Motion Planning

The lowest layer requires a controller capable of generating the leg trajectory by moving the joints from a starting position to a desired position within the workspace of the leg. This step usually needs a good kinematic model for the hexapod to design a controller capable of guaranteeing that the tip of the leg will reach the desired final position [20]. As it was discussed in chapter 3 and 4, some reinforcement learning methods address the trajectory generation without a kinematic model. Which is one of the major motivations for using artificial intelligence for this stage.

A common trajectory is the parabolic trajectory (see Fig. 5) [15, 20]. However, other trajectories can be replicated at this stage based on the analysis of real legged animals.

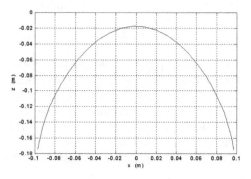

Fig. 5. Parabolic leg trajectory for an ant hexapod robot in [15].

3 Reinforcement Learning in the Context of Hexapod Robots' Locomotion

3.1 Problem Definition

Formally, reinforcement learning describes a problem and all methods that provide a solution are considered methods of reinforcement learning. This problem is composed of two elements [5]:

- A learning agent capable of taking actions from an action space A.
- An environment that, due to the action, changes its state $s_t \in S$ to a new state $s_{t+1} \in S$ and provides a reward value r_t to the agent as feedback (see Fig. 6).

The reward signal is usually numeric but reinforcement learning methods are usually interested in the long-term reward, therefore the problem consists of selecting the best actions from the action space A given the current state $s \in S$ such that the learning agent receives the maximum accumulated reward R_t.

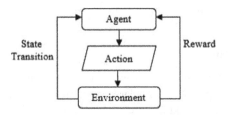

Fig. 6. Interaction between an agent and its environment [5].

The actions are selected from a policy $\pi(s)$. This policy is a mapping between actions and states. Therefore, the problem can be stated as, finding the optimal policy π^* that maximizes long-term reward signal R_t.

From the perspective of robot locomotion there is not a unique definition of the state it is more like a collection of the measurable variables of interest. One definition is [21]:

$$s = \left[q, \dot{q}, c, v\right] \tag{1}$$

That is the collection of the joints' positions, the joints' velocities, the contact with the ground vector and the travelling direction vector respectively [21]. Some other proposals incorporate a higher dimensional state space, that includes the robot's relative height and the orientation [4]. If the interest is to learn a controller for the leg trajectory generation then the actions are simply the torques applied to the joints [21] but if the purpose is to learn a gait pattern, then the actions are the steps that the robot must execute for the current state [22]. Similarly, there is not a unique definition for the reward signal. For example, in [4] the following reward signal model is proposed

$$R_t = \Delta x_t + s_t + \omega_0 C_t - \omega_1 \|\tau_t\|_2^2 - \omega_2 \|\phi_t\|_2^2 \tag{2}$$

Where Δx_t is the covered distance, s_t is the "survival reward" which is a positive reward if the episode has not been terminated, C_t is the number of legs making contact with the ground, τ_t is the squared sum of external forces and torques on each joint, ϕ_t are the actions, ω_0, ω_1 and ω_2 are weights [4]. Another model can be found in [21]:

$$r(s, a) = w_v E_v(s) + E_u(s) + w_l E_l(s) + E_a + w_e E_e(a) \tag{3}$$

Where each term is defined in such a way that encourages one different feature. $E_v = -|\bar{v} - \hat{v}|$ encourages the agent to move at the desired velocity, E_u encourages the agent to maintain its torso and head upright, E_l gives positive reward when the robot is moving in the forward direction, $E_a = -||a||$ gives negative reward if the torques are excessive to minimize energy consumption. In some reinforcement learning methods there are reward signal models suggested to benchmark the algorithms.

3.2   Value Based Methods

It is possible to define a value function as the expected total reward given a state $s \in S$ and following the policy π.

$$V^\pi(s) = E\{R_t | s_t = s\} \tag{4}$$

This associates the state with a numeric value that measures "how good" it is to be in that state. The value based methods allow to find the optimal policy π^* through finding the optimal value function $V^*(s)$. Some classical approaches are: Dynamic Programming, Monte Carlo methods and Temporal-Difference learning [5].

Dynamic Programming offers a set of algorithms for computing policies assuming that the problem can be modeled as a Markov Decision Problem [5, 23], where the value function can be written as:

$$V^\pi(s) = E_\pi\{R_t | s_t = s\} = \sum_a \pi(s, a) \sum_{s'} P^a_{ss'} [R^a_{ss'} + \gamma V^\pi(s')] \tag{5}$$

Where γ is a discount factor, $P^a_{ss'}$ is the state transition model and $R^a_{ss'}$ is the reward model [5].

Two of these algorithms are Policy Iteration and Value Iteration algorithms. The Policy Iteration algorithm has two main processes, Policy Evaluation and Policy Improvement. The Policy Evaluation process computes the function $V^\pi(s)$. Secondly, the Policy Improvement step improves the current policy π, which is now called π'. Then Policy Evaluation is called again to compute the new $V^{\pi'}(s)$. Following this loop will yield the optimal value function V^* and the optimal policy π^*. The main drawback is shown in 6. The factor $P^{\pi(s)}_{ss'}$ is the transition model of the system. Therefore, these methods require an accurate system model to compute the value function [5].

Monte Carlo methods are model-free algorithms that enable the agent to learn from experience through episodic tasks. Like the definition of the value function, an action-value function is defined as

$$Q^\pi(s, a) = E\{R_t | s_t = s, a_t = a\} \tag{6}$$

Which measures "how good" it is to be in the s state under the action a. Monte Carlo methods – as well as other reinforcement learning algorithms – use this action-value function to generate optimal policies. The classic idea behind Monte Carlo algorithms is to start with a greedy random policy, take actions until we reach the end of an episode and collect the reward given by each pair of states and actions present in the episode to build the $Q(s, a)$ function. This way the improved policy can be obtained by

$$\pi'(s) = \arg\max_a Q^\pi(s, a) \tag{7}$$

The major drawback for these algorithms is that the agent needs to wait until the final of the episode to improve the policy [5]. In terms of locomotion this implies to wait until the robot falls to improve the policy.

Finally, Temporal-Difference methods combine Dynamic Programming with Monte Carlo methods. They enable the agent to learn from experience and update the policy after each immediate iteration without waiting for the episode to end [5].

3.3 Q-Learning

In the context of robot locomotion, we can notice that Q-Learning and Deep Reinforcement Learning are the two most visited methods for addressing the walking learning problem for six-legged robots [4, 21, 22, 24–28]. Q-Learning is similar to a Temporal-Difference method [8]. It requires to start with a greedy policy. Take actions from the action space, measure the reward. Update the Q-values and then generate a new policy based on the updated Q. The update of Q is usually defined as [7, 8]

$$Q(s, a) \leftarrow r_t + \gamma \max_a Q(s_{t+1}, a) \tag{8}$$

Where r_t is the immediate reward and γ is a discount factor to weight the immediate and the future rewards. From here the improved new policy can be computed using 7.

Trying to apply classical Q-Learning to the hexapod locomotion problem can be difficult since multiple actions need to be output for a single state and the reward will depend on the complete system response. Therefore, to successfully apply the algorithm a few variations have been proposed. First, we can consider a multi-agent problem where each agent represents one leg, therefore there will be six policies to compute based on the same reward for each iteration [22]. Nevertheless, decomposing the global task into individual and smaller problems with only one reward signal implies that if the global system fails, it will give a negative reward to the agents that complete their tasks positively. To overcome this issue, in [24] a hierarchy architecture is proposed where if a state transition happens for a level controller d, the lower level controller $(d - 1)$ that caused the state change for d will be rewarded independently. Similarly, in [22] a special memory with the best rewards for a particular pair state-action is implemented to promote the cooperation between agents to achieve the most reward. This modifies the reward definition by

$$r_{max}(s, a) \leftarrow \max[r_{max}(s, a), r(s, a)] \tag{9}$$

These methods will be further discussed in Sect. 4.

3.4 Policy Search Methods

Another alternative for finding good policies is to search for the policy directly in the policy space instead of building the value function. Usually policies have lower parameters than value functions and better scalability [7]. Most of these algorithms start with an existing policy π, parametrized by a set of parameters θ_i and then they locally optimize the policy by small changes in the parameters looking for the most long-term reward [29].

Policy Gradient methods are commonly used for problems with continuous action spaces. There, the policy π is represented as a probability distribution that selects actions given a state according to a parameter vector θ [29].

$$\pi(a|s) = P[a|s; \theta] \tag{10}$$

The actor-critic architecture [5] consists of an actor that adjusts the parameters of the policy through the stochastic gradient ascent:

$$\theta_{k+1} = \theta_k + \alpha_k \nabla_\theta J(\pi_\theta) \tag{11}$$

Where α is a step size, and $\nabla_\theta J(\pi_\theta)$ is the gradient of the cumulative discounted reward.

And a critic that estimates the action-value function $Q(s, a)$.

Similarly, in [29] it has been demonstrated that it is possible to build deterministic policy gradient algorithms, this implies that the states are directly mapped to concrete actions and not to a probability distribution.

An interesting application for this kind of algorithms is the trajectory generation for a six-legged robot controller. The trajectory generation of a leg has a continuous action space, since it deals with the torques that should be applied to each joint. Proximal Policy Optimization [30] is a family of algorithms of policy gradient mostly focused on improving the data efficiency that has been applied in [21] to learn walking patterns for bipeds, quadrupeds and hexapods.

A list of value based, and policy search methods applied for a wide range of robotic tasks can be found in [7].

3.5 Deep Reinforcement Learning

Recently, it has been proven that it is possible to integrate deep neural networks to the classic reinforcement learning methods. This combination has been successful for solving decision-making problems [10, 11] and they are the state-of-art methods for solving locomotion problems of legged robots as well [4, 28]. The deep neural networks scale the reinforcement learning methods by being trained to learn the value functions or the policy directly [31]. For example, the "Q-Learning" algorithm, which is a value-function method, has been escalated to Deep Q-Network by parametrizing an approximation of the Q function, $Q(s, a; \theta_i)$ where the parameters are weights from the Q-network. The neural network used in DQN is a deep convolutional network [11]. Similarly, policy gradient methods have been scaled, such as Deterministic Policy Gradient to Deep Deterministic Policy Gradient (DDPG) [32] and Soft Actor Critic (SAC) [33].

The locomotion problem is usually decomposed in different stages as seen in Sect. 3. Therefore, classical reinforcement learning algorithms are usually designed to address specific tasks and then coordinated to achieve a successful locomotion solution as seen in Sect. 4. In contrast, deep reinforcement learning is robust enough to provide an end-to-end solution for the locomotion learning of walking robots as shown in [34], where the SAC algorithm was implemented to learn policies for walking in different directions with minimal human interaction and no hierarchical architecture as seen in the Q-Learning algorithms. Nevertheless, it was tested on a quadruped platform and it has not been benchmarked for a six-legged robot.

4 Applications of Reinforcement Learning for the Locomotion Problem

4.1 Q-Learning Based Applications

Efforts for solving the locomotion problem through reinforcement learning have been present since late 90's. Around 1998 Hierarchical Q-Learning (HQL) was applied to a hexapod robot with 2 degrees of freedom per leg [24]. Their proposed architecture tries to address the three layers of locomotion by considering a set of learning agents per layer. This strategy allows to have one learning agent learning at the highest level (Path planning), one agent learning at the intermediate level (Gait planning) and six agents learning at the lowest level (Leg motion planning) and permits that each agent has its own reinforcement signal. To relate the agents, a special decomposition of the state space is done. Assuming that each agent has a state space X^d and a goal state space $G^d \subseteq X^d$ where d is the layer level. Then, if the problem is recursively decomposed, $X^{d+1} = G^d$ [24].

Each agent per layer will follow its own policy which will generate actions based on

$$Policy\left(x_t^d\right) = \arg \max_{a^d \in A^d}\left(Q\left(x_t^d, a^d\right)\right) \tag{12}$$

Where x_t^d is the state in time t and layer d. This implies that the Q function will be updated for different levels of state spaces and action spaces and that the algorithm will be recursive. The highest-level action will be passed down to lower level layers until the last layer is reached. The final layer will perform the action in the real world, receive its reward, update its value in the Q function and then return to the previous layer so it can compute its reward and update the Q function as well, until the first level layer is reached again [24].

The constraints presented in [24] are that, the lowest level layer, which is the leg motion planning, only accepts discrete actions: move the leg up, move the leg down to the ground, swing the leg forward and stance the leg backwards and is not generating a smooth trajectory as discussed in Sect. 2.3. The experiments in [24] were only limited to learn the stance and swing movements. The stance movement was learnt generally after 50 trials. The real state space was strongly reduced from 90×90 to 10×10 due to the hardware limitations and the coordination between legs is not shown experimentally (Gait planning). Nevertheless, it is shown how to decompose a complex problem into smaller less complex tasks to enable a multi-agent Q-learning algorithm with particular reinforcement signals [24].

Similarly, a Distributed Q-Learning algorithm was proposed in [25] to address the Gait planning stage whenever the robot is initialized in a random orientation and position and needs to correct its walking pattern to move itself to a predefined straight path. If each leg is considered an individual agent with individual policy, reward signal and Q function then, the Q function of one agent may depend on the actions taken by other agents as well. It is assumed that an individual agent has no visibility of other agents' actions and Q values a priori but it can see the actions and rewards of each agent a posteriori. To consider the observable variables the proposal is to consider groups of M agents and their actions as new state variables. This implies a redefinition of the $Q(s, a)$ function as $Q^i(s, a^1, a^2, \ldots, a^M)$ where Q^i is the Q function for the agent i and each a is the action taken by other agents in the group. The effect of including more states is that the cost of computing the Q function increases considerably. To mitigate this effect, the authors suggest combining it with Self-role Organizing Maps (SOM) [25].

The conducted experiments in [25] are run on a simulator. The limitations implemented there are that the state space is limited to the orientation variable which was discretized by dividing the orientation range into 4 sections and 6 regions resulting in a state space of size equal to 24. The action space depends on the amplitude of the leg, which is the distance between the reference contact point of the leg and the final contact point of the leg. The main objective of their experiment is to correct the robot orientation; therefore the tripod gait pattern is used as the base locomotion algorithm. To correct the orientation the reinforcement learning algorithm will modify the amplitude of each leg [25].

Similar experiments are presented in [22] where each leg is seen like a learning agent. The difference is that the coordination of the legs is encouraged through the reward signal instead of having a hierarchy or looking at the actions from other agents. A memory is added to the system that will store the maximum reward given a state-action pair. This implies the creation of a function $r_{max}(s,a)$ of the same size as the Q function. The reward will be updated under the rule

$$r(s, a)_{max} = \max(r_{max}(s, a), r(s, a)) \tag{13}$$

In other words, the reward for a specific state-action pair will only be updated if it is the greatest reward seen for that state-action pair. This way, the effect of seeing multiple variations on the reward signal due to other agents is minimized [22].

The constraints in their experiments are the limited action space, which is confined to two options, don't move or move the joint to the next preprogramed position, and a limited number of learning agents set to three under the condition that the contralateral leg will behave identically. The reward signal was limited also as positive for forward movement and negative for backwards movement. Their experiments were conducted for learning to move forward [22].

As we mention in Sect. 2, the reward signal model may vary between implementations of the same reinforcement learning algorithm. In [26] a fuzzy system is designed to provide the reward values. The Q-Learning algorithm is used with a reduced state space: it is assumed that each leg can be in front of the body, behind the body or not in the ground. The actions chosen by the reinforcement learning algorithm are sent to a lookup table of actions and inverse kinematic solutions. This will translate the action into the joint position values, similarly, the states are passed through a lookup table of states and inverse kinematic solutions to map them to joint position values. This bypasses the use of a multi-agent Q-Learning architecture [26].

Fuzzy logic has been combined differently with Q-Learning in [27]. Where the main objective is path planning in an environment with obstacles. Fuzzy Q-Learning uses fuzzy logic to convert the measured distances to the obstacles into a finite set of states then Q-Learning is used to learn the control rules for the fuzzy system. The distances to the obstacles are discretized in three categories through the fuzzification process: far, middle and near. Since the robot incorporates three ultrasonic sensors there are 27 possible states after fuzzification. The action space is also discrete: move forward, turn left and turn right. The reward signal proposed is blurred as well using a gaussian model since it depends on the measurement of the three sensors for a particular state [27].

$$r(s) = 20e^{-\frac{(s-2)^2}{2}} \tag{14}$$

Where

$$s = min(a, b, c)$$

Here a, b and c are the individual rewards from each of the sensors.

The standard Q-Learning process described in Sect. 3.3 is executed three times in a particular timestamp to evaluate each of the sensors readings. This will provide three possible actions; the best action is selected with a fusion process [27].

As seen in the reviewed articles. Q-Learning can be applied to any layer of the locomotion problem independently. Nevertheless, it has important drawbacks since most of the times it requires to reduce the state space and the action space. Most of the algorithms modify the architecture of the Q function to incorporate a multi-agent scheme. An end-to-end solution is not presented yet. Most of work focus on a particular task in a specific layer of the walking problem.

4.2 Deep Reinforcement Learning Based Applications

As we have discussed, there are different walking patterns for a hexapod robot and the selection of a pattern depends on the application. Map-based Multi-Policy Reinforcement Learning (MMPRL) is a method proposed in [4] mainly designed to store multiple policies. Their idea is that, instead of having only one strong policy for one walking pattern, several policies can be trained based on the behavioral features that the robot needs, i.e., walking, running and jumping. This way the robot will have a better adaptability to different environments. MMPRL combines the Deep Deterministic Policy Gradient method (DDPG) with the Intelligent Trial and Error (IT&E) which is an evolutionary algorithm and therefore not discussed before. DDPG learns a policy and the state-action value function $Q(s, a; \theta)$ and its performance depends of the initialization of weights. Therefore, the algorithm may converge to different policies during different training if initialization is different. This instability is an advantage for MMPRL since multiple policies will be generated describing different behaviors. Those policies are stored in a map using the IT&E algorithm [4].

Their experimental setup consists on a hexapod with three degrees of freedom per leg and a height of 0.2 m. The joints have a valid range from −0.785 to 0.785 radians. The state space has 41 dimensions and includes the height of the robot, the orientation in quaternions, the joint angle positions, the indication if each leg is making contact with the ground and the relative height. The reward signal is defined in Eq. 2 [4]. The neural network architecture used is a Multilayer Perceptron with three hidden layers (400, 400, 200) for estimating the policy and a two layer Multilayer Perceptron (400, 200) for estimating the Q function, both with a ReLU activation. The training phase contains an environment with randomly placed obstacles of random height. And when testing the adaptation phase some modifications were applied to the robot such as: removing one or two tips of the toes, making the robot climb stairs or providing delayed observations [4].

Their results show that the algorithm generated 9030 policies in two weeks of training. The robot was able to move forward without obstacles for more than 25 m. In adaptation, testing shows better performance than a pure DDPG approach in most of the cases. It is remarked that the robot learnt a policy that does not need the joint 4 and that policy is selected commonly when the joint 4 is disabled [4].

In [28], DDPG has been applied in a modular fashion. First for learning a controller for an individual leg in the task of standing up. The same controller was programmed to every leg to enable the robot to execute the standup process. Secondly, two individual leg controllers were trained to learn how to walk forward, one controller was applied to the first and last leg from one side and the middle leg for the other side of the robot. The second controller was programmed for the remaining legs. With this configuration the robot should learn a tripod gait pattern. The action space for this last task consists on the six joint torques that can be applied to the two trained legs and the state space considers variables such as position and velocity of each joint as well as the height, pitch and roll of the torso of the robot. Their experimental results are still preliminary for this modular approach. The standing up tasks was completed successfully with the single leg and the two leg controllers. But the walking forward tasks was not completely achieved since the height of the body remained near ground [28].

It is clear that Deep Reinforcement Learning techniques easily enable the incorporation of continuous action spaces and state spaces and allow us to work with higher dimensional problems in contrast with the Q-Learning based algorithms were several state space reductions and discretization should be made. See Table 1 for a summary which shows the locomotion layers where each algorithm was applied. In the deep reinforcement learning based methods it is not that evident where the separation between the gait planning layer and the leg motion layer is, since it provides a more comprehensive solution. It enables the robot to learn more complex tasks such as overcome obstacles or operate when a joint is damaged. Table 2 shows the main task that each agent learnt.

Table 1. Main focus of the reviewed reinforcement learning algorithms from the hexapod walking problem perspective.

Algorithm	Path planning	Gait planning	Leg motion planning	Year
Hierarchy Q-Learning [24]		x	x	1998
Distribute Q-Learning [22]		x		2004
Cooperative Q-Learning [25]		x		2006
Q-Learning with Fuzzy Reward Signal [26]		x		
Fuzzy Q-Learning [27]	x			2017
MMPRL [4]		x	x	2017
Modular DDPG [28]		x	x	2019

Table 2. Summary of principal tested behaviors in each work.

Algorithm	Movement along a single axis	Orientation Correction	Swing and/or stance	Obstacle evasion	Obstacle climbing
Hierarchy Q-Learning [24]			x		
Cooperative Q-Learning [25]	x				
Distribute Q-Learning [22]		x			
Q-Learning with Fuzzy Reward Signal [26]	x				
Fuzzy Q-Learning [27]				x	
MMPRL [4]	x				x
Modular DDPG [28]	x		x		

4.3 Open Questions

The work discussed previously shows that reinforcement learning can be successfully applied to six-legged robot locomotion, nevertheless, a few points are identified from the discussion.

1. There is not a standard platform to benchmark the algorithms performance for six-legged robots. (See Fig. 7).
2. Although there are several approaches and successful use cases for reinforcement learning in locomotion there is still not a comprehensive learning algorithm for completely solving the walking problem in any situation.
3. There are other walking algorithms based on reinforcement learning that have not been benchmarked for hexapod robots. i.e., [34].
4. There is no direct comparison of performance in a six-legged robot platform between value based methods against policy gradient methods.
5. Q-Learning is the most common algorithm implemented – with several variations. There are still a set of algorithms that have not been translated to the walking problem domain. i.e., [35].
6. The effects of the robot morphology in the learning algorithms is not completely shown in the discussed work.
7. Analysis of the statically and dynamical stability is not explicitly discussed.
8. Movement along lateral and curved trajectories have not been extensively analyzed in comparison with forward movement.

Fig. 7. Example of hexapod CAD model that can be included in a simulator such as Gazebo [36].

5 Conclusion

As we have discussed, reinforcement learning has importantly contributed to solve the locomotion problems of hexapod robots. The benefits of using reinforcement learning include the generation of leg trajectories in the leg motion planning stage without a kinematic analysis of the robot, the coordination of legs in unknown environments without the hardcoding of a specific pattern and the autonomous obstacle evasion learning for path planning. Similarly, we have discussed the algorithms constraints and limitations during implementation to show gaps that need to be addressed in future research. There are many reinforcement learning methods in the literature that are still not benchmarked and compared against the discussed approaches.

The problem of locomotion can be seen from several perspectives and granularities. Thus, there are several ways to apply learning algorithms. A unified testing setup is needed to truly evaluate the performance for hexapod robot locomotion at each layer.

Finally, deep reinforcement learning algorithms are promising for developing an end-to-end solution to the locomotion problem since they allow the use of continuous action and state spaces with high dimensions. Hence, they enable the robot to learn how to overcome obstacles, learn to walk when a joint is damaged and adapt to environment changes. Those methods are considered part of the state-of-the-art and active research field.

References

1. Tedeschi, F., Carbone, G.: Design issues for hexapod walking robots. Robotics **3**(2), 181–206 (2014). https://doi.org/10.3390/robotics3020181
2. Devjanin, E.A., et al.: The six-legged walking robot capable of terrain adaptation. Mech. Mach. Theory **18**(4), 257–260 (1983). https://doi.org/10.1016/0094-114X(83)90114-3
3. Cully, A., Clune, J., Tarapore, D., Mouret, J.B.: Robots that can adapt like animals. Nature **521**(7553), 503–507 (2015). https://doi.org/10.1038/nature14422
4. Kume, A., Matsumoto, E., Takahashi, K., Ko, W., Tan, J.: Map-based multi-policy reinforcement learning: enhancing adaptability of robots by deep reinforcement learning. arXiv:1710.06117 (2017)
5. Sutton, R.S., Barto, A.G.: Reinforcement Learning: An Introduction. The MIT Press, London (1998)
6. Watkins, C.J.C.H..: Learning with delayed rewards. Ph.D. thesis, King's College (1989)
7. Kober, J., Bagnell, J.A., Peters, J.: Reinforcement learning in robotics: a survey. Int. J. Robot. Res. **32**(11), 1238–1274 (2013). https://doi.org/10.1177/0278364913495721
8. Watkins, C.J.C.H., Dayan, P.: Q-learning. Mach. Learn. **8**(3–4), 279–292 (1992)
9. Mnih, V., et al.: Playing atari with deep reinforcement learning. arXiv:1312.5602 [cs] (2013)
10. Silver, D., et al.: Mastering the game of Go with deep neural networks and tree search. Nature **529**(7587), 484–489 (2016). https://doi.org/10.1038/nature16961
11. Mnih, V., et al.: Human-level control through deep reinforcement learning. Nature **518**(7540), 529–533 (2015). https://doi.org/10.1038/nature14236
12. Delcomyn, F., Nelson, M.E.: Architectures for a biomimetic hexapod robot. Robot. Auton. Syst. **30**(1), 5–15 (2000). https://doi.org/10.1016/S0921-8890(99)00062-7
13. Pfeiffer, F., Eltze, J., Weidemann, H.-J.: The tum-walking machine. Intell. Autom. Soft Comput. **1**(3), 307–323 (1995). https://doi.org/10.1080/10798587.1995.10750637
14. Graham, D.: A behavioural analysis of the temporal organisation of walking movements in the 1st instar and adult stick insect (Carausius morosus). J. Comp. Physiol. **81**(1), 23–52 (1972). https://doi.org/10.1007/BF00693548
15. Gorrostieta, E., Vargas-Soto, E.: Algoritmo difuso de locomoción libre para un robot caminante de seis patas. Comput. Sist. **11**(3), 260–287 (2008)
16. Nonami, K., et al.: Development and control of mine detection robot COMET-II and COMET-III. JSME Int J. Ser. C **46**(3), 881–890 (2003). https://doi.org/10.1299/jsmec.46.881

17. Tedeschi, F., Carbone, G.: Hexapod walking robot locomotion. In: Carbone, G., Gomez-Bravo, F. (eds.) Motion and Operation Planning of Robotic Systems. MMS, vol. 29, pp. 439–468. Springer, Cham (2015). https://doi.org/10.1007/978-3-319-14705-5_15

18. Klein, C.A., Olson, K.W., Pugh, D.R.: Use of force and attitude sensors for locomotion of a legged vehicle over irregular terrain. Int. J. Robot. Res. **2**(2), 3–17 (2016). https://doi.org/10.1177/027836498300200201

19. Zhao, Y., Chai, X., Gao, F., Qi, C.: Obstacle avoidance and motion planning scheme for a hexapod robot Octopus-III. Robot. Auton. Syst. **103**, 199–212 (2018). https://doi.org/10.1016/j.robot.2018.01.007

20. García-López, M.C., Gorrostieta-Hurtado, E., Vargas-Soto, E., Ramos-Arreguín, J.M., Sotomayor-Olmedo, A., Morales, J.C.M.: Kinematic analysis for trajectory generation in one leg of a hexapod robot. Proc. Technol. **3**, 342–350 (2012). https://doi.org/10.1016/j.protcy.2012.03.037

21. Yu, W., Turk, G., Liu, C.K.: Learning symmetric and low-energy locomotion. ACM Trans. Graph. **37**(4), 144:1–144:12 (2018). https://doi.org/10.1145/3197517.3201397

22. Barfoot, T.D., Earon, E.J.P., D'Eleuterio, G.M.T.: Experiments in learning distributed control for a hexapod robot. Robot. Auton. Syst. **54**(10), 864–872 (2006). https://doi.org/10.1016/j.robot.2006.04.009

23. Ross, S.M.: Introduction to Probability Models. Academic Press, Berkeley (2014)

24. Kirchner, F.: Q-learning of complex behaviours on a six-legged walking machine. Robot. Auton. Syst. **25**(3), 253–262 (1998). https://doi.org/10.1016/S0921-8890(98)00054-2

25. Youcef, Z., Pierre, C.: Control of the trajectory of a hexapod robot based on distributed Q-learning. In: 2004 IEEE International Symposium on Industrial Electronics, vol. 1, pp. 277–282 (2004)

26. Shahriari, M., Khayyat, A.A.: Gait analysis of a six-legged walking robot using fuzzy reward reinforcement learning. In: 2013 13th Iranian Conference on Fuzzy Systems (IFSC), pp. 1–4 (2013)

27. Hong, J., Tang, K., Chen, C.: Obstacle avoidance of hexapod robots using fuzzy Q-learning. In: 2017 IEEE Symposium Series on Computational Intelligence (SSCI), pp. 1–6 (2017)

28. Konen, K., Korthals, T., Melnik, A., Schilling, M.: Biologically-inspired deep reinforcement learning of modular control for a six-legged robot. In: 2019 IEEE International Conference on Robotics and Automation Workshop. Montreal, CA (2019)

29. Silver, D., Lever, G., Heess, N., Degris, T., Wierstra, D., Riedmiller, M.: Deterministic policy gradient algorithms. In: Xing, E.P., Jebara, T. (eds.) Proceedings of the 31st International Conference on Machine Learning, pp. 387–395. PMLR, Bejing (2014)

30. Schulman, J., Wolski, F., Dhariwal, P., Radford, A., Klimov, O.: Proximal policy optimization algorithms. arXiv:1707.06347 (2017)

31. Francois-Lavet, V., Henderson, P., Islam, R., Bellemare, M.G., Pineau, J.: An introduction to deep reinforcement learning. FNT Mach. Learn. **11**, 219–354 (2018). https://doi.org/10.1561/2200000071

32. Lillicrap, T.P., et al.: Continuous control with deep reinforcement learning. arXiv:1509.02971 [cs, stat] (2019)

33. Haarnoja, T., Zhou, A., Abbeel, P., Levine, S.: Soft actor-critic: off-policy maximum entropy deep reinforcement learning with a stochastic actor. arXiv:1801.01290 (2018)

34. Ha, S., Xu, P., Tan, Z., Levine, S., Tan, J.: Learning to walk in the real world with minimal human effort. arXiv:2002.08550 (2020)

35. Lagoudakis, M.G., Parr, R.: Least-Squares Policy Iteration. J. Mach. Learn. Res. **4**, 1107–1149 (2003)

36. Gazebo Homepage. http://gazebosim.org/. Accessed 07 Apr 2020

Lockdown or Unlock in COVID-19 Disease? A Reinforcement Learning Approach

Jacobo Gerardo González León$^{(\boxtimes)}$ and Miguel Félix Mata Rivera$^{(\boxtimes)}$

Avenida Instituto Politécnico Nacional No. 2580, Col Barrio la Laguna Ticomán,
Gustavo A. Madero, Ciudad de Mexico, 07340 Mexico City, Mexico
jgonzalezl1007@alumno.ipn.mx, mmatar@ipn.mx

Abstract. Since the big arrival of COVID-19 in our lives and from the lockdown as a solution that, as an organized society we have proposed in most populations to control the epidemic, it could generate in us a series of questions: how do we know that we have made the best decision? what value do our decisions have? In terms of what could we measure such effectiveness? This article presents the first results of an IA-driven approach, to tries to answer these questions from different simulations generated using reinforced learning and real data experience.

Keywords: Reinforcement learning · COVID-19 · AI-Driven

1 Introduction

Being able to imagine moving in time, and memory, either backward (towards the past) or projecting oneself, forward (towards the future) has been an idea widely explored over time since the existence of consciousness, some they describe it as a human capacity [1]. Regardless of the linguistic label that we can put on it, humans, we can realize our ability to perceive, that function that our brain has to recognize itself, first, as an individual body that is within an environment, the world; this reality is always built from data that can capture and recover our senses, later this data reaches the brain and it reconstructs reality (the present) from its perception, stores some memories, structures, and abstract rules (the past). With all this information stored, in the environment, we can control our actions, not only that, but we can also modify these abstract rules if we see fit.

We also have been able to abstract this process in computational solutions in two ways, on the one hand, we can predict and inference, as a result of statistical learning theory, through the inductive learning process [2] where a machine learning method can estimate these unknown relationships, from the historical experience that the data can offer. This results in a multivariable model in terms of an explained variable, or target; and one or more explanatory variables, or features. Once these relationships have been accurately estimated (it is then necessary to measure), they can be used to predict future expected results from new data, that is, the generalization is used as a prediction method.

M. F. Mata-Rivera et al. (Eds.): WITCOM 2020, CCIS 1280, pp. 202–214, 2020.
https://doi.org/10.1007/978-3-030-62554-2_15

On the other hand, and based on the theories of optimal control applied in automation, and the cognitive and psychological theories on the behavior and conditioning of intelligent beings (humans, monkeys, dogs, rats, and other species), so vastly studied over time by various authors, today, we can abstract control through a dynamic system that is able of mapping situations to actions, based on the optimization of some type of gain over time.

In a given environment, an agent will collect some immediate rewards that will be again in the long term from his actions. The union of control, making decisions about a certain environment, and prediction, given the historical knowledge of the past, calculating the future, is called Reinforcement Learning (RL) [3]. RL is a set of design strategies to solve combinational, sequential, and/or decision-making problems. This framework, and amazing study area, seeks to re-create simulations given certain information of the problem, to observe the relationships between control and prediction [4], that is, to generate the simulation where an agent has to behave in a given environment This environment can be designed discretely or continuously, through states. In its purest version, a state must contain the information necessary to make inferences in the future without accumulating a history, since the result of the RL is an intelligent system that makes decisions from the present, without memory.

Since coronavirus disease (COVID-19) is a newly discovered coronavirus informed by the World Health Organization (WHO), a few reports have been found about works in reinforcement learning. In summary, first in [5] reports a review of how new technologies, like data science, machine learning, and artificial intelligence, are used to tackle the COVID-19 disease. In this article reports 3 worked related to the Drug Discovery problem with reinforcement learning. Then in [6] shown an interesting real-time forecasting approach to get into the problem of public health intervention policies with the focus on the spread of COVID. Lastly, in [7] they used RL to create simulations and so they can detect the infection rate by the early identification through the Social Internet of Things. Finally, in [8] they create an AI-Driven approach to generate optimal lockdown policies counting in balance health and economic costs based on graph theory, much of our modeling approach is taken from this great article.

1.1 Problem Statement

Following the current problem of the incessant mortality that is taking place worldwide due to COVID-19 (see Fig. 1), a deep question arises: if we had the possibility of knowing the impact of our decisions, then could we find an optimal way to calculate the cost of our actions and reduce the COVID-19 consequences through humanity? This article is the first approach to this big and complex problem and answer first the following question: in what terms do we want to measure the results of these actions? using RL as a framework to calculate the profit of the possible actions. Through this AI-Driven approach, we try to answer this specific question by simulation-based with the data experience, Reinforcement Learning, and real data.

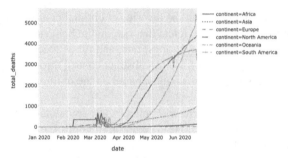

Fig. 1. A line plot for each continent showing the increase in total deaths over time.

2 Searching the Best Rewards Function

The key question that is intended to be answered with the results of this work is: in the face of the entry of COVID-19 in all the populations of the whole world as a possible pandemic, and assuming we only have two possible actions (lockdown or unlock), what would be the best action to take to minimize the COVID-19 impact in humanity? and to answer it satisfactorily, we should first ask the following two questions: how to measure the actions that could be taken over time leave? And in what terms do we want to measure the results of these actions? To answer this first question, and since this problem is multidimensional, it depends on time and space, and we propose to analyze it as a sequential decision-making problem and real data; since we had not a real model of the disease, we found a model based on data experience. In this first approach to the problem, it is proposed to find the best variables that characterize the phenomenon, and in a second approach, we simulated a dynamic system that, in time and space, moves and makes decisions, and the calculation of the future, given the past, as an approximation solution for know the result of possible actions. So, the following solutions are proposed and will be discussed throughout this section:

- Feature selection of the COVID-19 phenomenon, through a basic implementation of the classic Knowledge Discovery in Databases (KDD) [9] knowledge discovery methodology widely used throughout the years in Data Mining [10] and which is also a key piece of Data Science recently [11].
- Reinforcement Learning (RL) as a framework to model the sequential problem of decision-making, and which, among all its benefits, provides a dynamic system that can move in time and space, a policy Optimal control and estimate of values associated with states in discrete time using any approximation paradigm, including machine learning methods. This allows us to find the value of the different actions that could be taken shortly.
- Feed-Forward Back-Propagation Artificial Neural Network (ANN) as said approach method in the RL framework for calculating the value of the pair (discrete-time, action) in the absence of a real epidemiological model of COVID-19.

2.1 Getting Data

One of the main problems when carrying out any analysis based on data is precisely finding the most reliable open data source, and many times this can be a limitation to finding valuable information. Fortunately, and in the case of this project, the data set "Coronavirus Pandemic (COVID-19)"[1] from the "Our World in Data" initiative was found, which is supported by researchers from the University of Oxford, who are those in charge of the scientific edition; and the Global Change Data Lab organization, who maintain the site. The data provided there every day, and for this work, they were used from 2019-12-31 to 2020-06-19. In Fig. 2 we can see the completeness of the data set that has the following dimensions: 34 features and 24,395 observations. Within these variables, we can find temporal, geographic, counts, etc. For summary purposes, they can be grouped as follows:

- Time feature (date type):

  - {date}

- Geography features (categorical type):

  - {iso_code, continent, location}

- Count of cases, tests and deaths (numeric type):

  - {total_deaths, new_deaths, total_cases_per_million, new_cases_per_million, total_deaths_per_million, new_deaths_per_million, total_tests, new_tests, total_tests_per_thousand, new_tests_per_thousand, new_tests_smoothed, new_tests_smoothed_per_thousand, tests_units}

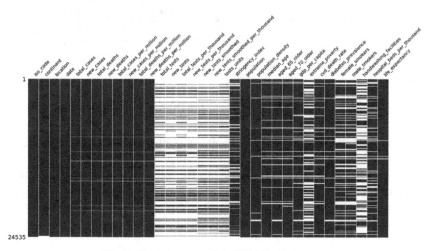

Fig. 2. Completeness of the COVID-19 data set.

---

[1] Coronavirus Pandemic (COVID-19) data source https://ourworldindata.org/coronavirus.

- Sociodemographic features (numeric type):

  - {stringency_index, population, population_density, median_age. aged_65_older, aged_70_older, gdp_per_capita, extreme_poverty, cvd_death_rate, diabetes_ prevalence, female_smokers, male_smokers, handwashing_facilities, hospital_ beds_per_thousand, life_expectancy}.

2.2 Data Wrangling

To carry out a good analysis based on data, and trying to take advantage of its vast and complex experience, through machine learning, the first step is to ensure that this is data quality and is understandable [12], for both humans and computers. Once we have the chosen data set to analyze, it is time to ensure quality through cleaning and preprocessing this data. As could be seen in the previous section, these data come with an evident lack of values for different variables. Figure 3 shows better what these variables are, the count of observations, and their percentage of completeness. The closer to 1 means that they are more complete, and the closer to 0 it means that they are emptier.

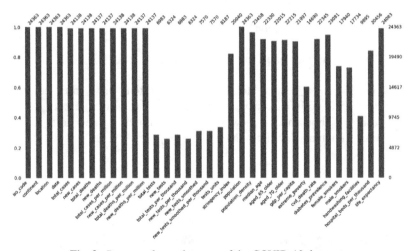

Fig. 3. Percent of completeness of the COVID-19 data set.

As a solution to the problem of missing values and other problems that could affect the quality of this data, there are methods of cleaning and preprocessing data [13]. This phase begins with a "dirty" data set, which means that the data set presents various symptoms such as the aforementioned incompleteness in its values, and also other ailments, such as duplicate observations, anomalous, or outliers, erroneous values, among others; and it ends with a "clean" data set, which means that the data set is closest to having a high quality.

The first step was to eliminate the columns that represented an incompleteness of 90% because for this project it was not necessary to carry out too much pre-processing of data, because the idea is hardly being built, this is a prototype of the solution. In Fig. 4 it can be seen that some columns, even though the threshold to discard incomplete variables was very close to 100%, there are still variables with incomplete values. In this case, there are usually two ways to solve it, or the observations with incomplete values are eliminated, but observations that in other variables may be very valuable to keep would-be lost; or are preserved and these missing values are calculated. As a solution, and since all these variables are naturally numerical, it was chosen to fill each one with the expected value of their distributions, that is, the average of each of these features.

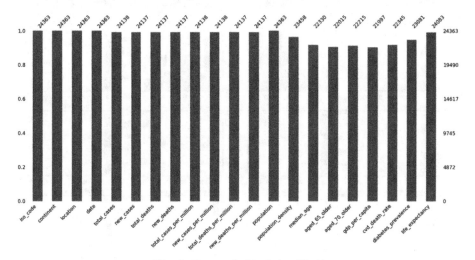

Fig. 4. Features before being filled.

At the end of this phase, and as already mentioned before, the main objective of cleaning and pre-processing is to increase the quality of the data, since they are the basic intake for machine learning methods to learn with the experience of these data. This step is also extremely necessary for humans to interpret the results found. Then, after submitting to a deep understanding of the data, since for the cleaning of the data we must enter into context with the case study being analyzed, we can now suggest modeling the problem by proposing machine learning methods as a helper for the approximation of a phenomenon given the data. This modeling always has to be done trying to take care of the trade-off between bias and variance, because in this type of multivariate analysis there is a "curse" when high dimensions are used to approximate a particular phenomenon, that is, in the space of features, the more the dimensions with which you want to approximate the relationship between the explained variable and explanatory variables are increased, the dispersion of your observations also increases and this leads to a low performance when making predictions with methods based on data [14].

Figure 5 shows the 16 features resulting from this already clean dataset, survivors of the previous processes. As can be seen, most of the variables that have greater variance and range in their values correspond to socio-economic features, while the features that correspond to the COVID-19 phenomenon count have few values accumulated in a range very short. Which of all these variables will be the "best"?

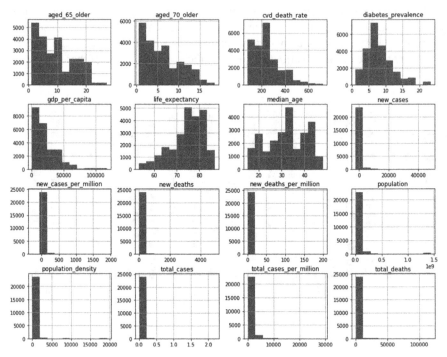

Fig. 5. Final 16 features before being selected by their importance.

2.3 Feature Selection

From the perspective of this first problem statement, when incorporating machine learning to correctly approach a particular phenomenon, it is necessary to find the balance between complexity and error; the so-called optimal complexity is shown in Fig. 6 is achieved by suitably increasing the complexity of the dimensions in which the problem is represented, without increasing as much variance, since this causes the "curse" of high dimensionality, but neither so few dimensions, as this causes a huge bias.

Then, once the data as close to "high quality" as much as possible were obtained, the phenomenon was modeled in a multidimensional way. From the 16 surviving variables of the previous preprocessing process, the most relevant features were selected when modeling the problem as a classification, that is, given these 16 features, finding an approximation function that is capable of accurately classifying the geographic provenance, at the level of continuous granularity, of new data presented. The classifier used

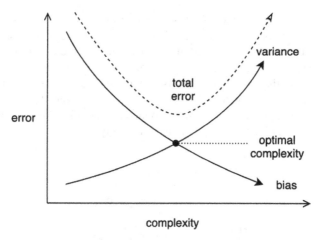

Fig. 6. Bias-variance trade-off to get the best optimal complexity multivariable model.

for this phase of the project was Random Forest, as one of its many advantages lies in its ability to calculate the most important features to describe the phenomenon from which it is learning.

Table 1 shows the increase in Accuracy of the classification, when all the data are presented, and when only the most important features found by the classifier itself are presented. As can be seen, selecting the 6 most important features presents a slight increase in the performance of the model compared to choosing all, also from the fact that this selection of characteristics also serves to lighten the calculation as it works as a method of reducing the dimensionality. These 6 best features generate the state space shown in RL formulation, to find the best complexity that reduces the error of the approximation found with the model from the data experience.

Table 1. Comparison between different experiments to find the best features.

Experiment	Accuracy
16 features	0.9220
5 features importance	0.8875
6 features importance	0.9244
7 features importance	0.9119

2.4 Measures

To answer the second question, in what terms do we want to measure the results of these actions? we use an RL approach to simulate these actions. So, two different measures were proposed, to compare between them what is the best way to measure the consequences of our supposed actions (lockdown or unlock). But first, we started with the following assumption that can be visualized in Fig. 7; going a little deeper into the population density, which is measured in how many people there would be per square kilometer, we could assume that, if at a certain point in time, our agent decided to unlock as a health measure, the probability that its population could move for all this square kilometer is 90%, as there is no mobility control; while if our agent decided to lockdown as a sanitary measure, the probability that its population could move in the area is 10%, since at most they could reach a close radius of mobility.

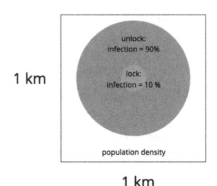

Fig. 7. Assumptions about COVID-19 disease spread.

Once the probability of expansion of the disease has been proposed, and based on the table "properties of the disease" in the research work reported in [8]. The following two ways of measuring the consequences of actions are proposed:

- Calculate the **possible deaths** through the following equation:

$$
\begin{aligned}
possible\ deaths = {} & people\ infected \times P(death) + population\ density \\
& \times P(infection|action) \times P(death) \times incubation\ days
\end{aligned} \tag{1}
$$

- Calculate the **possible recovered** through the following equation:

$$
\begin{aligned}
possible\ recovered = {} & people\ infected \times P(recovered) + population\ density \\
& \times P(infection|action) \times P(recovered) \times incubation\ days
\end{aligned} \tag{2}
$$

Where $P(recovered)$ is the probability that someone infected could be recovered, $P(death)$ are the probability that someone infected dies, $P(infection|action)$ is the probability of spreading the infection given one of the two actions.

2.5 Reinforcement Learning as a Framework to Control + Prediction

One of the features of this problem proposed in this article is that we are trying to model as sequential decision-making, and as this is a phenomenon of a dynamic but discrete nature over time (since the granularity of the problem is proposed for the different days for which there are historical data), it is proposed then to use an "off-policy" approach since we are much more interested in knowing the result of the actions than the value of the states, in addition to how the advantage of proposing an asynchronous approach, the "prediction" could be solved with a parametric approximation method, such as a neural network for example [15].

The Q-Learning algorithm [16] fits perfectly into the "control" solution where, through different episodes, in an environment given by the state space, an agent will take different actions using a ε-greedy mechanism, generating profits in the function of the two measures presented in the previous section. Choosing this algorithm also solves the "prediction" part of the pair values (state-action). So, the elements of the RL framework were defined as follows:

- The state space are the 6 most important features found in the Feature Selection, that is, {aged_70_older ',' aged_65_older ',' median_age ',' life_expectancy ',' diabetes_prevalence ',' cvd_death_rate '}.
- The action space is two, {lockdown, unlock}.
- Two possible rewards functions through actions are rewarded {possible deaths, possible recovered}.

3 Early Results

To achieve comparison of the results found from the simulation offered by the RL framework through the Q-learning algorithm, and to answer the great question of this research project, in what terms do we want to measure the results of these actions? the decision was made to choose half of the data to train the agent, to discover the value of the states, and the other half of the data to test that once the agent has learned. This results in four experiments, one for each measure proposed (possible deaths and possible recovered), one for each simulation (train and test).

The actions are taken over time, and space, are shown in Fig. 8 for each reward function and each simulation. It is remarkable to see, how in both training lap, these actions are predominantly unlocked, and at test time many of these decisions have been changed. In both test cases, there is more variation with both actions. This is how our agent decided to lock or unlock in the time and different populations. The size of each point is related to the population index of this world region.

In Fig. 9 we can see the result of each 2 measures proposed, for each train and test datasets. Here it is shown, that how our agent can minimize the possible deaths and maximize the possible recovered. Particularly, the possible recovered is also optimistic and had values very drastic [−500k, 400k] meanwhile the possible deaths shown a minimization in the range [−10k, 10k], this last measure is best that the original range for the total deaths [0, 60k] with an ascendant curve vs the flat curve generated by our agent's decisions.

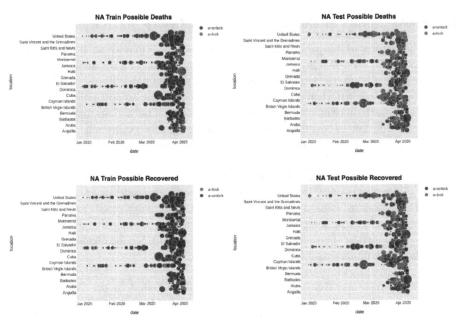

Fig. 8. First results of the 4 experiments in terms of the best actions through North America (NA) subset study case.

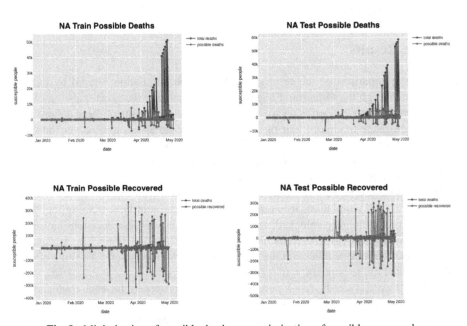

Fig. 9. Minimization of possible deaths vs maximization of possible recovered.

4   Conclusion and Discussion

Through a first approach to the problem, an effort was made to answer the question: in what terms do we want to measure the results of these actions (lockdown or unlock) derived from the COVID-19 pandemic? And the answer is: measure with possible deaths the impact. So, in this paper, we showed an RL approach that possible could help to minimize the COVID-19 disease and flatting the curve of possible deaths. This analysis has only been done in one region of the world, so experimentation with other regions of the world will continue. There are still many things to continue working and showing, the idea most close is to propose a multi-step lock-a-head mechanism in the variable incubation days to reach the calculation of these reward functions, to perform a variant calculation over time, since real life is stochastic; add the new action "hold", that will keep the previous action until there is a change of decision. Whatever this early result showed should be validated with more data to be a strong and serious solution approach.

References

1. Corballis, M.C.: Mental time travel, language, and evolution. Neuropsychologia **134**, 107202 (2019). https://doi.org/10.1016/j.neuropsychologia.2019.107202
2. Kantardzic, M.: Learning from data. In: Data Mining: Concepts, Models, Methods, and Algorithms, pp. 97–163. Wiley-IEEE Press (2019)
3. Sutton, R.S., Barto, A.G.: Introduction. In: Reinforcement Learning: An Introduction. MIT Press (2018)
4. Sugiyama, M., Hachiya, H.: Introduction to reinforcement learning. In: Statistical Reinforcement Learning, pp. 3–14. Chapman & Hall/CRC (2013)
5. Kumar, A., Gupta, P.K., Srivastava, A.: A review of modern technologies for tackling COVID-19 pandemic. Diabetes Metab. Syndr. Clin. Res. Rev. **14**, 569–573 (2020). https://doi.org/10.1016/j.dsx.2020.05.008
6. Ge, Q., et al.: Recurrent Neural Reinforcement Learning for Counterfactual Evaluation of Public Health Interventions on the Spread of Covid-19 in the world. medRxiv. 2020.07.08.20149146 (2020). https://doi.org/10.1101/2020.07.08.20149146
7. Wang, B., Sun, Y., Duong, T.Q., Nguyen, L.D., Hanzo, L.: Risk-aware identification of highly suspected COVID-19 cases in social IoT: a joint graph theory and reinforcement learning approach. IEEE Access **8**, 115655–115661 (2020). https://doi.org/10.1109/ACCESS.2020.3003750
8. Khadilkar, H., Ganu, T., Seetharam, D.P.: Optimising lockdown policies for epidemic control using reinforcement learning. Trans. Indian Natl. Acad. Eng. **5**(2), 129–132 (2020). https://doi.org/10.1007/s41403-020-00129-3
9. Han, J., Kamber, M., Pei, J.: Introduction. In: Data Mining, pp. 1–38. Elsevier (2012). https://doi.org/10.1016/b978-0-12-381479-1.00001-0
10. Nisbet, R., Miner, G., Yale, K.: Theoretical considerations for data mining. In: Handbook of Statistical Analysis and Data Mining Applications, pp. 21–37. Elsevier (2018). https://doi.org/10.1016/b978-0-12-416632-5.00002-5
11. Kotu, V., Deshpande, B.: Introduction. In: Data Science, pp. 1–18. Elsevier (2019). https://doi.org/10.1016/b978-0-12-814761-0.00001-0
12. Loshin, D.: Dimensions of data quality. In: Enterprise Knowledge Management, pp. 101–124. Elsevier (2001). https://doi.org/10.1016/b978-012455840-3.50005-4

13. Kotu, V., Deshpande, B.: Data science process. In: Data Science, pp. 19–37. Elsevier (2019). https://doi.org/10.1016/b978-0-12-814761-0.00002-2
14. Cohen, S.: The basics of machine learning: strategies and techniques. In: Artificial Intelligence and Deep Learning in Pathology, pp. 13–40. Elsevier (2021). https://doi.org/10.1016/b978-0-323-67538-3.00002-6
15. Bertsekas, D.: Parametric approximation. In: Reinforcement Learning and Optimal Control, pp. 126–171. Athena Scientific (2019)
16. Sewak, M.: Temporal difference learning, SARSA, and Q-learning. In: Sewak, M. (ed.) Deep Reinforcement Learning, pp. 51–63. Springer, Singapore (2019). https://doi.org/10.1007/978-981-13-8285-7_4

Cybersecurity Analysis on PACS-DICOM Servers in Chile

David Cordero Vidal(✉) and Cristian Barría Huidobro(✉)

Vicerrectoría de Investigación, Centro de Investigación En Ciberseguridad CICS,
Universidad Mayor, Santiago, Chile
david.cordero@mayor.cl, cristian.barria@umayor.cl

Abstract. Today the internet and the interconnection of equipment are a fundamental part of all organizations, payment systems, SCADA systems, medical equipment and others, and all are interconnected to facilitate data processing and thus optimize the work on these.

Services based on the DICOM protocol (Digital Imaging and Communications in Medicine) are used in medical equipment architectures around the world, because this is the universal format for exchanging medical images. PACS (Picture Archiving and Communication System) servers use this protocol to communicate.

The purpose of this work is to corroborate the information provided by recent research (2019–2020) regarding cybersecurity studies on PACS servers under the DICOM protocol, specifically the services that are operating in Chile.

The experimental design proposed by this research allows the passive, that is to say non-intrusive, discovery of operating nodes in Chile, the categorization of these nodes, the analysis of the data obtained, as well as the validation to create information from thus evidencing the exposure of these systems. Due to this problem, questions such as the following arise: Does the exposure of the data indicated in the related investigations turn out to be verifiable? A diagnosis of the current situation in the Country would allow us to identify the exposure of vulnerabilities in these services?

The following research aims to answer these questions, presenting an experimental search design and corroborating works presented in this area, which consider a specific geographical area such as Chile.

Keywords: PACS servers · Dicom protocol · Vulnerability · Country analysis

1 Introduction

Services based on the DICOM protocol (Digital Imaging and Communications in Medicine) are used in medical equipment architectures throughout the world, because this protocol is the universal format for the exchange of medical images. PACS (Picture Archiving and Communication System) servers use this protocol to communicate, however, this communication leaves them exposed to different threats, which are presented in various investigations that publicly expose vulnerabilities in these technologies, allowing I tend to third parties to obtain data from the presentations, mainly medical, that are made through these teams.

© Springer Nature Switzerland AG 2020
M. F. Mata-Rivera et al. (Eds.): WITCOM 2020, CCIS 1280, pp. 215–224, 2020.
https://doi.org/10.1007/978-3-030-62554-2_16

Considering the above, it is possible to find research based on the vulnerability of these protocols, such as the one published in early 2020 by Wang [1] where he exposes his risk edges from the use of Fuzzing technology, with which Failures in PACS servers were found, allowing the denial of services by third parties. Similarly, the one prepared by Desjardins [2] that indicates the importance of protecting DICOM images against vulnerable services.

On the other hand, different organizations contribute to the exposure of these risks, as is the case of Greenbone [3], who carried out a global security study in September 2019, publishing a list of PACS servers that operate under the DICOM protocol in the world, in addition to vulnerable nodes, from which patient examinations could be extracted, and eventually publish their results. Another contribution is that made by Samtani [4] who identified SCADA services connected to the internet, through massive recognition tools, such as Shodan (search engine for devices connected to the internet) [5] that supports the recognition process passive for node research. Without a doubt, through Shodan it is possible to carry out a massive search for certain services, identifying exposed ports, protocols, application names and even versions of these.

PACS servers that operate under the DICOM protocol normally operate on ports 11112 and 104, whose data storage operation on PACS servers (storage node) works from the interconnection from different sources (medical machinery) a laboratory, which can focus works from different organizations (radiographs, documentation, various files) even on the same server. This is how from a scan that uses combinations of search operators through Shodan, ports and protocols of a certain service are filtered, with which the nodes connected to the internet that meet this criterion are identified, thus obtaining information from of a passive scan of these services; It should be noted that this search is historical, since the data that Shodan provides is information that it collects over time.

Another edge to the vulnerabilities presented is the existence of the PACS Viewer that allows viewing the content of files in the DICOM format; These data are housed in PACS servers or devices with the ability to serve these antecedents, from a connection to one of these servers, some of the so-called PACS Viewers allow remote access to said nodes, if they are found. When configured without protection, password or security policies, it is possible to view the data from these servers without having to authenticate, allowing a third party to obtain the files and develop elaborate scripts to build a person's behavior, profile or situation in particular from the aforementioned vulnerabilities.

In this order of ideas, the purpose of the research is to corroborate the information provided by the research presented above regarding the study on cybersecurity in the PACS-DICOM servers, covering the active nodes that are currently operating in Chile.

In this way, it is expected to publicize the situation in the country, the dangers of the data when they remain exposed, and show the existence of vulnerabilities in critical systems such as medical systems, thus alerting organizations, companies or institutions so that they consider the necessary precautions and are in a position to mitigate this type of vulnerability, corroborating and counteracting the quantitative and technical antecedents applied in related works.

The data obtained in this work are compiled from a script developed exclusively for this research, which analyzed the availability of forty-seven (47) servers located in Chile, of which fourteen (14) allow obtaining of data; This procedure was applied based on a proposed experimental design to scan these security breaches, allowing the discovery, categorization, analysis and validation of the exposed nodes.

2   Experimental Design of Data Discovery, Categorization, Analysis and Validation

In order to diagnose the active nodes in Chile, it is necessary to collect the information available on the internet from the use of a massive protocol and port scanner such as Shodan; It is also necessary to develop a script in the Python programming language, which allows to automate the access verification, and the possible extraction and segregation of the data, to obtain information from the nodes. This whole process can be divided into four stages, namely: 1) scanning for the collection of information available on the internet; 2) categorization of the available nodes, making queries and requests for access to data and checking access to them; 3) analysis of data from their extraction, and 4) validation of the data obtained from vulnerable servers, which allows to demonstrate the risks that expose a node to the attack of a third party; All this process from an investigative point of view, without revelation or specific identification of the information associated with a node.

2.1   Discovery of Available Nodes

It is possible to point out that in our digital world the interconnection of services becomes essential, medical devices and their instrumentation need to be available on the internet for daily work, and within these services are the PACS-DICOM servers that store the results of each one of the exams that are applied every day, and whose information from medical centers, patient data, doctors and specialists in the area, can be scanned by third parties from any geographical location that allows a connection to cyberspace.

Consequently, Shodan (cited again) allows a massive and constant scan to devices connected to the internet, looking for services, servers, IOT devices, protocols, also classifying ports and even analyzing software versions and their ISP providers, among others. As this tool is similar to the service provided by Google (search engine), since these antecedents are stored in the Shodan database, thus facilitating access to consult this information in real time as well as historical information through its services API.

Therefore, just by searching through its website, using combinations of search operators, it is possible to filter all the computers connected to the internet that work under a certain protocol, even filtering it by country, port or program used. From its API it is possible to develop an algorithm that periodically automates the search for services and ports by regions, in order to keep a list of servers updated, in this case PACS-DICOM that requires monitoring.

Services Available in Chile: Through the service provided by Shodan by consulting its API and by means of an automated algorithm developed for this research, it is possible to show 47 (forty-seven) PACS-DICOM servers are operating in Chile through the Internet under the DICOM protocol, this sample of servers was filtered and studied from the daily scan of permanently and sporadic active services during the months of April, May and June 2020. Some of these services are operational intermittently (in some organizations these teams are turn off or disconnect from the network at specific intervals of days), and in others they correspond to computers for personal use which have DICOM services and store information related to clinical organizations, said number of servers (47) is the total number of servers detected with activity during the 3 months of follow-up and that were found in the region declared in this investigation (Chile). They also correspond to services that have ports 104 and 11,112 open which correspond to the scope of the investigation, these protocols are those defined by default in the DICOM protocol. The following is the information obtained from this passive quest through Shodan.

- IP of the nodes (servers that operate under the DICOM protocol).
- Open ports (Extended consultation of services by IP found).
- Operator (internet service provider).
- Approximate location.
- Search date (last update in the database by Shodan).

From the list of nodes found by the Shodan API, it is possible to determine a search path, automatically consulting each node and verifying if it is possible to obtain data.

2.2 Categorization of Nodes

By searching for available nodes on the Internet, periodic queries are made to the collected IP addresses. Through the Nmap scanning software, the open ports of the node are verified, thus storing the ports that are active, the software used by the node and their version. Once the results of the Shodan and Nmap scan have been verified, validation tests are performed based on the use of the WADO protocol, verifying access to the data by validating queries on port 104 and 11,112, without using access credentials or access method. authentication on the consulted server, the nodes that responded with information were classified as potential victims of third-party attacks, it should be noted that in the present investigation I only cover consultations on the previously named ports, without taking into account software versions and other protocols exposed in these vulnerable servers available on the internet.

2.3 Analysis of Data Collection

There are free access tools that allow viewing medical images (DICOM). These are known as PACS Viewers and allow you to see, study and categorize these images. Some of these viewers can be connected to third-party servers in order to extract information through internal networks or the internet.

There are open source development projects that allow connection to PACS-DICOM servers. from public algorithms; Libraries like Pynetdicom or Pynetdicom3 support the development of programs that allow connection to these nodes [6], thus allowing the creation of custom scripts that automate the download of data.

With the information obtained from the search and diagnosis of available nodes, it is possible to go through each studied IP, consulting whether access to the data does not have any type of authentication, through ports 11.112 and 104.

The DICOM communication protocol uses other protocols that are part of itself to perform communication between systems and information nodes, these allow the transmission of medical images between devices, the C-FIND protocol in charge of searching and retrieving available data and the C-GET, C-MOVE protocols which are very similar in their operation and are in charge of recovering the information from the nodes informing applications and integrated services of the performance of these operations, the information nodes that are available on the internet They use a data transmission protocol called WADO, this being the standard for the recovery of data in DICOMweb images with which it is possible to obtain image information, data related to patient examinations or information from the institution or body that stores them, these data defined from available PACS-DICOM servers.

This latest WADO protocol also allows the visualization of information from third-party software connections, the so-called PACS viewers as shown in the following figure (see Fig. 1), the operation of the aforementioned protocols which allow searching is summarized. and DICOM image retrieval [7], informing servers that an application wants to execute a file transfer, to transfer data and images from servers.

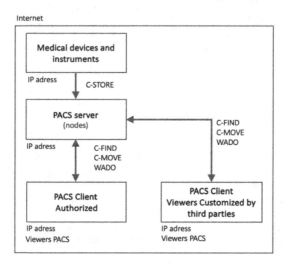

Fig. 1. C-FIND, C-MOVE -WADO methods to obtain information.

2.4 Validation of Data Obtained from Vulnerable Nodes

By obtaining the files (images) of each vulnerable node available on the internet (PACS-DICOM server), access to them can be validated through queries without sending authentication credentials, executing data transfer processes using the WADO protocol of DICOMweb. Below are some of the attributes retrieved from these files, which expose the metadata information for them.

- Unique identifier of the patient (Unique Tax Role).
- Date of birth.
- Sex.
- Name of the exam performed.
- Date of the exam performed.
- Time of the exam performed.
- Organization that stores the exam.
- Exam images.
- Professional in charge of the exam.

2.5 Experimental Design Process

This process of diagnosis, analysis, validation and extraction of data on vulnerable nodes can be applied in any region of the world. This process can be seen in the following figure (see Fig. 2).

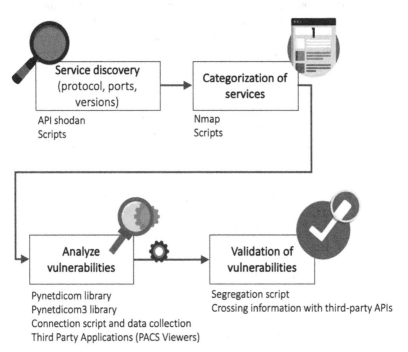

Fig. 2. The figure shows how the automation process is in the discovery, categorization, analysis and validation of the data obtained from vulnerable PACS-DICOM servers.

3 Metrics of the Data Obtained

From the data extraction by means of a Script (automated process), it is possible to determine the number of servers that are in a given region. This research focuses on the available nodes in Chile, so the following metrics only refer to this country. The following table shows the number of PACS-DICOM servers that are operating in Chile versus the servers that are vulnerable in that country, that is, servers from which data can be obtained from queries without the need for authenticate (Table 1).

Table 1. PACS-DICOM servers that are active in Chile vs. vulnerable PACS-DICOM servers in Chile.

PACS servers in Chile	Number of servers
Operational servers	47
Vulnerable servers	14

Table 2 refers to the number of vulnerable servers that operate in Chile under the DICOM communication protocol found during the months of April May and June 2020 and that work with the ports used by default in the DICOM protocol, port 104 and 11,112 During this study, a node that had both ports open was detected.

Table 2. PACS-DICOM vulnerable servers that are active in Chile separated by ports.

Port number	Number of servers
104	1
11.112	14

With the data obtained from the 14 vulnerable servers identified in this research, it is possible to validate studies such as those carried out by the Greenbone organization, since from this data and by running scripts that classify and filter the information obtained, it was possible to establish the number of Exposed Exams, in the case of this research the sum of the exams corresponds to 212,792 these distributed in the different active and vulnerable nodes in Chile, with this information the number of people identified by sex was identified as shown in the Table 3.

Table 3. Amount of men vs women.

Sex	Number of people identified
Man	46.824
Woman	109.653

It is also possible to segregate affected individuals by age ranges from the date of birth recorded in the data obtained from vulnerable servers, thus defining an age classification of the affected population, including minors (in Chile under 18 years of age)) young adults and older adults, within the information obtained examinations are recorded where the date of birth was not recorded (Table 4).

Table 4. Age range of patients.

Age ranges	Number of people identified
Minors	23.775
Adults	76.192
Elderly	53.020
No birth record	3.490

The exams registered in different medical centers and in organizations that have PACS-DICOM services sometimes identify the same type of exam with different names using small variants (shortened name, acronyms, etc.), the published samples corresponding to types of exams correspond to exams that exactly matched their name in their string format (Table 5).

Table 5. Most performed exams.

Exams performed	Number of exams
Abdominal echo tomography	12.604
Mammography	10.187
Bilateral breast echo tomography	8.322
Echo tomography soft parts or skeletal muscle	7.212

4 Future Work

It is essential that work be carried out covering the entire spectrum of cybersecurity in the country, considering critical infrastructure as that of medical services, as essential, since both its malfunction and the exposure of data can affect directly to the population, and even more so when the current situation of health crisis due to Covid-19 has all these entities at their maximum capacity. Clearly, a cyberattack in these circumstances can cause considerable damage and serious loss.

In the present investigation, we only work from ports 104 and 11,112, considered these as a basic or default installation during the implementation of PACS-DICOM servers in organizations, however, from the discovery of services (first process in the experimental design exposed), other services in common were evidenced, these not related to the DICOM protocol but vulnerable to third parties, these being a source of new research on critical services exposed to targeted attacks.

It is necessary to carry out investigations that include implementation methodologies in the face of data leaks from the services named in this investigation. Validate these implementations and check risk mitigation. Carry out work that shows the flow of risks that directly affect people (exposure of medical data), and the connections of data sources with third parties. Finally, collect stratified information on the people affected, and carry out analyzes that cover other edges of cyber attacks on critical infrastructures [8].

5   Conclusions

With the current health crisis that the world is facing due to the Covid-19, medical services become more fundamental and their availability directly affects people, which highlights their quality of critical infrastructure. The possibility of obtaining data from services that store patient information undoubtedly represents a considerable risk for people who are indexed. Data mining can allow third parties to create user profiles of these systems, increasing risk on an even larger scale, by creating new cybersecurity gaps. It is clear that this information can be used by new intermediaries in illicit crimes that are difficult to foresee, all of which will end up directly affecting a significant percentage of the national population.

The present investigation validated reports and written works referring to vulnerabilities of PACS-DICOM servers, demonstrating that obtaining data from vulnerable nodes is a reality. This allowed us to outline the risk situation in which Chile currently finds itself, all from internet connected services that share medical file data and are exposed, as they lack security or access restrictions for unauthorized personnel.

Also, from the analysis of these data, it was shown that information can be obtained allowing a specific study of a certain percentage of the Chilean population, such information can influence the decision making of organizations that are related to medical systems, insurance or contracts, which ultimately affects the people whose data is stolen.

In short, it is crucial to implement systems that support the mitigation of these types of vulnerabilities, since they can be the gateway to attacks of greater importance, which in the long run allows the taking of control of medical systems, the denial of services, adulteration of results, and the like.

References

1. Wang, Z., et al.: DICOM-Fuzzer: research on DICOM vulnerability mining based on fuzzing technology. In: Gao, H., Feng, Z., Yu, J., Wu, J. (eds.) ChinaCom 2019. LNICSSITE, vol. 312, pp. 509–524. Springer, Cham (2020). https://doi.org/10.1007/978-3-030-41114-5_38
2. Benoit, D., et al.: DICOM images have been hacked! Now what? Am. J. Roentgenol. **214**(4), 727–735 (2020)
3. Greenbone Networks GmbH: Information security report confidential patient data freely accessible on the internet. Ciber resilience report (2019)
4. Samtani, S., Yu, S., Zhu, H., Patton, M., Matherly, J.: Identifying supervisory control and data acquisition (SCADA) devices and their vulnerabilities on the internet of things (IoT): a text mining approach. IEEE Intell. Syst. 1 (2018). https://doi.org/10.1109/mis.2018.111145022

5. Shodan. https://www.shodan.io/. Access 20 June 2020
6. Yepes-Calderon, F., et al.: Extending PACS functionality: towards facilitating the conversion of clinical necessities into research-derived applications. In: Proceedings of SPIE 10160, 12th International Symposium on Medical Information Processing and Analysis, p. 1016015 (2017). https://doi.org/10.1117/12.2264350
7. César, H.V., Cordeiro, S.D.S., dos Santos, E.E.D., Azevedo-Marques, P.M.: Computational tool for estimation of effective dose in computed tomography exams based on DICOM header data extraction. In: 23 Brazilian Congress on Medical Physics, Brazil (2018)
8. Sametinger, J., Rozenblit, J., Lysecky, R., Ott, P.: Security challenges for medical devices. Commun. ACM **58**(4), 74–82 (2015)

Experimental Based-Analisis of the Optimal Transmission Thresholds for WSNs in Noisy Channels

Edgar Romo-Montiel[✉], Mario Eduardo Rivero-Ángeles,
Ricardo Menchaca-Méndez, Herón Molina-Lozano,
and Rolando Menchaca-Méndez

Computer Research Center – Instituto Politécnico Nacional, Mexico City, Mexico
eromom0900@alumno.ipn.mx, mriveroa@ipn.mx,
{ric,hmolina,rmen}@cic.ipn.mx

Abstract. WSNs are a set of autonomous and tiny nodes deployed on a specific area to collect data from the environment. These nodes are limited in energy and processing resources, therefore a correctness planning in the transmission schemes of the nodes improves the WSN performance. Since WSNs are commonly deploy in non-ideal environments, the nodes usually communicate their data messages in a noisy channel.

Specifically, we propose three unscheduled transmission schemes for control packets: Fixed Scheme (FS), Adaptive by Estimation Scheme (AES) and Adaptive by Gamma Scheme (AGS), they are based on contention mechanisms such as the CSMA-NP protocol (Carrier Sense Multiple Access No Persistent). Thus, this study focuses on the sending of control packets where channel conditions are unfriendly, for instance, with presence of noise, interferences and attenuations of the signal. As such, we looked for mechanisms that adjust the nodes' transmission to the channel conditions to reduce energy consumption and reduce the delay in the network due to this process of sending of control packets.

The experimental results of this study suggest that adaptive schemes are preferable for the transmission of the nodes in noisy channels, such that energy consumption and delay are reduced significantly when it carefully chooses setting parameters, as in this work is made.

1 Introduction

A Wireless Sensor Network (WSN) is a set of tiny and autonomous devices called nodes with capabilities to sense environment conditions in the area where is deployed. WSNs also have at least one base station, commonly named as sink node which collects the data from each node.

One node is a device composed by a transceiver, a sensor, a battery and a processing unit (in its most basic format). However, the sink node is a specific device with higher processing, memory and energy capabilities (either with high capacity batteries or with no constraints at all when connected to an electric outlet or by renewable unlimited sources like solar [5] or energy harvesting

© Springer Nature Switzerland AG 2020
M. F. Mata-Rivera et al. (Eds.): WITCOM 2020, CCIS 1280, pp. 225–243, 2020.
https://doi.org/10.1007/978-3-030-62554-2_17

techniques [10]). Since a comercial node is equipped by a typical battery as the energy supply, it is crucial to take care of the energy consumption as much as possible to extend the lifetime of the network [2,3].

Building on this, the use of optimal mechanisms to transmit information have proven that better energy consumption is achieved [8,12]. Thus, we present a proposal to limit the transmission of the nodes to reduce the energy consumption of the nodes. In previous work the limitation of transmissions under thresholds was presented with a significant improvement in the network performance [9,11].

We denoted two kinds of information: *control packets* and *data packets*. The former packets are information of the own nodes which are shared to the network to be discovered and update the network's state. Meanwhile, the second packets are used to send the information collected from the environment [13]. Additionally, control packets commonly are sent in a contention scheme on non-ideal channels, and their information allows to create schedules to assign time periods for each node to guaranty the correct transmission of the data packets (which are the most important because they contain the sensed information).

Mainly, we studied three contention scheme based on the well known CSMA-NP protocol (Carrier Sense Multiple Access - No Persistent) for the transmission of control packets of each node. Specifically, we found and reported the optimal parameters by which the network achieves the best performance. This performance measured through the energy consumption and the delay in the sharing of control packets. To this, we considered a non-ideal channel where noise, interference or others issues are presented and usually are impossible to avoid. Note that [11] is a study in ideal channels, and the work and results in this paper are adding the presence of errors during the transmission of control packets. This work is part of our study of the WSNs and how to improve its performance, initially we looked for the reduction in energy and was solved by minimizing the power of the transmission of nodes through clustering techniques, however, it still required proceses with high energy consumption and delay to create the groups. Based on that, we proposed alternative solutions to improve the performance of WSNs and the controlling of transmission probability of nodes gave a good result, initially it was studied for free-error channels, and subsequently we studied the affect of unfriendly channels. In this work we report the results of this last research, where basically, it is observed that controlling the transmission of the nodes based on the conditions on the channel, highly improves the energy consumption and the delay in the network.

The rest of the paper is organized as follows: Section 2 presents related work, Sect. 3, explains in detail the proposed mechanisms. Then, Sect. 4 presents the system model as well as the main suppositions in this work. We finish this paper presenting relevant numerical results and conclusions.

2   Related Work

Currently, the use of WSNs is taken to solve multiple monitoring tasks, its implementation allows to carry on repetitive tasks in a fashion way such that less man hours are required. Additionally, with the expansion of Internet of the Things, (IoT), WSN take a roll of collectors of information to impulse a more sophisticated system. Based on that, it is crucial to design more efficient systems, specifically, WSNs need to be robust enough to interact with more and more devices but they require energy strategies that extend the lifetime of the network.

In the literature there exist multiple algorithms that look for improvement of energy consumption, such case is data transmission reduction presented in [6] which analyzes reduction transmission in clustering algorithms to improve the energy. This take advantage of the correlation of the information to avoid to transmit repetitive data from different nodes, although they use learning techniques based on Neural Networks, it is no taking care neither in the sending of control packets process, nor the channel conditions.

Recent works use classical clustering techniques with significant improvements, such is the case of [1] which presents a framework to improve the performance of clustering algorithms in WSN by tuning setting parameters such as number of cluster members, the radius of cluster, among others. However it is not considering the control process and the presence of errors in the channel.

Additionally, in [7] it is presented a work which control the transmission rate of nodes based on the traffic in the channel to prevent congestion and fault detection, they are using data science algorithms which demand highly computation, although nowadays the capabilities of devices are enough to process these algorithms, it still is preferable the use of low power techniques to prevent early dead of the nodes. As such they are dealing with techniques to prevent some errors in the channel but not prevent directly the energy consumption issues and do not consider the case where the errors in channel are inevitable.

In summary the state of the art, does not considere the process of sending control messages and the presence of channel errors, although they are obtaining good results, our work presented here contributes to the improvement of the network performance in that process.

3 Proposed Mechanisms

Along this section, we present the mechanisms proposed for the process of sending control packets. Similar to the proposed in [11] these mechanisms were developed in order to reduce energy consumption. It is important to consider that in [9], we also studied the scheme presented here considering noisy channel with a contention scheme based on the CSMA-NP protocol and time slots to divide the channel. In these projects the main idea is to restrict the transmission of control packets employing a *transmission probability*. The main deference with previous work is that the first one does not consider the non- ideal channels and in the case of the second one, the effect on the system due to the presence of errors in the channel is not finely detailed. Therefore, in this work we study various error scenarios and how the parameters for such cases behave.

In error prone channels, it is susceptible to occur collision and idle slots, due to nodes are transmitting in a contention scheme. These events are a big issue by two main reasons: collisions demands retransmission of the nodes and idle slots impacts in reporting delay. Both cases damage resources of the network. Although the network uses a schedule protocol for the transmission of data packets, control packets are sent by a random access protocol, as is considered in LEACH (Low Energy Adaptive Clustering Hierarchy) [4] therefore, the higher energy consumption is in the process of sending control packets.

Specifically, we denote that one node will transmit with *transmission probability* τ in each time slot. However, the value of τ increases as the number of nodes attempting to transmit decreases, and viceversa. Additionally, in the presence of errors like in non-ideal channels, the value of τ also is based on the likelihood of such errors.

For each proposal, we assume that a probability models the existence of errors. We know that unwanted events in the channel are due to many issues like noise, interference, fading, among others. However, we classified all of them in two events: False Positive errors and False Negative errors. The first one occurs with probability P_{e+} while the second occurs with P_{e-}. Commonly a False Positive error is detected as a transmission in the system, but no one of the nodes has transmitted, and a False Negative takes place at the time the network does not detect a transmission.

Below we present our proposal for transmission of nodes in noisy channels.

3.1 Fixed Scheme (FS)

It a simple solution which no considers the conditions of the channel and the nodes will transmit in each time slot with a fixed probability τ. This probability is the setting parameter for this scheme and is the inverse of the total nodes inside the network N, computed as $\tau = \frac{1}{N}$.

We assume that nodes have to transmit only one control packet in determined periods of time called *rounds* where the network state is updated with the information of all the nodes. Until the last node sends its control packet the network monitor the area, consequently, it is desirable that nodes spend the lowest time as possible sending packets due to it increases the delay of the information.

We modeled this as a stochastic process, where nodes transmit their control packets successfully with probability P_s. With probability P_f, the nodes do not transmit a packet in determined time slot. As such P_s is the probability of fulfilling the following sentences:

– Only one of the k remaining nodes transmits, and the rest does not. This behaves as a binomial random variable with parameter k and τ which follows the equation below:

$$P(X = j) = \binom{k}{j}\tau^j(1 - \tau)^{k-j} \qquad (1)$$

Where j is the number of nodes that transmit in a time slot and k is the current number of nodes attempting to transmit. Replacing the value of j

and solving (1) we found that the probability of only one node transmits is:

$$P(X = 1) = \binom{k}{1}\tau(1-\tau)^{k-1} = k\tau(1-\tau)^{k-1} \tag{2}$$

- It needs that there are no errors in the channel, namely neither False Positive nor False Negative occur. It achieves with probability $(1 - P_{e+})(1 - P_{e-})$
- Observe that False Positive and False Negative are mutually exclusive events, therefore, we assume that the presence of both events at the same time means a free-error channel. This occurs with probability $(P_{e+})(P_{e-})$

Then, the value of $P_s(k)$ for k nodes attempting to transmit is computed as follows:

$$P_s(k) = P(X = 1)[(1 - P_{e+})(1 - P_{e-}) + (P_{e+})(P_{e-})] \tag{3}$$

On the other hand, no one node successfully transmits if any of the following events is presented:

- A collision occurs because two or more nodes transmit in the same time slot.
- No one node transmit but errors occur, mainly, noisy is detected as a transmission. This does not change the state of the network because the same quantity of nodes are still attempting to transmit.
- One node transmits but a False Negative occurs, and a False Positive does not occur. This causes that the network does not detect such transmission.

Observe that this set of statements are the complement of the events that makes susceptible a successful transmission. Therefore the probability of a no successful transmission occurs is called $P_f(k)$. Then, the value of $P_f(k)$ for k nodes attempting to transmit is computed as following:

$$P_f(k) = 1 - P_s(k) \tag{4}$$

Build on that, a model using a Markov chain of one dimension is proposed to represent the number of nodes attempting to transmit. As such a state is the number of nodes with pending transmission, this starts in the state N and finishes in the absorbing state 0, meaning no more nodes will transmit. In each new state is computed the probability to going at the following state where the number of nodes attempting to transmit is reduced (if a successful transmission occurs) and the probability of the chain remains in the same state (if does not occur a successful transmission) following the equations previously described. Figure 1 presents this Markov chain.

Although this strategy seems very simple, it could not be effective enough since the channel conditions are not constant along all the time. To solve that problem, we present the proposal described in the following subsections.

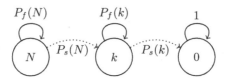

Fig. 1. Markov chain for control packets sending with fixed transmission probability

3.2 Adaptive by Estimation Scheme (AES)

We present this strategy obeying the fact that the number of nodes attempting to transmit is not the same along the time. Let us give an example: when no one node has sent control packets, the total amount of active nodes are attempting to transmit, conversely, when the majority of nodes has transmitted successfully their control packets, in future time slots the number of nodes attempting to transmit decreases.

Base on that we suggest a mechanism such that when the amount of nodes attempting to transmit is high, they compete for the channel with low probability to avoid collisions and with a low number of nodes attempting to transmit they compete for the channel with high probability to avoid idle time slots such that the delay decreases.

Build on the fact that only one node must transmit in each time slot, the ideal transmission probability should be inversely proportional to the number of nodes attempting to transmit. We denote this as $\tau_{ae} = 1/k'$, where k' is the current estimated number of nodes with pending transmission.

Thus, the value of τ_{ae} will be update in each time slot such that it increases as the estimated number of nodes attempting to transmit decreases. This means that in each successful transmission detected, the system estimates a value of k' of one unit lower that its previous value.

Hence, inside ideal error-free channels, this scheme seems to fit perfectly that in each time slot one transmission is performed. The main problem is when the network deploys in a conflictual environment where noise, interferences, and other not desirable events are susceptible to occur.

Considering such environments, we note the following issues:

- If the nodes do not detect the transmission of one of them, they do not update their transmission probability correctly.
- If the channel presents a high probability of False Positive presence, the nodes are prone to estimate that less of them are attempting to transmit since they detect errors as successful transmissions. This fact impacts when it estimates one node attempting to transmit and actually there is more than two nodes waiting to transmit. The nodes with pendent transmission assume that the channel is free because they estimate that no one more of them is attempting to transmit. Eminently, this causes that the successive slots present collisions and the network will never be able to collect information from the environment.

For this new model it is considered three main events: successful transmission, being in the same state or a false successful transmission. Below they are described.

- Successful transmission: Occurs when only one of the k nodes attempting to transmit performs a transmission and the channel presents neither False Positive nor False Negative, or one node transmits and it presents False Positive and False Negative (it is assumed as error-free channel), similar to the described in (3) but now it is depending on the current value of k and the estimation of the remaining nodes attempting to transmit k'. Additionally, this event reduces k and k' in one unit, therefore, the following value of τ_{ea} updates with the new value of k' for the future time slot. This event occurs with probability $P_s(k, k')$ computed as:

$$
\begin{aligned}
P_s(k, k') &= P(X = 1)[(1 - P_{e+})(1 - P_{e-}) \\
&\quad + (P_{e+})(P_{e-})] \\
&= k\tau_{ae}[1 - \tau_{ae}]^{k-1}[(1 - P_{e+})(1 - P_{e-}) \\
&\quad + (P_{e+})(P_{e-})]
\end{aligned}
\tag{5}
$$

- False successful transmission: This event occurs when none one node transmits in the slot, but the nodes detect one transmission in the channel. It is because one False Positive occurred and no a False Negative. This occurs with probability $P_{fs}(k, k')$ computed as:

$$
\begin{aligned}
P_{fs}(k, k') &= P(X = 0)(P_{e+})(1 - P_{e-}) \\
&= [1 - \tau_{ae}]^k (P_{e+})(1 - P_{e-})
\end{aligned}
\tag{6}
$$

By this event, the estimated number of nodes attempting to transmit k' decreases but not the value of k. Consequently, the transmission probability is increased by the new value of k' for future slots.
- Being in the same state: It is an event which implies that neither the value of k nor the value of k' change and it is because different events which are appointed now. When one node transmits but errors in the channel are presented such that the transmission is not detected; when none one node transmits and errors are presented (except the case of occurs False Positive and not a False Negative); and when two or more nodes transmit in the same time slots causing a collision. This event occurs with probability $P_{ss}(k)$ which is computed below:

$$
\begin{aligned}
P_{ss}(k, k') &= P(X = 0)(1 - P_{e+}(1 - P_{e-})) \\
&+ P(X = 1)(P_{e+} + P_{e-} - 2P_{e+}P_{e-}) \\
&+ \sum_{j=2}^{k} P(X = j)
\end{aligned}
\tag{7}
$$

Again, we modeled the transmission of the nodes in the network using a Markov chain. In this case, it chose a three dimensions chain such that each state is named with the number of nodes attempting to transmit k, the estimated number of nodes attempting to transmit k' and the j nodes transmitting in the time slot, thus, the state is (k, k', j).

Figure 2 shows the Markov chain used to model this proposal where each state tell us the current value of nodes attempting to transmit and the estimated of them. It considers that for the first slot they have same value $k = k' = N$, but as the time runs, it is possible that $k' \leq k$. Additionally, both values have to be equal to or higher than 0 and, when k' reaches a threshold value, the probability transmission is the value fixed by τ_{th}. We choose that value experimentally such that the energy consumption and the delay reduce for the sending of control packets process. In following it is explained the use of such threshold.

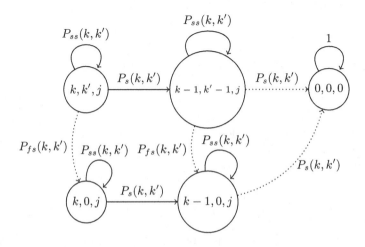

Fig. 2. Markov chain for the adaptive by estimation transmission probability scheme.

3.3   Threshold for AES

Note that it is highly relevant to have a threshold that limits the channel access to the nodes to avoid collisions. In this case, the threshold τ_{th} works once the estimated value of k' reaches a number n_{th} of nodes attempting to transmit. However, the value of the threshold depends on the presence of False Positives and False Negatives. Thus, the value of τ_{ae} is computed as describes the following equation.

$$\tau_{ae} = \begin{cases} 1/k' & \text{if } k' > n_{th} \\ \tau_{th} & \text{if } k' \leq n_{th} \end{cases} \tag{8}$$

Now the value of the current estimated nodes attempting to transmit is considered since it directly impacts to the transmission probability of the nodes.

Based on that, we developed a new model to describe the transmission evolution of control packets of the nodes using this proposal of τ adaptive since the probability $P(X = j)$ is computed as follows:

$$P(X = j) = \begin{cases} \binom{k}{j} 1/k'(1 - 1/k')^{k-1} & \text{if } k > n_{th} \\ \binom{k}{j} \tau_{th}(1 - \tau_{th})^{k-1} & \text{if } k \leq n_{th} \end{cases} \tag{9}$$

This threshold prevents undesirable events that damage the performance of the network, for instance, if $k' = 0$, mathematically and at computing level it is an error. Another example is if there is a $k' = 1$ and $k > 1$, this represents that two or more nodes are trying to transmit in the successive time slots and a set of collisions will be present in the network. It causes mistakes in the energy usage and the network will never gather data from the environment.

Additionally, we observed that this strategy does not describe exactly the conditions of the channel, therefore, we present the Adaptive by Gamma Scheme described as following.

3.4   Adaptive by Gamma Scheme (AGS)

To follow the line of an adaptive transmission scheme, we present the Adaptive by Gamma Scheme which is looking for fitting the transmission of the nodes based on the conditions of the channel. Therefore, this scheme only regards three possible events: successful transmission, collision and idle slot.

For this scheme we want the nodes adjust softly their probability to transmit such that they could increase or decrease this probability to according to the channel conditions. Conversely to AES which only increases the transmission probability along the time, in this scheme nodes are able to reduce this probability to prevent future collisions.

Then the transmission probability of nodes is updated by a factor called γ which increases or decreases the value of $t\tau$ (we now call it τ_{ag}) according to the events that we detail below.

- Successful transmission: This event occurs with the same probability $P_s(k)$, in this, we assume that conditions in the channel are good enough such that only one node is transmitting in the slot, therefore, nodes transmit with an *optimal* probability that we want to it be equal for the future slot in hope of the conditions do not change quickly.
- Collision: A collision occurs when two or more nodes transmit in the same time slot and when one node transmits and a False Positive but not a False Negative is presented at the same time. This event occurs with probability $P_c(k)$ computed as follows:

$$P_c(k) = P(X = 1)(P_{e+})(1 - P_{e-}) + \sum_{j=2}^{k} P(X = j) \tag{10}$$

In this event, the transmission probability is higher than the optimal such that causes collisions. To avoid a potential collision in the following slot, this probability transmission updates by a soft reduction by a factor of γ, thus the new value of τ_{ag} for the time t is computed as follows: $\tau_{ag}(t) = \gamma\tau_{ag}(t-1)$ where $0 < \gamma < 1$.

– Idle slot: Is the event where the channel is free due to the absence of transmissions and errors, or for the transmission of one node but it presents a False Negative and not a False Positive. In this event, nodes must to increase their probability to transmit because it assumes that current value of τ_{ag} is small for the conditions of channel. As such, iIdle slot occurs with probability $P_I(k)$ which is computed as follows:

$$P_I(k) = P(X = 0)[(1 - P_{e+})(1 - P_{e-}) + P_{e+}P_{e-}] \\ + P(X = 1)P_{e-}(1 - P_{e+}) \tag{11}$$

The form that τ_{ag} updates is increasing softly in a factor of gamma as $\tau_{ag}(t) = \frac{1}{\gamma}\tau_{ag}(t-1)$ where $0 < \gamma < 1$ and t is the number of slot.

Moreover, a False Success occurs when none one node transmits and it presents a False Positive but no a False Negative. In such case, the value of τ_{ag} and nodes attempting to transmit are conserved. This event occurs with probability $Pfs(k) = P(X = 0)P_{e+}(1 - P_{e-})$.

3.5 Threshold of AGS

The updating of τ_{ag} is thought to prevent collisions and idle slots. As such, we know that it decreases as is detected the first event and increases in the case of the second one. Unfortunately, there exists an issue for consecutive slots with the same type of that unwanted events, for that reason we include this subsection to expose the use of thresholds that prevent such events.

First, in case of continuous collisions, the value τ_{ag} will continually be decreased such that $\tau_{ag} \approx 0$ then, in future time slots, no one node is going to transmit causing a set of idle slots that implies high delay in the packets. To solve this issue, we propose a minimum value admissible to take τ_{ag} which is named τ_{min} such that once the updated value of τ_{ag} reaches it, this is conserved in case of a new collision, or if the event changes to a idle slot, it instantly increases by a γ factor. The value of τ_{min} is experimentally computed and showed in the following section.

On the other hand, if the events that constantly occurs are idle slots, the value of τ_{ag} increases each time a new of this event is presented. That causes $\tau_{ag} \approx 1$ or greater than 1, which in probability it is an inconsistency. A probability of 1 represents the complete assignation of the channel to all the nodes trying to transmit. Such is feasible when there is only one node attempting to transmit, but this is a big issue in the case of 2 or more nodes wit pending transmission. This last case entails future collision in the slots, increasing in the energy consumption by nodes and the delay. To solve this issue we proposed a threshold τ_{max} for the maximum value that could take τ_{ag} which is presented and computed experimentally in the following section.

Although it is more common to reach τ_{max} in first slots and τ_{min} in last slots, this is not discarded to be reach those thresholds in intermediate slots.

Building in previous statements we can establish the manner to compute the value of τ_{ag} in each time slot t, then this is:

$$\tau_{ag}(t) = \begin{cases} \frac{1}{\gamma}\tau_{ag}(t-1) & \text{if a idle slot is presented} \\ \gamma\tau_{ag}(t-1) & \text{if a collision is presented} \\ \tau_{max} & \text{if } \frac{1}{\gamma}\tau_{ag}(t-1) \geq \tau_{max} \\ \tau_{min} & \text{if } \gamma\tau_{ag}(t-1) \leq \tau_{min} \end{cases} \tag{12}$$

Markov chain of Fig. 3 models this scheme and shows an arbitrary state of the chain which is composed by two dimensions with the number k of nodes attempting to transmit and the current value of τ_{ag}. We suggest the state at the beginning of the process $k = N$ and $\tau_{ag} = \frac{1}{N}$ to dispose of one transmission by slot. Consider that shifting to a new state, it updates the value of k or τ_{ag} then, such new values are assigned as current, and the state in Fig. 3 is still a valid representation.

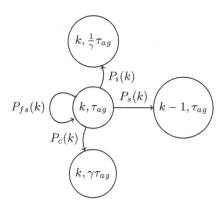

Fig. 3. Arbitrary state of the Markov chain for the adaptive by Gamma scheme.

4   System Model

We performed this study under a non-ideal channel scenario where it considers noise and interferences as probabilities that either a False Positive (P_{e+}) or a False Negative (P_{e-}) occurs.

The nodes are located uniformly in the network area and transmit with the power enough to be heard by each one of the network members independently of its position. Once that it is set the position of the nodes and the number of them, it does not change along the time.

We focus our study on the sending of control packets process under a CSMA/NP scheme (this process is named in different forms depending of the protocol used, per example in LEACH is known as Cluster Formation State). To study the performance of the schemes presented, we used the parameters in the Table 1 to find the average values for the thresholds mentioned in the previous section such that the average of energy consumption and delay due to this process reduces.

Additionally, we compared the performance of the three schemes to observe which one has the best performance under the same channel conditions such that network's administrators have a guideline to their scheme setting selection.

Table 1. Parameters

Parameter	Value
Nodes in the network	$N = 5, 10, 20, 50, 100$
Network size	100 sqr meters
Sample size	100000 networks of 100 nodes
Probability P_{e+}	from 0.1 to 0.5
Probability P_{e-}	from 0.1 to 0.5
Time of transmission	1 unit (1 time slot)
Energy consumption for Tx	1 unit(50nJ/bit)
Energy consumption for Rx	1 unit(50nJ/bit)

5   Numerical Results

The numerical results shown in this sections were obtained through extensive numerical simulations and solving the chain presented in each scheme. Through these experiments, we evaluated the performance of different values for the thresholds mentioned to obtain one which is optimal for the channel conditions.

First, we evaluated the parameters that impacts the performance of the Adaptive by Estimation Scheme. This evaluation was for the values of N previously described under a conflictive channel with False Positive and False Negative probabilities. In this scheme the settings parameters of the network are n_{th} and τ_{th}. The results presented in Fig. 4 shows that the value of n_{th} is higher as the number of nodes in the network increases. Hopefully, this parameter is not directly affected by the presence of errors since it only is an indicator of where high probability transmission creates collisions. Additionally, we observe that this parameter is linearly approximated to $n_{th} = round(2.1N + 1.4)$

As such, τ_{th} is affected by the presence of errors and the number of nodes in the network as it shows Fig. 5 where we observe that as the number of nodes in

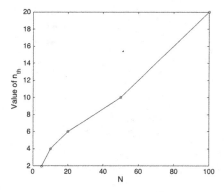

Fig. 4. Threshold of number of nodes attempting to transmit.

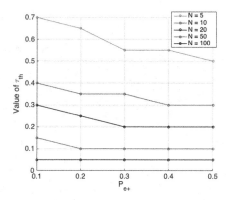

Fig. 5. Value of τ_{th} in error-prone channels.

the network increases, τ_{th} has lower values, this is intuitive since n_{th} is high for huge networks, then as the remaining nodes attempting to transmit is high, the probability must be small to prevent collisions. Additionally, it is notable that presence of False Positives impacts the value of τ_{th} more than False Negative.

We observe particularly how False Positive probability changes τ_{th} in Fig. 5. In network of $N = 100$ is a constant $\tau_{th} = 0.05$, but for networks with $N \leq 20$, as probability of False Positive increases, this threshold takes lower values. This is because the transmission of nodes are susceptible to collide with False Positives, then, reducing the transmission probability increases the network performance.

In Adaptive by Gamma Scheme exist three setting parameters for the scheme that have a significant role in the network performance: $\tau_{min}, \tau_{min}, \gamma$. We present the experimental results to assign this values below.

First, Fig. 6 shows τ_{min}, where we observe that networks with $N > 10$ presents a quasi-constant value. Additionally, as the number of nodes increases in the network, τ_{min} is lower. This is because with more nodes in the network is better to limit the transmission probability to avoid collisions, such that a lower

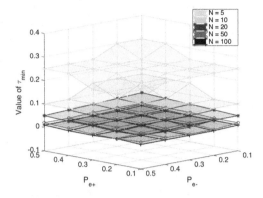

Fig. 6. Value of τ_{min} in error-prone channels.

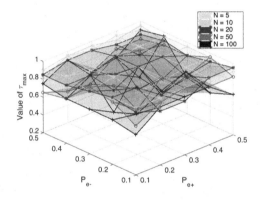

Fig. 7. Value of τ_{max} in error-prone channels.

value of τ reduces the number of transmissions in each time slot since nodes have a low probability to transmit.

Similar behavior is observed in results for τ_{max} as shows Fig. 7 where networks with a low number of nodes tends to reach $\tau_{max} = 0.95$ even the presence of False Positive and False Negative with high probability. This is because fewer nodes in the network compete for the channel, consequently, it is feasible to assign a high probability to transmit.

Notice that $\tau_{max} > \tau_{th}$ (they are analogs since both restrict to a maximum probability to transmit). This is because in AGS reaching τmax does not indicate that for all future slots nodes will transmit with that probability, and in AGS consecutive collisions are prevented by reducing in a γ factor the transmission probability. This fact is a plus point to AGS since could seem more tolerable to errors in the channel. We observe the specific case of $N = 100$, in AES the maximum probability is 0.05 meanwhile in AGS is higher than 0.6, which means, for transmission of the last node, it is more probable to present idle slots using AES than the case of AGS.

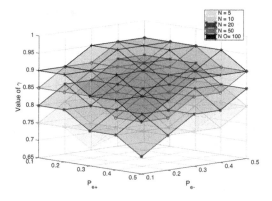

Fig. 8. Value of γ in error-prone channels.

On the other hand, we observe that γ is a setting parameter with a relevant role in the performance of the network because it is the factor which updates the transmission probability, namely its value will change the probability slowly or quickly. Figure 8 shows the result for the values of γ that increase the network performance. Mainly we observe that errors and number of nodes in the network impact the value of γ, note networks with a high number of nodes present higher value of γ. That means changes in τ_{ag} are smaller as γ has high values, that is desirable in huge networks because as more nodes are attempting to transmit the probability of transmitting is similar in following slots (if we think that ideal transmission probability is $1/k$ to ensure only one transmission per slot and for higher value of k, $1/k \approx 1/(k-1)$).

As was mentioned previously, these schemes were proposed and studied theirs setting parameters to gain a lower delay and less energy consumption in the control packets sending process. Base on that in Fig. 9 and Fig. 10 are presented the energy consumption of nodes per bit to send packet controls and the delay in slots for this process for a network of 5, 20 and 100 nodes.

Clearly, it shows that adaptive schemes improve over 40% of the energy consumption. Moreover AGS is the best scheme for networks with $N > 5$. With those results is confirmed that AGS is more tolerable to errors since it improves energy consumption even in the presence of errors, except for the case of $N = 5$, $P_{e+=0.1}$ and $P_{e-<0.5}$ where AES achieves the fittest performance in energy consumption.

A similar result obtains the delay measurement. The improvement of delay is view as a reduction of this. Clearly we observe that the delay reduces with the use of adaptive strategies since this decreases to a 40% of the delay in fixed scheme. Additionally, we observe that AGS is which achieves the lowest for any N independently of the presence of errors, except for the case of $N = 5$ and $P_{e+=0.1}$ and $P_{e-<0.5}$ where AES is a bit better. Based on both results energy consumption and delay, we observe that AGS is the best performance scheme

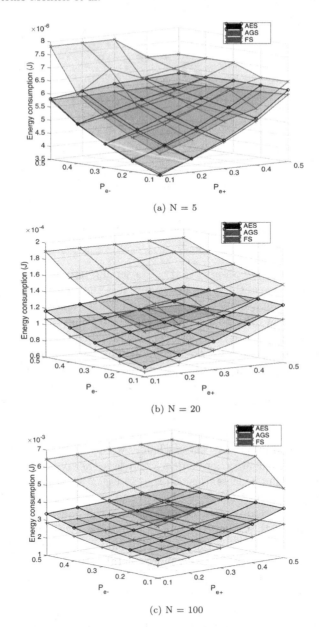

(a) N = 5

(b) N = 20

(c) N = 100

Fig. 9. Energy consumption in control packets sending process

and adaptable to the presence of errors even the network has a large number of nodes.

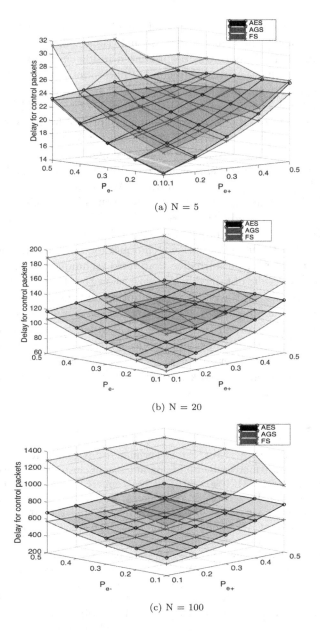

(a) N = 5

(b) N = 20

(c) N = 100

Fig. 10. Delay in control packets sending process

6   Conclusion

In this paper, we study, analyze and evaluate three contention schemes for transmission of control packets for WSNs in no free-error channels. We select two types of schemes: fixed and adaptive. In the former, the nodes transmit with the same probability along the control packets sending process, such that they do not take care about conditions in the channel. Hence, in fixed scheme a huge set of collisions and idle slots will be presented inside since channel conditions changes along the time and transmissions of nodes are not fit to this changes. However, adaptive techniques better adjust to changes in the channel, from the number of nodes in the network until the presence of errors. The price to pay is a correct selection of setting parameters for adaptive schemes. For the case of AES the setting parameters are n_{th} and τ_{th}, and for AGS three parameters are required: τ_{max}, τ_{min} and γ. AES uses n_{th} as the number of nodes with pending transmission that set the transmission probability to the threshold τ_{th}, i.e. the maximum value of τ to transmit. Meanwhile, AGS updates the current value of the transmission probability by a factor γ between the values of the thresholds τ_{min} and τ_{max}. In this study we choose these parameters through experimental methods of try and error, even they are restricted to the system model presented here, it proves that the use of adaptive techniques for the transmission of control packets achieves a better performance than fixed techniques.

The numerical results obtained in this work show that the scheme that has the best performance base on the energy consumption and the delay in the Wireless Sensor Networks composed by 5, 20 and 100 nodes in a 100×100 m area and with the presence of errors in the channel is the Adaptive by Gamma Scheme, followed by Adaptive by Estimation Scheme. Then Fixed Scheme achieves the lowest performance. Moreover Adaptive by Estimation Scheme performs well for particular cases of 5 nodes networks, based on that, this may be viable to use as an easy solution for small networks.

References

1. Alchihabi, A., Dervis, A., Ever, E., Al-Turjman, F.: A generic framework for optimizing performance metrics by tuning parameters of clustering protocolsin WSNs. Wirel. Netw. **25**(3), 1031–1046 (2019). https://doi.org/10.1007/s11276-018-1665-8
2. Baronti, P., Pillai, P., Chook, V.W., Chessa, S., Gotta, A., Hu, Y.F.: Wireless sensor networks: a survey on the state of the art and the 802.15.4 and zigbee standards. Comput. Commun. **30**(7), 1655–1695 (2007). https://doi.org/10.1016/j.comcom.2006.12.020. http://www.sciencedirect.com/science/article/pii/S0140366406004749. Wired/Wireless Internet Communications
3. Bokare, M., Ralegaonkar, M.A.: Wireless sensor network: a promising approach for distributed sensing tasks. Excel J. Eng. Technol. Manag. Sci. **1**(1), 1–9 (2012)
4. Fanian, F., Rafsanjani, M.K., Bardsiri, V.K.: A survey of advanced leach-based protocols. Int. J. Energy Inf. Commun. **7**(1), 1–16 (2016). https://doi.org/10.14257/ijeic.2016.7.1.01. http://www.sersc.org/journals/IJEIC/vol7_Is1/1.pdf
5. Islam, M.S., Hoq, M., Haque, M.A.S., Akand, M.A.R., Hasan, M.R., Basher, M.K.: Challenges and prospects of cost-effective SI-based solar cells fabrication in Bangladesh. In: 2014 International Conference on Electrical Engineering and Information Communication Technology (ICEEICT), pp. 1–6 (2014). https://doi.org/10.1109/ICEEICT.2014.6919168
6. Jarwan, A., Sabbah, A., Ibnkahla, M.: Data transmission reduction schemes in WSNs for efficient IoT systems. IEEE J. Sel. Areas Commun. **37**(6), 1307–1324 (2019)

7. Kazmi, H.S.Z., Javaid, N., Awais, M., Tahir, M., Shim, S.O., Zikria, Y.B.: Congestion avoidance and fault detection in WSNs using data science techniques. Trans. Emerg. Telecommun. Technol. e3756 (2019). https://doi.org/10.1002/ett.3756. https://onlinelibrary.wiley.com/doi/abs/10.1002/ett.3756. E3756 ett.3756

8. Koubâa, A., Alves, M., Tovar, E.: Lower protocol layers for wireless sensor networks: a survey (2005)

9. Montiel, E.R., Rivero-Ángeles, M.E., Rubino, G., Molina-Lozano, H., Menchaca-Méndez, R., Menchaca-Méndez, R.: Performance analysis of cluster formation in wireless sensor networks. Sensors **17**(2902) (2017). https://doi.org/10.3390/s17122902

10. Resali, M.S.M., Salleh, H.: Comparison of energy harvesting power management techniques and application. In: 2010 34th IEEE/CPMT International Electronic Manufacturing Technology Symposium (IEMT), pp. 1–5 (2010). https://doi.org/10.1109/IEMT.2010.5746768

11. Romo-Montiel, E., Rivero-Ángeles, M.E., Molina-Lozano, H., Rubino, G., Menchaca-Méndez, R., Menchaca-Méndez, R.: Optimal transmission thresholds for QoS guarantees in WSNs. In: Proceedings of the 14th ACM International Symposium on QoS and Security for Wireless and Mobile Networks, Q2SWinet 2018, pp. 108–115. Association for Computing Machinery, New York (2018). https://doi.org/10.1145/3267129.3267137

12. Romo-Montiel, E., Rivero-Angeles, M.E., Villordo-Jiménez, I., Molina-Lozano, H.: Impact of the error sensing probability in wide coverage areas of clustered-based wireless sensor networks. Revista Facultad de Ingeniería (79), 63–74 (2016)

13. Sundararaj, V., Muthukumar, S., Kumar, R.: An optimal cluster formation based energy efficient dynamic scheduling hybrid mac protocol for heavy traffic load in wireless sensor networks. Comput. Secur. **77**, 277 – 288 (2018). https://doi.org/10.1016/j.cose.2018.04.009. http://www.sciencedirect.com/science/article/pii/S0167404818303754

A Parallel Rollout Algorithm for Wildfire Suppression

Mauro Montenegro$^{(\boxtimes)}$ ⓘ, Roberto López ⓘ, Rolando Menchaca-Méndez ⓘ,
Emanuel Becerra, and Ricardo Menchaca-Méndez

Centro de Investigación en Computación, Ciudad de México 07738, Mexico
{b191114,a190467,a180968}@sagitario.cic.ipn.mx,
{rmen,ric}@cic.ipn.mx

Abstract. In this paper, we formulate the problem of optimal Wildfire Suppression as an infinite horizon Decision Process (DP) problem where an agent (e.g., a robotic firefighter) decides which areas to intervene to extinguish the fire. The dynamics of the wildfire is modeled by a cellular automaton whose state at time k is defined as a bi-dimensional grid x_k where each cell in this grid describes the state of a rectangular geographic region of the wildland. The proposed algorithm, which is based on a non-parametric reinforcement learning (RL) methodology, computes optimized control policies that determine the agent's actions that minimize a cost function that aims to preserve most of the cells with trees. From a given state x_k, the proposed algorithms employs rollout to take advantage of heuristic solutions to approximate, in polynomial-time, the future cost function. Two different heuristics approaches were applied: A *corrective*-based model that only takes into account surrounding burning cells, and a *predictive* strategy that calculates a coefficient-based metric over nearby trees and empty cells. We implemented a parallel sampler using CUDA to simulate the trajectories that rollout generates. This parallel implementation allows us to increase the number of lookahead steps without incurring in large computing times. Our experimental results show that the rollout strategy outperforms the base heuristics and that effectively suppresses wildfires.

1 Introduction

Wildfire models based on cellular automata are a type of *Probabilistic Cellular Automata* (PCA) that try to capture the dynamics and general patterns of tree clusters that emerge from an evolving forest subject to perturbations. They have been proved to be a valuable tool for ecological and natural hazard sciences because they are simple but powerful modeling tools [17]. Wildfire models help to tackle questions like: Will the tree population eventually die out?, what is the general shape of tree clusters?, what is the shape of the boundary between the forest and a wildfire?

At first glance, wildfire models seem similar to epidemiological cellular automata models though, they emphasize finite population and the persistence

M. F. Mata-Rivera et al. (Eds.): WITCOM 2020, CCIS 1280, pp. 244–255, 2020.
https://doi.org/10.1007/978-3-030-62554-2_18

of pathology over time, which contrasts with the infinite forest population and the emphasis on the spatial extension of the fire. In this work, we adapt this model to a *Reinforcement Learning* (RL) problem and suggest a rollout strategy to suppress a wildfire in this kind of PCA.

Reinforcement Learning involves a class of solution methods for problems associated with learning to map states to actions to optimize a cost function. Sutton and Barto [14] underline three key features that distinguish RL problems: closed-loop system, learning by experience, and future consequence. RL problems are closed-loop because the learning system's actions influence their later inputs. Furthermore, at a given state, the agent is not told which actions to take and needs to learn by experience, and these actions could affect immediate and future costs.

In an RL system, typically, we find an agent that interacts with the environment through actions and obtains a cost signal that determines the quality of control. These actions are taken following a *policy*(π) that maps observed states of the environment to actions. Sometimes this policy could be only a lookup table or includes a searching process.

RL problems are suitable to be solved with the *Dynamic Programming* (DP) paradigm, as both aspire to optimize some cost function. DP could accommodate the optimal or sub-optimal solution depending on the type of problem and deals with scenarios where is necessary some optimization. At each stage, it ranks over all possible actions based on the sum of present cost and expected future cost, assuming an optimal decision making in the future [2].

The rest of the paper is organized as follows. Section 2 presents a formulation of the problem of wildfire suppression as a Markov Decision Process. Section 3 the proposed solution methodology which is based on Rollout. Section 4 presents the results of a series of experiments that characterize the performance of the proposed solution. Lastly, Sect. 5 presents our concluding remarks.

2   Reinforcement Learning Formulation

A dynamic system expresses the evolution of the system state under the influence of decisions made at discrete instances of time. In this work, the dynamic system is a wildfire spreading over a forest, and it is model as a stochastic DP problem that involves a discrete-time system of the form:

$$x_{k+1} = f_k(x_k, u_k, w_k), \; k = 0, 1, ..., N - 1 \tag{1}$$

where k is the step-index, and x_k is the state of the system at that time. In a wildfire automaton, this state is represented by a forest lattice with each cell representing the state of the field (e.g., fire, empty, tree), together with the position of a robotic firefighter position. Given x_k, the robotic firefighter (in this case a helicopter) could select an action or control (u_k) from some the set $U_k(x_k)$ that will determine his next position in the grid (Fig. 1).

The wildfire model proposed by Drossel [6] is defined by a set of rules that include a probabilities f and p for all cells that at each time determines if a tree

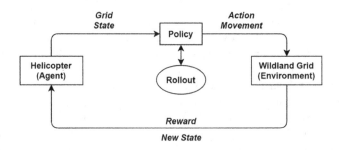

Fig. 1. Wildfire control formulated as a reinforcement learning problem.

ignites or empty cell fills with a tree respectively. The variable w_k includes this last form of disturbance that governs the evolution of the state x_k. This disturbance is characterized by a probability distribution $P(*|x_k, u_k)$ that is only affected by x_k and u_k, but not on prior values. Future state of the forest grid x_{k+1} only depends on x_k, w_k and u_k. This last property tells us that system dynamics is a *Markov Decision Process* (MDP) and is one of the strengths of DP methodology. The problem also involves a cost function $g_k(x_k, u_k, w_k)$ (e.g., total fire cells) that is additive in the sense that the cost at step k accumulates over time until a terminal value $g_N(x_N)$ added at the end of the process. Figure 2 displays this stochastic dynamics. An effect of uncertainty is the evaluation of various quantities such as cost function, which involves expected values. To handle these disturbances, we use a *Monte Carlo simulation*.

Formally, the expected cost of π starting at x_0 is as presented in Eq. 2.

$$J_\pi(x_0) = E\left\{g_N(x_N) + \sum_{k=0}^{N-1} g_k(x_k, \mu_k(x_k), w_k)\right\} \qquad (2)$$

A DP algorithm works under the principle of *optimality* [1], and it proceeds sequentially, by solving all the tail sub-problems of a given length, using the solution of the tail sub-problems of shorter length. The algorithm constructs a sequence of optimal values J^* starting from the last state N (Eq. 3), and solving backwards (Eq. 4).

$$J^*(x_N) = g_N(x_N) \qquad (3)$$

$$J^*(x_k) = \min_{u_k \in U_k(x_k)} E\left\{g_k(x_k, u_k, w_k) + \alpha^k * J^*_{k+1}(f_k(x_k, u_k, w_k))\right\} \qquad (4)$$

where $\alpha < 1$ is a positive scalar that assigns weight to future costs with respect to costs incurred at the present time.

In order to reduce time complexity, we can define a forward algorithmic process by replacing the optimal cost of J^*_k by an approximation function $\tilde{J}_k$. When $\tilde{J}_k$ arises, we need to use sub-optimal solution methods, which are the main subject of RL.

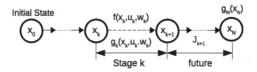

Fig. 2. Evolution of a stochastic finite optimal control problem. Starting from x_0 and following the system dynamics $f(x_k, u_k, w_k)$

Some approximation approaches in RL are problem approximation, on-line approximate optimization, parametric approximation, and aggregation [5,10].

Although RL algorithms have been used in several areas, their implementation to mitigate wildfires has only be studied in some recent works. Vulcano [12] uses a multi-agent deep reinforcement learning actor-critic algorithm with a local reward extension using a centralized training and a decentralized execution approach to handle the incremental number of agents outperforming traditional methods. Furthermore, Haksar and Schwager [9] proposed a distributed deep reinforcement learning (RL) based strategy for a team of Unmanned Aerial Vehicles (UAVs) to autonomously fight forest fires. Both works rely on and off-line framework using Q-methods. We aim to develop an off-line methodology that effectively mitigates a wildfire spread using a rollout optimization strategy.

In this work, our goal is to optimize a policy π that controls the agent behavior in a wildfire cellular automata model. A stochastic behavior governs the automata dynamics and determines his state and transitions. Also, the model has no terminal state. According to last considerations, we face a stochastic infinite horizon DP problem. To approximate cost functions J_k^*, we use an on-line non-parametric approximation method called *rollout* [3] [11], which consists of making an exact optimization over the first l-controls (l-*lookahead*) and let a heuristic, called the *base heuristic*, work for the next m-steps to obtain $\tilde{J}_k$.

3 Methodology

In this section, we shortly explain the *rollout* architecture, which consists of three main components given a state x_k: an exact cost minimization for the first $k + l$ steps, a cost approximation using a base heuristic for the next m steps, and a final cost approximation $\tilde{J}$. Then, we analyze the wildfire environment and propose two base heuristics.

3.1 Rollout Algorithm

The rollout strategy is a sub-optimal approximation algorithm that sequentially solves intractable DP problems. It employs problem-dependent heuristics to approximate the future cost by running simulations on subsequent steps (i.e., the rolling horizon) [15].

Rollout works under the framework of policy improvement [2], namely, it starts with a sub-optimal policy, based on a heuristic called the base heuristic, then, we produce an improved policy by a limited look ahead using the heuristic for m-steps and some form of cost approximation at the end. Formally, Eq. 5 describes rollout with l-step lookahead at state x_k.

$$\min_{u_k,\mu_{k+1},\ldots,\mu_{k+l-1}} E\left\{ g_k(x_k,u_k,w_k) + \sum_{m=k+1}^{k+l-1} g_m(x_m,\mu_m(x_m),w_m) \right.$$
$$\left. + \tilde{J}_{k+l}(x_{k+l}) \right\} \tag{5}$$

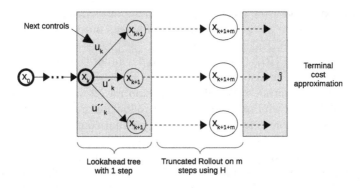

Fig. 3. Schematic of rollout with 1-step lookahead

The approximate cost $\tilde{J}_{k+l}(x_{k+l})$ is integrated by the base policy (H) running m-stages and a terminal approximation function.

Following a 1-step lookahead architecture and given a state x_k, this algorithm considers all the tail sub-problems considering every possible next state x_{k+1}, according to $u_k \in U_k(x_k)$ and solves sub-optimally by using some heuristic, referred to as the base heuristic. Then, the rollout algorithm applies the control that minimizes over $u_k \in U_k(x_k)$.

Using Q-factors, at state x_k the algorithm applies the control $\tilde{\mu}(x_k)$ following the minimization in Eq. 6.

$$\tilde{\mu}(x_k) \in arg \min_{\mu_k \in U_k(x_k)} \tilde{Q}_k(x_k,u_k,w_k) \tag{6}$$

where $\tilde{Q}_k(x_k,u_k,w_k)$ is the approximate Q-factor defined by Eq. 7.

$$\tilde{Q}_k(x_k,u_k,w_k) = g_k(x_k,w_k) + \alpha^k * H_{k+1}(f_k(x_k,u_k)) \tag{7}$$

with $\alpha^k * H_{k+1}(f_k(x_k,u_k))$ denoting the cost of the base heuristic starting at x_{k+1} with a penalty cost of α for a infinite horizon problem as stated in Sect. 1. This process defines a sub-optimal policy called the rollout policy. A 1-step lookahead architecture with truncated rollout using $\tilde{J}$ as his final cost approximation is illustrated in Fig. 3.

A heuristic needs to be sequentially consistent if we expect the rollout policy to outperform the base heuristic [2,7]. A heuristic is sequentially consistent if it has the property that, when it generates the sequence $\{x_k, x_{k+1}, ..., x_N\}$, and then we start from state x_k, it also generates the sequence $\{x_{k+1}, ..., x_N\}$ [2]. Our proposed heuristics follows a greedy behavior in their decisions and achieve this sequential consistency property.

We generate S simulated trajectories for each possible control $u_k \in U_k(x_k)$. The costs of the trajectories corresponding to a pair(x_k, u_k) can be represented as samples of the Q-factor (Eq. 8).

$$Q_k(x_k, u_k) = E\{g_k(x_k, u_k, w_k) + H(f_k(x_k, u_k, w_k))\} \tag{8}$$

By Monte Carlo averaging of the costs of the sample trajectories, we obtain an approximation of the Q-factor $Q_k(x_k, u_k)$ for each possible control at state x_k which we will denote by $\tilde{Q}_k(x_k, u_k)$. We then compute the approximate rollout control $\tilde{\mu}_k(x_k)$ with Eq. 6.

3.2   Cellular Automata Environment

Formally, a cellular automata is represented by the 4-tuple (Z, S, N, f), where Z refers to a finite or infinite lattice, and S is a finite set of states. Set N is a finite neighborhood, and f is a set of transition rules that govern the dynamics of the system [4].

In this paper, we work with a cellular automata environment that emulates a wildfire dynamics under the gym framework for RL. The source code is available on GitHub[1].

The environment consists of a configurable size 2-D lattice Z (Fig. 4), with each cell having 3 types of states: {fire, empty, tree}, giving a 3^{M*N} total possible states in S. It uses a 2-D Moore Neighborhood N described by directions on the compass N $= \{$N, W, C, E, S$\}$.

Formally, a Moore neighborhood [8] of C_{x_0,y_0} with a cell range r is described by Eq. 9.

$$N_{x_0,y_0}^M = \{(x,y) : |x - x_0| \leq r, |y - y_0| \leq r\} \tag{9}$$

Given a cell $C_{x,y}^k$ at time k and his neighborhood N, the automata follows 4 main transition rules:

1. Spontaneous fire on a tree cell: $P(C_{x,y}^{k+1} = fire \mid C_{x,y}^k = tree) = f$
2. A tree grows on an empty cell: $P(C_{x,y}^{k+1} = tree \mid C_{x,y}^k = empty) = p$
3. A fire cell becomes empty: $P(C_{x,y}^{k+1} = empty \mid C_{x,y}^k = fire) = 1$
4. Neighborhood with r $= 1$ becomes fire: $P(N_{x,y}^M = fire \mid C_{x,y}^k = fire) = 1$

---

[1] https://github.com/elbecerrasoto/gym-forest-fire.

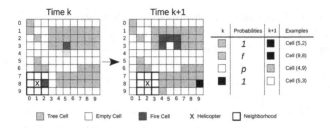

Fig. 4. Random environment with a 10×10 lattice at time k. Agent starts at position $C_{1,8}$ and transitions to $k+1$ moving right

3.3 Heuristics

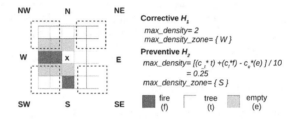

Fig. 5. An example of H_1 and H_2 calculating their max Burning Neighborhood Zone (BNZ)

We propose two greedy base heuristics $(H_1 \& H_2)$ based on fire density in the neighborhood N^M of the agent at state x_k and cell range r. We divide by 8 zones in this neighborhood.

Given the agent position C_{x_i, y_i} and his Moore neighborhood $N^M_{x,y}$, with r acting like his cell-range vision, we define a set Z that consists of 8 different zones in $N^M_{x,y}$, corresponding to 8 possible moves of the agent in the environment (excluding the "not move" action). We define a function $F(z)$ that returns a coefficient, based on which Heuristic was selected for a given zone $z_i \in Z$. Heuristics work greedy and returns an action based on the scores obtained applying $F(z_i)$ for each $z_i \in Z$.

Function $F(z)$ depends on which H was selected, in this work we proposed a *corrective* and a *preventive* model (Fig. 5). A corrective heuristic (H_1) only consider fire cells by each zone and returns a control u_k that corresponds to the zone with **max** fire density. A preventive heuristic (H_2) Calculates a fire coefficient c_f that sums a factor for fire cells (actual fire, f_i) tree cells (potential fire expansion, t_i), then subtracts a value for empty cells (stops propagation, e_i). Finally we divide by total cells in respective zone to normalize c_f.

Once we get a zone with max fire density, heuristic maps to a respective action.

3.4 CUDA Implementation

As discussed in Sect. 3, our implementation for the on-line rollout algorithm uses Monte-Carlo sampling starting from all the possible trajectories depending on the *l-steps* of the lookahead configuration and the stochastic nature of the environment. To accelerate the sampling process we use a kernel function in CUDA written in Python and compiled with the Numba package, this for ease to read the resulting code. Using CUDA is effective to accelerate this type of parallel workload [16].

This kernel has an equivalent of the Helicopter environment with its stochastic behavior, cost function, and of all the heuristics embedded on it to use on this work. The essence of its performance is to divide and execute the task in a parallel manner, taking each possible trajectory previously calculated for the given parameters, repeat to calculate the mean cost for taking the actions to apply the action with the minimum cost associated. An overall overview can be seen in Fig. 6 and a logic diagram showing the parallel process of truncated rollout can be seen in Fig. 7.

The source code is available on GitHub[2] under Open Source License and version 1.1.0 is archived in Zenodo [13].

4 Experimental Study

We evaluate the proposed rollout algorithm using different lookahead sizes with the heuristics described in Sect. 3.3. We use CUDA 10.1 and Numba 0.49 for parallelization. The algorithm is coded in Python 3.6 while using the environment on the Open AI Gym framework.

A summary of environment and algorithmic parameters can be viewed in Tables 1 and 2. Our goal is to minimize the total cost that the environment returns, which in this work is as shown in Eq. 10.

$$
\begin{aligned}
\text{cost}(x_k) = -\big\{ & \text{c\_tree} \cdot \text{sgn}(\#\text{Tree}_k - \#\text{Fire}_k) \cdot [\#\text{Tree}_k - \#\text{Fire}_k]^2 \\
& + \text{c\_hit} \cdot (2 \cdot \text{Hit}_k - \text{Move}_k) - \#\text{Empty}_k \cdot \text{c\_empty} \big\}
\end{aligned}
\tag{10}
$$

Our proposal encourages the algorithm to maintain tree cells in the grid as much as possible while introducing a sense of urgency to put down the fire. A cost is added to penalize roaming through the grid but is not large enough to discourage exploring the wild area without extinguishing a fire cell.

We made tests for incremental values of lookahead $l = \{1, \ldots, 6\}$ and a vision range of $r = 3$ for both heuristics. The objective in is to preserve most of the cells containing a tree in the environment. We evaluate this last aspect by establishing a metric called *Forest Preservation Area* (FPA), which calculates a ratio (Total tree cells/Total cells) in each environment. We evaluate the final value of FPA applying different sizes of lookahead and compare the performance against he

---

[2] codebase: https://github.com/Bobobert/gym-forest-fire.

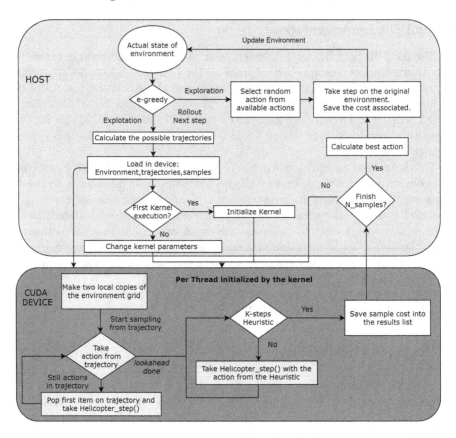

Fig. 6. CUDA sampler diagram

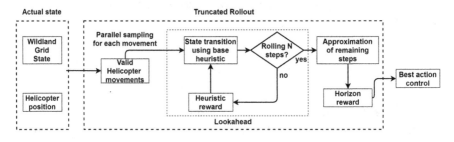

Fig. 7. Logical diagram of parallel truncated rollout process

base heuristics (dashed line) and the natural evolution of the environment without the agent (dotted line); see Figs. 8a, 8c. From the figures we can observe that increments in number of lookahead steps make FPA increase and outperforms both heuristics that are represented by the baseline. The results also show that H_1 obtain better results, but seems to over estimate values as we increase the lookahead from 5 to 6, while H_2 still increments his FPA. Also, as a consequence of Eq. 10 that rewards extinguishing fire cells, we are interested in measuring the fire that is active while the agent is interacting with the environment. We calculate a value called *Wildland Fire Density* (WFD), which measures the ratio (Total fire cells/Total cells) in each environment. We can observe in Figs. 8b and 8d, the WFD for each lookahead value and both heuristics. Lookahead steps and WFD are inversely proportional, inducing our rollout algorithm to outperform heuristics.

<table>
<tr><td colspan="2">Table 1. Algorithm parameters</td></tr>
</table>

Parameter	Value
K	24
Samples	30
α	0.90
Vision	3
Steps	200
Freeze	8
Tests	15

Table 2. Environment parameters

Parameter	Value
p_fire	0.01
p_tree	0.05
c_tree	3
c_fire	0
c_empty	1
c_hit	1
grid	16 × 16 cells

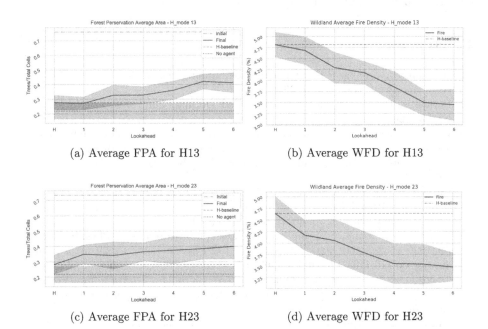

(a) Average FPA for H13

(b) Average WFD for H13

(c) Average FPA for H23

(d) Average WFD for H23

Fig. 8. Average Forest Preservation Area (FPD) and Wildfire Density (WFD) for the base heuristics (H_1 and H_2) with $r = 3$ and 6 lookahead steps

5   Conclusion

In this paper, we propose a non-parametric Dynamic Programming strategy called rollout to suppress wildfires modeled by a cellular automata environment. Rollout optimizes over the first l-control steps and approximate future costs by applying a greedy base heuristic. We proposed a corrective and a predictive heuristic (H_1 & H_2). The corrective type focuses its attention on fire cells in the neighborhood of the agent. Meanwhile, the predictive ones consider a possible fire propagation or extinction by the tree and empty cells in the surrounding neighborhood.

To evaluate all possible controls of the agent, given a state x_k, it is necessary to generate and sample all the trajectories determined by l-*lookahead*. This evaluation could be very time-consuming as the cardinality of the trajectories set increases exponentially with l. Additionally, we need to sample each trajectory a fixed number of times. By using CUDA to parallelize the sampling process, we handle this exponential time increase.

We demonstrate that an off-line rollout strategy achieves better performance than using only the base heuristics. Moreover, as we increase the number of lookahead steps, we can obtain even better values of FPA and WFD. This is reflected in better preservation of trees in the forest and, at the same time, more effective suppression of fire in the area.

References

1. Bellman, R., Kalaba, R.E.: Dynamic Programming and Modern Control Theory. Academic Press, New York (1965)
2. Bertsekas, D.: Reinforcement Learning and Optimal Control. Athena Scientific, Nashua (2019)
3. Bhattacharya, S., Badyal, S., Wheeler, T., Gil, S., Bertsekas, D.: Reinforcement learning for pomdp: partitioned rollout and policy iteration with application to autonomous sequential repair problems. IEEE Robot. Autom. Lett. 5(3), 3967–3974 (2020)
4. Codd, E.F.: Cellular Automata. Academic Press, New York (2014)
5. Dimitri, B.: Biased Aggregation, Rollout, and Enhanced Policy Improvement for Reinforcement Learning. preprint, pp. 1–26 (2019)
6. Drossel, B., Schwabl, F.: Self-organized critical forest-fire model. Phys. Rev. Lett. 69, 1629–1632 (1992). https://doi.org/10.1103/PhysRevLett.69.1629, https://link.aps.org/doi/10.1103/PhysRevLett.69.1629
7. Goodson, J.C., Thomas, B.W., Ohlmann, J.W.: A rollout algorithm framework for heuristic solutions to finite-horizon stochastic dynamic programs. Eur. J. Oper. Res. 258(1), 216–229 (2017)
8. Gray, L., et al.: A mathematician looks at wolfram's new kind of science. Notices Am. Math. Soc. 50(2), 200–211. Citeseer (2003). http://www.ams.org/notices/200302/fea-gray.pdf
9. Haksar, R.N., Schwager, M.: Distributed deep reinforcement learning for fighting forest fires with a network of aerial robots. In: 2018 IEEE/RSJ International Conference on Intelligent Robots and Systems (IROS), pp. 1067–1074 (2018)

10. Joseph, A.G., Bhatnagar, S.: An online prediction algorithm for reinforcement learning with linear function approximation using cross entropy method. Mach. Learn. **107**(8–10), 1385–1429 (2018)
11. Nagórko, A.: Parallel nested rollout policy adaptation. In: 2019 IEEE Conference on Games (CoG), pp. 1–7. IEEE (2019)
12. Pais, C.: Vulcano: operational fire suppression management using deep reinforcement learning. In: Proceedings of the 19th International Conference on Autonomous Agents and MultiAgent Systems, pp. 1960–1962 (2020)
13. Roberto López, M.M.: Rollout implementation with CUDA, June 2020. https://doi.org/10.5281/zenodo.3922856
14. Sutton, R.S., Barto, A.G.: Reinforcement Learning: An Introduction, 2nd edn. The MIT Press, Cambridge (2018). http://incompleteideas.net/book/the-book-2nd.html
15. Yue, X., Kontar, R.A.: Why non-myopic bayesian optimization is promising and how far should we look-ahead? a study via rollout (2019)
16. Zhang, S., Buro, M.: Improving hearthstone AI by learning high-level rollout policies and bucketing chance node events. In: 2017 IEEE Conference on Computational Intelligence and Games (CIG), pp. 309–316. IEEE (2017)
17. Zinck, R.D., Grimm, V.: Unifying wildfire models from ecology and statistical physics. Am. Naturalist **174**(5), E170–E185 (2009)

Safety Instructions in a Virtual Machining Process: The Use of Motion Capture to Develop a VR App for Industrial Safety Purposes

Anna Lucía Díaz Vázquez⬛ and Óscar Hernández-Uribe^(✉)⬛

CIATEQ AC, Av. del Retablo 150, Col. Constituyentes-Fovissste, 76150 Querétaro, Mexico
oscar.hernandez@ciateq.mx

Abstract. Safety in industry has always been an important issue since 1950, following safety standards can reduce incidents and accidents throughout the manufacturing process, for instance, in the operation of a lathe. On the other hand, the prices for modern HMDs (ex. Oculus, HTC VIVE) have decreased, and, the amount of developers have increased around the world, so, the virtual reality on the last decade has been used across a wide range of sectors. This works shows a process flow to build a virtual environment for training operators on safety instructions for the lathe operation, where motion capture is used. The virtual environment is according to our real facilities where the building was modeled by using a laser scanner to maintain physical measures and distribution, the trainer body shape was also modeled, and, their motions were captured in order to make the virtual environment more immersive for training operators (i.e., they will see the virtual environment the same as the real facilities). Based on the developed methods, and, the capture motion to build the avatar which will teach operators to follow safety instructions, we found that participants felt immersed and comfortable while walking around the virtual environment, they also listened very carefully to the safety instructions given by the trainer's avatar. This was due to the emotional link built between the trainer and the participants by meeting each other before the test.

Keywords: Virtual reality · Motion capture · Industrial safety

1 Introduction

Safety in industry has always been promoted to minimize the number of incidents through the introduction of standards and compliance since 1950. Also, in the nineteen seventies, safety management systems had a new twist and started to focus on risk assessment and mitigation. Nowadays, the application of all the safety information gathered through all these years, is commonly transmitted with paper-based documentation like two dimensional drawings or verbal communication [1]. Even though, accident rates were reduced since 1950, they were not enough to have a totally safe environment. As a new strategy, industrial safety is trying to include emotional intelligence to manage cognitive failures, which are very common in workplaces. Cognitive failures are defined as cognitive-based

© Springer Nature Switzerland AG 2020
M. F. Mata-Rivera et al. (Eds.): WITCOM 2020, CCIS 1280, pp. 256–267, 2020.
https://doi.org/10.1007/978-3-030-62554-2_19

errors resulting from problems with memory, attention or action, these errors occur in simple tasks that a person should do without mistakes [2].

Also, cognitive failures have an important impact in workplace accidents or working performance. With all the changes industrial safety is having, the way of teaching it must change too. Nowadays, regular safety training doesn't show workers how to react emotionally and mentally to different types of scenarios, as a solution, these scenarios can be recreated in a virtual environment, making VR as a new option for safety training.

2 Literature Review

2.1 The Impact of VR

VR has become popular across many industries, such as entertainment, architecture, military, manufacturing and medicine. Even though that the concept of VR appeared since 1963, it became popular in 1989 by the founder of the Virtual Programming Languages research company, Jaron Lanier [3]. Nowadays, VR is defined as an "inducing targeted behavior in an organism by using artificial sensory stimulation, while the organism has little or no awareness of the inference" [4], this definition applies to any life forms such as cockroaches, monkeys, etc. The idea of being aware or not in VR comes from the idea of fooling the user in a neurobiology level (ex, when animals explore their environment, neural structures composed of place cells are formed to encode spatial information about their surroundings, our brains may fire place cells too while experiencing VR).

There are different types of devices to experience a virtual environment, the most common are Head Mounted Displays (HMD) and the Cave Automatic Virtual Environment (CAVE). There are some advantages and disadvantages between these two environments, the most important are the price and immersion level. Thanks to massmedia market, the prices for modern HMDS, like the Oculus Rift or the HTC VIVE have decreased but also, with all the technological development, "low-cost" CAVEs have been created tool [5]. Even though, the CAVE field of view is closer to the values of the human field view, the HMD offers a virtual environment that is visible all around the subject and gives an "everywhere" immersion notion. The decision of choosing one from another must rely in the characteristics of the project, like workspace, the wanted immersion level or budget.

For the development of VR simulations, a VR engine would be ideal but unfortunately, they are not yet available. In exchange of VR engines, developers use game engines like Unity or Unreal Engine, these engines are adapted for VR and sometimes need the special use of software development kits (SDK). These kits include particular headsets, device drivers, head tracking and display output. The main software components that are needed to produce a VR experience are matched motion (the correspondence between user motions on the real world and the virtual world), physics (for the virtual world to behave as the real) and networked experiences (interactions in the virtual world).

2.2 The Impact of VR in Training

VR applications are possible thanks to the immersion and presence level the user experiences, when we talk about immersion, we are referring to the sensorial stimulation that the virtual system offers, the feeling of presence is the psychological response to it [6].

Users of VR technologies have higher levels of immersion when the design of the Virtual Environment includes authentic images of the real place that is tried to simulate [7]. Nowadays, immersive systems are applied in different types of sectors. In case of the construction sector, immersive systems are used for the building information models (BIM) [8]. One of the advantages of this application is that the user walks through an unbuild building, in case there's something unwanted in the design, the building can be virtually changed, saving time and money. Also, the Human Resources (HR) sector applied immersive systems to improve recruiting. An example is the Jaguar company, they developed a mixed reality application to attract talent and test skills. Besides Jaguar, in 2016, the British financial agency Lloyds Banking Group announced the use of VR technology for job interviews [9].

The level of immersion and presence often changes with the type of technology that is used (AR, VR or CAVE). For example, it is reported that the experience in a simulation of a virtual piston with the same haptic feedback, feels more real with VR conditions than AR conditions [10]. Some VR applications also have challenges like picking or moving virtual objects, the level of immersion in these types of simulations depend on how similar the grabbing technique is to the hand grabbing movement [11]. Another area that impacts the level of immersion and presence, is the realism of how a common phenomenon is appreciated in a virtual simulation, like smoke or fire [12]. In most of the scientific literature, questionnaires and surveys are applied to participants in VR experiments to evaluate immersion, and the graphical and physical realism of the VE that the simulation offers. It is known that the success of VR applications relies in the realism that the virtual experience can offer, even, evidence suggests that human responses to virtual characters are similar to their responses to real people where emotion help people to establish a better relation with virtual avatar based on past interactions [13–15]. Moreover, the feeling of presence is greater in the "emotional" environments [16, 17], and, the ability of avatars to transmit and provoke an emotional state provides a very flexible and accurate manipulation of emotional induction [18, 19]. In this work, we reinforcement an emotional link by allowing participants meet the trainer in real life before meet in the virtual environment as an avatar.

Applications of VR go from military training to the healthcare sector. In case of the military sector, VR is applied for the training of military strategies that can't be done in some urban environments, making the training cheaper and safer. In the healthcare sector, VR is used in some hospitals to reduce chronic pain or anxiety in their patients [20]. This technology is also used in phobia treatments, making therapy cheaper and with less risk for the patient. Besides phobia treatments, VR has also been applied to evaluate the impact of vision loss in glaucoma patients, leading to a new technique of diagnosis for the detection of vision loss caused by this type of disease [21]. Simulations are commonly used in healthcare training, even though nurses and doctors share the same space, the academic content in each training can't be the same. Technologies like VR or AR come as a solution for new surgery learners, the common method of surgery training can lead to ethical problems and limited reality, also, additional training in an operating room costs time and can endanger the patient [22]. For nurses, VRS is used to train them for hospital evacuation process of the most vulnerable patients in case of a natural disaster or emergency [23].

Besides healthcare, VR training in the driving and manufacturing sector is very important, their activities involve people, which represent a major risk of accidents. VR offers driving training for automated cars, even though this type of car is not available for many people, in a future might be, getting used to the system will prevent accidents or any distraction while driving [24]. In the manufacturing area, the number of VR applications increased thanks to the digitization of manufacturing, the combination of cyber-physical systems and the internet of things (IoT) create less wasteful and smart processes. Also, it can help factories to increase their efficiency and productivity. This digitization is called Industry 4.0 and represent the fourth revolution that has occurred in manufacturing [25]. Table 1, show additional applications of VR in the manufacturing field.

Table 1. Application of VR in the manufacturing field.

VM Virtual Manufacturing	VR can support the representation of objects, processes, activities and principles providing enhanced graphic interface, this representation helps to the rapid understanding and decisions making by visualization experience. The Ford Motor Company uses VR as a technology to present their new car models and to improve their cars design [26, 27].
VP Virtual Prototyping	VP is the application of virtual reality for prototyping physical mock-ups (PMUs) using product and process data, it can be used to identify potential problems in a faster, less expensive and safer way than with traditional physical prototypes. Rolls-Royce Aero Engine Services used VP to demonstrate the company's Trent 800 engine [28].
VF Virtual Factory	These simulations are able to show the design of production facilities, individual manufacturing processes or total manufacturing enterprises. Some plants simulators use VR to evaluate the performance of industrial operators when facing abnormal situations that represent a potentially risk of accident, and, opens the opportunity to develop certifications in VF [29].
VT Virtual Training	Is a form of training done in a virtual or simulated environment that can improve the process of acquiring skills, it can be useful in the time reduction needed for assembly implementation [30]. In the aviation industry is applied for operators to learn how to detect cracks in the maintenance of aircrafts engines [31]. In the manufacturing industry, human-robot collaborations (HRC) are becoming very common, VT helps operators to learn new techniques of collaboration without risking their own safety [32–35]

3 Materials and Methods

This research aims to create a VR app that simulates a machining area to safely interact with a universal lathe machine. Safety instructions were recorded with a motion capture equipment, these recordings were applied in a virtual environment, the model for this environment was taken from the machining area at CIATEQ Bernardo Quintana. The universal lathe machine because it has more tendency to accidents than the other types of tool machines at CIATEQ. Figure 1 summarize mainly steps to build this VR app.

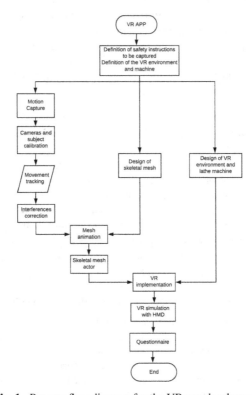

Fig. 1. Process flow diagram for the VR app development.

3.1 Motion Capture

Motion capture can be applied to track objects, animals, facial expressions or people. For this methodology, five Vicon Vero 1.3 MP cameras were used, the software for motion capture was run on a HP Z8 G4 Workstation with 32 GB of RAM and an NVIDIA Quadro P5000 GPU. A Vicon software, named "Shogun Live" was used for the motion capture and cameras calibration. The first part of the calibration consists in using a "wand v2" to test the range of the cameras and to set an origin in the reference axis at Shogun Live. Then, the setting of the floor plane and the delimitation of the working area has to be made, for these final steps, instead of the wand, spherical reflective markers (14 mm size) were used. After calibrating the cameras, the subject calibration has to be made, this subject will be recognized at any moment by the software for the motion capture, for this step a tracking suit with 54 spherical reflective markers along the body extremities and head was used. At the same time the Shogun Live software was running, the "Vicon Eclipse" software was used to create a data base with all the movements Shogun Live detects. With a T-pose, the subject calibration started until it detected at least 52 markers, after calibrating the subject, the safety instructions were recorded and saved as videos at the data base created with Vicon Eclipse (Fig. 2). The lack of a huge number of cameras and the workspace conditions created interference in our motion captures, these interferences were corrected with the Vicon "Shogun Post" software so that movements in the safety instructions would be able to look as natural as possible. After the videos were corrected, the files were exported as animations to the Autodesk Motion Builder software, the version used was the 2019.

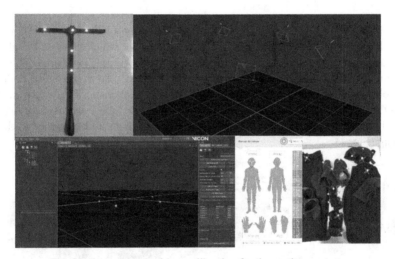

Fig. 2. Cameras and subject calibration for the motion capture.

3.2 Design of Virtual Environment

Before using Motion Builder, a skeletal mesh was designed in Autodesk Maya (also used the 2019 version) for the animation of the safety instructions performance. The skeletal mesh type has an underlying skeleton of joints that are controlled by data from an animation, for this research purposes, the motion captures that were already corrected in Shogun Post were used to animate the skeletal mesh (Fig. 3). In the Autodesk Motion Builder software, the motion captures were detected as a set of vertices and joints, this set helped to synchronize the videos with the mesh by using a vertex skinning process, where each vertex position is built up from a number of points of references [36], for this case, the points of references were the spherical markers in the tracking suit. After synchronizing the skeletal mesh with the motion captures, the animations were exported to Unreal Engine as skeletal mesh actors, this type of actors are different to static meshes and are generally used to display complex motion [37].

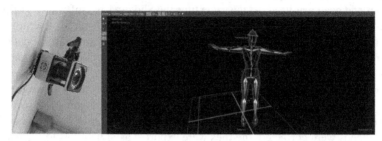

Fig. 3. Vicon Vero 1.3 MP camera with the visualization of the motion capture at the Autodesk Motion Builder software.

The 3D modeling technique chosen for the recreation of the machining area and universal lathe machine was the box modeling technique, which consists on taking a basic shape, like a box, cylinder, etc. and sculp it out until you reach a desired model [38] it is commonly used to make hard surfaced objects like desks, doors, furniture, buildings or any object that requires to be modeled with this characteristics. The software used to apply the box modeling technique was Autodesk Maya, also, photos were taken to the machining area and universal lathe machine to use them as a reference to the 3D modeling (Fig. 4).

Fig. 4. Comparison between the machining area and the universal lathe machine at CIATEQ Bernardo Quintana with the virtual recreations for the VR app.

4   Application and Discussion

4.1   VR App

As the use of VR becomes more popular with time, the number of HMD brands is increasing too. For example, Google launched a pair of VR glasses made with cardboard and focal distance lenses, the device was named as "Google CardBoard" and can be used with a smartphone. Even though Google CardBoard appears as a new and cheap option for VR, the top brands in the market of HMD are HTC Vive and Oculus Rift, the VR app for this project was designed to be used by an Oculus Rift S HMD (Fig. 5).

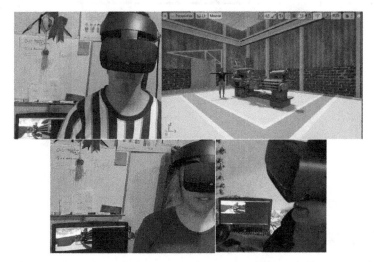

Fig. 5. Participants visualizing safety instruction for the virtual lathe machine in the VR with the use of Oculus Rift S.

The app showed to the users the virtual machining area taken from CIATEQ Bernardo Quintana and the skeletal mesh actor performing the following safety instructions:

1. To put on the safety helmet
2. To stay at the safety lane of the machining area
3. A "no" signal to disapprove unsafely actions at the working area
4. A "yes" signal to approve a behavior or action in the working area
5. To wear the appropriate clothes for the use of the lathe

For the VR tests, 10 participants were randomly chosen, the number of participants was chosen according to the number needed and used in the scientific community for this type of experiments, which is in a range of 8−10 participants. At the end of the simulation a questionnaire was applied, the questionnaire was divided in three sections, the first was to collect demographic information, the second section was about the knowledge of the lathe and industrial safety, the last section was about VR, participants were asked about how familiar VR was for them (Fig. 6). Also, giving a scale from 1 to 5 (being 5 the highest grade) the participants were asked about the realism that the render offers in the simulation, they were also asked about how immerse and comfortable they felt with the VE, other types of questions in this last section were about how useful they considered VR as a learning tool and how easily was to understand the instructions from the avatar.

Fig. 6. An online questionnaire to support findings about the VR app.

4.2 Discussion

In the present study, participants were not very familiar with VR simulations, they only related it with videogames. When we asked them to walk around the virtual machining area before introducing them to the universal lathe machine, participants perceived the render of the virtual machining area as very realistic. Even though, participants had no experience with industrial safety and the universal lathe machine, they understood clearly the instructions for its safety use and considered that the movements of the skeletal mesh actor were very natural. They also adapted very easily to the Oculus Rift S hardware and have short time simulations. The VR app developed for this project can be considered as a solution for constant training about safety issues in the machining area at CIATEQ.

5   Conclusions and Future Work

This work shows a potential use of motion capture for training operators on safety instructions, we followed our process flow to the end with a virtual environment by using motion capture, we captured our building facilities, the trainer's shape and body expressions. In these few tests, the emotional link that was built between the trainer and the operator, and, the model of the virtual environment close to the real facilities has revealed that the user feels immersive and comfortable with the simulation, and, listened carefully the safety instructions given by the trainer's avatar.

Now that we have an approach to our building facilities by this virtual environment, we will continue doing more tests by building an emotional link between the trainer and the operators for future tests. We are working on recreating more virtual scenarios in order to test different cases under stress and look for several main causes of accidents that can be a misunderstood content on a traditional classroom training. As an internal project, the app was not uploaded to any store, it was only designed for Oculus hardware, in a future, industrial safety projects could be uploaded to the Oculus Store as a commercial VR app. Finally, some advantages we have found by working on this app are:

- Different VR scenarios can be built to ensure and enhanced different learning paths.
- Real time tours in virtual factories can be made with the technology that motion capture offers.
- Since VR prevents user's equipment damage, mistakes are allowed, and, injures to users are avoided.
- VR allows to have a realistic training for industrial purposes.

References

1. Cheng, T., Teizer, J.: Real-time resource location data collection and visualization technology for construction safety and activity monitoring applications. Autom. Constr. **34**, 3–15 (2013)
2. Petitta, L., Probst, T., Ghezzi, V., Barbaranelli, C.: Cognitive failures in response to emotional contagion: their effects on workplace accidents. Accid. Anal. Prev. **125**, 165–173 (2019)
3. Muhanna, M.: Virtual reality and the CAVE: taxonomy, interaction challenges and research directions. J. King Saudi Univ.-Comput. Inf. Sci. **27**(3), 344–361 (2015)
4. Lavalle, S.: Virtual Reality, 1st edn. Cambridge University Press, University of Oulu, Cambridge (2019)
5. Mestre, D.: CAVE versus head-mounted displays: ongoing thoughts. J. Electron. Imaging **2017**(3), 31–35 (2017)
6. Bowman, D., McMahan, R.: Virtual reality: how much immersion is enough? Computer **40**(7), 36–43 (2007)
7. Jang, Y., Park, E.: An adoption model for virtual reality games: the roles of presence and enjoyment. Telematics Inf. **42**(February), 1–9 (2019)
8. Wang, C., Li, H., Kho, S.: VR-embedded BIM immersive system for QS engineering education. Comput. Appl. Eng. Educ. **26**(3), 626–641 (2018)
9. Zhao, H., Zhao, Q., Ślusarczyk, B.: Sustainability and digitalization of corporate management based on augmented/virtual reality tools usage: China and other world IT companies' experience. Sustainability **11**(17), 1–17 (2019)
10. Gaffary, Y., Le Gouis, B., Marchal, M., et al.: AR Feels "Softer" than VR: haptic perception of stiffness in augmented versus virtual reality. IEEE Trans. Visual Comput. Graph. **23**(11), 2372–2377 (2017)
11. Lin, J., Schulze, J.: Towards naturally grabbing and moving objects in VR. Electron. Imaging **2016**(4), 1–6 (2016)

12. Liu, S., Yu, Z.: Sounding fire for immersive virtual reality. Virtual Reality **19**(3-4), 291–302 (2015). https://doi.org/10.1007/s10055-015-0271-7
13. Freeman, D., Slater, M., Bebbington, P.E., et al.: Can virtual reality be used to investigate persecutory ideation? J. Nervous Mental Disease **191**(8), 509–514 (2003)
14. Vinayagamoorthy, V., Garau, M., Steed, A., Slater, M.: An eye gaze model for dyadic interaction in an immersive virtual environment: practice and experience. Comput. Graph. Forum **23**(1), 1–11 (2004)
15. Qu, C., Brinkman, P.W., Ling, Y., et al.: Human perception of a conversational virtual human: an empirical study on the effect of emotion and culture. Virtual Reality **17**, 307–321 (2013)
16. Riva, G., Mantovani, F., Capideville, C.S., et al.: Affective interactions using virtual reality: the link between presence and emotions. CyberPsychol. Behav. **10**(1), 45–56 (2007)
17. Slater, M., Lotto, B., Arnold, M.M., et al.: How we experience immersive virtual environments: the concept of presence and its measurement. Anuario de Psicología **40**(2), 193–210 (2009)
18. Causse, M., Pavard, B., Senard, J.M., et al.: Positive and negative emotion induction through avatars and its impact on reasoning performance: cardiovascular and pupillary correlates. Studia Psychologica **54**(1), 37–51 (2012)
19. Chirico, A., Gaggioli, A.: Virtual-reality music-based elicitation of awe: when silence is better than thousands sounds. In: Cipresso, P., Serino, S., Villani, D. (eds.) Pervasive Computing Paradigms for Mental Health. LNICST, vol. 288, pp. 1–11 (2019). https://doi.org/10.1007/978-3-030-25872-6_1
20. Wiederhold, B., Miller, I., Wiederhold, M.: Using virtual reality to mobilize health care: mobile virtual reality technology for attenuation of anxiety and pain. IEEE Consum. Electron. Mag. **7**(1), 106–109 (2018)
21. Daga, F., Macagno, E., Stevenson, C., et al.: Wayfinding and glaucoma: a virtual reality experiment. Invest. Ophtalmol. Vis. Sci. **58**(9), 3343–3349 (2017)
22. Maier, J., Weiherer, M., Huber, M., et al.: Imitating human soft tissue on basis of a dual-material 3D print using a support-filled metamaterial to provide bimanual haptic for a hand surgery training system. Quant. Imaging Med. Surg. **9**(1), 30–42 (2019)
23. Farra, S., Miller, E., Hodgson, E., et al.: Storyboard development for virtual reality simulation. Clin. Simul. Nurs. **12**(9), 392–399 (2016)
24. Sportillo, D., Paljic, A., Ojeda, L.: Get ready for automated driving using virtual reality. Accid. Anal. Prev. **118**(June), 102–113 (2018)
25. What is Industry 4.0? Here's a super easy explanation for anyone. https://www.forbes.com/sites/bernardmarr/2018/09/02/what-is-industry-4-0-heres-a-super-easy-explanation-for-anyone/#7708b5f49788, Accessed 18 Nov 2019
26. Ford presenta el Mustang más potente de la historia. https://www.milenio.com/negocios/ford-presenta-el-mustang-mas-potente-de-la-historia, Accessed 02 Jul 2019
27. Innovación de Diseño de Autos en 3D. https://www.ford.mx/blog/innovacion/diseno-autos-tecnologia-3d-ford-nuevos-modelos-201902/, Accessed 02 Jul 2019
28. Schina, L., Lazoi, M., Lombardo, R., Corallo, A.: Virtual reality for product development in manufacturing industries. In: De Paolis, L.T., Mongelli, A. (eds.) AVR 2016. LNCS, vol. 9768, pp. 198–207. Springer, Cham (2016). https://doi.org/10.1007/978-3-319-40621-3_15
29. Colombo, S., Golzio, L.: The plant simulator as viable means to prevent and manage risk through competencies management: experiment results. Saf. Sci. **84**, 46–56 (2016)
30. Gabajová, G., Furmannová, B., Medvecká, I., et al.: Virtual training application by use of augmented and virtual reality under university technology enhanced learning in Slovakia. Sustainability **11**(23), 1–16 (2019)
31. Eschen, H., Kötter, R., Rodeck, T., et al: Augmented and virtual reality for inspection and maintenance processes in the aviation industry. In: 6th International Conference on Through-life Engineering Services, TESConf2017. Procedia Manufacturing, vol 19, pp. 156–163 (2018)

32. Nalepka, P., Lamb, M., Kallen, R., et al.: Human social motor solutions for human–machine interaction in dynamical task contexts. Proc. Nat. Acad. Sci. U.S.A. **116**(4), 1437–1446 (2019)
33. Wang, Q., Cheng, Y., Jiao, W., et al.: Virtual reality human-robot collaborative welding: a case study of weaving gas tungsten arc welding. J. Manuf. Process **48**, 210–217 (2019)
34. Matsas, E., Vosniakos, G., Batras, D.: Prototyping proactive and adaptive techniques for human-robot collaboration in manufacturing using virtual reality. Robot. Comput.-Integrated Manuf. **50**, 168–180 (2018)
35. Oyekan, J., Hutabarat, W., Tiwari, A., et al.: The effectiveness of virtual environments in developing collaborative strategies between industrial robots and humans. Robot. Comput.-Integrated Manuf. **55**, 41–54 (2019)
36. Tutorial 9 : Skeletal Animation. https://research.ncl.ac.uk/, Accessed 01 Jul 2020
37. Skeletal Mesh Actors|Unreal Engine Documentation. https://docs.unrealengine.com/en-US/Engine/Actors/SkeletalMeshActors/index.html, Accessed 30 Jun 2020
38. Box Modeling: The 3D Modeling Technique. http://thilakanathanstudios.com/2016/10/box-modeling-the-3d-modeling-technique/, Accessed 01 Jul 2020

The Effect of Bilateral Filtering in 3D Reconstruction Using PSP

Luis Arturo Alvarado Escoto$^{(\boxtimes)}$, Jesús Carlos Pedraza Ortega,
Juan Manuel Ramos Arreguin, Efren Gorrostieta Hurtado,
and Saúl Tovar Arriaga

Facultad de Ingenierías, Universidad Autónoma de Querétaro,
Santiago de Querétaro, Querétaro, Mexico
luis.a.alvarado.e@gmail.com, caryoko@yahoo.com, jsistdig@yahoo.com.mx,
efrengorrostieta@gmail.com, saul.tovar@uaq.mx

Abstract. Phase-shifting profilometry is among the most popular techniques in optical measurement due to its numerous advantages such as high resolution and low computational cost. Although, high quality 3D reconstructions can be achieved by phase-shifting profilometry, Moiré pattern noise may appear during the image acquisition stage and be carried out during the entire reconstruction process. Thus, resulting in noisy reconstructions and uncertain or unreliable height estimations. Moiré noise can be attenuated, however, or even removed in the frequency domain of the reconstructed scenes. By analyzing the spectrum of the image, we can discard the high frequencies cause by the Moiré patterns. Furthermore, a band-pass filter is applied in order to suppress such frequencies. This paper focuses of the use of a bilateral filter as a post-processing stage in phase-shifting profilometry. Moreover, we discovered that by filtering these high frequencies, Moiré pattern noise is reduced, resulting in smoother surfaces and better height estimations.

Keywords: Phase shifting profilometry · 3D reconstruction · Bilateral filter · Phase unwrapping · Fringe projection

1 Introduction

Over recent years, a significant area of research in computer vision has been dedicated to the extraction of 3D information from a 2D scene. The extraction of depth information can be used in a number of applications such as facial recognition, virtual reality, video games and medical equipment. Although many different techniques may extract the 3D shape of an object, a post-processing is empirical in order to reduce the noise generated in the extraction process. Moiré patterns have been observed in 3D extraction techniques, inducing significant error in the measurements obtained by the reconstructed scenes. In phase-shifting profilometry, PSP, Moiré patterns are carried throughout the reconstruction process from the image acquisition stage. Thus, reducing the accuracy in the obtained results even after the phase unwrapping process.

© Springer Nature Switzerland AG 2020
M. F. Mata-Rivera et al. (Eds.): WITCOM 2020, CCIS 1280, pp. 268–280, 2020.
https://doi.org/10.1007/978-3-030-62554-2_20

1.1 Phase-Shifting Profilometry

Phase-shifting profilometry is one of the most popular techniques in 3D extraction, since it can achieve high resolution at a low cost. Moreover, PSP is less sensitive to variations in the reflection and ambient light[1]. PSP is considered a non-contact technique, since no contact is required with the subject under study. It is also considered an active technique, since it depends on triangulation and the projection and detection of light. In contrast, passive methods use ambient illumination during data acquisition [2]. In phase-shifting profilometry at least three fringe patterns, created from sinusoidal or periodic signals, of light and dark fringes are projected onto the object and the background plane. These fringes are deformed by the shape of the object[3]. Every fringe pattern is projected onto the object and then captured by a camera from a different angle. The object's 3D information is then obtained from these images through phase extraction[4–6].

A number of PSP methods have been developed over the years, *three-step* and *four-step* methods are the most popular ones, their names based on the number of patterns projected. In these methods, every fringe pattern projected has on offset in phase of $2\pi/N$, where N represents the number of patterns used. The true phase is then encoded in the variations of the intensity pattern of the fringes, and can be recovered by a point-to-point calculation. To obtain the object's height estimation, the phase map must be extracted from the images and then unwrapped[1, 4, 5]. Accurate phase extraction, however, is a challenging task, since it can significantly influence on measurement results. Many research have improved phase shifting algorithms by changing the configuration of the fringe patterns, succesfully reducing the errors in phase-shifting extraction. In 2018 Zhai[8] proposed a method based on lest-squares algorithm and general eclipse fitting, which can effectively suppress random phase-shifting errors.

The recovered phase is then limited to the interval $[-\pi, +\pi]$ given the principle of the arctan function, which is used in the phase extraction process[4, 7]. As a result, the phase must be unwrapped in order to eliminate the artificial discontinuities created by the phase extraction. Phase unwrapping is the process of finding the integer unknown multiple of 2π that must be added to each pixel in the wrapped phase map to make it continuous[6]. Although, phase unwrapping may seem as a trivial task, the presence of noise, low illumination, undersampling, and the conditions of the object under study , make phase unwrapping a complex and difficult process. In reality, the unwrapping of the phase is considered and NP-Hard problem, for which, an approximate solution is devised[9]. There are a number of phase unwrapping techniques that have been developed over the years. In this paper, we focus on the use of Graph-Cuts algorithm[9], since it is a robust algorithm and presents a fast and accurate phase unwrapping[3].

1.2 Moiré Patterns

Moiré patterns occur when two or more figures with periodic rulings are made to overlap. For the Moiré patterns to appear, the two patterns must not be completely identical, but must be displaced, shifted or rotated[11,12]. Moiré patterns usually appear as stripes, ripples, or curves or intensity and color superimposed on an image. These patterns can dramatically lower the visual quality of the image[13]. Although the presence of Moiré patterns is unwanted, the patterns may be useful in some applications. In 2015, Garcia [14] created a solution for face-spoofing detection based on Moiré patterns. Here, face detection is carried out by searching for Moiré patterns and the detection of peaks in the frequency domain of the image.

Over the years, given the increasing demand for high-resolution and detailed clear images, the demand for post-processing techniques capable of reducing Moiré patterns has been on the rise. Several methods have been proposed to remove Moiré patterns. Liu[15] proposed a Moiré pattern removal method via low rand and sparse matrix decomposition. However, this techniques is used exclusively on texture images with the premise that textures are locally well-patterned. Sun[13] proposed a more robust techniques based on convolutional neural networks, achieving state of the art performance to similar image restoration techniques.

In PSP, Moiré patterns appear given the nature of the fringe patterns used. Furthermore, given the complex origination of the noise, it is very difficult to control its appearance during the data acquisition stage. Therefore, a post-processing method must be carried out in order to remove or reduce the noise. Typically, Moiré noise can be filtered in the Fourier domain of the image by correcting the amplitude spectrum components altered by the noise. Noise filtering can result in smoother surfaces and reduces the error in height estimation since less peaks are present, resulting in better estimations[12]. The present work focuses on the correction of Moiré patterns in 3D reconstruction using *three-step* phase-shifting profilometry, by applying a bilateral filter as a post-processing technique.

2 Principle of the Method

The *three-step* method projects three fringe patterns onto the object. These patterns can be described by the following equations:

$$I_1 = I'(x,y) + I''(x,y)Cos(\phi(x,y)) \tag{1}$$

$$I_2 = I'(x,y) + I''(x,y)Cos(\phi(x,y) + \alpha) \tag{2}$$

$$I_3 = I'(x,y) + I''(x,y)Cos(\phi(x,y) + 2\alpha) \tag{3}$$

where $I'(x,y)$ is the intensity, $I''(x,y)$ is the intensity modulation, $\phi(x,y)$ is the true phase and α is the offset in phase[4,5,10]. Here, a value of $2\pi/3$ is used for α.

The proposed methodology requires to capture two sets of images. The first set are the fringe patterns projected onto the object, while the second set are the fringe patterns projected without the object. This, will create a reference plane over the true phase without the distortions created by the object. The complete methodology is described by Fig. 1.

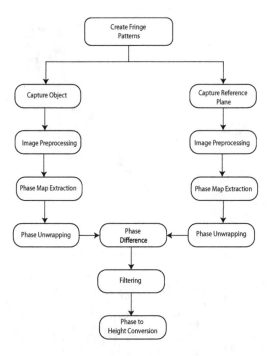

Fig. 1. Methodology used for 3D reconstruction.

Image acquisition is carried out by using a setup as the one shown in Fig. 2. Here, a projector is set above the object and a camera captured the projected patterns from a different angle. Normally, a distance between 18 to 30 cm between the projector and the camera is used, assuring that the angle between the object and the camera is about 10°. The captured images are then set through a pre-processing. All the images are set to an equal size and a perspective correction is carried out. Later, a gamma correction is applied to the images and a histogram equalization is done, if and only considered necessary.

The phase map to solve is then given by Eq. 4. From this equation the phase map can be obtained applying the same process point-to-point or pixel-to-pixel. Figure 3 shows an example of the captured images and the phase maps retrieved for the object and the reference plane.

$$\phi(x,y) = tan^{-1}\left(\sqrt{3}\frac{I_1(x,y) - I_3(x,y)}{2I_2(x,y) - I_1(x,y) - I_3(x,y)}\right) \tag{4}$$

Due to the arctan function, the retrieved phase map will be wrapped. There-fore, the next stage must consist in implementing a phase unwrapping technique. Here, *Graph Cuts* algorithm was implemented for the phase unwrapping stage. This algorithm, more commonly known as *PUMA*, is based on the premise of energy minimization which is reached by a finite sequence of binary minimiza-tions. Each of this sequence is efficiently solved by a max-flow/min-cut calculus

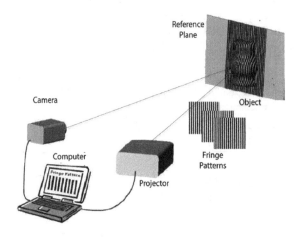

Fig. 2. Setup used for image acquisition

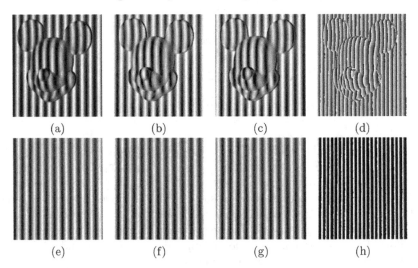

Fig. 3. (a) Step 1: 0°. (b) Step 2: 120°. (c) Step 3: 240°. (d) Object phase map. (e) Reference step 1: 0°. (f) Reference step 2: 120°. (g)Reference step 3: 240°. (h) Reference plane phase map.

in certain graphs[9]. Finally, the 3D reconstruction can be obtained trough the difference in phase of both, the object unwrapped phase map and the reference plane unwrapped phase map.

2.1   Notch Filtering

The purpose of a notch filter is to exclude the noise components from images by removing isolated noise or distorted frequencies[12]. Figure 4 shows a 2d representation of an object reconstructed using PSP and presents Moiré pattern noise.

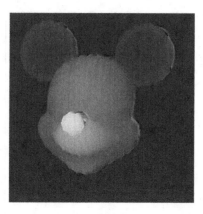

Fig. 4. Reconstructed object using PSP presenting Moiré pattern noise.

The noise is present in vertical lines, which are caused by the fringe analysis used in image acquisition. In Fig. 5 the entire process implemented for the reduction of moiré patterns is described. As shown, the noise is filtered in the frequency domain, and a band-pass filter is used in order to eliminate the high frequencies which are responsible for causing the Moiré patterns.

The analysis of the image's spectrum allow to visualize the coordinates where the unwanted frequencies are present. In Fig. 6 a 2D and a 3D representation of the spectrum is shown. Here, is noticeable that the unwanted frequencies are close to the center in the horizontal axis. In the 3D representation, the unwanted frequencies are visible as small peaks close to the main peak.

In this paper, a band-pass filter was chosen to attenuate the peaks of noise that are close to the center. To represent the band-pass filter, a 2D mask of ones was created, the same size as the spectrum, placing zeros in the coordinates where the unwanted frequencies are located. The mask is then multiplied by the spectrum, eliminating the values of the high peaks. In Fig. 7 the resulting spectrum can be visualized. Here, the peaks that were previously found along the horizontal axis are no longer present.

In order to evaluate the effect of the proposed filter in PSP reconstructed images, two types of objects were used: symmetrical objects and objects with complex surfaces. The symmetrical objects have known dimensions, which means that a digital representation of the object can be created, in contrast to the objects of unknown dimensions. The effects of the filter was evaluated by comparing the results of the reconstructed image before and post-filtering.

3   Results

The effect of the bilateral filter was evaluated by using two types of object, symmetrical with known dimensions and objects of unknown dimensions and complex surfaces. For the experimental setup the equipment used was a Dell G3

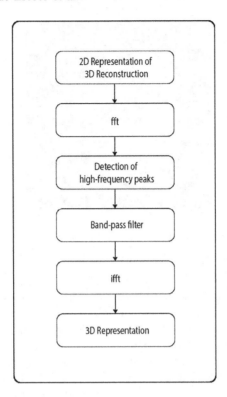

Fig. 5. Steps followed to suppress Moiré noise using a notch filter.

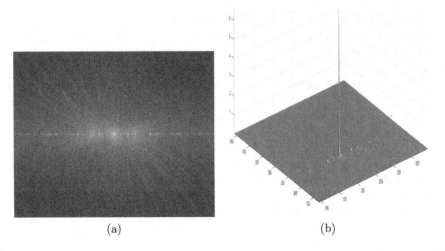

(a)   (b)

Fig. 6. (a) 2D visualization of the spectrum of an image with Moiré pattern noise. (b) 3D representation of the spectrum. The image was magnified for better visualization of spectral components around the center.

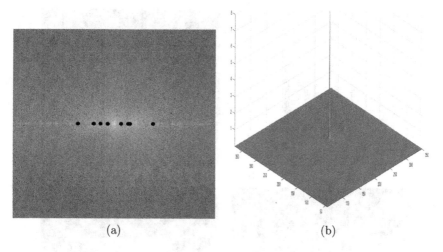

Fig. 7. (a) 2D visualization of the spectrum of an image with Moiré pattern noise. (b) 3D representation of the spectrum. The image was magnified for better visualization of spectral components around the center.

with 16GB RAM computer with an Intel® Core™ i7-8750GHz and Windows 10 64 bits. Matlab R2018 was utilized, as well as a DLP projector brand Asus S1 and a webcam Logitech model C920 Pro. The fringe analysis was carried out using 32 gray-scale fringes in every pattern. To evaluate the effect of the filter in the PSP process, we tested more than 10 different objects. The objects were reconstructed using *three-step* PSP and *Graph Cuts* phase unwrapping.

Figure 8 shows some of the results obtained during experimentation. Here, it's visible that Moiré pattern noise is heavily present after the phase unwrapping stage. In the 3D representation, seen in Fig. 9 of the object, these patterns are even more visible. Thus, the surface of the object seems to have peaks, when ideally it would be flat. When analyzing the spectrum of the image, these high frequencies are very noticeable, appearing mostly along the horizontal axis of the image. When, we filtered the noise using the band-pass filter, we can see a considerable improvement on the quality of the image. Most of the noise patterns have been smoothed out, creating a flatter surface in the 3D representation.

This reconstruction was chosen specifically, since it presents high levels of Moiré pattern noise. As shown in the Fig. 9 a high frequencies are present specially on the side of the object. This, due to the fact that shadow regions were captured during the image acquisition stage. The implemented filter does remove the noise created by the shadow regions. But, as can be seen in the spectrum, these regions created high level frequencies in zones of the spectrum outside of the horizontal axis.

Figure 10 shows a profile of the reconstructed object before and after the filter was applied. Here, we can see that the overall outline does present less jumps in value, creating a somewhat smoother area. However, the noise is heavily present,

Fig. 8. (a)Original Object. (b) 2D visualization of object reconstructed using PSP. (c) Filtered spectrum. (d) 2D visualization of reconstructed object post-filter.

as observed by the spectrum of the image, the Moiré patter extends beyond the horizontal axis, which means that a further analysis would be required to improve on the image. However, the results presented do improve on the result obtained after the phase unwrapping stage.

In Fig. 11 a second reconstruction was performed to test the effect of the filter. Here, there is less noise present after the phase unwrapping stage. In this particular case, the high frequencies can be seen as regions along the horizontal axis. The spectrum of the image showed certain coordinates where the frequencies presented higher peaks. After using the band-pass filter, we removed these frequencies from the image's spectrum. As a result, in Fig. 12 we can see that the surface has been smoothed out, and there was no major loss of information. In the 3D representation of the reconstructed object in Fig. 12, the post-filter result clearly presents less phase jumps, resulting in a much smoother area.

Figure 13 shows a profile of the reconstructed object, as a way of analyzing the impact of the filter. Here, we can observe that the entire outline has been somewhat smoothen. The post-filtering profile does present improvements in the overall shape, which would result in a more accurate estimation of height. Although, noise is still present, it certainly improves on the result obtained without the filter.

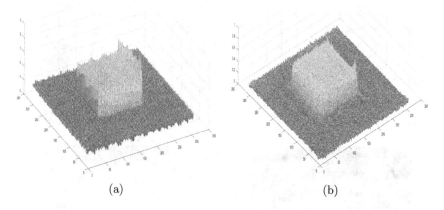

Fig. 9. (a)3D visualization of reconstructed object using PSP. (b) 3D visualization of reconstructed object post-filter.

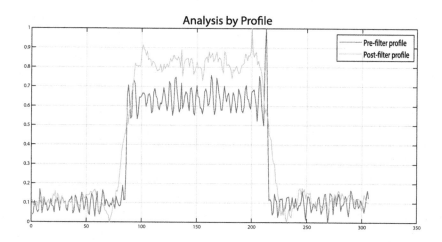

Fig. 10. Profile of the reconstructed object pre and post filtering

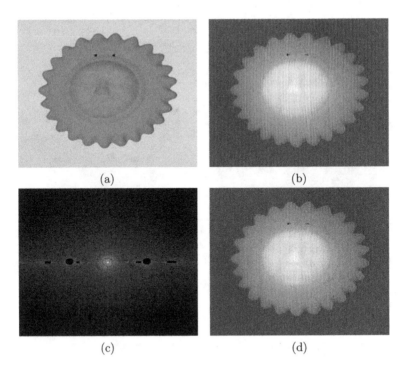

Fig. 11. (a)Original Object. (b) 2D visualization of object reconstructed using PSP. (c) Filtered spectrum. (d) 3D visualization of reconstructed object post-filter.

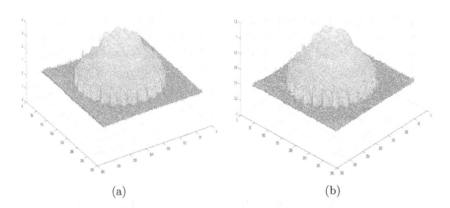

Fig. 12. (a)3D visualization of reconstructed object using PSP. (b) 3D visualization of reconstructed object post-filter.

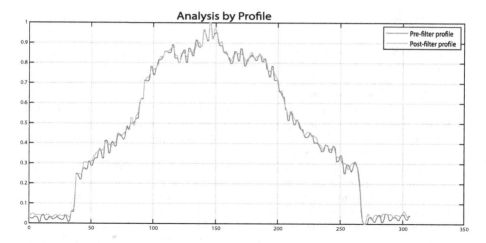

Fig. 13. Profile of the reconstructed object pre and post filtering

4   Conclusions and Future Work

In this paper we developed an experiment to test the effects of bilateral filtering as a post-processing stage in 3D reconstruction by phase-shifting profilometry, specifically the three-step algorithm. This techniques consists in projecting three fringe sine patterns, each with an offset in phase, onto the object, in order to extract the 3D information encoded in the phase shift. Given the nature of the overlapping patters, Moiré pattern noise is present during the image acquisition process and is carried through the entire reconstruction process, resulting in noisy reconstructions and less accurate height estimations. To reduce the present of Moiré noise, a notch filter was proposed as a post-processing stage in the PSP process.

At least 10 objects were tested, to evaluate the effect that the filter has on the obtained reconstructions. By analyzing the reconstructed image in its frequency domain and examining its spectrum, we can filter the frequencies that may cause some of the noise. Using a 2D mask, we created a band-pass filter which would suppress the unwanted frequencies in the image's spectrum. Here, we chose to suppress only the high peaks, as to reduce the loss of information. The results showed that by doing this, we can obtained flatter, smoother surfaces of the reconstructed objects. Furthermore, the resulting reconstructed images have better visual quality than the results obtained without the filter.

As future work, we hope to improve on the obtained results, by doing a more detailed analysis of the spectrum and applying a filter in both axis of the image. Research is been done as well, in a comparison of different filters for Moiré patterns and test their effect in PSP.

References

1. Guerrero, R.E.D., Morales, J.C.M., Arreguin, J.M.R., Soto, J.E.V., Ortega, J.C.P.: Comparative analysis of phase unwrapping in PSP using depth images. In: International Conference in Mechatronics, Electronics and Automative Engineering (ICMEAE), Prague, pp. 20–24 (2015)
2. Pedraza Ortega, J.C.: Image processing for 3D reconstruction using a modified Fourier transform profilometry method. In: Gelbukh, A., Kuri Morales, Á.F. (eds.) MICAI 2007. LNCS (LNAI), vol. 4827, pp. 705–712. Springer, Heidelberg (2007). https://doi.org/10.1007/978-3-540-76631-5_67
3. Lopez-Torres, C., Salazar Cortes, S., Kells, K., Pedraza-Ortega, J., Ramos-Arreguin, J.: Improving 3D reconstruction accuracy in wavelet transform profilometry by reducing shadow effects. IET Image Process. 14(2), 310–317 (2020)
4. Kato, J.: Fringe Analysis. In: Yoshizawa, T. (ed.) Handbook of Optical Metrology, Principles and Applications, pp. 541–554. CRC Press, Boca Raton (2015)
5. Schreiber, H., Brunning, J: Phase shifting interferometry. In: Malacara, D. (eds.) Optical Shop Testing, pp. 547–667. Wiley Interscience (2007)
6. Gorthi, S., Rastogi, P.: Fringe projection techniques: whither we are? Opt. Lasers Eng. 48(2), 113–440 (2010)
7. Zuo, C., Feng, S., Huang, L., Tao, T., Yin, W., Chen, Q.: Phase shifting algorithms for fringe projection profilometry: a review. Opt. Lasers Eng. 109, 23–59 (2018)
8. Zhai, Z., Li, Z., Zhang, Y., Dong, Z.: An accurate phase shift extraction algorithm for phase shifting interferometry. Optics Communications 429, 144–151 (2018)
9. Bioucas-Dias, J.M., Valadao, G.: Phase unwrapping via max flows. IEEE Trans. Image Process. 16, 698–709 (2007)
10. Garcia, J.: Review in digitization of solid through structured light. Centro de investigaciones en optica, A.C. (2015)
11. Oster, G., Nishijima, Y.: Moiré patterns. Sci. Am. 208(5), 54–63 (1963)
12. Wei, Z., Wang, J., Nichol, H., Wiebe, S., Chapman, D.: A median-Gaussian filtering framework for Moiré pattern noise removal from X-ray microscopy image. Micron 43(2–3), 170–176 (2012)
13. Sun, Y., Yu, Y., Wang, W.: Moiré photo restoration using multiresolution convolutional neural networks. IEEE Trans. Image Process. 27(8), 4160–4172 (2018)
14. Garcia, D.C., Queiroz, R.L.: Face-spoofing 2D-detection based on Moiré-pattern Analysis. IEEE Trans. Inf. Forens. Secur. 10(4), 778–789 (2015)
15. Liu, F., Yang, J., Yue, H.: Moiré pattern removal from texture images via low-rank and sparse matrix decomposition. In: 2015 Visual Communications and Image Processing (VCIP), pp. 1–4 (2015)

Regulation of a Van der Pol Oscillator Using Reinforcement Learning

Carlos Emiliano Solórzano-Espíndola$^{(\boxtimes)}$ (D), José Ángel Avelar-Barragán (D),
and Rolando Menchaca-Mendez (D)

Centro de Investigación en Computación, Mexico City, Mexico
carlosemiliano04@gmail.com, angelavelarb.94@gmail.com, rmen@cic.ipn.mx

Abstract. In this work, we propose a reinforcement learning-based methodology for the regulation problem of a Van der Pol oscillator with an actuator subject to constraints. We use two neural networks, one who learns an approximation of the cost given a state, and one that learns the controller output. We employ a classic PID controller with compensation as base policy in a rollout scheme. This policy is further improved by a neural network trained on trajectories from random initial states. The results show that the resulting control policy reduces the cost for a minimal energy trajectory given an initial state.

Keywords: Van der Pol · Reinforcement learning · Rollout · Controller · Neural networks

1 Introduction

Balthazar van der Pol studied the phenomena of oscillations in a vacuum tube, obtaining that for any set of initial conditions the system converges to the same periodic orbit (a stable limit cycle). But this behavior was different from the solutions of linear models. Balthazar then proposed the differential equation known as 'the unforced van der Pol oscillator' [18].

This differential equation is now a basic model for the oscillatory process, van der Pol for himself tried to study the stability of the heart mechanics comparing it to circuit models. The van der Pol equation describes an autonomous system and for the sinusoidal forced case can derive into a chaotic oscillator. The unforced case is taken as a first approach to the problem, trying to perform the convergence to a certain point before convergence to trajectories.

Among the different ways to control non-linear systems, for the analytical case, solving a Lyapunov function is the most usual. But for more complex cases, where is not trivial get the analytical solution, there are some numeric approximations, and as is mentioned in [15] were they apply a fuzzy control and hyperbolic system control as a universal approximator of the original system.

About the optimal control for forced van der Pol oscillator the work of T.P. Chagas, *et al.* present an approach using proportional feedback and a delayed feedback controller [5].

© Springer Nature Switzerland AG 2020
M. F. Mata-Rivera et al. (Eds.): WITCOM 2020, CCIS 1280, pp. 281–296, 2020.
https://doi.org/10.1007/978-3-030-62554-2_21

Instead of using an approach based on other numeric solvers for least mean squares optimization, as in the work of Zheng Ji and Xuyang Lou [10]. An algorithm based in an Actor-Critic model is proposed that solves the optimal control (using the minimum energy for the control signal) to converge to a certain state of the system.

1.1   Reinforcement Learning

Reinforcement Learning proposes methods to find solutions to non-trivial problems. Given that we know a cost/reward function, reinforcement-learning solutions obtain optimized *control policies* such that, given the state x_k of the system, determine an action $u_k = \mu(X_k)$ that optimize the long term cost [2]. For this, each state in the system

$$J(x_k) = g(x_N) + \sum_{k=0}^{N-1} g(x_k, u_k) \tag{1}$$

Where $f(x_k, u_k)$ defines the next state reached by the system upon using the control u_k and $g(x_k, u_k)$ is the cost of using the control u_k while begin in the state x_k. $J(x_k)$ is the cumulative long term cost of the sequence starting from the state x_k. It assumes that for all the states in the problem, the cost J is finite.

$$J(x_k) = g(x_N) + J(f(x_k, u_k)) \tag{2}$$

Where $f(x_k, u_k)$ defines the next state reached by the system upon using the control u_k and $g(x_k, u_k)$ is the cost of using the control u_k while begin in the state x_k, $g(x_N)$ is the cost of being in the terminal state, which commonly is 0. $J(x_k)$ is the long term cost of the sequence to arrive to the next state given by $f(x_k, u_k)$ considering N steps. It assumes that for all the states in the problem the cost J is finite and will arrive in $s \leq N$ steps.

A policy $\mu(X)$ is optimal if it produces the controls u such that,

$$J^*(x) = \min_{u \in U(x)} g(x, u) + J^*(f(x, u)) \tag{3}$$

for all the states x considered in the problem. The Reinforcement Learning methods have shown promising advantages for control systems either when we do have a model of the system or in a model-free setting [4].

There are two main approaches for Reinforcement Learning in control theory; the first one is to use it to tune the parameters of a given controller [7]; the second one is to use a parametric architecture, commonly a neural network, to obtain a controller. In this work, we show how a standard method from classic control can be used as a basis to build a better controller using two neural networks for the given problem.

1.2 Van der Pol Oscillator

The Van der Pol oscillator is defined by the second order differential equation

$$\frac{d^2x}{dt^2} - \alpha(1 - x^2)\frac{dx}{dt} + x = 0 \tag{4}$$

where the parameter α is a constant that defines the damping with $(1 - x^2)$ resulting in a non-linear behavior of the system. It is common to find it in a two-dimensional form, where the state X is defined as $[x_1 = x, x_2 = \dot{x}]^T$. Thus, the differential form of the system is defined as described in 5.

$$\dot{X} = \begin{bmatrix} \dot{x_1} \\ \dot{x_2} \end{bmatrix} = \begin{bmatrix} x_2 \\ \alpha(1 - x_1^2)x_2 - x_1 \end{bmatrix} \tag{5}$$

Where x_1 corresponds to position, and x_2 to velocity in case of a mechanical system. If this parameters have initial values equal to 0, the system will stay in that position; any other value will converge into an stable oscillation (or orbit in a phase diagram) [18] (Figs. 1 and 2).

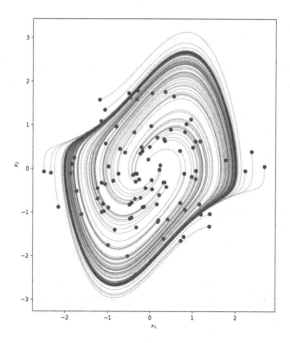

Fig. 1. Examples of trajectories, plotted in blue, for a Van der Pol oscillator with random initial states, plotted in red. Without external forces, the oscillator converges to a stable cycle in the phase diagram. (Color figure online)

The system is useful for the modeling of nonlinear phenomena such as biological signals (ECG, EEG), analysis of electrical circuits, and circadian cycles [6,13].

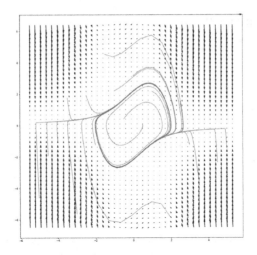

Fig. 2. Examples of trajectories, plotted in red, and the vector field which generates for a Van der Pol oscillator converging into a stable limit cycle [11] (Color figure online)

1.3   Optimal Control Problem

Assuming an input u, external to the system that is given by a policy $\mu(X)$ the system becomes:

$$\dot{X} = \begin{bmatrix} x_2 \\ \alpha(1 - x_1^2)x_2 - x_1 + u \end{bmatrix} \tag{6}$$

Also expressed as differential matrix equation in 7.

$$\dot{X} = FX + Gu \tag{7}$$

where F and G are matrices, respectively:

$$F = \begin{bmatrix} 0 & 1 \\ -1 & \alpha(1 - x_1^2) \end{bmatrix}, G = \begin{bmatrix} 0 \\ 1 \end{bmatrix} \tag{8}$$

This paper does not consider the problem of the forced van der Pol oscillator; the more general problem considers a perturbation signal that affects the behavior of the system. The proposed problem is to find a policy $\mu(X)$ such that it minimizes the expression in 9.

$$\min_u \int_{t_0}^{t_f} x_1(t)^2 + x_2(t)^2 + u(t)^2 dt \tag{9}$$

$$s.t. \quad |u| \le c$$

Where, for this problem, we consider to set the variables to $t_0 = 0s$, $t_f = 50s$, step length of $0.1s$, and the limit for the control signal of $c = 10$. The variable u is the control signal, which in this case is identical to the policy to improve.

The c bound for the control signal is motivated by real-world applications where the actuator is limited or to reduce the energy consumption of the system. The results from the policy $\mu(X)$ may output values that are not within the range of allowed values, in those cases they are clipped to stay within range as in 10.

$$u = sgn(\mu(x)) \cdot min(c, |\mu(x)|) \tag{10}$$

This result derives from the solution to the problem of finding an optimal control μ which minimize, for the stochastic case, ¿the following expression? 11 [8].

$$J(t, X(t), \mu(t)) = \mathbb{E}\left[\int_t^{t_f} C[s, X(s), \mu(s)]ds + D[X(t_f)]\right] \tag{11}$$

Solving for the minimum μ, that is: $V(t, X(t)) = \underset{\mu}{min}[J(x, X(t)], \mu(t))$ the equation is called dynamic programming principle, for the deterministic case 12. The result derived from this expression is the Hamilton–Jacobi–Bellman (HJB) Equation 13.

$$V(t, X(t)) = \underset{\mu}{min}\left[\int_t^{\eta} C[s, X(s), \mu(s)]ds + V(\eta, X(\eta))\right], \text{for all } \eta \in [t, t_f] \tag{12}$$

$$V(t, X(t)) = \underset{\mu}{min}\left[\int_t^{t_f} C[s, X(s), \mu(s)]ds + D[X(t_f)]\right] \tag{13}$$

In this case, the system is already known and following the result of [10] is proposed the same cost function. In this setting of the problem, the state $[0, 0]$ becomes a cost-free and absorbing state.

1.4 PID Control

Reinforcement Learning using approximations such as neural networks by policy iteration has been found useful even when starting with a random policy. A useful technique for Reinforcement Learning is to use a *base policy*, that allows faster improvements. In this case, a well-known method of classic control is proposed, that being a PID controller with compensation.

A PID controller is a technique for linear systems with feedback, it considers the actual state $x(t)$ measured by a sensor and the reference state or trajectory $r(t)$, and calculates the error $e(t) = r(t) - x(t)$. To guarantee asymptotic stability, so that $e(t) \to 0$ as $t \to \infty$, the controller also considers the *derivative* error $e_d(t)$ and *integrative* error $e_i(t)$.

The integral error was calculated by using the numeric approximation $e_i(t) = e_i(t-1) - e(t)\Delta_t$ and the derivative error $e_d(t) = \frac{x(t) - x(t-1)}{\Delta_t}$, where Δ_t refers to the step of the solver and correspond to an Euler solver. Then using the coefficients k_p, k_i and k_d the PID controller is defined in 14.

$$u_{PID} = k_p e + k_i e_i + k_d e_d \tag{14}$$

The objective of compensation is adding zeros and poles to the system, forcing these to change to desired ones [16]. The compensation part was designed following the dynamic system of the oscillator, considering the errors as the inputs (a series compensation), described by the Eq. 15.

$$u_c = -e + \alpha(1 - e^2)e_d \tag{15}$$

The output of the controller is given by $u = u_c + u_{PID}$. The complete system is illustrated in the Fig. 3. The parameters proposed for the PID controller are $k_p = 2$, $k_d = 1$, $ki = 0.001$, as they are enough for the system to arrive to the desired state.

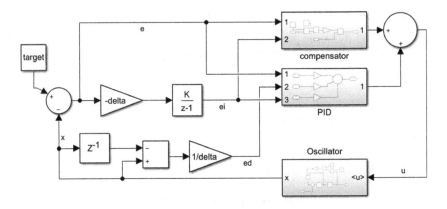

Fig. 3. System diagram with the proposed controller.

1.5   Rollout

Rollout is a method for reinforcement learning where a base policy or heuristic is used to obtain a better policy $\tilde{\pi}$ [2]. The idea is that for each possible action $u \in U_k(x_k)$ that the actuator can perform given the current state x_k, the system runs each action u for l number of steps (possibly 1), and upon arriving to each possible state x_{k+l} the base policy is run until termination to obtain an estimate of the cost $\hat{J}(x_k + 1)$. The cost approximation of the state then becomes,

$$\min_{u_k \in U_k(x_k)} \left[g(x_k, u_k) + \sum_{m=1}^{l} g(x_m, u_m) + \hat{J}(x_{k+l}) \right] \tag{16}$$

and the control for the new policy at x_k is found as the,

$$\arg \min_{u_k \in U_k(x_k)} \left[g(x_k, u_k) + \sum_{m=1}^{l} g(x_m, u_m) + \hat{J}(x_{k+l}) \right] \tag{17}$$

That is the action that minimizes the cost according to the base policy.

In order to make Rollout more computationally efficient, there are some alternatives to the original [3]. The first variant is to not run until termination, but for a limited number of steps and add an approximation of the cost function for the remaining steps. Another variant is to evaluate only some candidate actions $\bar{U}_k$ that have been found useful (Fig. 4).

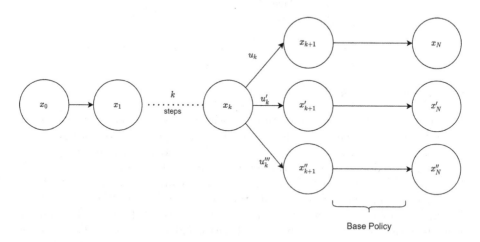

Fig. 4. Rollout for one step in the future. A set of actions are performed and the base policy is used to estimate the long term cost for the remaining $N - k - 1$ steps.

An important factor, although not completely necessary, is that to apply the Rollout scheme the base policy is an effective one for the problem. A property that can verify that is that the policy is sequentially consistent. That is that the policy only requires the current state to get the control. As the policy requires the errors as inputs, in order to guarantee this property, the errors are added to an *extended* state conformed by the vector $[x_1, x_2, e, e_d, e_i]^T$ and from this point a state x is conformed by those elements.

2   Methods

In order to improve the base policy, an optimistic scheme composed of two neural networks is proposed. The first neural network learns an optimistic approximation of the J function given the base policy. The second network learns a new policy that improves the current one by simulating trajectories and evaluating actions with the first network. In the first iteration, the current policy corresponds to the PID controller.

This approach is known as Actor-Critc (AC) methods in Deep Reinforcement Learning, and has been proven useful in diverse settings [9,14].

Both networks will share the same architecture, a fully connected neural network (FCNN) with ELU as activation function. This architectures are shown in Table 1.

Table 1. Table describing the architecture of the proposed FCNN.

Layers	Neurons per layer
Input	5
Hidden layer 1	256
Hidden layer 2	128
Hidden layer 3	64
Hidden layer 4	32
Output	1

2.1 Value Network (Critic)

Using the base policy, a neural network $\tilde{J}_\mu$ with a set of parameters r, is trained to obtain an approximation of the cost optimistically, this will be known as the *value network* or *critic*. That is, to simulate the system using the base policy from some initial state, and get the total cost after a limited number of steps l. We propose a range of 10–20 steps in the future, equivalent to 1 to 2 s, of the simulation to improve the initial trajectory cost given by the PID controller.

The system is simulated to train the neural network from random initial states For each one of them, the cost $g(x, u)$ is calculated by the ODE solver and by an auxiliary function $\hat{J}(x, l)$ that calculates a trajectory of the desired length where all the controls u are the output of the PID controller given the state. The final cost is then defined as,

$$\gamma^s = g(x^s, u^s) + \hat{J}(f(x^s, u^s), l) \tag{18}$$

The network is then trained to minimize the cost function where r is the set of parameters of the architecture $\tilde{J}_\mu(x, r)$ for the training samples pairs (x^s, γ^s) (Fig. 5).

$$\bar{r} \in \arg\min_r \sum_{s=1}^{q} (\tilde{J}(x^s, r) - \gamma^s)^2 \tag{19}$$

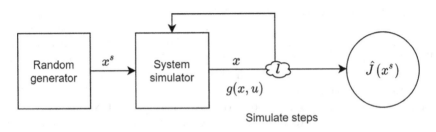

Fig. 5. Methodology to obtain the training samples for the cost approximation.

To acquire the training set composed of pairs (x^s, β^s), we simulated 10,000 trajectories with random initialization within the considered range. A total of 20 s is simulated for each trajectory. We collected a total of 2,000,000 training samples. For the training, we used the ADAM optimizer [12] with an initial learning rate of 0.001. Dropout is used after every hidden layer in the network with $p = 0.5$ for regularization, and it is turned off after training.

2.2   Policy Network (Actor)

The *policy network*, or *actor*, needs to minimize the cost of the policy by evaluating actions given the current state. It can be computationally expensive as all the possible actions are the real values in the range of $[-10, 10]$. For this purpose, we propose a method where the previous policy is evaluated and returns a control $\bar{u}$. Random noise is added to the control such that a set $R(x) = \{u_1, ..., u_r\}$ of r random controls are obtained.

The random set $R = \{\bar{u} + \epsilon | \epsilon \sim \mathcal{N}(0, \sigma)\}$ comes from a normal distribution centered around 0 and with a standard deviation decreasing with time. The simulator then evaluates the next step of the system, given all the random actions, and once it arrives at the next state, the approximation function $\tilde{J}_\mu$ returns a cost that is added to the cost g of performing the corresponding control.

$$\beta^s = \min_{u \in R(x)} g(x^s, u^s) + \tilde{J}(f(x^s, u^s)) \tag{20}$$

The action with the lowest approximate cost, according to $\hat{J}(x, l)$, is selected and becomes part of the training set (i^s, β^s). The policy network $\mu(\tilde{x}, r)$ is then

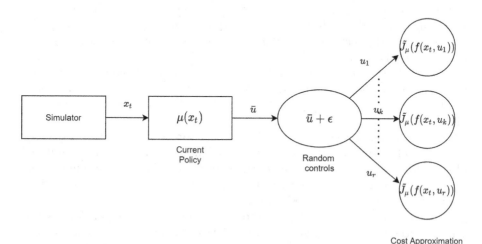

Cost Approximation

Fig. 6. Randomization of the current policy by adding Gaussian noise to the output of the current policy. The random control with the lowest approximate cost is selected according to the critic network.

fitted by minimizing 21, given a total of q training samples, to obtain the new set of parameters $\bar{r}$ (Fig. 6).

$$\bar{r} \in \arg\min \sum_{s=1}^{q} (\tilde{\mu}(x^s, r) - \beta^s)^2 \tag{21}$$

To acquire the training set composed of pairs (x^s, β^s), we simulated 1,000 trajectories with random initialization and within the considered range. We collected a total of 500,000 training samples. As in the case of the Critic network, we used the ADAM optimizer with Dropout as a regularizer.

The implementation of the simulator for the system was done using the function *odeint* of the scipy library for the Python programming language [19]. The rest of the functions were written for the *numpy* library [20]. The codes were implemented in a computer with an Intel i7-8750 CPU and an Nvidia GTX 1060 GPU.

3   Results

The first step was to determine the number of l steps that are large enough for a policy to improve its cost using a random set of controls where $|R| = 15$. With a lower number of steps, the approximation will behave more like a greedy algorithm, but a larger number will be more computationally expensive. It was done by testing for 100 initial random states produced with the same seed, and obtain the total cost of those trajectories. With $l = 20$ it was enough to satisfy the improvement of the cost.

Using that parameter and, as stated in the methods section, a total of 2,000,000 training samples of the form (x^s, β^s) were obtained. This was done simulating trajectories with random initial states of the form $[r_1, r_2, 0, 0, 0]^T$. The actor and the critic networks were programmed and trained using the *PyTorch* library for Python [17].

The resulting fit of the critic network once results in the comparison of the curves in Fig. 7. The most important part of this fit is to retrain the shape and not the exact values, as its importance is its ability to determine which state has a lower cost.

Figure 8 illustrate the result of training the actor for the complete trajectory of the control signal. In both cases, the resulting fit of the architecture introduces a bias. Although in the case of the critic network, the shape is more important than the output value, in the actor, this bias term creates an effect that does not allow to converge to the desired value.

For the policy evaluation step, and to be the same for all the policies, a set of random initial points were generated with the same seed for the pseudo-random number generator. In this case, it was used the *numpy* random number generator with the seed 34. The actor-network is trained with new random trajectories until it stops improving the policy evaluation cost. The table with the evaluations is in the Table 2, with the original policy and the AC policy after n iterations.

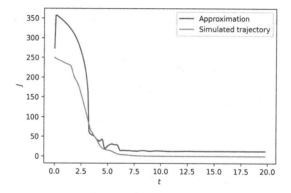

Fig. 7. Comparison of the cost function with the simulated trajectory and the output of the Critic network.

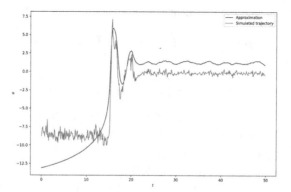

Fig. 8. Comparison of the control signal with the simulated trajectory and the output of the Actor network. A bias above 0 can be seen for the Actor network.

Additionally, the Table 3 shows the performance of the AC algorithm starting with a random policy for comparison with the same number of updates as the proposed method. In this case, the cardinality of the set of random control R was increased to 20 as with fewer the policy never improved.

Given the initial states considered in the policy evaluation step of the problem, a comparison of the final costs for the simulated trajectories can be seen in Fig. 9.

The result of only using the PID controller is illustrated in Figs. 10 and 11. From the figures, we can observe that the system converges to zero, but tends to oscillate and reach the limits of the control signal. Meanwhile, the result of the AC networks, for the same initial state can be seen that converges without oscillations, and the controller signal stays within the range of $|c|$ proposed, this can be seen in Figs. 12 and 13.

Table 2. Total cost and improvement of each policy using PID as the base policy.

Policy	Total cost	Improvement
PID (base)	803,689.38	0
AC 1	660,619.02	143,070.36
AC 2	641,343.51	19,275.51
AC 3	629,074.52	12,268.99
AC 4	606,293.73	22,780.79
AC 5	604,487.07	1,806.66
AC 6	591,575.41	12,911.66
AC 7	585,803.2	5,772.21

Table 3. Total cost and improvement of each policy starting with a random policy.

Policy	Total cost	Improvement
Random (base)	2,083,834.7	0
AC 1	2,466,408.71	−382,574.01
AC 2	1,017,857.41	1,448,551.29
AC 3	907,639.33	110,218.07
AC 4	928,788.87	−21,149.53
AC 5	916,518.73	12,270.13
AC 6	916,779.81	−261.07
AC 7	915,169.69	1,610.11

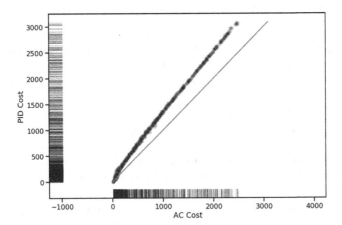

Fig. 9. Terminal costs for the simulated trajectories using the initial (PID) and final policies (AC). Most of the points fall within the upper part of the diagonal as the PID costs are greater for the same initial states.

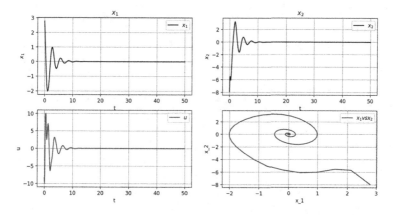

Fig. 10. Example of the control sequence of the system using the PID controller. It will tend to oscillate before arriving to the final state.

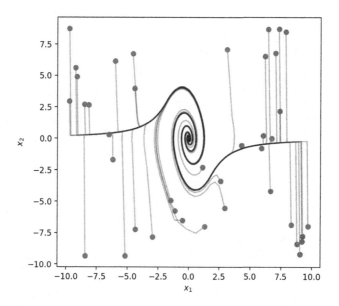

Fig. 11. Examples of trajectories of the system using the PID controller. The trajectories converge [0, 0] with some oscillations.

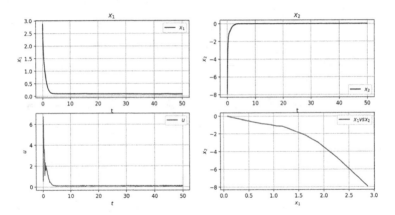

Fig. 12. Example of the control sequence of the system using the actor after the training process. It converges without oscillations, and the control signal is slightly noisy.

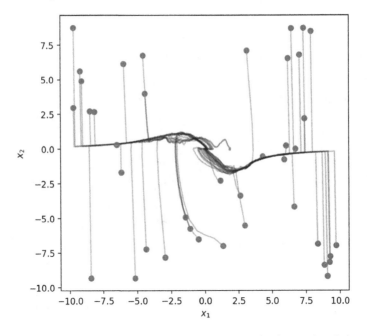

Fig. 13. Examples of trajectories of the system using the last pair of Actor Critic networks. The trajectories converge without little oscillations to a point near to [0, 0].

4   Conclusions

The usage of a method of classic control such as PID is still useful to derive a better control policy for a non-linear system in conditions where the controller does not consider the constraints. Although it introduces some bias in the first iterations of the policy improvement being similar to the PID controller, the final controller behaves differently to the original policy.

A problem with pure Reinforcement Learning applied to robotics is that by starting with a completely random policy it is possible to damage the actuators. In this case, the new policies will behave at least as good as the method of classic control, becoming a viable alternative for robotics implementation.

A current problem found with this method is the bias that the proposed architecture produces after the fitting in the *actor* network, especially for states near the desired point, not allowing to converge to that point. Further work can be done by using different architectures and regularization schemes to solve this. An alternative could be the usage of Differential Equation Neural Networks, which have been used to predict the trajectory of the system [1]. Also, as a continuation of this work is suggested perform the optimal control of a forced van der Pol oscillator to certain trajectories, in order to deal with the chaotic version of this problem.

Although the base policy was not optimized for the minimal energy problem, each iteration of the policy returns an improved result with less cost and that converges faster to the desired state. When compared with the random initial policy, besides the lower final cost, it also requires less exploration in order to improve in each update.

The proposed system performs a more complex control (feedback and series compensation) compared with the suggested PID, because of the use of the extended state, and is the actor that selects the parameters for the control.

Checking the values of the weights in each layer of the actor could help to understand the way in which the actor controls the van der Pol oscillator, and could lead to a methodology to automatically adjust parameters for a proposed control.

References

1. Avelar, A., Salgado, I., Ahmed, H., Mera, M., Chairez, I.: Differential neural networks observer for second order systems with sampled and quantized output. IFAC-PapersOnLine **51**(13), 490–495 (2018). https://doi.org/10.1016/j.ifacol.2018.07.327
2. Bertsekas, D.: Reinforcement Learning and Optimal Control. Athena Scientific Optimization and Computation Series, Athena Scientific (2019). https://books.google.com.mx/books?id=ZlBIyQEACAAJ
3. Bhattacharya, S., Badyal, S., Wheeler, T., Gil, S., Bertsekas, D.: Reinforcement learning for POMDP: partitioned rollout and policy iteration with application to autonomous sequential repair problems. IEEE Robot. Autom. Lett. **5**(3), 3967–3974 (2020)
4. Buşoniu, L., de Bruin, T., Tolić, D., Kober, J., Palunko, I.: Reinforcement learning for control: performance, stability, and deep approximators. Ann. Rev. Control **46**, 8–28 (2018). https://doi.org/10.1016/j.arcontrol.2018.09.005
5. Chagas, T., Toledo, B., Rempel, E., Chian, A.L., Valdivia, J.: Optimal feedback control of the forced van der pol system. Chaos Solit. Fractals **45**(9), 1147–1156 (2012). https://doi.org/10.1016/j.chaos.2012.06.004. http://www.sciencedirect.com/science/article/pii/S0960077912001282

6. El Cheikh, R., Lepoutre, T., Bernard, S.: Modeling biological rhythms in cell populations. Math. Modell. Nat. Phenom. **7**(6), 107–125 (2012). https://doi.org/10.1051/mmnp/20127606

7. el Hakim, A., Hindersah, H., Rijanto, E.: Application of reinforcement learning on self-tuning PID controller for soccer robot multi-agent system. In: 2013 Joint International Conference on Rural Information Communication Technology and Electric-Vehicle Technology (rICT ICeV-T), pp. 1–6 (2013)

8. Fabbri, G., Gozzi, F., Święch, A.: Stochastic Optimal Control in Infinite Dimension. Probability Theory and Stochastic Modelling. Springer, Heidelberg (2017). https://doi.org/10.1007/978-3-319-53067-3. https://link.springer.com/book/10.1007/978-3-319-53067-3

9. Grondman, I., Busoniu, L., Lopes, G.A.D., Babuska, R.: A survey of actor-critic reinforcement learning: standard and natural policy gradients. IEEE Trans. Syst. Man Cybern. Part C (Appl. Rev.) **42**(6), 1291–1307 (2012)

10. Ji, Z., Lou, X.: Adaptive dynamic programming for optimal control of van der pol oscillator. In: 2018 Chinese Control And Decision Conference (CCDC), pp. 1537–1542 (2018)

11. Khalil, H.K.: Nonlinear Systems, 3rd edn. Prentice-Hall, Upper Saddle River (2002). https://cds.cern.ch/record/1173048. The book can be consulted by contacting: PH-AID: Wallet, Lionel

12. Kingma, D.P., Ba, J.: Adam: a method for stochastic optimization. In: Bengio, Y., LeCun, Y. (eds.) 3rd International Conference on Learning Representations, ICLR 2015, San Diego, CA, USA, 7–9 May 2015, Conference Track Proceedings (2015). http://arxiv.org/abs/1412.6980

13. Kinoshita, S.: 1 Introduction to Nonequilibrium Phenomena. Elsevier Inc. (2013). https://doi.org/10.1016/B978-0-12-397014-5.00001-8.

14. Li, Q., Li, G., Wang, X., Wei, M.: Diffusion welding furnace temperature controller based on actor-critic. In: 2019 Chinese Control Conference (CCC), pp. 2484–2487 (2019)

15. Noori Skandari, M., Ghaznavi, M., Abedian, M.: Stabilizer control design for nonlinear systems based on the hyperbolic modelling. Appl. Math. Modell. **67**, 413–429 (2019). https://doi.org/10.1016/j.apm.2018.11.006. http://www.sciencedirect.com/science/article/pii/S0307904X1830533X

16. Ogata, K.: Modern Control Engineering, 4th edn. Prentice Hall PTR, Upper Saddle River (2001)

17. Paszke, A., et al.: Automatic differentiation in PyTorch. In: NIPS 2017 Workshop (2017)

18. Tsatsos, M.: Theoretical and numerical study of the Van der Pol equation. Undergraduate thesis, Aristotle University of Thessaloniki (2008)

19. Virtanen, P., et al.: SciPy 1.0: fundamental algorithms for scientific computing in Python. Nat. Methods **17**, 261–272 (2020). https://doi.org/10.1038/s41592-019-0686-2

20. van der Walt, S., Colbert, S.C., Varoquaux, G.: The NumPy array: a structure for efficient numerical computation. Comput. Sci. Eng. **13**(2), 22–30 (2011). https://doi.org/10.1109/mcse.2011.37

Flow Velocity Estimation by Means Multi-layer Perceptron in a Pipeline

José Francisco Uribe Vázquez, Héctor Rodríguez Rangel,
Mario Cesar Maya Rodríguez[✉], René Tolentino Eslava,
and Eduardo Yudho Montes de Oca

Departamento de Ingeniería en Control y Automatización, ESIME Zacatenco–IPN,
07738 Ciudad de México, Mexico
{juribev1500,hrodriguez1501,eyudhom1300}@alumnno.ipn.mx,
{mmayar,rtolentino}@ipn.mx

Abstract. In this work, the use of the multiple advantages of a multi-layer perceptron to predict the average flow velocity in a pipeline for a centrifugal fan operating at different frequencies is presented. The learning process was with data acquired from the velocity profile gotten by the measuring of a hot wire anemometer, carrying out a different angular speed of the centrifugal fan. To experiment was carried out with different waves inputs to flow speed estimation, the first one is a ramp wave of frequencies with a single hidden layer the second one is a sinus wave of frequencies with the comparison between a single hidden layer and two hidden layers. In the first part, the simulations results showed the error between the real data and the output of the multi-layer perceptron, with a maximum error of 4 m/s, and the second part the accuracy of the two hidden layers in respect to a single hidden layer with a maximum error of ± 2.81 m/s.

Keywords: Multi-layer perceptron · Average flow velocity · Estimation · Pipeline

1 Introduction

Artificial Neural Networks (ANN) also known as simple as "Neural Networks" (NN); are inspired by the form than the human brain works. The theory and modeling of the NN are based on the natural systems and processes that are developed on the human brain, even the structure of the NN is based on a biological neuron. The Multi-Layer Perceptron (MLP) [1], uses the proposed inputs which, in combination with weights, hidden layers, nodes, bias, activation function, and epochs, estimates an output to compare to the actual data associated with the input. In this way the error is calculated, which is fundamental for the change of hyperparameters mentioned above through a training algorithm, i.e. Backpropagation [2], whose function is the minimization of a cost function, i.e., mean square error (MSE), resulting in the model being able to estimate with a certain precision in the testing stage.

For many years in the industry, in the area of process control, advances and implementations have been made with neural networks to solve specific problems, such as carrying

M. F. Mata-Rivera et al. (Eds.): WITCOM 2020, CCIS 1280, pp. 297–308, 2020.
https://doi.org/10.1007/978-3-030-62554-2_22

out predictive controls [3], or carrying out system identifications [4]; also besides, the advantages of ANN such as universal approach capabilities, flexibility, and parsimony have been of great importance for applications to be found in areas such as the steel industry and water treatment, as mentioned in [5]. That is why the use and implementation of ANN not only MLP but from areas of interest such as Deep-Learning, Convolutional Neural Networks, accommodate more works that seek to obtain a reference model and develop additional applications for automatic control.

The flow rate is one of the most common variable measures in the industry. Flow measurement and control of liquids and gases in pipelines can be improved due to the increasing needing for accuracy. Even an MLP can provide the mathematical model of a system and its own tuning PID control in real-time due to the slow of the variable and the difficulty to achieve a set-point on the system [6].

Climate change required rigid environmental laws for monitoring pollution emissions produced in combustion processes. In chimney monitoring, the gas velocity is an important variable to compute the bulk velocity of the combustion gases, and in consequence of the volumetric flow of pollutant emissions. The gas velocity in this application is measure by a type-S Pitot tube than is calibrated against a type-L Pitot tube. The calibration according to the standards ISO 10780 [7], ASTM D-3796 [8], and the EPA method are done [9]. These standards provide calibration methodologies in a range from 3 m/s to 50 m/s and need to know the velocity profile behavior in the calibration site at different operation conditions. Airspeed measurement is necessary for ventilation systems and air conditioning, applications that have enormous potential for energy saving. Other needs of airspeed measurements are in performance curves of blowers and fans and compressors, where Pitot tube type-L following AMCA 201-74/ASHRAE 51-74 standards are employed [10]. To test a water heater that uses natural gas and LPG, standard NOM-011-SESH-2012 sets that the pilot must not turn off when is exposed to an air stream of 21 km/h $\pm$ 2 km/h [11].

There are some researches about velocity behavior in different aspects like experimental and simulations. In [12], showed a volumetric flow measurement in a pipeline technique, for developed flow conditions using the wall defect wall to this purpose, they characterized the installation using velocity profiles using a type-L Pitot tube and a laser Doppler anemometer. In [13], carried out numeric research to study the air behavior in pipelines with disturbs as elbows on different planes in circular and rectangular pipelines. To validate the simulation, the results were compared with the ones that [14], for one and two elbows in the same plane in a circular pipeline.

In [15] developed a theoretical analysis and experimental research related to the flow measurement method by Pitot tube carried out tests in an air blower using IRAM standard 19004 about Blowers Test Laboratory methods. They used a static Pitot tube in a pipeline located at the fan pressure side a transversal plane was at 8.5 diameters from the blower outlet, 24 measurement points to get the volumetric flow was measured, flow in that point was developed based on the behavior of the velocities profiles.

Air and gas speed measurement is a variable in industrial processes such as air pollution emissions in chimneys, mine ventilation systems, air conditioning, and drying processes. This variable is measured through differential pressure instruments are their corresponding equation is employed to compute the speed in a point; other instruments used are anemometers that directly measure speed, which can be thermal, propeller, ultrasonic, to name a few. The speed measurement with those instruments is punctual, so when measuring different points in a cross-section the speed profile is known, and if it is integrated volumetric flow is computed. For flow measurement is necessary to measure from 10 points to 36 points distributed in the cross-section of the duct; the above takes time and their subsequent treatment for analysis when the measurements are carried out. On the other hand, the flow relates to the power consumed by the machines that move gases and air in various processes, so an accurate flow measurement leads to determine the energy consumption of fans, compressors, and blowers to implement energy-saving strategies in the industry.

So, a solution to this problem is to use an instrument to measure the volumetric flow direct, but by the dimensions and shapes of the ducts, this solution is costly. One solution is to use Artificial Neural Networks (ANN). Thus, the use of an MLP to estimate the flow velocity at a specific point in a pipeline according to different frequencies in an air blower is proposed in this paper. The information used for the learning and training of the MLP was provided by the velocity profiles measured through a hot wire anemometer at different velocities from 3.96 m/s up to 35.8 m/s, those experimental data are gotten from reference [16]. The MLP will provide a minimum error between experimental data and the estimation model depended on a hyper-parameter selected.

2 System Identification

The NN structure used is shown in Fig. 1, and is formed by three layers. It is mandatory to define the nodes and neurons to reach the planned task in layers, the estimation of the flow velocity profiles in a pipeline. The first one is the input layer, where the quantity of information with which one of the NN will work is defined. In this case, 6 data at the input to get the estimation by a training process were used. The second one is the hidden layer that is then responsible for developing the performance. In this layer, each input is operated through multiple neurons on the hidden layer and through it, an estimation at the output is gotten. The last one is the output layer that contains the estimated data necessary for the testing process.

The MLP output equation according to Fig. 1 for the estimation of flow velocity profiles is given by,

$$\hat{y}(k) = g_j \left[\sum_{j=1}^{m} V_j f_j \left(\sum_{i=1}^{n} W_i u_i + b_{Ii} \right) \right] + b_{Oj} \tag{1}$$

where the vectors V_j and f_j are the weights of the MLP, the bias are given by b_{Ii} and b_{Oj}, the index n and m are the neurons number in each layer, and f_j are g_j the active functions. The input function is given by

$$u = f_{Hz}(Hz) \tag{2}$$

where u is a wave function that depends on frequencies given in Hz.

The error equation is given by:

$$e(k) = \hat{y}_j(k) - y_j(k) \tag{3}$$

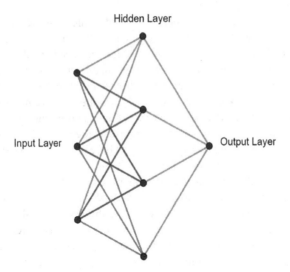

Fig. 1. Feedforward neural network graphic structure

The index that minimizes is,

$$J(k) = \frac{1}{n} \sum\nolimits_{j=1}^{n} \left(\hat{y}_j(k) - y_j(k) \right)^2 \tag{4}$$

The backpropagation equation is given by:

$$w(k+1) = w(k) + \eta \frac{\partial J(k)}{\partial w(k)} \tag{5}$$

And the gradient is defined by:

$$\Delta w(k) = w(k+1) - w(k) = \eta \frac{\partial J(k)}{\partial w(k)} \tag{6}$$

where η is the learning rate. In [17] you can find information about the MLP and the learning process.

3 Experimental Data

The experimental data used in this paper were acquired in a centrifugal fan test bench, integrated by three centrifugal fans with different impellers (backward inclined, backward curved, and radial). The three fans have a free inlet, ducted outlet, and according to AMCA standards [18] are type B facility. The fans with backward inclined and radial impellers have a circular duct of 3.91 m (12 ft 10 in) length and 254 mm (12 in) diameter and have a conical damper installed at the end of the duct. Data for this work were measured in the backward curved impeller fan that has a duct of 308 mm (12 in) diameter and a length of 5.1 m (16 ft 8 in). Every fan is driven by an 11.19 kW (15 hp) electric motor, controlled by a variable frequency drive to have different flow conditions; test bench details are in [16].

A hot-wire anemometer operated at constant temperature was used to measure the velocity profiles in the duct. The velocity and turbulence profiles were measurement in the developed flow zone located at 12 diameters from the fan outlet. The anemometer used is DANTE 90C10 model and a general-purpose probe 55P11. The probe was calibrated in the unit flow of the system in a range from 0.5 m/s to 50 m/s and moved using a traverse system. The velocity profiles were measured at frequencies of 11.8 Hz, 27.5 Hz, 43.4 Hz, and 58.5 Hz, and are present in Fig. 2. The nearest point to measure the velocity in the duct was at 4 mm from the upper and lower wall. The other velocity point was carried out with increments every 10 mm. By the no-slip velocity condition, in both walls a velocity of 0 m/s was considered, experimental details about velocity data acquired are showed in [16].

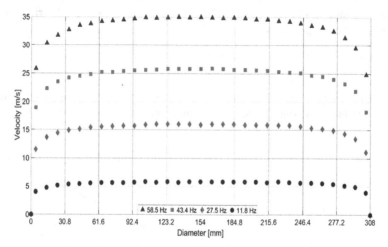

Fig. 2. Velocity Profiles at different operating conditions

Volumetric flow (q_v) and average velocity as a function of frequency and angular speed are shown in Table 1. Equation (7) represent the relation between frequency (f) and angular speed (ω), the nominal angular velocity at 60 Hz is 3460 rpm, the poles number (NP) is 2, and the electric motor sliding is 0.0389.

$$\omega = \frac{120f}{NP}(1 - S) \tag{7}$$

The average speed ($V_{average}$) was computed with Eq. (8) [19]. Where V, represents the velocity at a different distance from the pipe wall.

$$V_{average} = \frac{\int_A VdA}{A} \tag{8}$$

Once the average velocity was computed, the volumetric flow is obtained by Eq. (9). The International System of Units is used in Eq. (7) to Eq. (9).

$$q_v = AV_{average} \tag{9}$$

Table 1. Average conditions at Different Frequencies

Frequency [Hz]	Angular speed [RPM]	Volumetric flow [m³/s]	Average velocity [m/s]
11.8	680	0.382	5.13
27.5	1586	1.062	14.25
43.4	2503	1.717	23.04
58.5	3374	2.327	31.24

To have enough data to train the NN, affinity law for flow in turbomachinery was used, represents the relationship between flow delivered by the fan and the angular speed as presented in Eq. (10) [20]. In the above equation, 1 and 2 subscripts indicate the starting and ending conditions.

$$\frac{q_{V1}}{q_{V2}} = \frac{\omega_1}{\omega_2} \tag{10}$$

Figure 3 shows the fan volumetric flow as a function of an angular speed predicted by the affinity law (blue line), experimental data obtained from Eq. (9) are shown too.

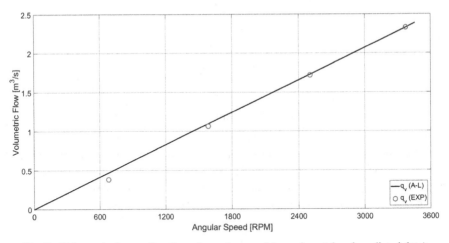

Fig. 3. Volumetric flow as function of angular speed (experimental and predicted data)

Average velocity in the duct at different angular speed are shown in Fig. 4, velocity computed from affinity law Eq. (10) are in the blue line, and experimental data are indicated by (□).

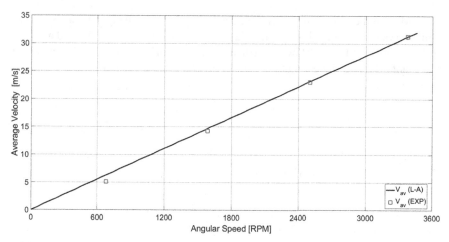

Fig. 4. Average velocity variation with angular speed (experimental and predicted data)

4   Simulation

Taking the data from the previous section, two experiments were considered to show the advantages of using an MLP to estimate the average flow velocity over a pipe. The first one constant of using a ramp type input, directly associates the value of an input frequency in (Hz) and the average speed in m/s, using a single hidden layer MLP. We selected $x_i = (y(k-1), y(k-2), (y(k-3), u(k-1), u(k-2))$, the neurons of the hidden layer (nh = 15), the output is given by average flow velocity and the learning rate $\eta = 0.1$. The epoch's number is 50. Figure 5 shows a comparison of real data with an estimated response of the MLP.

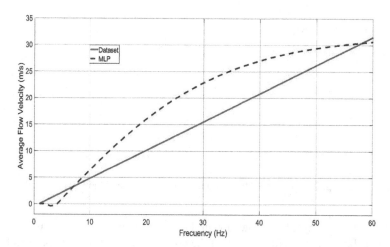

Fig. 5. Ramp input response of the MLP perceptron

To evaluate the performance of the neural network, the following is proposed.

The MSE and error are shown in Fig. 6 and Fig. 7, respectively, with a ramp input. The first one shows that the lost function (MSE) was not minimized with good accuracy. Moreover, the second one shows that it has an error of about ±7 m/s, which is an unacceptable error in the estimation stage. Therefore, the error performance does not converge to zero.

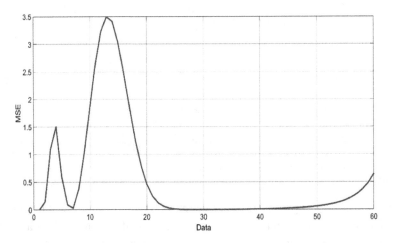

Fig. 6. Mean Square Error under the ramp input with a single hidden layer

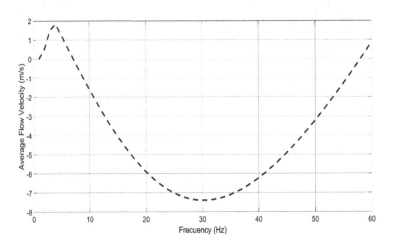

Fig. 7. Error under the ramp input with a single hidden layer

The results of a single hidden layer neural network show that it is difficult to achieve good results because it is difficult to find the correct combination of hyper-parameters according to the universal approximation theorem.

Otherwise, according to the identification theory [21], it is necessary to look for an input excitation that allows better performance in obtaining the model, which is why for the second experiment the following input is presented, in addition to the comparison between a hidden layer and two hidden layers. Keeping the same hyperparameters of the previous network.

$$x_i(k) = 30 \cdot sin(k) + 30 \tag{11}$$

Figure 8 shows the comparison of actual data with those estimated by the MLP by a single hidden layer.

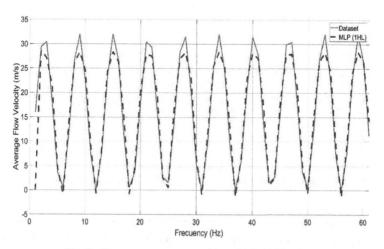

Fig. 8. Sinus wave response with a single hidden layer

And the output of MLP with two hidden layers, with 30 nodes for the first layer and 20 nodes for the second layer, Fig. 9.

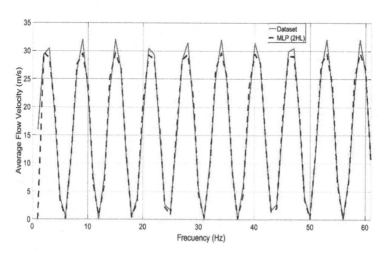

Fig. 9. Sinus input response of MLP with two hidden layers

The error produced by an MLP with two hidden layers, maximum error ±2,81 m/s, is less than that obtained by a single hidden layer, maximum error ±3,84 m/s, as shown in Fig. 10.

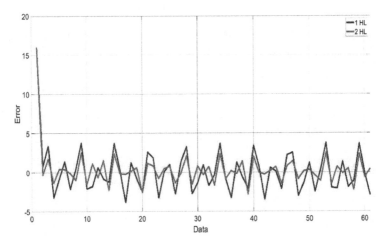

Fig. 10. Comparison of the unnormalized error of one hidden layer and two hidden layers

Figure 10 shows the improvement in the performance of estimation response by means two hidden layers compared to a single hidden layer. Furthermore, a sinus wave of the input excitation improves the accuracy response of an MLP in the testing stage. Figure 11 shows than lost functions are minimized by two experiments.

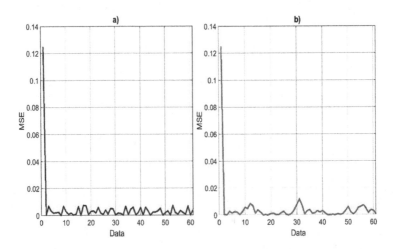

Fig. 11. Mean Square Error of training stage, a) one hidden layer, b) two hidden layer.

5   Conclusions

Affinity law allowed to predict volumetric flow at different frequencies conditions, and therefore the average velocity in the duct to have enough data to train the MLP. The maximum error between experimental and predicted data was 22.7% and 15.4% for volumetric flow and average velocity, respectively.

The average flow velocity estimation of a pipeline can be achieved with an MLP and will depend on hyper-parameters and the excitation input. In this work, the estimation of average flow velocity with a maximum error of ±7 m/s was gotten. The error is higher than expected because the data was taken from a real process with some disturbs. Through the data acquisition with the hot wire anemometer, the learning process of the MLP allowed us to get an estimation of the average flow velocity.

In some points, a considerable error persists in experiment one, for this reason, the input wave excitation was changed, and a comparison between one and two hidden layers, two hidden layers is made to improve the average flow velocity estimation by MLP and with this reducing the error (experiment two). Further, the maximum error for two hidden layers MLP was ±2.81 m/s. Therefore, by selecting other hyper-parameters it is possible to obtain better results.

References

1. Shiblee, M., Kalra, P.K., Chandra, B.: Time series prediction with multilayer perceptron (MLP): a new generalized error based approach. In: Köppen, M., Kasabov, N., Coghill, G. (eds.) ICONIP 2008. LNCS, vol. 5507, pp. 37–44. Springer, Heidelberg (2009). https://doi.org/10.1007/978-3-642-03040-6_5
2. Šíma, J.: Gradient learning in networks of smoothly spiking neurons. In: Köppen, M., Kasabov, N., Coghill, G. (eds.) ICONIP 2008. LNCS, vol. 5507, pp. 179–186. Springer, Heidelberg (2009). https://doi.org/10.1007/978-3-642-03040-6_22
3. Wang, T., Gao, H., Qiu, J.: A combined adaptive neural network and nonlinear model predictive control for multirate networked industrial process control. IEEE Trans. Neural Networks Learn. Syst. **27**(2), 416–425 (2016)
4. Nidhil, K.J., Sreeraj S., Vijay, B., Bagyaveereswaran, V.: System identification using artificial neural network. In: 2015 International Conference on Circuits, Power and Computing Technologies [ICCPCT-2015], Nagercoil, India, pp. 1–4. IEEE (2015)
5. Bloch, G., Denoeux, T.: Neural networks for process control and optimization: two industrial applications. ISA Trans. **42**(1), 39–51 (2003)
6. Hu, K., Li, Y., Guan, X.: Research of the pipe flow measurement and control system on bp neural networks PID. In: Kim, H. (eds.) Advances in Technology and Management. Advances in Intelligent and Soft Computing, vol 165, pp. 25–35. Springer, Berlin, Heidelberg (2012). https://doi.org/10.1007/978-3-642-29637-6_4
7. ISO. 10780: 1994. Stationary Source Emissions–Measurement of Velocity and Volume Flow Rate of Gas Streams in Ducts (1994)
8. ASTM D3796–90 (Reapproved 1998). Standard Practice for Calibration of Type S Pitot Tubes (1998)
9. EPA Method 2. Determination of Stack Gas Velocity and Volumetric Flow Rate (Type S Pitot Tube)
10. ANSI/AMCA Standard 201-74/ASHRAE 51-74. Laboratory methods of testing fans for rating (1974)

11. NOM-011-SESH-2012. Calentadores de agua de uso doméstico y comercial que utilizan como combustible Gas L.P. o Gas Natural. - Requisitos de seguridad, especificaciones, métodos de prueba, marcado e información comercial (2012)

12. Geropp, D., Odenthal, H.J.: Flow rate measurements in turbulent pipe flows with minimal loss of pressure using a defect-law. Flow Meas. Instrum. **12**(1), 1–7 (2001)

13. Care, I., Bonthoux, F., Fontaine, J.R.: Measurement of air flow in duct by velocity measurements. In: EPJ Web of Conferences, vol. 77, p. 00010 (2014)

14. Bonthoux, F., Fontaine, J.R.: Measurement of flow rate in a duct by investigation of the velocity field. Uncertainty linked to the position and number of measurement points. In: Proceedings of Room Vent (8th International Conference on Air Distribution in Rooms), Copenhagen, Denmark, pp. 373–376 (2002)

15. Pesarini, A.J., Bigot, R., Mora Nadal, V.J., Di Bernardi, C.A., Ringegni, P.J.: Theoretical analysis related to aspects of the Pitot tube methodology in flow rate determination for blower's performance test. Flow Meas. Instrum. **12**(5–6), 373–377 (2002)

16. Tolentino-Eslava, R., Tolentino-Eslava, G., Polupan, G., Abugaber-Francis, J.: Análisis del flujo en una instalación para calibrar tubos de Pitot tipo S. En: 8vo Congreso Iberoamericano de Ingeniería Mecánica. Federación Iberoamericana de Ingeniería Mecánica, Cusco, Perú (2007)

17. Haykin, S.: Neural Networks and Learning Machines, 3rd edn. Pearson Education, Ontario, Canada (2008)

18. AMCA Fan Application Manual, Air Systems (1987)

19. Fox, R.W., McDonald, A.T., Pritchard, P.J.: Introduction to Fluid Mechanics, 6th edn. John Wiley, Hoboken, NJ (2004)

20. Splitzer, D.W.: Variable Speed Drives: Principles and Applications for Energy Cost Savings, 2nd edn. Instrument Society of America, Research Triangle Park, NC (1990)

21. Ljung, L.: System Identification: Theory for the User, 2nd edn. Prentice Hall PTR, Upper Saddle River, NJ (1999)

Evolution of COVID-19 Patients in Mexico City Using Markov Chains

Ricardo C. Villarreal-Calva[1], Ponciano J. Escamilla-Ambrosio[1(✉)],
Abraham Rodríguez-Mota[1], and Juan M. Ramírez-Cortés[2]

[1] Instituto Politécnico Nacional, Centro de Investigación en Computación,
Mexico City 07738, Mexico
carlos.calva@gmail.com, {pescamilla,arodrigm}@cic.ipn.mx
[2] Instituto Nacional de Astrofísica Óptica y Electrónica,
Tonantzintla, Puebla 72840, Mexico
jmram@inaoep.mx

Abstract. In this work a Markov process model has been conceived using public data from patients that have experienced symptoms associated with the COVID-19 disease. The data published by the health system of Mexico City was used to fit the model with seven different states. The probabilities of death or recovery at every state are calculated to understand the severity of the novel disease compared to other respiratory diseases. The model provides information to asses the risk of staying at a hospital in Mexico City for patients with respiratory illnesses either positive or negative to SARS-COV-2 virus.

Keywords: Markov process · COVID-19 · Disease model · Bayesian inference

1 Introduction

The severe COVID-19 disease discovered at the end of year 2019 has spread around the world. Caused by the severe acute respiratory syndrome coronavirus 2 (SARS-COV-2), this disease was declared a pandemic by the World Health Organization (WHO) in March 2020. As it is causing a global health crisis, the scientific community is working towards understanding its dynamics. One set of tools available to scientists are the mathematical models used to characterize the disease dynamics and predict the pressure on the health systems around the world [4,10,11]. These models have proven difficult to get right [1], as there are many unknowns about the virus, but after several months of transmission more data is feed to the scientific community from the health systems contributing to the improvement of the accuracy of the models.

There have been many approaches to understand how the COVID-19 disease affects people all around the world, some have researched over the disparities in the risk and outcomes of COVID-19 related to ethnicity and race [6], but there is also increased evidence that such disparities might have stronger relation to

M. F. Mata-Rivera et al. (Eds.): WITCOM 2020, CCIS 1280, pp. 309–318, 2020.
https://doi.org/10.1007/978-3-030-62554-2_23

the presence of comorbidities [7]. The present work aims to create a model of the different stages that an ill individual might experience from the time she/he approaches a medical health center and she/he is identified with COVID-19 symptoms to the time she/he recovers or dies. The methodology followed provides information over the relation of comorbidity with the severity of COVID-19 sickness. The public data available from the health system of Mexico City was used, which is composed of thousands of cases. These cases were partitioned, for each partition a model is created to compare the predictions of the health state evolution of patients from different groups.

The goal of the model is to understand the path a case might follow after a patient reach the health system with COVID-19 symptoms. Hence, this paper presents the data set in Sect. 2, the Markov process model applied is described in Sect. 3. The result's discussion is presented in Sect. 4 and finally, Conclusions are presented in Sect. 5.

2   The Data Set

In order to create a Markov chain model, the data from The Mexico City Health System was used [3]. The data set was published on July 2nd 2020, it has a total of 155,722 cases of people that have presented symptoms compatible with the COVID-19 disease in Mexico City. For each case there are 93 registries containing patient information such as immigrant status, travel information, place of residence, comorbidities, laboratory test, sickness symptoms, medical treatment, among others.

2.1   Registries for the Study

The registries selected for the study discussed in this work are related to the health of the patients and the medical infrastructure required for their treatment:

- Type of patient
- Definitive result
- Comorbidities of the patient
- Case evolution
- Intubation
- Intensive Care Unit

Type of Patient. This registry has two possible values: *Hospitalized* or *Ambulatory.*

Definitive Result. This registry has 17 possible values related to the result of the laboratory test done to the patients. From those values there is one of interest, *SARS-COV-2*, which is the virus known to cause the COVID-19 disease. If a a case has the value *SARS-COV-2* on this registry, then the patient is confirmed to the COVID-19 disease, otherwise the patient sickness is not COVID-19.

Comorbidities of the Patient. There are diseases that contribute to the severity of COVID-19 symptoms. The data set contains 11 registries for such diseases with yes/no values. The Mexican health minister has informed during press conferences that among Mexicans, hypertension, diabetes, overweight and tabaquism are the worst. Therefore, patients that report any of those four diseases are considered as having comorbidity, all other diseases reported are not considered as comorbidity for this study.

Case Evolution. This registry has 12 possible values, which indicates status such as "Hospital discharge", "in treatment", "Severe case", "Death", "Follow up at home", "Follow up at home ended" among others. From this registry it is possible to know if the patient has recovered, died or is still in treatment.

Intubation. This is a yes/no value registry for hospitalized patients, and it indicates if the patient was intubated to receive mechanical aid for breathing. By default ambulatory patients have this registry empty.

Intensive Care Unit. This registry with yes/no values indicates if hospitalized patients used an intensive care unit for her/his treatment. By default ambulatory patients have this registry empty.

One of the limitations of the data set is that it is not possible to know for how many days a patient stayed at any state. It is only possible to know if a given patient was or not at some state.

2.2 Data Partitions

The 155,722 cases are divided into two partitions: active cases and closed cases. The registry *case evolution* from the data set is used to determine if a case is active or is closed. A case is classified as closed if this registry value is any of: "ALTA - CURACION" (discharge - recover), "ALTA - MEJORIA" (discharge - improvement), "ALTA - VOLUNTARIA" (discharge - voluntary), "SEGUIMIENTO TERMINADO" (follow up end) or "DEFUNCION" (death). A closed case indicates that the patient has already recovered or died. A total of 50,042 cases are found closed and those are used to create the Markov models presented. All active cases are discarded and are not used for this study as it is not possible to know for those cases if they will end in the recovery or death of the patient.

The set of closed cases is further divided in those cases positive to SARS-COV-2 virus and those cases negative to it. To drive this partition the registry *Definitive result* is used. If this registry has value of "SARS-COV-2", then this case is classified as positive to SARS-COV-2, otherwise the case is classified as negative to SARS-COV-2. A total of 28,520 cases are negative to SARS-COV-2. Those cases are the baseline to understand the difference between COVID-19 and other respiratory diseases.

A further partition of closed cases positive to SARS-COV-2 is done, this partition is defined by the presence or absence of comorbidity sickness. For this study, a case is considered to have comorbidity illness when at least one of the following sickness is present: hypertension, diabetes, overweight and tabaquism. A total of 10,922 cases are positive to SARS-COV-2 that do not present comorbidity illness. As summary, Table 1 presents the size of each partition done to the data set.

Table 1. Data set partitions.

Partition	Elements
Active cases	105,680
Closed cases, negative to SARS-COV-2	28,520
Closed cases, positive to SARS-COV-2 without comorbidity	10,922
Closed cases, positive to SARS-COV-2 with comorbidity	10,600
Total	155,722

The data set was downloaded in CVS format and was partitioned using some scripts written in the Python Language.

3 Markov Process Model

The framework used to create the model is The Markov Process. The Markov process is a stochastic process, which is a mathematical tool used for modeling time-dependent random phenomena. The Markov property states that the distribution of the forthcoming state X_{n+1} depends only on the current state X_n and does not depend on the previous ones $X_{n-1}, Xn - 2, ..., X_1$ [9].

3.1 Markov Process States

For the Markov process seven states are defined: Sickness,Ambulatory, Hospitalized, Intensive Care Unit (ICU), Ventilated, Death and Recovered. States death and recovered are absorbing states. The process will stay at death or recovered forever if one of this states is reached [2].

Sickness. All cases from the data set are originated on health centers. Sick people with symptoms compatible with the COVID-19 disease approach a health care facility to receive medical aid. Those patients are not necessarily infected with SARS-COV-2, but are probable cases. On our model, *Sickness* is the start state for every case.

Ambulatory. Some sick people do not stay at hospitals, their symptoms are not severe and they are allowed to recover at home.

Hospitalized. Some sick people stay at the hospital for treatment. This stage represents that the patient required hospitalization and used a general bed.

ICU. This stage represents patients acutely ill that receive treatment in an ICU, where their health is constantly monitored, but are not receiving mechanical aid for breathing.

Ventilation. Some patients lose the ability to breath by their own, so they are intubated to receive mechanical assistance to keep breathing.

Recovered. Patients that recovered from their illness. In the model presented, this is an absorbing state.

Death. Patients who did not recover and died, this is an absorbing state.

3.2   Observed Process of the Markov Chain

A Discrete Time Markov Chain (DTMC) can be fit from observed data through statistical analysis [8]. Each of the 50,042 closed cases of the data set is expressed as one of the process observations shown in Table 2. Every observed process starts with the state *Sickness* and end with either of the absorbing states *Recovered* or *Death*.

The information from the registries of the data set is used to determine the observed process for each closed case. The observed process considers that there is a natural sequence in the evolution of a patient. The patient first needs to be sick, then she/he could either get hospitalized or allowed to go home. Once hospitalized, on a general bed, he could be translated to an ICU or get ventilation or both. A patient from any given state different from the start state might die

Table 2. Process observations derived from the closed cases of the data set.

Sickness → Ambulatory → Recovered
Sickness → Ambulatory → Death
Sickness → Hospitalized → Recovered
Sickness → Hospitalized → Death
Sickness → Hospitalized → Ventilated → Recovered
Sickness → Hospitalized → Ventilated → Death
Sickness → Hospitalized → ICU → Recovered
Sickness → Hospitalized → ICU → Death
Sickness → Hospitalized → ICU → Ventilated → Recovered
Sickness → Hospitalized → ICU → Ventilated → Death

or recover. It is natural to think that once a patient is at ventilation, before recovering he will go to ICU, then to a general bed before recover, this type of reverse steps are omitted from the model.

3.3   Markov Chain Process Fitting

The 50,042 observed process are used to fit a DTMC model for each of the data set partitions. The fitting process was done under the R Software Environment for Statistical Computing and Graphics [5]. The R package used to fit the sequences was *markovchain* with the function *markovchainFit* configured to use the method *map* for Bayesian inference [8].

The Markov Chain process graph from each of the three data partitions are shown in Fig. 1, Fig. 2 and Fig. 3. The confidence level reported for the three models is 0.95.

From the DTMC model it is possible to get the probability to reach the absorbing states of death and recovery from every state of the chain. This is done elevating to the power of fourth each of the DTMC probabilities matrix. Table 3 shows these probabilities.

Table 3. Probability to reach death or recovery from each state of the DTMC for the partitions considered.

State	Negative to SARS-COV-2		Positive to SARS-COV-2			
			No comorbidity		With comorbidity	
	Recover	Death	Recover	Death	Recover	Death
Sick	0.79	0.21	0.79	0.21	0.58	0.42
Ambulatory	0.96	0.04	0.96	0.04	0.88	0.12
Hospitalized	0.40	0.60	0.51	0.49	0.36	0.64
ICU	0.19	0.81	0.20	0.80	0.12	0.88
Ventilated	0.07	0.93	0.14	0.86	0.09	0.91

4   Discussion

In this section an interpretation of the DTMC models obtained is given. The model obtained from the negative to SARS-COV-2 partition is used as base line. The graph of the DTMC process for this group of individuals is shown in Fig. 1.

From Figs. 1, 2 and 3 we observe that the group of sick people with higher probability to get hospitalized is the one with *SARS-COV-2 with comorbidity illness*. This group has a probability of 59% to get hospitalized, against 39% for the people with *SARS-COV-2 without comorbidity*. Sick patients *without SARS-COV-2* virus have the lower probability to get hospitalized with only 30%.

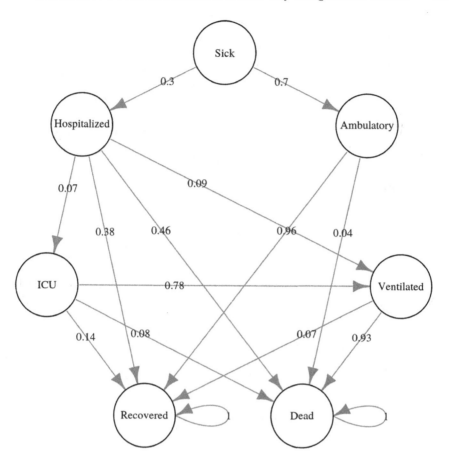

Fig. 1. The Markov Chain process graph for cases with negative test for SARS-COV-2

From data in Table 3 we observe that for sick people that are not hospitalized (ambulatory state) there is a high probability to recover, with 96% for people *without SARS-COV-2* as well as people *positive to SARS-COV-2 without comorbidity illness*. It is worth to mention that, even tough those *positive to SARS-COV-2 and comorbidity illness* have an 88% probability to recover from the ambulatory state, they have three times the probability to die with respect to those on the other partitions considered.

Once people is hospitalized, their probabilities to recover start to drop. The data analyzed shows that the group of patients with higher probability to recover is the one with *SARS-COV-2 and no comorbidity*, followed by the group of patients *without SARS-COV-2* and at the end patients *with SARS-COV-2 and comorbidity* with 51%, 40% and 36%, respectively. Data shows that COVID-19 sickness is worst than the average of other respiratory diseases that require hospitalization only on the presence of comorbidity illness.

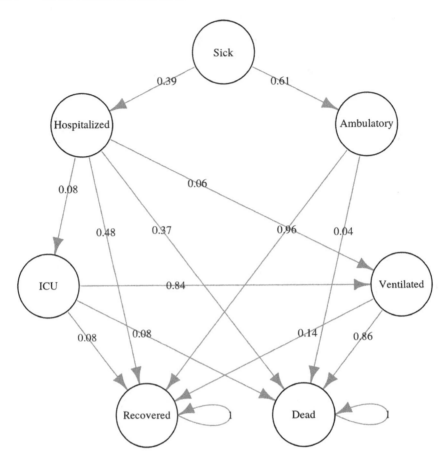

Fig. 2. The Markov Chain process graph for cases with positive test for SARS-COV-2 and no comorbidity

Patients moved to ICU lower their probabilities to survive to 20%, 19% and 12% for people *positive to SARS-COV-2 without comorbidity, negative to SARS-COV-2* and *positive to SARS-COV-2 with comorbidity*, respectively. At ICU COVID-19 disease is worst than the average of other respiratory diseases if a comorbidity illness is present.

Finally, once ventilation is required, surprisingly for the authors, the group with the higher probability to die is the one *negative to SARS-COV-2* with 93%; followed by people *positive to SARS-COV-2 with comorbidity* which have 88% of probability to die; patients *positive to SARS-COV-2 without comorbidity* have the lower probability to die with 86%. Although this is later discussed, a plausible explanation for this, may be that these patients got sick with another respiratory infection with higher lethality than that for COVID-19. However, this needs a further and deeper investigation.

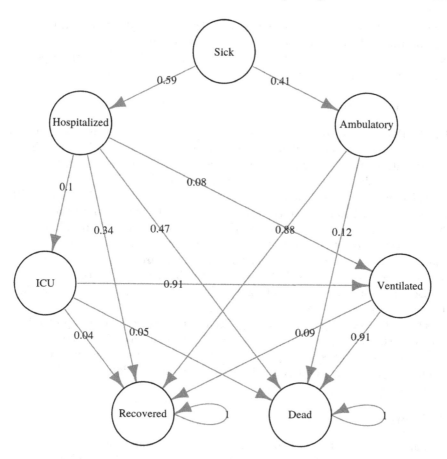

Fig. 3. The Markov Chain process graph for cases with positive test for SARS-COV-2 and comorbidity

The graphs of the DTMC on Figs. 1, 2, 3 show that patients hospitalized with SARS-COV-2 and comorbidity have 47% of probability to die without being translated to ICU, almost the same as those patients without SARS-COV-2, which have 46% of probability. The group with less probability to die on a general bed is the one of patients *positive to SARS-COV-2 without comorbidity* with a 37% of probability.

From the analysis done, it is clear that people *positive to SARS-COV-2 with comorbidity* have the higher probability to reach death from most states, being the exception on ventilation, for which the higher probability to reach death is for the group of patients *negative to SARS-COV-2*.

The advantage of people that test negative to SARS-COV-2 is that they have lower probabilities to get hospitalized, but data shows that once they reach hospitalization their probabilities to survive drops even more than for people with SARS-COV-2. This is something that require further research to explain, but one possible explanation is that they might get infected with SARS-COV-2 at the hospital with their immune system already compromised; another plausible explanation is that those patients may have acquired some other respiratory illness with higher lethality than COVID-19.

5   Conclusions

The Markov Chain process was used to model the probabilities that a person with respiratory illness will recover or die once they approach a health care facility with COVID-19 symptoms in Mexico City. The model was fitted with a data set published by the government of Mexico City.

The model states that people negative to COVID-19 and positive to COVID-19 without comorbidity have the same probability to recover from the sick and the ambulatory states. Nevertheless, the probability to die for people negative to COVID-19 from the ventilated state is the higher and the authors consider that this behaviour requires further and deeper research.

From most states COVID-19 is worst to the average of other respiratory diseases only with the presence of comorbidity, being the exception the ventilated state as mentioned above.

The methodology presented can be used to understand how the probabilities change on time and space configuring the proper partitions for the fitting process. Therefore, the analysis can be done at different scales from health care facility, municipality, state or country level proved that there is data available at those scales for the fitting process.

References

1. Carletti, T., Fanelli, D., Piazza, F.: Covid-19: The unreasonable effectiveness of simple models. Chaos, Solitons and Fractals: X 5 (2020). https://doi.org/10.1016/j.csfx.2020.100034
2. Ching, W.K., Ng, M.K.: Markov Chains: Models, Algorithms and Applications, vol. 83. Springer, US, Boston, MA (2006)
3. City, M.: Datos abiertos de la Ciudad de México covid-19 sinave (2020)
4. Davies, N.G., et al.: Effects of non-pharmaceutical interventions on covid-19 cases, deaths, and demand for hospital services in the UK: a modelling study. Lancet Publ. Health 5(7), e375–e385 (2020)
5. Gentleman, R., Ihaka, R.: The R project for statistical computing (2020)
6. Pareek, M., et al.: Ethnicity and covid-19: an urgent public health research priority. Lancet 395(10234), 1421–1422 (2020)
7. Ravi, K.: Ethnic disparities in covid-19 mortality: are comorbidities to blame? Lancet (Br. Ed.) 396(10243), 22–22 (2020)
8. Spedicato, G.A.: Discrete Time Markov Chains with R. R J. 9(2), 84–104 (2017)
9. Spedicato, G.A., Kang, T.S., Yalamanchi, S.B., Yadav, D., Cordón, I.: The markovchain package: a package for easily handling discrete markov chains in R
10. Verity, R., et al.: Estimates of the severity of coronavirus disease 2019: a model-based analysis. Lancet Infect. Dis. 20(6), 669–677 (2020). https://doi.org/10.1016/S1473-3099(20)30243-7
11. Çakan, S.: Dynamic analysis of a mathematical model with health care capacity for covid-19 pandemic. Chaos Solitons Fractals 139, 110033 (2020)

Design and Development of Photovoltaic Power Automatic System

Jaime Vega Pérez[1], Blanca García[2], and Nayeli Vega García[3(✉)]

[1] Escuela Superior de Ingeniería Mecánica y Eléctrica – Ticoman, IPN, 07738 Mexico City, Mexico
jvegape@hotmail.com
[2] Centro de Estudios Científicos y Tecnológicos 1, IPN, 07738 Mexico City, Mexico
blgarcia16@yahoo.com.mx
[3] Escuela Superior de Cómputo, IPN, 07738 Mexico City, Mexico
nvegag0126@gmail.com

Abstract. In this paper the design, building and test of the photovoltaic power automatic system prototype is reported, the electronic system is developed using the capacitive technique to reduce the power loss of the photovoltaic module. The property of variable resistance reflected by the capacitor during its discharge–charge process is toke in advantage to sweep the module I-V curve wile module current and voltage are sensed. An electronic system is designed using a microcontroller target to get the digital voltage signal and. Also, a personal computer is used to automatize the measurement. So that, a software base on Mat Lab was designed and developed to operate the electronic system since the computer. Experimental results gotten since the prototype electronic developed, the I-V and P-V curves can be measured for different modules until 60 V and 8 A, the efficiency is about 98%. The system simple and cheaper and it can be manufactured easily.

Keywords: PV module · P-V curve · Maximum power

1 Introduction

Nowadays, the conventional electric energy is used minus in whatever country due to its great environmental contamination basically. So that renewable energy sources have started to be used. The renewable energy is until now the energy sources most known are the photovoltaic energy which use the sum energy, and the win energy it transforms the win energy among others. Particularly the sum energy is transformed with photovoltaic (PV) modules, these are electronics devises done of silicon basically contaminate with phosphorus and they work based on the photovoltaic effect. The PV modules (Fig. 1) supplies direct current electric, and due to the PV cell is integrated by the union of two electrical semiconductors, it has electrical characteristics of series resistance, parallel resistance, current source then it can be represented by the electrical circuit showed in Fig. 2. The VP modules are being used due to their advantage such as: Clean energy source, low maintenance and they do not pollute, although they are of low efficiency.

© Springer Nature Switzerland AG 2020
M. F. Mata-Rivera et al. (Eds.): WITCOM 2020, CCIS 1280, pp. 319–332, 2020.
https://doi.org/10.1007/978-3-030-62554-2_24

Due to the PV cell supplies 0,56 V and variable current because it depends of its area and the incident solar radiation basically, then the PV cells are connection in series to increase the voltage to obtain the PV module and when the PV modules are connected serial or parallel the PV array is gotten.

Fig. 1. Photovoltaic module IUSASOL Mexico

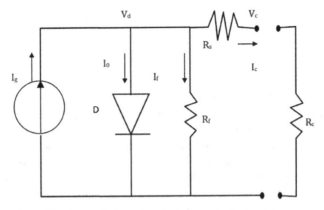

Fig. 2. Equivalent electrical circuit f solar module

The PV cell or PV module can be represented by the electrical circuit in Fig. 2.

The PV cell or module power is obtained for the mathematic equation obtained from equivalent electronic circuit in Fig. 2, that indicates the supplied current changes exponentially, then the PV cell or module supplies a maximum power point (MPP) and it is changing during the day because the solar radiation is changing. It is necessary to locate and follow the MPP using an electronic system to improve the efficiency of the PV module, this kind of system are named Maximum Power Point Tracker (MPPT), and also the PV module output maximum power must be measured on installation place, because the modules are electrically characterized by the manufacturer in standard conditions (i.e. solar power of 1000 W/m^2, temperature of 25 °C), but in real working conditions the photovoltaic module is subjected to environmental changes all time. To measure photovoltaic modules of higher power and voltage, for example up to 60 V and 5 A it is necessary to research about new measurements techniques. Then, in this paper the design and development of a measurement technique of PV modules is reported.

2 State of Art

Due to the I-V curve of solar module is nonlinear, then it is not easy to locate the maximum power point (MPP). So it is necessary to develop techniques and prototypes to measure the PV module maximum power. Some researchers have been reporting different techniques and methods to obtain the PV module I-V curves and development system to locate the module MPPT. Mohamed AL-Emam, Mostafa I. Marei, and Walid El-khattam [1] proposed MPPT technique for tracking the global MPP under partial shading conditions. It consists of FLC and scanning system implemented using a simple microcontroller. The system was tested under different shading conditions. Simulation of PV system under partial conditions was doing using Matlab/Simulink.

Anas Al-rawashdeh, Saleh Al-Jufout [2] done an evaluation of using Distributed Maximum Power Point racking (DMPPT) architecture to reduce power losses caused by shadow effect. They compared the simulation results of applying shadow on the existing multi string architecture system with their redesigned system by using DMPPT architecture, their results showed that the system energy improved by using DMPPT architecture during shadow effect condition

Mustafa Engin Başoğlu [3] developed a power processing unit (PPU) connected between PV module and load to extract more power from PV modules, he guess DC-DC converters are used for impedance matching between PV module and load also he design steps of the boost converter for an MPPT application have been presented. Mustafa Engin Başoğlu [4] analyzed the lost power due to partial shading of photovoltaic (PV) modules the entire surface of the PV, them he developed an improved version of a 0.8 VOC model based global maximum power point tracking (GMPPT). He used an ended primary inductance converter (SEPIC) is used as a power converter between PV module and load. He proved the proposed GMPPT strategy outperforms than full scanning-based algorithm known. Alfredo Oliver Batu, Harsono Soepardjo and Prawito Prajitno [5] analyzed the disadvantages of photovoltaic module is when irradiation from the sun changes which moves the maximum power point in P-V curve, so the output power obtained become not at its maximum power. Then, he used Arduino Uno as microcontroller to process the readings from voltage and current sensor while also controlling DC-DC Booster which able to move the operating voltage of the system.

He proved experimental results yield the output power from system greater than output power from photovoltaic module without using MPPT as result from the system working at operating voltage when the voltage of maximum power exists. Ankit Chowdhury, Tanmay Rout, Sarita Samal and Manoj Kumar Maharana [6]. They analyzed The PV module maximum power point in random change irradiance for various irradiance levels, using simulation models with Simulink software to study the change of PV module current-voltage and power-current, and they determined Maximum power point decrease linearly with decrease in irradiance from 1000 W/m^2 to 250 W/m^2. Muhammad Hanan1, Xin AI, Muhammad Yaqoob Javed, Muhammad Majid Gulzar4, and Saqib Ahmad [7], a hybrid combination of variable-step sized Incremental Conductance with Fractional Short Circuit Current (FSCC) technique is proposed in this research work. Initially, the FSCC forces the PV system to work near MPP and then InC technique track the exact peak. MatLab/Simulink software is used to implement the proposed hybrid technique. Finally, the results verify its superior performance under rapidly changing environmental conditions.

Muhammad Hanan1, Xin AI, Muhammad Yaqoob Javed, Muhammad Majid Gulzar, and Saqib Ahmad [8]. In this paper, the distributed maximum power point tracking (DMPPT) techniques used to track the maximum power under partial shading condition, both series and parallel connected DC-DC converters are considered to track the MP from panels by use of a DMPPT algorithm, the efficacy of the proposed system was verified with Matlab/Simulink simulations. J. Vega, B Garcia and N. Vega [9] developed an electronic system to measure the MPP of the PV module using the variable resistance technique. L. Navinkumar Rao and S. Gairola [10],. Studied a 50 W PV module electrical characteristics was studied with the focus on control of boost converter to achieve maximum power point tracking by Perturbation and Observation method uniquely used with PI so This paper has presented the MPP tracking algorithm controller the simulation was done using MATLAB.

Issam A. Smadi*, Rana AL-Qudah [11] developed an accurate, simplified, explicit, and fast computing one-step model for a practical photovoltaic (PV) module without the need of heavy offline calculations, lookup tables, or iterative methods. A closed-form expression of the model shaping factor is provided, which paves the way to explicitly locate the maximum power point (MPP), and also, they adaptive maximum power point tracking (MPPT) algorithm is proposed. Hadj Araba et al. [12], presented the results of maximum power performance measurements of PV modules of the first grid-connected PV system installed at Centre de Development des Energies Renewables The analysis has shown that all the PV modules are producing power, but less than rated value. Sonam Dorji, et al. [13], have studied the Maximum Power Point Tracking using Perturb & Observe and fuzzy logic controller for boost converter and quadratic boost converter is carried out for the purpose of comparison of its performance and analysis thereof. Both techniques are simulated in Matlab/Simulink software and 80 W solar photovoltaic module. F. Almonacid et al. [14] proposed a model based on Artificial Neural Networks (ANNs) to predict the maximum power of an HCPV module using easily measurable atmospheric parameters, atmospheric parameters and the PV maximum power have been measured Spain research Centre.

Based on the articles reviewed and reported above and due to the output power of the photovoltaic module changes constantly with the temperature and the level of solar radiation basically and also the voltage current characteristic curve of the module is an exponential law. then the location of the maximum power point continues to be the subject of research. several researchers have developed electronic systems called MPPT using different techniques [1, 2, 4], others have elaborated mathematical algorithms [6, 7] and other scientists have simulated using different software based on Matlab-Simulink, other have use microcontrollers as Arduino 1 [5] among others, some of these studies we have reported to. Also, the PV module I-V curve had been measured using an electronic device to generate variable resistance to PV module [9] but using this technique the PV module power has to be dissipated so that his technique is appropriate to measure low levels power up 100 W. Other researchers have developed techniques for detecting and monitoring the maximum power point of the cell, module or photovoltaic arrangements [10], also reported new mathematical models [11, 12], using neural networks [14] and fuzzy logic [13] to control the point of maximum power of the module. Then, to measure high powers is necessary to lock forward other techniques. In this work the design and developed of an electronic system using capacitive technique to measure PV modules is reported.

3 Proposal

In this paper a new measurement electronic system based on capacitive impedance technique of photovoltaic modules is proposed. An electrolytic capacitor is used to be connected through current sensor to module, then it is possible measure modules of higher power and voltage, for example the photovoltaic modules of 60 V, and 5 A will be measures easily on the installation place, In this paper, the design, development and test of electronic meter using capacitive impedance is reported. The electronic system developed is integrated for an electrolytic capacitor connected through an electronic switch to photovoltaic module, during the charge process of capacitor the current voltage of PV module are sampled, then an electronic must adequate the current and voltage signals sensed from the photovoltaic module.

The electrical signals are inter-connected to micro control unit to be converted to digital signals, after they are sent to a personal computer to automate all the electronic system. Also control electronic circuit it is necessary to design to operate the switch and to synchrony al electronic circuit and the measurement process. Whit this technic it is possible to measure high voltage module avoiding dissipating the measured power. The proposal system is showed in Fig. 3.

The proposed method takes advantage of the electrical property of the capacitor, because the capacitor reflects variable resistance value during its charging process. At the beginning when the capacitor is discharged it reflects zero ohm, then it acts as a short circuit and the photovoltaic module is placed in a short circuit condition sending its maximum current to the capacitor. While the capacitor is charged it increases its resistance reducing the charge current sent by the module, then the voltage current

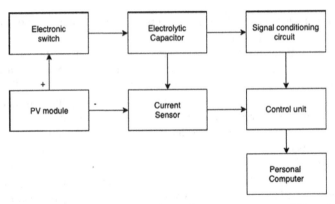

Fig. 3. Block diagram of proposal electronic system to measure PV modules

curve of the photovoltaic module is swept, until when the capacitor is fully charged its resistance is infinite, and then the photovoltaic module is set to the open circuit condition, and therefore no current passes from the module to the capacitor. The charge current of the capacitor follows an exponential law (Eq. 1).

$$I(t) = \left(\frac{V}{R}\right) e^{-\frac{t}{RC}} \tag{1}$$

From Eq. 1, V is the module voltage, R is the cable resistance between PV module and the electrolytic capacitor it is about 5 Ω, t is the capacitor charge time, C is the capacitor value and $I(t)$ the current variation during charge capacitor.

Whit this method is possible to measure PV modules up 300 W, 40 V and 8 A the measurement time is about 4 ms (Fig. 4).

3.1 Electronic Design

Electronic circuit designed is integrated for two electrical sensors one of them for current and other for voltage, the electrical signals sensed are send to amplifiers to adequate el output voltage level to be sent to digital analogic converter. Also, a microcontroller is used to link the electronic circuit with the computer. A synchrony electronic circuit using different integrated circuit digital and analogic signal transistor as BC547 [15] and electronic switch were used, to control the charge and discharge of the capacitor and also electronic comparators to detect the time. Based on the controller time response it was proposed 3 s was proposed complete reading, then due to the cable resistance is 5 Ω it was calculated the electrolytic capacitor was of 60000 micro farad [15]. The microcontroller target Arduino was used to engage the electronic system with the personal computer [16]. Also, a software was designed it was based on Matlab.

To begin the measurement and the instant when the maximum power point the PV modules is detected (Fig. 5).

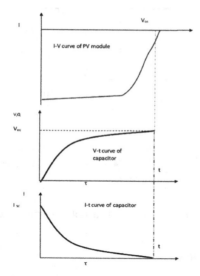

Fig. 4. Capacitor I-t and V-t curves and PV module I-V curve.

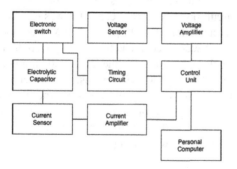

Fig. 5. Block diagram of proposal electronic system

To ensure that the module I-V curve is swept at the same time that the capacitor is charged, and the switch is activated, a control and synchrony electronic circuit is designed, and this is activated from the laptop. This electronic circuit is integrated with an electronic switch to discharge the electrolytic capacitor activated from a digital circuit and an analogic comparator (Fig. 6). To start the measurement the computer sent a high voltage pulse by port A to activated the digital circuit and discharge the capacitor, check the comparator output if its voltage level is cero them the lap top send high voltage level pulse to switch A and the capacitor charge is started, at the same time the current and voltage from PV module are sampled, at the same time the PV module voltage is compared and when is equal at the open circuit voltage, the process is finished.

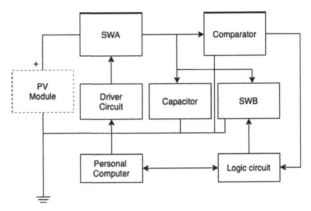

Fig. 6. Block diagram of control and timing circuit

4   Experimental Work

To get the PV module I-V curve is necessary to generate an enough delay so that the control unit and the laptop can capture the sample of current and voltage since short circuit point to open circuit point, so that el capacitor was implemented with capacitor bank of 20 electrolytic capacitor of 4700 μF at 100 V were used to get 94000 μF. Power MOSFET transistors were used as electronic switch. High impedance operational amplifier with Jfet technology were used as the integrated circuit TL081 also, precision operational integrated circuit like LM308 were used as differential amplifier. Digital integrated circuits and different small signal transistors and discrete electronic devices were used to develop the timing control circuit to power on the switches. The Arduino I was used as microcontroller, and as power supply, two 9 V battery were used. The prototype electronic system is showed in Fig. 7.

Fig. 7. Prototype electronic system developed.

5 Measurement

The prototype electronic system developed was calibrated to get right results, so that the capture time was of 500 ms, the output signal amplifier was from 0 to 5 V. The capacitor discharge delay was 1 s, the prototype was calibrated to measure up 300 W and PV modules of 60 V. The error found with measurements was o 1.8%.

I-V curves were measured for different photovoltaic modules under real conditions of solar radiation and temperature, the result is in Fig. 8.

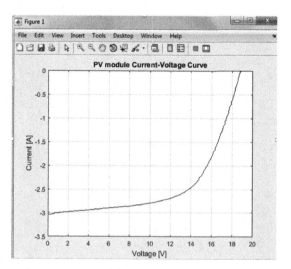

Fig. 8. I-V curve of photovoltaic module measured with the electronic system developed.

Also, the P-V curve of photovoltaic module was measured, the result is showed in Fig. 9.

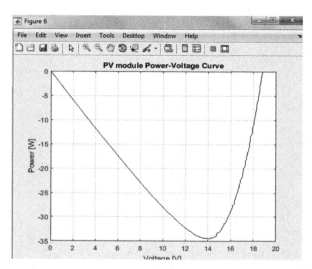

Fig. 9. P-V curve of photovoltaic module measured with the electronic system developed.

Although the PV module power curve was gotten it is necessary analyses the current variation from open circuit condition to short circuit condition and confirmed if the developed electronic prototype can be able to obtain the I-V and P-V curves for PV module with voltage more than twenty, so that also a PV module of 35 W and 38 V of open circuit was measured under real environmental condition; the level of solar radiation was 480 W/m^2. The I-V and P-V curves were measured, and they are reported in Fig. 10 and Fig. 11.

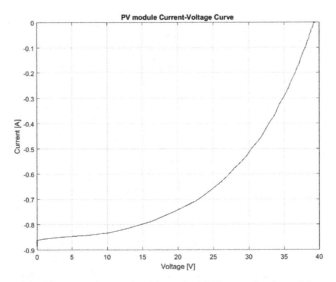

Fig. 10. I-V curve obtained from the 38 V open circuit module

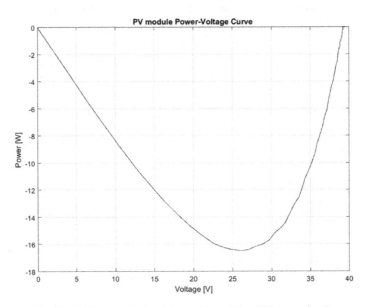

Fig. 11. P-V curve obtained from PV module of 38 open circuit

The power and their coordinate current and voltage were measures and the power was obtained to test the correct operation of the software, the results are showed in Table 1.

Table 1. Current and voltage sample values captured during measurement of the I-V curve

Voltage (V)	Current (A)	Power (W)
39.23712	0	0
39.287424	−0.00497694	−0.19553116
39.23712	−0.00497694	−0.1952808
39.186816	−0.00995388	−0.39006087
39.136512	−0.01493082	−0.58434023
39.086208	−0.01990776	−0.77811887
38.9856	−0.0248847	−0.97014499
38.834688	−0.02986164	−1.1596675
38.884992	−0.03483858	−1.35469794
38.683776	−0.04479246	−1.73274154
38.633472	−0.0497694	−1.92276477
38.532864	−0.06470022	−2.49308484
38.331648	−0.0746541	−2.86161476
38.23104	−0.08460798	−3.23465115
37.97952	−0.10451574	−3.96945774
37.778304	−0.11446962	−4.32446822
37.577088	−0.12940044	−4.86249185
37.375872	−0.14433126	−5.39450684
37.174656	−0.16423902	−6.10552923
36.872832	−0.17916984	−6.60649959
36.621312	−0.19907761	−7.2904831
36.269184	−0.21898537	−7.94242053
35.917056	−0.23889313	−8.5803378
35.665536	−0.25880089	−9.23027235
35.2128	−0.28368559	−9.98936386
34.810368	−0.30359335	−10.5681962
34.357632	−0.32350111	−11.114732
33.904896	−0.35336275	−11.9807273

(*continued*)

Table 1. (*continued*)

Voltage (V)	Current (A)	Power (W)
33.552768	−0.37327051	−12.5242588
32.898816	−0.39815521	−13.098835
32.395776	−0.42303991	−13.7047062
31.792128	−0.45290155	−14.3987041
31.238784	−0.47280931	−14.769988
30.43392	−0.49769401	−15.1467798
29.729664	−0.52755565	−15.6840523
28.9248	−0.55244035	−15.9792268
27.969024	−0.57732506	−16.1472183
27.013248	−0.6071867	−16.4020848
26.057472	**−0.6320714**	**−16.4701827**
24.950784	−0.6569561	−16.3915697
23.793792	−0.6818408	−16.2235781
22.536192	−0.7067255	−15.9269015
21.12768	−0.72663326	−15.352075
19.668864	−0.74654102	−14.6836138
18.008832	−0.76644878	−13.8028473
16.3488	−0.78635654	−12.8559858
14.58816	−0.80128736	−11.6893082
12.726912	−0.81621818	−10.387937
10.412928	−0.831149	−8.65469472
7.79712	−0.84110288	−6.55818011
5.080704	−0.84607982	−4.29868114
2.76672	−0.85105676	−2.35463577
1.00608	−0.8560337	−0.86123839
0	−0.86101064	0

PV module maximum power as function real environmental conditions were measured to test the correct operation of the software. The results are in Table 2.

Table 2. Maximum power measured with different insolation levels.

Solar radiation (W/m^2)	Voltage (V)	Current (A)	Maximum Power (W)
125	12.173568	−0.21898537	−2.66583324
138	11.06688	−0.23391619	−2.58872236
135	22.435584	−0.11446962	−2.56819284
218	24.447744	−0.1741929	−4.25862354
217	21.479808	−0.19410067	−4.16924502
215	23.844096	−0.1741929	−4.15347234
220	27.16416	−0.21898537	−5.94855352
390	28.270848	−0.49271707	−13.9295295
490	24.950784	−0.6569561	−16.3915697
423	25.453824	−0.58727894	−14.9484947
420	23.240448	−0.64202528	−14.9209551
450	24.246528	−0.62211752	−15.0841898
405	23.8944	−0.58727894	−14.0326778
408	24.90048	−0.56239424	−14.0038864

6 Conclusions

Based on preliminary experimental results showed in Figs. 8, 9, 10 and 11, it can assure the prototype electronic system developed to measure the current, voltage and power o photovoltaic module at the same time the measurement of its characteristics curves works rightly. From Table 1 results the prototype developed determinates well the power and detects the maximum power o PV module with 70 mW of error, 35 mA of current and 25 mV of voltage. Base on experimental results showed in Table 2 it is right to ensure the prototype electronic system can measure low power levels up to 2.5 W for 300 W full scale, so that the measurement error of prototype developed is near to 1%. Although it necessary to make more measurements to precise the error percent. Also, the measurement technique using electrolytic capacitor is adequate to measure the electric characteristics of the photovoltaic module of high level of current and voltage. The prototype developed is simple, light, cheap and easy to manufacture.

Acknowledgments. The authors are thankful to National Polytechnic Institute from México, and also grateful to the project No. 20201335 SIP-IPN by their financial support.

References

1. Abdourraziq, S., Abdourraziq, M.A., Darab, C.: Maximum power point tracking applied to PV systems under partial shading conditions. In: 2017 International Conference on Electromechanical and Power Systems (SIELMEN), Iasi, pp. 286–290 (2017)

2. Al-rawashdeh, A., Al-Jufout, S.: Evaluation of energy harvest increase by distributed maximum power point tracking. In: 2019 IEEE Jordan International Joint Conference on Electrical Engineering and Information Technology (JEEIT), Amman, Jordan, pp. 145–149 (2019)

3. Başoğlu, M.E.: Realization of a low cost and fast boost converter based MPPT for PV system. In: 2019 4th International Conference on Power Electronics and their Applications (ICPEA), Elazig, Turkey, pp. 1–6 (2019)

4. Başoğlu, M.E.: Module level global maximum power point tracking strategy. In: 2019 4th International Conference on Power Electronics and their Applications (ICPEA), Elazig, Turkey, pp. 1–5 (2019)

5. Batu, A.O., Soepardjo, H., Prajitno, P.: Arduino uno-based maximum power point tracking for pv module using perturb and observe algorithm. In: 2019 International Conference on Mechatronics, Robotics and Systems Engineering (MoRSE), Bali, Indonesia, pp. 213–216 (2019)

6. Chowdhury, A., Samal, S., Rout, T., Maharana, M.K.: Effect of irradiance during foggy days and clear climatic conditions in maximum power point in PV characteristics for photovoltaic systems. In: 2018 4th International Conference on Electrical Energy Systems (ICEES), Chennai, pp. 67–71 (2018)

7. Hanan, M., Ai, X., Javed, M.Y., Majid Gulzar, M., Ahmad, S.: A two-stage algorithm to harvest maximum power from photovoltaic system. In: 2018 2nd IEEE Conference on Energy Internet and Energy System Integration (EI2), Beijing, pp. 1–6 (2018)

8. Nitesh, Y., Malakondareddy, B., Kumar, S.S., Anand, I.: Experimental investigation of distributed maximum power point operation for solar PV system. In: 2018 20th National Power Systems Conference (NPSC), Tiruchirappalli, India, pp. 1–6 (2018)

9. Vega Pérez, J., García, B., Vega García, N.: Design and development of photovoltaic power meter. In: Mata-Rivera, M.F., Zagal-Flores, R., Barría-Huidobro, C. (eds.) WITCOM 2019. CCIS, vol. 1053, pp. 130–141. Springer, Cham (2019). https://doi.org/10.1007/978-3-030-33229-7_12

10. Rao, L.N., Gairola, S.: Maximum power point tracking issues in control of a low power photovoltaic (PV) module. In: 2015 International Conference on Energy Economics and Environment (ICEEE), Noida, pp. 1–6 (2015)

11. Issam, A., Smadi, R.: Explicit one-step model and adaptive maximum power point tracking algorithm for a photovoltaic module. Comput. Electr. Eng. **85**, 106659 (2020)

12. Hadj Araba, A., et al.: Maximum power output performance modeling of solar photovoltaic modules. In: 6th International Conference on Energy and Environment Research, ICEER 2019, University of Aveiro, Portugal (2019)

13. Dorji, S., Wangchuk, D., Choden, T., Tshewang, T.: Maximum power point tracking of solar photovoltaic cell using perturb & observe and fuzzy logic controller algorithm for boost converter and quadratic boost converter. Mater. Today Proc. 1224–1229 (2020)

14. Almonacid, F., Fernández, E., Rodrigo, P., Pérez-Higueras, P.J., Rus-Casas, C.: Estimating the maximum power of a high concentrator photovoltaic (HCPV) module using an artificial neural network. Energy **53**, 165–172 (2013)

15. Smith, S.: Microelectronic Circuits. Oxford University Press Inc., New York (1998)

16. Marckus, J.: Electronic Circuit Manual. Mcgraw-hill, New York (1987)

Availability Vulnerabilities Evaluation to LoRaWAN

Pamela Beltrán-García, Ponciano Jorge Escamilla-Ambrosio$^{(\boxtimes)}$, Eleazar Aguirre-Anaya, and Abraham Rodríguez-Mota

Cybersecurity Laboratory, Centro de Investigación en Computación, Instituto Politécnico Nacional, Mexico City, Mexico
`pam.belt.g@gmail.com`, `{pescamilla,eaguirre,arodrigm}@cic.ipn.mx`
`http://www.cic.ipn.mx`

Abstract. LoRaWAN as one of the newest protocols in the Internet of Things ecosystem represents a whole new area in cybersecurity research. In this protocol, security is focused on data integrity and confidentiality and most the research that analyse its security only examined the availability property of the protocol from the performance or join-procedure perspective. In this paper we aim to provide evidence supporting a major interest in the availability property. Therefore we describe five identified vulnerabilities that have not been thoroughly analysed in the literature together with exemplification of how to exploit them to perform cyberattacks, specifically for bidirectional communication. We also make the case for IoT gateway as a main target for the Committing Uplink/Downlink Communication, Theft the Gateway for Packet Monitoring, Data Loss, Delay in Data Reception and Battery Consumption attacks. We also provide details of the experiments and discussion of the obtained data. Finally, we include a discussion of some mitigations activities for such vulnerabilities.

Keywords: Vulnerabilities · LoRaWAN · Cyberattacks · Availability · Cybersecurity

1 Introduction

The acronym IoT *(Internet of Things)* defines an interconnected network of "smart objects" that collect information from the environment through sensors and interact with the physical world through actuators; such objects use the Internet to transfer and analyse information [1].

Therefore, an IoT system is integrated by IoT devices that process and transmit information using a variety of protocols. Lately, some of the more used protocols are those used in the so-called Low Power Wide Area Networks (LPWAN), designed to connect IoT devices with low power consumption, long-range and low cost; for example, NB-IoT, Sigfox, and LoRaWAN; with LoRaWAN as one is one of the most suitable technology for short-range applications [2, 17].

Long-Range Wide-Area Network (LoRaWAN) is a new MAC layer protocol in the LPWAN family, which is standardised by the LoRa-Alliance. A LoRaWAN network

© Springer Nature Switzerland AG 2020
M. F. Mata-Rivera et al. (Eds.): WITCOM 2020, CCIS 1280, pp. 333–351, 2020.
https://doi.org/10.1007/978-3-030-62554-2_25

consists of a star-of-stars topology, see Fig. 1, which involves specific access restrictions to unlicensed bands, 902–928 MHz for the US. It can use channels with a bandwidth of either 125 kHz or 500 kHz, depending on the region. An Adaptive Data Rate (ADR) mechanism is used for optimising data rates, airtime, and energy consumption in the network, which are used by individuals nodes through MAC commands [9, 18]. Therefore, the three classes of end-devices have different possible characteristics of communication.

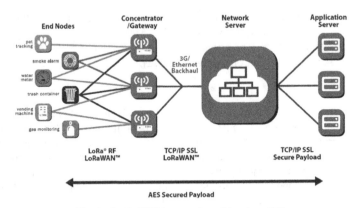

Fig. 1. LoRaWAN network architecture [13].

The default class which must be supported by all LoRaWAN end-devices is class A, based on the ALOHA family of protocols that take into account duty cycle restrictions; this is the percentage of time that a given node occupies a particular frequency band, choosing a random channel for each transmission [21]. Once the uplink is finished, the end-device opens two short receive windows (RX1 and RX2) to listen to downlinks, 1 and 2 s after the end of the uplink transmission, respectively. Downlink transmissions at any other time must be buffered at the network server until the next uplink. For class B, in addition to class A, end-devices are synchronised to the network using periodic beacons, they must enable extra receive windows at scheduled times by receiving a time-synchronised beacon from the gateway. Finally, in class C, end-devices have almost continuous receive windows, reducing latency on the downlink by keeping the receiver of the device open at all time, meaning no transmission. Based on this, the network server can initiate a downlink transmission at any time [13].

Along with the new protocols, due to the rapid development and limited resources of IoT devices, security has become an essential factor. Even with these new protocols for IoT, such as LoRaWAN, which has the particularity of providing data security relayed on cryptographic key generation [19], vulnerabilities that can be exploited by a threat actor may be introduced due to the topology and the type of communication used.

In the rest of this work, related works are discussed in Sect. 2. In Sect. 3, as a result of the performed analysis, five protocol vulnerabilities, along with the selected devices for testing, are introduced. The methodology starts with protocol vulnerability analysis; in the first place, reviewing the components of a LoRaWAN network; moreover, official documentation of the LoRaWAN protocol, especially the bidirectional communication, in addition to attacks already studied at the literature were reviewed. Next, for validation and after identifying the vulnerabilities based on the previous analysis, all attack vectors in a proof-of-concept were designed and performed, considering device characteristics such as model, datasheets, and specifications; eventually displayed in an attack tree presented at Sect. 4. After verifying and exploiting the vulnerabilities identified, a discussion on how these attacks can be mitigated in Sect. 5 is provided. Results and conclusions are presented in Sect. 6. Finally, in Sect. 7 future work is proposed.

2 Related Work

This section presents a set of analysis of protocol vulnerabilities investigations reported in the literature, most of them focused on data integrity and confidentiality, and some which analyse vulnerabilities that compromise nodes availability.

Butun *et al.* [3] and Aras *et al.* [4], analysed vulnerabilities from a theoretical point of view, vulnerabilities that are counter used for join procedure and the usage of beacons. In first place, the paper discusses how the *Replay Attack* for Over-The-Air Activation (OTAA) nodes is achievable through the keys generation with the *DevNonce* field; where a first join-request from a legitimate end-device is intercepted and jammed by an attacker. Then after waiting for a timeout to receive the join-accept, the end-device retries to join to the network and sends another join-request with a new *DevNonce* value. The attacker replays the first join-request message bringing out the network server acceptance, as this first value has not been used before. From now on, the network server and the legitimate end-device are de-synchronised in terms of *DevNonce* until a new session is initiated. In second place, the attack *Beacon Class B Synchronisation* is described, as beacons are not in any way secured, an attacker can set up a gateway to send fake beacons, resulting in class B end-devices having received windows out-of-sync. Regarding the *wormhole* attack, packets are captured by the attacker from one node and transmitted to another distantly located device; then she/he replays the packet in a different time, this is due to the lack of timestamp usage or signatures to validate packet time.

Iskhakov *et al.* [5] theoretically analysed the *Replay* attack for Activation-By-Personalisation (ABP) nodes as well as *ACK Spoofing* attack, and Yang *et al.* [6] performed experimentation and verification of such attacks. In the case of the first attack, incorrect use of the counter is identified as a vulnerability, as intercepting packets with the highest counter value of the last session, so forwarding them in a new session causes the no messages acceptance response for messages with a smaller counter value. In the second case, as the data-acknowledgment mechanism in LoRaWAN is made optional to reduce the time ratio required to power up, ACK messages are generated without message source identification. For such reason, the same ACK is used to confirm the successful receipt of another unrelated message, even when it has not arrived at the backend provider.

Finally, Yang *et al.* [5] proved the *Eavesdropping* attack in which, when capturing different packets from different sessions and comparing those with the same counter, the text or data sent is decrypted due to the AES algorithm in the counter mode used for confidentiality. Finally, the *Bit Flipping* attack is discussed, in which when an attacker changes a bit of the message between the Network Server and the Application Server, the

Application Server incorrectly decrypts the message. The first attack is accomplished through the data encryption counter mode, and the second attack is accomplished since integrity is only verified on the Network Server.

In the works reviewed above, authors analysed all the vulnerabilities described for the LoRaWAN protocol version 1.0.2, regardless of the type of equipment used. From a security perspective, all these vulnerabilities analyses are not complete as the availability property is not considered, and they were mainly focused on the confidentiality and integrity properties.

3 LoRaWAN Vulnerabilities and Attacks

In this section a vulnerabilities and attacks analysis to the LoRaWAN protocol is presented. We restricted this analysis to consider only threats within the assumptions stated in the version 1.0.2 specification of the protocol. Additionally, according to the Request for Comments 8376 (RFC) [7] and the LoRa-Alliance standardisation document [8], all devices must have Class A support.

The *LoRa Family Kit* [14] is used to perform the attacks. The kit includes an IoT *LoRa Gateway Hat* and five *IoT LoRa Nodes pHat* for the *Raspberry Pi* development board, for frequencies 902–928 MHz. All evaluations were released in a controlled LoRaWAN environment, Fig. 2, with *The Things Network (TTN)* as the public network server and *Ubidots* as the application server.

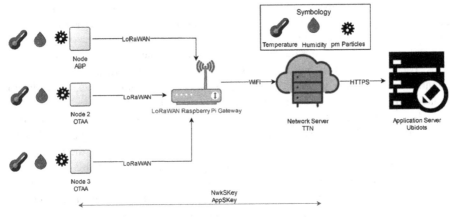

Fig. 2. LoRaWAN network scenario.

3.1 Uplink and Downlink Communication Committing

As mentioned in Sect. 1, a LoRaWAN network consists of nodes, gateways, a network server, and an application server. According to the protocol, communication is achieved when gateways relay messages between end-devices and the central network server; that is, nodes do not have direct communication with the network server. The gateway acts as a transparent bridge, converting the data obtained by the nodes to IP packets and vice versa.

Communication is bidirectional, as uplink messages going from end devices to the network server, and downlink messages are transmitted from the network server to the end-devices; this communication is only possible if the data is sent through the gateway [8]. For this reason, the gateway has been selected as the element of interest from where it is investigated if vulnerabilities can be identified on this device and, in the case vulnerabilities are identified, assessing the possibility for them to be exploited in order to interrupt the up and down communication link. For this analysis it was proposed a small LoRaWAN network, consisting of one gateway, a node, and a network server; plus extra hardware and software required to perform the analysis, including devices and tools that help the attacker to identify and exploit the vulnerabilities of the target.

For the interruption of uplink/downlink communication attack, the attacker goal is to disable the gateway. After the attack, node's data will not be sent to the network server; therefore, data will be unreachable at the network server. From the attacker perspective, it only knows that the LoRaWAN gateway is assembled onto a Raspberry Pi. This attack is designed based on the information gathered by applying penetration test techniques. In this case the MAC address identifies the gateway; as LoRaWAN uses MAC EUI-64 standard. After scanning devices connected to the network, a second scan is performed to identify the IP and active services. Identifying the LoRaWAN gateway with a web service that requires user/password authentication to access different web sections, a dictionary is generated with the credentials based on the device model. Finally, once credentials have been obtained, the control section can be accessed where the gateway can be turned off; in this attack scenario is knowed as "System Control". Another method to perform the attack, once the credentials are obtained, is achieved by sending a *get* request to the specific URL associated to the control of the shutdown gateway button. Figure 3 shows the attack setup.

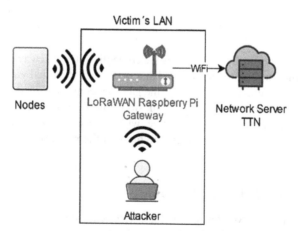

Fig. 3. LoRaWAN setup for uplink/downlink communication committing attack.

Table 1 shows the disruption effect over the communication; this happens while receiving data up to counter with value 5 after the attacker shutdown the LoRaWAN gateway, indicating disruption of communication.

Table 1. TTN Console non-receiving data after cnt = 5

Time	Frequency	Mod.	CR	Data rate	Airtime (ms)	Cnt
18:00:45	904.7	Lora	4/5	SF8 BW125	92.7	5 dev addr: 26 02 2C 09 payload size: 17 bytes
18:00:39	904.3	Lora	4/5	SF8 BW125	92.7	4 dev addr: 26 02 2C 09 payload size: 17 bytes
18:00:33	905.3	Lora	4/5	SF8 BW125	92.7	3 dev addr: 26 02 2C 09 payload size: 17 bytes
18:00:27	904.1	Lora	4/5	SF8 BW125	92.7	2 dev addr: 26 02 2C 09 payload size: 17 bytes
18:00:21	903.9	Lora	4/5	SF8 BW125	102.9	1 dev addr: 26 02 2C 09 payload size: 21 bytes
18:00:17	925.1	Lora	4/5	SF10 BW500	92.7	0 dev addr: 26 02 2C 09 payload size: 22 bytes
18:00:16	904.5	Lora	4/5	SF10 BW125	329.7	0 dev addr: 26 02 2C 09 payload size: 17 bytes

In this case, as long as the attacker has the credentials, the gateway can be shutdown n-times, and communication is interrupted due to the two identified vulnerabilities. For the first vulnerability, it is considered that the gateway configuration default credentials are not changed; and in the second one, the web interface uses HTTP protocol. The authentication mechanism is of a *basic* type, where credentials (ID and password) are in Base64 encoding, allowing the attacker to monitor the network and exfiltrate a valid request credentials.

3.2 Gateway Theft for Packet Monitoring

With a fake gateway, it is possible to monitor devices that connect through it, allowing to collect data such as the time at which nodes send data. However, an attacker can use the victim's gateway to achieve these tasks. To analyse how such attack can be performed, we set a small LoRaWAN network, consisting of one gateway, a node, and a network server, including also some extra hardware and software elements required to perform the analysis, also devices and tools that help the attacker identify and exploit the target's vulnerabilities. Figure 4 shows the attack setup used to test the following attack methods next described.

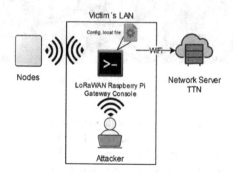

Fig. 4. LoRaWAN setup for gateway theft attack.

The first proposed attack starts by running the first three stages of the attack previously described in the section above, with a difference in the last stage when credentials are obtained, in this case the configuration section is changed to the attacker's values: the "Packet Forwarder Config" section, the parameters "Gateway ID" and "TTN Gateway Key" are modified, see Fig. 5.

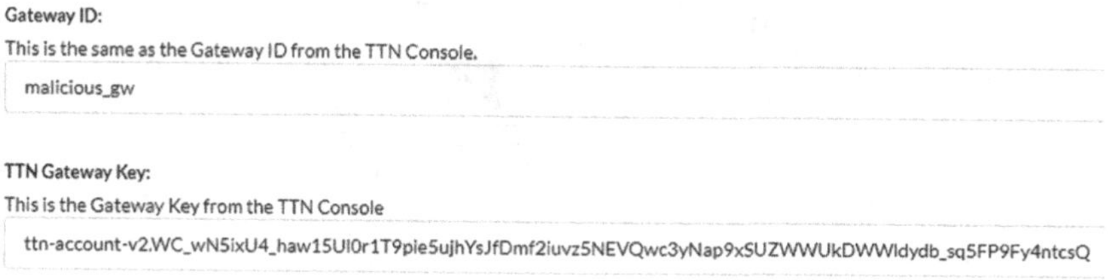

Gateway ID:

This is the same as the Gateway ID from the TTN Console.

    malicious_gw

TTN Gateway Key:

This is the Gateway Key from the TTN Console

    ttn-account-v2.WC_wN5ixU4_haw15UI0r1T9pie5ujhYsJfDmf2iuvz5NEVQwc3yNap9xSUZWWUkDWWldydb_sq5FP9Fy4ntcsQ

Fig. 5. "Packet Forwarder Config" Section modified by the attacker.

Once access to the console of the gateway device is gained, it is possible to use a different method to perform the attack, by changing the configuration file with data that has been obtained during the creation of a gateway in TTN. Figure 6 shows the local file of the LoRaWAN gateway modified by the attacker.

Similarly, as long as the attacker has the credentials, she/he can change the value of those fields to disable the gateway. Therefore for the identified vulnerabilities of default credentials and the HTTP protocol in the web service, a LoRaWAN gateway can be taken by an attacker.

3.3 Data Loss Caused by the Gateway

As discussed in Sect. 3.1, the gateway is a critical point for bidirectional communication in a LoRaWAN network. According to the LoRa-Alliance specification, download messages are sent by a single gateway [8].

```
GNU nano 3.2                                                local_conf.json

"gateway_conf": {
    "gateway_ID": "5049530055de840F",
    "contact_email": "lora.ciseg@gmail.com",
    "description": null,
    "servers": [
        {
            "serv_type": "ttn",
            "server_address": "",
            "serv_gw_id": "another_gw",
            "serv_gw_key": "ttn-account-v2.WC_wN5ixU4_haw1SU1Or1T9pie5ujhYs3fDmf2iuvz5NEVQwc3yWap9xSuZwWUkDWW1dydb_sq5FP9Fy4ntcsQ",
            "serv_enabled": true,
            "serv_port_up": 1700,
            "serv_port_down": 1700
        }
    ]
}
```

Fig. 6. Configuration file *local_config.json*.

Additionally, a gateway cannot receive upload transmissions while it is transmitting downlinks. If a gateway transmits to nodes 10% of the time, it cannot receive anything during the same time; therefore, data sent by nodes at the same time are lost [9].

For this reason, in order to analyse whether or not data loss can be caused by action of an attacker due to these operational conditions, we proposed a LoRaWAN network scenario shown in Fig. 7.

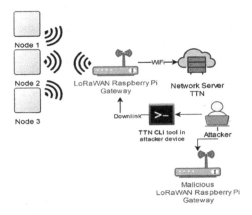

Fig. 7. LoRaWAN setup for data loss attack.

In this case, the attacker's goal is to make the gateway unable to transmit uplinks by sending downlinks to different nodes at the same time. After the attack, node's data will be lost at the time at which the gateway transmits the downlinks. From the attacker perspective, she/he must be able to send downlinks to the nodes by the TTN CLI tool and to monitor the time when nodes send data using a LoRaWAN gateway. The design of the attack begins with the authentication in the TTN CLI tool using the code provided by the victim's TTN server. The attacker monitors the network with the malicious gateway in order to identify the ID of each device and the time they send data. Once identified, the attacker sends, using the TTN CLI tool, the *ttnctl downlink* command to the specific node with the defined ID in the network, see Fig. 8.

A proof-of-concept was performed with a LoRa node sending data every 4 s including downlinks to other nodes, causing a 16 s of no data received from node 1. This is, node

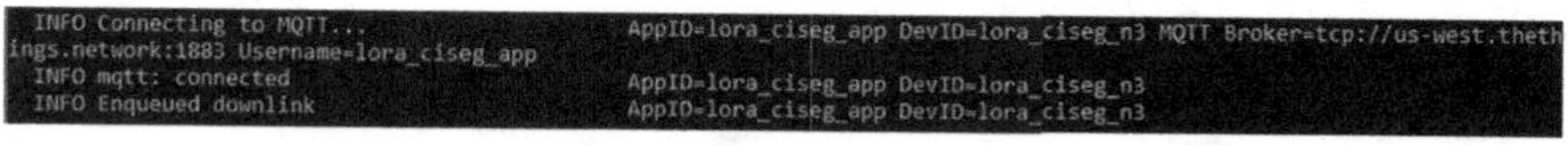

```
INFO Connecting to MQTT...                    AppID=lora_ciseg_app DevID=lora_ciseg_n3 MQTT Broker=tcp://us-west.theth
ings.network:1883 Username=lora_ciseg_app
INFO mqtt: connected                          AppID=lora_ciseg_app DevID=lora_ciseg_n3
INFO Enqueued downlink                        AppID=lora_ciseg_app DevID=lora_ciseg_n3
```

Fig. 8. Downlink queued to node *lora_ciseg_n3* with ttnctl command.

1 stops receiving data while the gateway sends downlinks to the other nodes of the network, see Table 2.

Table 2. Data Loss of node *lora_ciseg_n1* for 16 s

Time	Packet Number	Node ID	Payload
21:13.37	11	1	Payload: 01 02 3A 60
21:13:33	10	1	Payload: 01 02 42 93
21:13:29	9	1	Payload: 01 02 6A F0
21:13:13	5	1	Payload: 01 02 24 BD
21:13:08	4	1	Payload: 01 02 61 AE
21:13:04	3	1	Payload: 01 02 6B 67

Therefore, it can be observed that the system is vulnerable when an attacker is sending multiple downlinks to different nodes in the network, and the time in which downlinks are performed, is going to be proportional to the time that the data transmitted by the other nodes is lost.

3.4 Delay in Data Reception

A LoRaWAN node can be programmed to send specific data types such as temperature, humidity, etc., and so the node must ignore any unrecognised data or commands [8]. However, it consumes its window time to discard the unrecognised data, causing the no reception of legitimate data; in this case it also has to be considered that a node class A opens its receive windows only when sending an uplink; which can provoke delay in data reception. To analyse how can be performed, an attack under this conditions, we proposed the LoRaWAN scenario shown in Fig. 9.

In this attack, the attacker goal is to force the node to consume its window time processing unrecognised data, additionally by requesting acknowledgment of the unrecognised data reception takes most of the time. In the proposed scenario, from the attacker perspective, she/he must have access to send downlinks to the nodes by the TTN CLI tool and to monitoring the network with a LoRaWAN gateway. The design of the attack

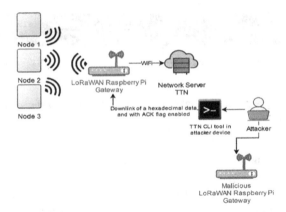

Fig. 9. LoRaWAN setup for testing a delay in data reception attack.

begins by sending a downlink data after performing authentication into the TTN CLI tool using the code provided by the victim's TTN server; and, by monitoring the network, she/he must identify the node's ID. Additionally, the ACK flag of the frame is enabled due to the presence of confirmed traffic which can significantly degrade the performance of the network [20]. With both conditions, it provokes a delay when new data is sent to the network server. This vulnerability can be exploited by sending the *ttnctl downlink node_id hex –confirmed* command with a hexadecimal data to the victim's node, which sends data every 5 s.

According to Eq. 1, one of the variables considered when thinking about data delay is the payload size. Therefore, there exists a correlation between time-on-air (ToA) and maximum payload sizes in each Spread Factor (SF). Time increases, as seen in Fig. 10, meaning that the node's receiver is active occupying its window time while receiving data due to the lack of a time restriction on receiving a downlink. In other words, the larger the payload size, the longer the time spent for the reception.

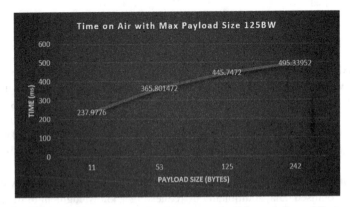

Fig. 10. Payload vs. time on-air with max payload for each Spread Factor.

$$\text{ToA} = (\frac{2^{SF}}{BW}((NP+4.25) + (SW + max(ceil\left(\frac{(8*PL) - (4*SF) + 28 + (16*CRC) - (20*IH)}{4(SF - (2*DE))}\right)$$
$$* (CR + 4), 0))) \tag{1}$$

Where NP = Number preamble symbols (NP = 8); SW = Sync Word Length (SW = 8); PL = PHY payload size; CR = Code Rate (CR = 4/5); DE = Rate optimization. DE = 1 when "LowDataRateOptimize" is enabled, DE = 0 otherwise; IH = Inserting frame header; CRC = Cyclic Redundancy Check with value 4/5; BW = Bandwidth; SF = Spread Factor. LoRaWAN specifications prescribes CRC = 1 and IH = 0 for uplinks; and for downlinks CRC = 0 and IH = 0.

3.5 Battery Consumption

To maximise battery life, LoRaWAN employs the Adaptive Data Rate (ADR) mechanism, which sets a data rate associated with a Spread Factor (SF), and in turn, the amount of data that can be sent. In other words, depending on the packet size, the transmission time increases, meaning that the higher the SF value becomes the longer it will take to send data. The defined data rate values in North America can be seen in Table 3 and Table 4, associated to packet size and SF values, respectively.

Table 3. Packet Size (N) Vs. Data Rate for US902-928.

DataRate	N
0	11
1	53
2	125
3...4	242
5...7	Not Defined
8	33
9	109
10...13	222
14..15	Not Defined

According to Semtech [12], for a combination of Spread Factor (SF), Data Rate (DR), and Bandwidth (BW), the total time-on-air (ToA) of a transmission for a packet can be calculated using Eq. (1).

Therefore, as the attacker goal is to consume a node's battery by making the node receiver to stay active while retransmitting its data in every SF as long as the node does not receive the confirmation of the data by the network server, the node will change its SF to a higher one in a mayor range. To analyse the feasibility of such attack, we propose a particular LoRaWAN network scenario, as shown in Fig. 11, where nodes retransmit once in each SF while the network server did not receive data.

Table 4. US 902-928 TX Data Rate.

DataRate	Configuration
0	LoRa: SF10/125 kHz
1	LoRa: SF9/125 kHz
2	LoRa: SF8/125 kHz
3	LoRa: SF7/125 kHz
4	LoRa: SF8/500 kHz
5:7	RFU
8	LoRa: SF12/500 kHz
9	LoRa: SF11/500 kHz
10	LoRa: SF10/500 kHz
11	LoRa: SF9/500 kHz
12	LoRa: SF8/500 kHz
13	LoRa: SF7/500 kHz
14	RFU
15	Defined in LoRaWAN

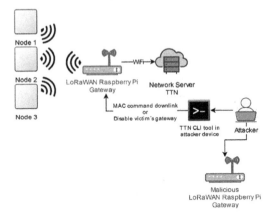

Fig. 11. LoRaWAN setup for battery consumption attack.

The attack design starts by performing authentication into the TTN CLI tool using the code provided by the victim's TTN server. The attacker could execute the attack by two methods. The first method implies the use of MAC commands, in which the attacker sends the MAC *LinkADRReq* command with the highest coding rate possible value, e.g., CR = 13; or, with the *RXTimingSetupReq* MAC command which allows she/he to adjust the duration of the node's time reception windows to a higher value. The second method requires to disable the LoRaWAN gateway which have the consequence of having unconnected nodes due to continuously verification of its connection to the server. An SF adjustment is made each time the node does not receive a response from the server, so the time the data in the air increases. In all cases, it means that the receiver is active longer than necessary, causing higher battery consumption.

As a proof-of-concept to test this vulnerability in a system, it was proposed to perform a calculation of the one packet transmission time-on-air sent twice in every SF; this is by modifying Eq. (1) to obtain Eq. (2). In this new equation, in addition to the variables in Eq. (2); m is included representing the case number, i.e., case 1 data rate is 0, case 2 data rate is 1, etc.; and n representing the number of nodes. A multiplication by 2 is also included to represent the transmission and retransmission actions, and the sum of the terms to get the total time-on-air. Table 5 presents the results obtained by calculation of the total time-on-air using Eq. (2) and with the minimum packet size that can be sent (11 bytes), as defined in Table 3. Figure 12 depicts a plot of data on Table 5 for each SF and a 125BW value.

Table 5. Time-on-Air (ToA)

DR	SF	BW	PL	ToA(ms)	Total ToA retransmission (ms)	Total ToA (ms)	ToA with 600 nodes
0	10	125	11	278.93	557.87	2195.18	1317113.24 ms
1	9	125	11	150.35	300.70		=
2	8	125	11	82.43	164.86		21.95 min
3	7	125	11	46.29	92.59		
4	8	500	11	20.60	41.21		
8	12	500	11	248.46	496.92		
9	11	500	11	131.00	262.00		
10	10	500	11	69.73	139.46		
11	9	500	11	37.58	75.17		
12	8	500	11	20.60	41.21		
13	7	500	11	11.57	23.14		

$$\text{ToA} = 2n\Sigma \left(\frac{2^{SF_m}}{BW}\left((NP + 4.25) + \left(SW + \max\left(\text{ceil}\left(\frac{(8 \cdot PL_m) - (4 \cdot SF_m) + 28 + (16 \cdot CRC) - (20 \cdot IH)}{4(SF_m - (2 \cdot DE))}\right) \ast (CR + 4), 0\right)\right)\right)$$

$$(2)$$

As seen in Figs. 12 and 13, if data is retransmitted at least a second time, the time is doubled. Therefore, for a 600-node network where each node tries to retransmit twice for each SF, the time-on-air will be 21.95 min.

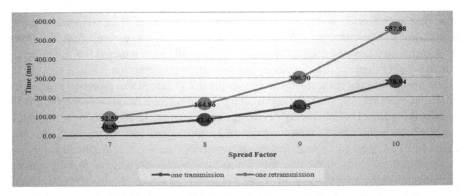

Fig. 12. ToA for one transmission vs ToA retransmission with 125BW.

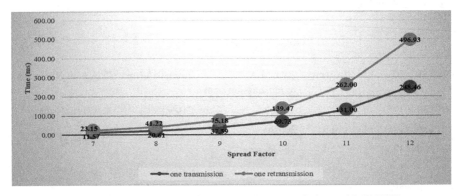

Fig. 13. ToA for one transmission vs ToA retransmissions with 500BW.

4   Attack Tree

An attack can be modelled graphically, mathematically, or as a decision tree called attack tree. It provides a methodical and formal way to describe the insecurity of a system so that an attack tree can be built from the point of view of an attacker/adversary. Attack trees are represented by a diagram with a single *root node* at the top, which represents the attacker overall target, that root branches down by expanding through *leaves* and *branches,* which represent the sub-targets. With the proper selection of the target, it is possible to analyse an entire system with a single attack tree being a useful tool to define the attack surface of a particular system. Events in an attack tree are connected by logical operators, such as AND/OR, these act as connector functions; where the AND connector indicates that all input sub-targets must be completed for the attack execution, and an OR connector indicates that with a single input sub-target the attack can be completed [15].

The interpretation of a tree of this type is done from the bottom to the top, sub-objectives or lower leaves must be performed to advance to the next branches and achieve the overall goal. Additionally, when certain sub-goals must be met sequentially, the action is represented by an arrow indicating the order of the sub-goals/sheets [16].

An attack tree representing all attacks performed in Sect. 3 is shown in Fig. 14. The root node represents the final goal: compromising LoRaWAN network communication. The second level represents any specific attack performed. The remaining levels represent the different steps that the attacker needs to follow in order to achieve her/his goal. This attack tree also summarises the design of each performed attack. As a result of this process it can be observed that by analysing LoRaWAN bidirectional communication considering the gateway as a highly vulnerable point in a LoRaWAN network it is possible to reduce various security threats by increasing security on the gateway or nodes devices. Moreover, the attack tree presented and the discussed results provide evidence that these attacks are possible and successful under the default settings of the LoRaWAN devices due to a lack of security mechanisms on the device itself and in the downlink communication. Additionally, the risk of any of the discussed attacks, as long as the objective is desired, is high as they can be performed as long as the identified vulnerabilities are not corrected.

5   Attack Mitigation

In order to mitigate exploitation of the identified vulnerabilities, see Sect. 3, it is recommended to follow a set of countermeasures:

- Change default passwords to strong passwords according to the NIST SP 800-118 about the proper use of passwords.
- Use HTTPS instead of HTTP, and a secure authentication mechanism that does not transmit the user ID and password unencrypted. This is, avoid the "basic" authentication mechanism.
- Use a Web Application Firewall (WAF) in the gateway, this must be in "server resident" mode [10], otherwise gateway's functionality would be disabled given the design to be public so different LoRaWAN devices make use of it. Since we use a public network server, we do not have access to its set up for our own purposes, meaning that the WAF rules to be considered into the gateway setting up mainly are restricted to limiting the access to the application on port 80 to the administrator IP only, and accept all UDP traffic over port 1700 in order to not affecting the redirection, using TTN for communication. It is important to notice that with a gateway mounted on a Raspberry Pi, computational resources allow to run a WAF in many cases.
- Use the data provided by the *ttnctl* tool, specifically "last seen information", to monitoring the gateway connection via *ttnctl gateway status,* paying attention to parameter values greater than 20 min, as they indicate that there is a problem with the gateway; pointing towards a possible *uplink and downlink communication committing* attack. According to information regarded to *gateway theft for packet monitoring* attack, additional to the three first points, monitoring a change in the configuration file, described in Sect. 3, can alert a malicious behaviour. Also, change default configurations settings to give permissions to the superuser only; this will decrease the probability of change by any unauthorised user.
- According to Bor *et al.* [11], one gateway provides suitable performance to 120 nodes, so by increasing the number of gateways (one for every 3.8 ha), downlink outages can decrease.

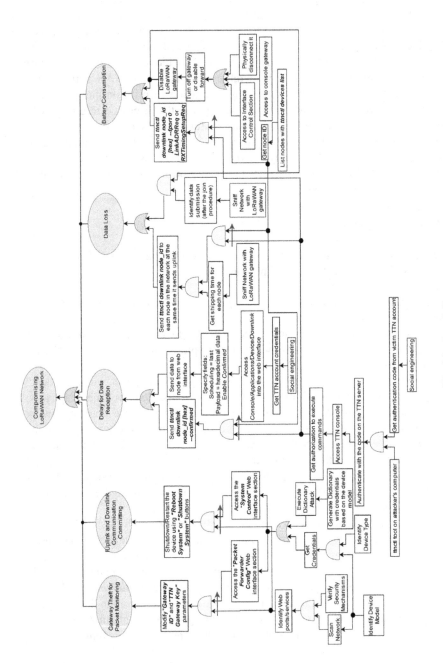

Fig. 14. Attack Tree.

- The code provided for access has no time limitation for using the CLI once it has been authenticated. So, by establishing time limits to 1 day, this can be mitigated. Also, by the creation of a "collaborator" profile so that the LoRaWAN network owner could delate at any time or limit the access to this new profile.
- Once removed the access to the attacker using the code, devices must be restarted. As settings set by commands are cleared and adjusted to the default settings, it is necessary to readjust them to the corresponding values according to the network needs.
- Finally, if two frames are retransmitted by all SF values and are not successful, it can be coded into the program node, once the device reaches the lowest transmission data rate, stop the process and minutes later try the retransmission. If the problem persists, an increase of the timeout before retrying transmitting can be a useful approach.

6 Results and Conclusion

In this paper, a vulnerability analysis of the LoRaWAN protocol v1.0.2 was presented. Also, presenting the corresponding assessment of bidirectional communication was executed in an adversarial scenario. As a result, we identified five noteworthy vulnerabilities that mainly compromise the availability in a LoRaWAN system. As part of the vulnerability analysis, a set of attack vectors were designed and performed, allowing us to include countermeasures in order to mitigate these attacks.

In more detail, the *battery consumption* attack showed to have the greatest impact in terms of time in data communication; since it takes several minutes even with a payload size that can be sent in all SF, i.e., performing it once, with a payload of 11 bytes the receiver will be active for 21.95 min trying to transmit one data in all SF twice. Thereby, in one day, a node is going to try the data transmission 72 times.

On the other hand, *data loss* and *delay in data reception* attacks are performed during about 16 and 0.49 s, respectively. So, the times an attacker must execute them to achieve the goal increases, given the durability of the attack, meaning that for *data loss* attack, the attacker needs to perform the attack during 76 times, since in one hour the data lost are ≈ 4 packets. In terms of the *delay in data reception* attack, to achieve the goal, this must be performed ≈ 123 times in one hour. However, any of the three attacks can be persistently performed under the conditions defined in Sect. 3, because nodes will continue receiving valid commands and data to process.

Additionally, we observed that in the *battery consumption* and *delay in data reception* attacks, besides time, the payload size is meaningful secondary variable, which affects the time-on-air equation as described in Sect. 3.4 and 3.5.

Finally, it can be observed that these attacks provoke a reduction in the lifetime of the device related to the fact that the device receiver keeps active longer than it will be if it sends data at the first attempt or, in a second case, while the node tries to regain connection if the gateway is disabled. Moreover, when a node discards received unrecognised data and processed it in the corresponding receive windows. Therefore, if the node is waiting to an ACK and the data sent was lost caused by the gateway, the node will be waiting for the acknowledgment of its data; due to the presence of confirmed traffic, this result in the degradation of the node's battery lifetime. In either case, it was proved the exploitability of the bidirectional communication vulnerabilities analysed represents a high risk in which nodes lifetime is severely compromised.

7   Future Work

According to the result of this investigation, the described process can be used to analyse different devices belonging to different device classes, such as class B or C, whose characteristics are different from class A devices in terms of communication. Furthermore, the results are a good reference point for other studies aiming to evaluate security from different perspective, for example approaches where the adversary, that does not have access to the victim's LoRaWAN network by social engineering, attack the network by sending data or MAC commands from its own network server.

Nevertheless, further analysis of other IoT protocols seems suitable to be performed following the process described in this research, providing a reference point to identify the existence of new vulnerabilities associated to the configuration of the network or connected devices, as well as intrinsic protocol design.

Acknowledgment. The authors would like to thank the Instituto Politécnico Nacional (IPN), the Centro de Investigación en Computación (CIC) and the Consejo Nacional de Ciencia y Tecnología (CONACYT) for the support in this research, under grants SIP-20200480 and CONACYT-264087.

References

1. Escamilla-Ambrosio, P., Salinas-Rosales, M., Acosta-Bermejo, R., Rodríguez-Mota, A.: Internet de las Cosas: 50 Mil Millones de Puntos Inseguros. In: SOMI XXX Congreso de Instrumentación, pp. 1–12 (2006)
2. García, P.B., Escamilla-Ambrosio, J., Anaya Eleazar, A.: Vulnerabilidades de LoRaWAN (Long Range Wide Area Network). INAOE Ciberseguridad para la Industria 4.0, pp. 1–4 (2019)
3. Butun, I., Pereira, N., Gidlund, M.: Analysis of LoRaWAN v1.1 security. In: Proceedings of the 4th ACM MobiHoc Workshop on Experiences with the Design and Implementation of Smart Objects, pp. 1–6 (2018)
4. Aras, E., Ramachandran, G.S., Lawrence, P., Hughes, D.: Exploring the security vulnerabilities of LoRa. In: 3rd IEEE International Conference on Cybernetics CYBCONF 2017 - Proceedings (2017)
5. Iskhakov, S., Meshcheryakov, R., Iskhakova, A., Bondarchuk, S.: Analysis of vulnerabilities in low-power wide-area networks by example of the LoRaWAN. In: IV International Research Conference" Information Technologies in Science, Management, Social Sphere and Medicine (ITSMSSM 2017), vol. 72, no. Itsmssm, pp. 334–338 (2017)
6. Yang, X.: LoRaWAN: Vulnerability Analysis and Practical Exploitation. Delft University of Technology. Master of Science (2017)
7. Farrell, S., (ed.): Internet Engineering Task Force (IETF). ISSN: 2070-1721, Low-Power Wide Area Network (LPWAN) Overview. RFC8376, pp. 4–10 (2018)
8. LoRa Alliance Technical Commitee. LoRaWAN 1.0.2 specification. LoRaWAN 1.0.2 Specification no. 1.0.2 (2016)
9. TheThingsNetwork Homepage. LoRaWAN. https://www.thethingsnetwork.org. Accessed 30 June 2020
10. Prema Sindhuri, B., Kameswara Rao, M.: IoT security through web application firewall. Int. J. Eng. Technol. 7(2), 58–61 (2018)

11. Bor, M.C., Roedig, U., Voigt, T., Alonso, J.M.: Do LoRa low-power wide-area networks scale? In: Proceedings of the 19th ACM International Conference on Modeling, Analysis and Simulation of Wireless and Mobile Systems, pp. 59–67 (2016)

12. Sol, C.E.: Telematics and Computing, vol. 944 (2018). https://semtech.my.salesforce.com/sfc/p/#E0000000JelG/a/2R00000010Ks/Bs97dmPXeatnbdoJNVMIDaKDlQz8q1N_gxDc gqi7g2o. Accessed 27 June 2020

13. T.M. Workgroup: A technical overview of LoRa ® and LoRaWAN TM What is it? Technical Report. LoRa Alliance (2015)

14. LoRa Family Kit. https://uk.pi-supply.com/products/iot-lora-family-kit?variant=183196979 36454. Accessed 30 June 2020

15. Ingoldsby, T.R.: Attack Tree Threat Risk Analysis, pp. 3–9. Amenaza Technologies Limited (2013)

16. Sonderen, T.: A manual for attack trees. Master Thesis University of Twente, pp. 104 (2019)

17. Ikpehai, A., et al.: Low-power wide area network technologies for internet-of-things: a comparative review. IEEE Internet Things J. 6(2), 2225–2240 (2019)

18. Marais, J.M., Malekian, R., Abu-Mahfouz, A.M.: Evaluating the LoRaWAN protocol using a permanent outdoor testbed. IEEE Sens. J. 19(12), 4726–4733 (2019)

19. Xu, W., Jha, S., Hu, W.: LoRa-Key: secure key generation system for LoRa-based network. IEEE Internet Things J. 6(4), 6404–6416 (2019)

20. Magrin, D., Capuzzo, M., Zanella, A.: A thorough study of LoRaWAN performance under different parameter settings. IEEE Internet Things J. 7(1), 116–127 (2020)

21. Sandoval, R.M., Garcia-Sanchez, A.J., Garcia-Haro, J., Chen, T.M.: Optimal policy derivation for transmission duty-cycle constrained LPWAN. IEEE Internet Things J. 5(4), 3114–3125 (2018)

LoRa and LoRaWAN Protocol Analysis Using Cupcarbon

Esau Bermudez Sanchez$^{(\boxtimes)}$ (ID) and Djamel Fawzi Hadj Sadok(ID)

Federal University of Pernambuco (UFPE), Recife, PE 50740-560, Brazil
ebs2@cin.ufpe.br
https://www3.cin.ufpe.br/br/

Abstract. In the Internet of Things (UIoT) universe, LoRa and its
LoRaWAN protocol have become a representative technology in Low
Power Wide Area Networks (LPWAN). This article discusses the
LoRaWAN protocol, which runs on the spectrum that is below the Giga
Hertz. The analysis begins with an overview of its range, performance,
useful time to charge, sensor analysis, airtime, and comparisons of some
of its processes and performance. On the other hand, the concept of
energy is approached superficially but with great interest for future work,
since it is one of the most commented topics and has gained special interest in this type of technology. The analysis is carried out with the Cup-
Carbon platform, since it has a very user-friendly graphic environment
and its final result is in accordance with what is required for this type of
technology.

Keywords: Computational geometry · IoT · LoRa · LoRaWAN ·
Radio frequency

1 Introduction

When we talk about IoT, better known as the Internet of Things (IoT) [1], we
are referring to that scenario in which connectivity in red and computing power
are intertwined with everyday objects, sensors and articles that are generally not
considered computers [2]. Thus, these devices are allowed to generate, exchange
and consume data with minimal human intervention [3]. However, there is no
single definition. We can say that LoRa [4,5] is a promising low-power long-
range technology, operating in the 868–915 MHz ISM band that allows bit rates
between 0.37 kbps and 46.9 kbps and promising ranges. up to 25 km [6]. On the
other hand, LoRaWAN, the MAC protocol for wide area networks, is based on
the ALOHA protocol, it becomes the standard, multiple access by carrier detection [7]. Ideal for applications with sporadic communication requirements and
low traffic. Energy efficiency makes LoRa attractive for up-link communication
while reaching a long range [8]. In LoRaWAN, battery-powered distributed sensor nodes send data directly to an always-on gateway. In this way, a detailed
analysis of the RF spectrum is performed using equations and specialized Cupcarbon software [9,10].

© Springer Nature Switzerland AG 2020
M. F. Mata-Rivera et al. (Eds.): WITCOM 2020, CCIS 1280, pp. 352–376, 2020.
https://doi.org/10.1007/978-3-030-62554-2_26

On the other hand, different companies and organizations such as the LoRa Alliance Institute and Semtech dedicated to research have published a wide range of projections on the potential impact that the IoT will have on the Internet and on the economy in the coming years [4]. The term internet of things was first used in 1999 by the British Kevin Ashton to describe a system in which objects in the physical world could be connected to the Internet by means of sensors [11]. Ashton coined this term to illustrate the power of connecting radio frequency identification (RFID) tags that are used in corporate supply chains to count and track merchandise without the need for human intervention [12]. Today, the term internet of things has become popular to describe scenarios in which internet connectivity and computing power are extended to a variety of everyday objects, devices, sensors, and items, thus creating that dimension that at that time was unknown, and that now we can see it consolidated in UIoT to be able to converge in a point called the communications universe and affect it in a positive way as shown in the Fig. 1.

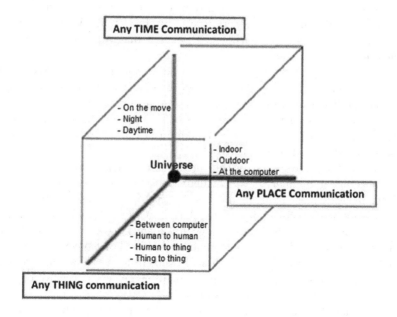

Fig. 1. UIoT - Universe of the Internet of Things

The objective of low-power wide area networks has become a topic of great interest in the technology of the IoT, since these are a fundamental part of the development of new emerging technologies [13]. LPWAN is a broad term where there are a variety of technologies used to connect sensors and controllers to the Internet without the use of WiFi or traditional cellular networks. Thus, two main standards emerged for low-power wide area networks [14], those based on cellular phones, for example, NB-IoT or LTE-M; and those developed natively for IoT use

354 E. B. Sanchez and D. F. H. Sadok

cases such as LoRaWAN and SigFox [15]. The predominant design considerations are low power consumption (up to more than ten years of autonomy), strong penetration, the connection of a large number of sensors and devices with very low bandwidth [6].

A significant percentage of LoRaWAN's modeling and simulation research has been devoted to working on features such as collisions, coverage, scalability, delay, and power consumption [16–19]. However, when doing analysis with convex envelope algorithms [20–22] in an almost linear network in LoRaWAN, they have not been very popular. In [23] a LoRaWAN module is performed with the ns-3 simulator, where a LoRa-based IoT network was modeled for a LoRa network scenario, where packet delivery performance rates of over 90% are obtained. The vulnerability work has been carried out in the MAC and the upper layers [24,25]. They also analyzed measures that are primarily based on cryptographic algorithms.

On the other hand, the collision modeling in LoRaWAN networks where different points of view are exposed in the literature [26]. One of these considers that collisions in LoRaWAN occur mainly when simultaneous transmissions are carried out in the same SF. Detection systems in a LoRaWAN network [27] can also be simulated in CupCarbon with energy diagrams, related to sensors without the delay instruction.

This document provides an analysis of LoRa and its LoRaWAN protocol that employs convex envelope algorithms in an almost linear network using the CupCarbon multi-agent, discrete event wireless sensor network simulator. The purpose of this analysis is to understand the behavior of the LoRaWAN protocol, for a better optimization in its use in communication networks using a general purpose sensor provided by CupCarbon.

The Graham and Jarvis's algorithms are executed in a small WSN networks. In an almost linear manner, it was evident that hops are generated which are compared to each other. Thus, in Jarvis's algorithm, two hops forwards and one for back are evidenced, forming a triangulation in the communication, while in Graham's algorithm two hops are shown until reaching the destination node. From these evidences, different performances of the LoRaWAN protocol were analyzed and results were obtained that are shown in the results section, these results led to the conclusion regarding the use of these types of convex envelope algorithms in almost linear WSN networks.

The document is structured in four sections. The first section begins with conceptualizations concerning the internet of things and its development in LoRa. The second section is an analysis of LoRaWAN starting with concepts such as orthogonality, code rates, Shannon's theorem, link of budgets, mathematical analysis, P-ALOHA, signal and propagation. The third section presents the two proposed scenarios, the application of the theory presented in the second section and the obtained results. Finally, the fourth section shows the conclusions of the study.

2   LoRaWAN Review

2.1   Orthogonality

The spread spectrum technique used in LoRaWAN ensures a wider range of links, as well as better interference immunity. LoRaWAN uses a 125 kHz to transmit the signal but also allows the use of scalable bandwidth between 125 kHz, 250 kHz or 500 kHz [28]. The use of a wider band makes LoRaWAN resistant to noise, Doppler effects, long-term variations of oscillators and fading. However, the use of a narrow band signal in a much wider band means that the spectrum is used less efficiently, unless a perfectly orthogonal signal generation is achieved between the different transmitters [29].

Thus, with this feature (multiplexing of OFDM carriers), it becomes very robust against multipath that is very common in broadcasting channels, against selective frequency attenuations and against RF interference, being able to recover the information between the different signals with different delays and amplitudes that reach the receiver) [30]. One way to understand orthogonality in a mathematical way is described below:

$$A * B \rightarrow \int_{t_1}^{t_2} f_a(t) * f_b(t) dt = 0 \tag{1}$$

$f_a(t)$ is orthogonal with $f_b(t)$ if $f_a(t) = \cos(nwt)$ and $f_b(t) = \cos(mwt)$. How $\cos\alpha * \cos\beta = \frac{1}{2}[\cos(\alpha + \beta) + \cos(\alpha - \beta)]$ then

$$\frac{1}{2}[\cos(n+m) + \cos(n-m)wt]$$

$$\frac{1}{2}\int_0^T \cos(n+m)wt dt + \int_0^T \cos(n-m)wt dt$$

$$\frac{1}{2}\left[\frac{1}{(n+m)w}\sin(n+m)wt\right] + \frac{1}{2}\left[\frac{1}{(n-m)w}\sin(n-m)wt\right]$$

How $\sin(0) = 0, \sin(2\pi) = 0$ and $w = 2\pi/T$ then

$$\frac{1}{2}\left[\frac{T}{(n+m)2\pi}\sin(n+m)2\pi\right] + \frac{1}{2}\left[\frac{T}{(n-m)2\pi}\sin(n-m)2\pi\right] \tag{2}$$

$$\frac{1}{2}[\phi_1 \sin(n+m)2\pi] + \frac{1}{2}[\phi_2 \sin(n-m)2\pi] \tag{3}$$

$$\sin(n+m)2\pi = 0 \rightarrow k = 0, 1, 3, ... \forall k(2\pi) \tag{4}$$

When the relationship between two frequencies is an integer, they are said to be Harmonic and Orthogonal. Therefore, the transmitter forms signals by altering their frequency over time and constantly protecting the phase between adjacent symbols. The transmitted signal is a noise-like signal that is resistant to multipath and Doppler fade, and is robust against interference. The receiver can decode even a much-attenuated signal of 20 dB below the noise level [31].

2.2   Code Rate

If we talk about the error correction technique used by the LoRaWAN protocol, it should be known that to increase the sensitivity of the receiver further, it is the forward error correction (FEC) type, it must be done by using a Hamming code Adjustable length, the CR defines the amount of FEC and LoRaWAN offers CR values between 1 and 4. LoRaWAN uses code rates, $codingrate = 4/(4+CR)$ or $4/5, 4/6, 4/7$ and $4/8$. If the code rate is denoted as k = n, where k represents useful information and the encoder generates n number of output bits, then $n-k$ will be the redundant bits Redundancy allows the receiver to detect and correct errors in the message at the cost of decreasing the effective data rate [29].

It should be clear that in the LoRaWAN protocol, a variable spreading factor (SF) is taken as a function of the signal-to-noise (SNR) ratio received [4]. In order to tailor the length of the symbol, it also details the number of bits per symbol. This is why changing the spread factor generates a variable bit rate for the highest spread factor and for the lowest spread factor as shown below.

$$R_b = \frac{BW}{2^{SF}} * SF[bits/seg] \tag{5}$$

with coding:

$$R_b = \frac{\frac{4}{4+CR}}{\frac{2^{SF}}{BW}} * SF[bits/seg] \tag{6}$$

2.3   Shannon Theorem

For its part, the Shannon-Hartley theorem sets the maximum possible information rate for a channel with noise at a given bandwidth [32]. The recent development of various methods of modulation such a Pulse-code modulation (PCM) and Pulse-position modulation (PPM) which exchange bandwidth for signal-to-noise ratio has intensified the interest in a general theory of communication. A basis for such a theory is contained in the important paper of Nyquist and Hartley [33] on this subject. In the present paper, the theory to include a number of new factors is extend, in particular the effect of noise in the channel, and the savings possible due to the statistical structure of the original message and due to the nature of the final designation of the information.

As indicated above, Shannon [34] studies the general case of a communication system, consisting of a transmitter, a receiver, a transmission channel and a noise source, which in any real transmission system exists in greater or lesser measure. An example of these calculations will be shown follow.

Let $p(x)$ be one-dimensional distribution. The form of $p(x)$ giving a maximum entropy subject to the condition that the standard deviation of x be fixed at σ is Gaussian. To show this we must maximize

$$H(x) = -\int p(x) \log p(x) dx \tag{7}$$

with $\sigma^2 = \int p(x)x^2 dx$ and $\int p(x)dx = 1$ as a constraints. In order to maximize the Eq. 8, the condition in 9 is necessary.

$$\int \left[-p(x) \log p(x) + \lambda p(x)x^2 + \mu p(x) \right] dx \tag{8}$$

$$-1 - \log p(x) + \lambda x^2 + \mu = 0 \tag{9}$$

And consequently, adjusting the constants to satisfy the constraints,

$$p(x) = \frac{1}{\sqrt{2\pi}\sigma} e^{-(x^2/2\sigma^2)} \tag{10}$$

where

$$C = B * \log_2\left(1 + \frac{S}{N}\right) \left[\frac{bits}{seg}\right]$$

Taking into account that C = channel capacity, B = channel bandwidth, S = average signal strength in the receiver, N = average noise power in the receiver, S/N = signal/noise ratio in the receiver Therefore, if this logarithmic ratio of base 2 to the natural base is converted and it is also assumed that for an expanded spectrum application, the small signal-to-noise ratio and signal strength will be much lower than noise, then S/N << 1 and the previous Equation can be rewritten as 11.

$$\frac{C}{B} = 1.43 * \frac{S}{N} \tag{11}$$

Thus, we can deduce that in order to transmit error-free information at a given signal-to-noise ratio, we only need to increase the bandwidth of the channel, in order to transmit more information [35].

2.4 Link Budget

If you want to set the link budget, this is determined by 12:

$$Link Budget = MDS - MTP[db] \tag{12}$$

where MDB is the minimum detectable signal and MTP is the maximum transmit power. Sam and Miller assure that the maximum range is given by the link budget taking into account the attenuation of the signal in the free space (FSPL) [36].

$$FSLP = 20\log_{10}(d) + 20\log_{10}(f) + 20\log_{10}\left(\frac{4\pi}{c}\right) [dB] \tag{13}$$

And considering $f = 900$ MHz, then

$$FSLP = 32.45 + 20\log(d) + 20\log(f) \quad [dB] \tag{14}$$

LoRaWAN creates a package format, which shows that the greater the error correction, the longer the package will be for a given payload [31]. The emission time of a LoRaWAN package is given by 15:

$$T_{packet} = T_{preamble} - T_{payload} \quad [Sec] \tag{15}$$

Where $T_{preamble}$ is the preamble time of the LoRaWAN package given by 16. And, $T_{payload}$ is the total LoRaWAN payload time given by 17.

$$T_{preamble} = (n_{preamble} + 4.25)\, T_s \quad [sec]$$
$$T_s = \frac{1}{R_s}[sec], \quad R_s = \frac{BW}{2^{SF}} \tag{16}$$

With T_s, the time of a LoRaWAN symbol is related to the speed of the symbol and R_s the symbol rate related to the bandwidth of the channel and the SF.

$$T_{payload} = PL_{Symb} * T_s \tag{17}$$

The total time of a LoRaWAN package can be obtained through the following formula and these in turn are related to the channel bandwidth and the SF.

$$T_{packet} = (n_{preamble} + 4.25 + PL_{Symb}) * \frac{2^{SF}}{BW} \tag{18}$$

2.5   Aloha at LoRaWAN

Whereas the MAC of LoRaWAN is based on P-ALOHA [7]. Therefore, the following variables are defined as follows: S the average number of packets generated per interval; λ as the traffic source consisting of the number of users that form a Poisson source, which is independent, with an aggregate package rate of $X_{packages}/s$, the time and width of the package, are fixed with a period of T seconds. A node delays the transmission of a previously collided packet with a random time. Thus, the total sum of traffic is not just new packets, but the repetition of the re-transmission of collided packets.

$$S = \lambda T$$
$$G \geq S$$
$$G(n) = \lambda(n)T$$
$$S = G(n)P_{SUC} = \lambda(n)T * e^{-\lambda(n)2T}$$

The probability that the chosen packet will not suffer a collision is the probability that a Poisson random variable with mean $2(\lambda + \lambda_r)$ packets takes on the value 0, which is $e^{-2(\lambda+\lambda_r)}$. Because packet are transmitted on the channel at a total rate of $\lambda + \lambda_r$ packets/slot, it follows that packet are received correctly at a rate of $S = (\lambda+\lambda_r)e^{-2(\lambda+\lambda_r)}$ packets/slot, which is the throughput equation for pure ALOHA in statistical equilibrium. Differentiation on the right show that the throughput S is maximized by the total transmission rate $\lambda+\lambda_r = \frac{1}{2} packets/slot$. The resulting maximum throughput is indeed

$$S_{max} = \frac{1}{2e} \approx 0.184 \frac{packets}{slot} \tag{19}$$

2.6   Signal Propagation

Among the UHF signal propagation models, we find some propagation models for signals in the UHF frequency range, among the best known is Okumura-Hata [37]. This Okumura-Hata model gives the value of pathloss at a given distance between a base station and a mobile user. Consider several factors such as frequency, antenna height and others [38,39].

Taking into account the spectrum for the 915 MHz, ISM band will be divided into the channel plans shown in the Fig. 2 [4].

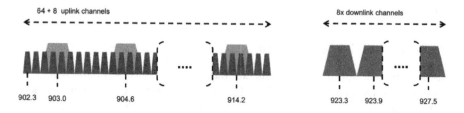

Fig. 2. LoRa Alliance, LoRaWAN regional parameters, 2019

2.7   Computational Geometry

The Computational geometry systematic study of algorithms and data structures for geometric objects, included computer graphics, computer vision and others [22].

Theorem 1. *Algorithm Graham's scan runs at time $O(n \log n)$.*

Test: The symbolization of the points (sensors) according to the x-coordinates provided in these scenarios with the LoRaWAN protocol of this work, can be done using any efficient classification algorithm $O(n \log n)$. Observing that Di denotes the number of points shown (removed) in the Pi processing. Because each orientation the test takes $O(1)$ time. The amount of time spent processing pi is $O(Di + 1)$. The extra +1 is for the last point tested, which is not removed. Therefore, the total execution time is proportional to:

$$\sum_{i=1}^{n}(D_i + 1) = n + \sum_{i=1}^{n} D_i \qquad (20)$$

To bound $\sum_i D_i$, observe that each of the n points is pushed onto the stack once. Once a point is deleted it can never be deleted again. Since each of n points can be deleted at most once, $\sum_i D_i \leq n$. Thus after sorting, the total running time is $O(n)$. Since this is true for the lower hull as well, the total time is $O(2n) = O(n)$.

Theorem 2. *Algorithm Jarvis March*

Jarvis march computes the $CH(Q)$ by a technique known as gift wrapping or package wrapping. Consider first, a base point $P_0(S1Detection)$ is selected. This is the point with the minimum y-coordinate provided in these scenarios with the LoRaWAN protocol. Select leftmost point in case of ti.e. The next convex hull vertices P1 has the least polar angle w.r.t. the positive horizontal ray from P_0. Measure in counterclockwise direction. If tie, choose the farthest such point. Vertices $P2, P3, ..., P_k$ are picked similarly until $Y_k = Y_{max}$. $Pi+1$ has least polar angle w.r.t. positive ray from P_0. If tie, choose the farthest such point. In practice, Jarvis march is normally faster than Graham's scan on most application. Worst case occurs when $O(n)$ points lie on the convex hull i.e., all points lie on the circle.

2.8   Sensors and Consumption

A node has the ability to transmit data to an access point using the LoRa/LoRaWAN radio module. But for this to happen, the sensor needs an integrated power source [40]. This source that provides this energy. It can be internal or environmental.

The hardware of a sensor node can be broken down into five main parts: the processor, the sensor, the storage module, the transmitter and the power supply. As it can be seen in the Fig. 3, all the elements of the sensor are using the power supply simultaneously.

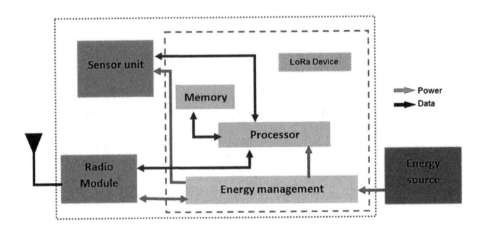

Fig. 3. Sensor structure

LoRa operates in different modes of a communication sensor [4]. It should be borne in mind that these LoRaWAN modes have as their main characteristics its Band, its dispersion factor and its CR, in order to find differences in distance for a slow data rate and range and a minimum range which provides a speed high data and a beneficial ratio for the battery.

The energy consumed by the communication sensor for one cycle is represented by the equation $E_T = E_S + E_A$, where E_S and E_A characterize the node in idle mode and the total power consumption during active mode of the microcontroller, respectively. E_S is expressed as $E_S = P_S + T_S$. Whereas PS and TS are characterizing power consumption and time keeping in sleep mode.

2.9   Software Tools

The purpose of this subsection is to present and compare some software tools to simulate LoRaWAN netowrks with their main characteristics and functionalities. Additionally, the reasons of the selection of the CupCarbon network simulator for this study are exposed. The comparison of the WSN network simulators is shown in the Table 1.

Table 1. WSN network simulators

Parameters	NS-2	NS-3	OMNeT++	TOSSIM	CupCarbon
Use research activities	High	Medium	High	Medium	Low
Sort of license	GNU GPL	Free	Academic Public License	BSD	GNU
Curve of learning	High	High	High	High	Medium
Platforms	FreeBSD, Linux,	Linux, OS-X,	Windows, Unix	Windows, Linux, Cywing	Windows, Linux, Mac
Graphical Interface	Low	Medium	High	High	High
Result through graphs	Not availab.	Acceptable	Acceptable	Acceptable	Acceptable
Supported technologies and layer 2–3 protocols	TCP/IP, UDP, FTP, RTP, GPRS, Mobile-IPv6, MPLS	IPv4/Pv6, 802.11a, 802.11b, 802.11g, OLSR	802.11, fair (ad-hoc routing)	Low (CSMA)	Low
Traffic modeled	High	Medium	Medium	High	–
Energy modeling	Yes	–	No	No	Yes
Programming language	C/C++, Otcl	–	Ned	Python, C++	Java, SenScript

NS-2 is a discrete event simulation tool and one of the most used [41]. It started as a general network simulator and later NS-2 added support for WSN. Its great success is due to its possibilities of use, its availability to the public and its characteristics that allow users to perform and test several types of network. A disadvantage of NS-2 is that the graphic support through the tool called Nam (AniMator) is very poor [42]. Finally, the latest version is more suitable for sensor networks since it includes power modeling [43].

NS-3 is a discrete network event simulator that arises after discovering a set of important failures in NS-2. NS-3 is not an update of NS-2. The simulations are based solely on C++ and it is also compatible with Python [44]. NS-3 provides an easy and quick way to create the topology through an intuitive interface, which allows adding nodes [45].

OMNeT++ is another popular discrete event simulation tool that owes its success to its extensibility and to being open source [46]. OMNET++ having a very powerful graphical interface. One disadvantage is the lack of protocols and energy modeling in its library compared to other simulators [47]. The modules that make up the tool are not fully developed. This implies that programmers should modify the existing code, so the learning curve is high.

TOSSIM is a discrete event simulator for TinyOS WSNs [48]. Its main objective is to provide high fidelity for the simulation of TinyOS applications. Although this simulator can be used to evaluate behavior in real cases. The main disadvantages of TOSSIM are the following: it is based on the assumption that all nodes execute the exact same code which makes it less flexible and does not model the power consumption. However, in the last versions in has added PowerTOSSIMz which solves this problem [49].

CupCarbon is a simulator specially designed for WSN networks [50, 51]. Its objective is the design and visualization of this type of networks, it has algorithms for environmental monitoring, data collection, among other characteristics. It also allows the creation of scenarios with stimulation generated by the environment where the network is built, such as fires, mobile objects for scientific and educational projects. It offers two simulation environments. The first allows the design of scenarios with mobility and generation of natural events and the second, the simulation of discrete events in WSN.

A network simulation can be designed through its graphical, intuitive and user-friendly interface, which uses OpenStreetMap (OSM), where you can search for specific scenarios for the network you want to run. One of its characteristics is that the sensors can be individually configured through its command lines, under a specially designed language called SenScript. CupCarbon does not implement all the layers of protocols, but for the analysis of this article, it counts as a tool with the main characteristics for LoRa sensors, its energy consumption, among others. It is there where its true outstanding functionality of the simulators is found, giving options to observe the consumption of natural resources and the effect of buildings and streets on urban and suburban networks. CupCarbon can simulate the ZigBee, LoRa and WiFi protocols.

Another important feature of CupCarbon is power consumption, which can be calculated and displayed graphically based on simulation time. In addition, it allows observing the visibility of the propagation and interference models in the (OSM). On the other hand, although it does not stand out for having a wide variety of integrated protocols, but because it has been implemented using Java, this allows the creation of different algorithms.

After studying some network simulators, CupCarbon has very interesting parameters that make it an avant-garde tool in its use today, such as its power modeling, its graphical interface, which are very important aspects when analyzing a sensor network, apart from having technologies as Zigbee, WiFi, LoRa and others. It is analyzed than other simulators different to CupCarbon do not

include tools for intuitive sensor design with an intuitive interface, design adaptability, Java programming and energy modeling. Also, it is important to have
a knowledge in WSN to understand how these simulators work. That's why
CupCarbon is shaping up to be a good option for working on WSN analysis.

3   Simulation and Results

This section provides a breakdown of the results and analysis of LoRaWAN in
CupCarbon and its performance in low power networks. A LoRaWAN network
composed of four sensors in an almost linear arrangement was proposed. The
network was located between the NIATE (Integrated Nuclei of Activities of
Ensino) and the CIn (Computer Center) of the UFPE University in Recife,
Brazil.

3.1   Simulation

The network has specific coordinates. Longitude: $-34.95020270\ 347595$ Latitude:
-8.054035008159962. The location and parameters of the nodes are shown in the
Table 2.

Table 2. Nodes parameters

Node	Latitude	Longitude	Distance/mts	Lfs
1	8.051.549.216.211.980	$-3.494.926.929.473.870$	168	75.726
2	8.052.760.244.966.250	34.949.880.838.394.100	168	75.726
3	8.054.035.008.159.960	$-3.495.019.197.463.980$	162	75.41
4	8.054.959.209.124.860	$-3.495.118.975.639.340$	151	74.799

The follow parameters are variables utilized in Cupcarbon with LoRa: Sensor
Radius: 20%; Energy Max: 19154.245939200744J; Data Rate UART: 9600 bits;
Drift (Sigma) Clock Freq MHz: $3.0E^{-5}$; Node Radius: 130.0; PL: 100.0; Send-
ing energy consumption (E_Tx): 5.92E-5; E_Rx: Receiving energy consumption:
$2.86E^{-5}$; Sleeping Energy: $1.0E^{-7}$; Listening Energy: $1.0E^{-6}$; Data Rate: the
sending/receiving data rate (250k bits/s); Spreading Factor: 7; and CH: 0.

In this study, the characteristics of the modes that LoRaWAN are represented
with a transceiver predetermined by CupCarbon. All peripherals are powered at
the same voltage level equal to 3.30 V, except the sensor unit which is powered
at 2.0 V.

Consequences of CR and SF regarding energy consumption taking into
account the equations already mentioned above we will carry out its implementation. The bit rate was finding using the Eqs. 5 and 6 and it are presented
in different bands graph in the Figs. 4 and 5.

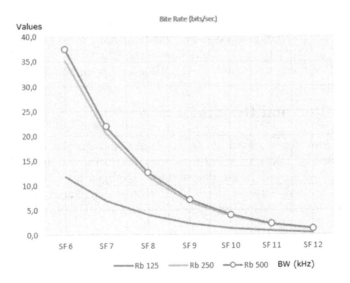

Fig. 4. Bit rate

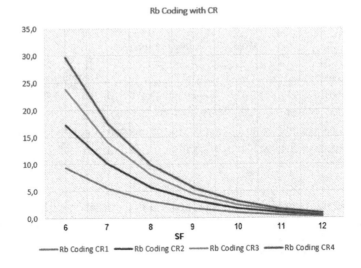

Fig. 5. Rb coding

In the use of the Eq. 13, FSL takes into consideration the parameters of the Table 2 according to what is established by the simulated nodes. In order to take into account the link budget of yhe Eq. 12.

It is important in LoRa's telecommunications and its LoRaWAN protocol to estimate the airtime of a packet, since this way we can know how effective our link is in the first layers of access. For this reason, the calculation of Eqs. 15, 16,

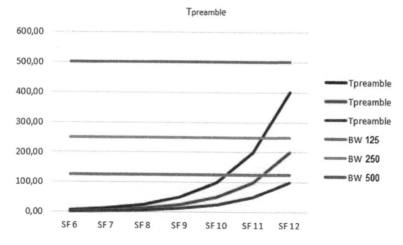

Fig. 6. Preamble time

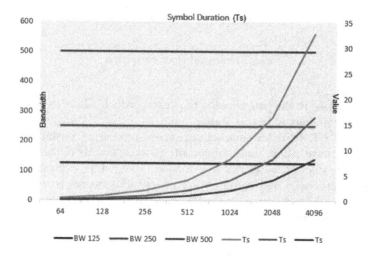

Fig. 7. Symbol duration

17 and 18 are performed and their graphical representation is presented in the Figs. 6, 7 and 8.

The time in air is shows in the Figs. 9 and 10 as a function of the size of the payload at different SF and CR values. The bandwidth channel is set to 125 kHz, 250 kHz, and 500 kHz in order to analyze each one. And it was analyzed that when the SF is high, the time in the air increases, which means that the sensor node consumes more energy to transmit. Analyzing CR about the time in the air, it is observed in the graph that if the number of encoding bits is increased, it

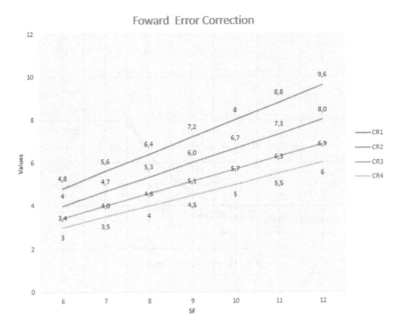

Fig. 8. Forward error correction

causes an increase in the transmission of packets, which allows the radio module to consume more energy in this state.

In the LoRa/LoRaWAN communication sensor energy consumption results, the basics were worked on touching certain relevant aspects of this type of technology that is part of many research focuses, but not in exhaustive research, since the energy issue and consumption of sensor networks is interesting and profound, it is clarified that the research focused more in part on the analysis of the operation of sensor networks.

Simulation 1: Jarvis's Algorithm. In this simulation, Jarvis's algorithm was used, which, despite being one of the simplest, has a computational complexity of $O(nh)$. The obtained triangulation is presented in the Fig. 11. When using Jarvis's algorithm in this sensor network, despite its simplicity, it is observed that the distance traveled from the S2SinkGateway sensor to the S1Detection sensor has a passage through the S4Router2 and when it reaches S1Detection it makes the same journey. This route makes that in reality the execution time is: $[O(nh)]$, where h is the number of points of the envelope. Thus obtaining an algorithm output sensitive.

ToA with different CR / 10 bytes vs SF

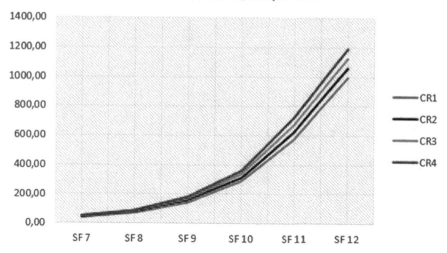

Fig. 9. Time on Air with different CR

ToA with BW and payload 10 bytes vs SF

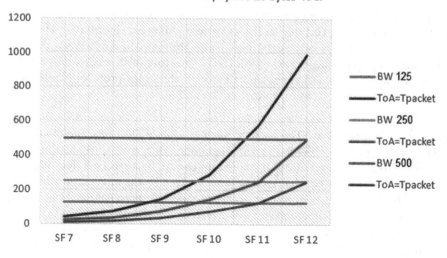

Fig. 10. Time on Air vs SF

Simulation 2: Graham Algorithm. Taking into account that when using the Graham algorithm, it is founded that it calculates the convex envelope in time $[O(nlogn)]$ which is the optimal time. The triangulation obtained in this simulation is shown in the Fig. 12. Executing this algorithm it is notable that the distance traveled from the S2SinkGateway sensor to the S1Detection sensor has a step through the S4Router2 and when arriving at S1Detection. It makes

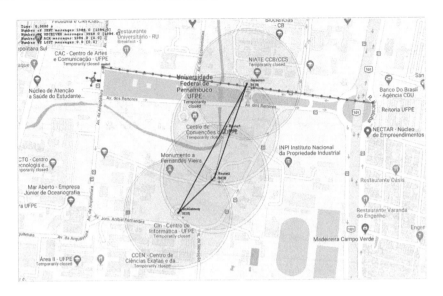

Fig. 11. Simulation 1: Jarvis algorithm (Color figure online)

the same route, but when going through the ordered list of the points it does not find the closing point, this due to the way these points are distributed. However, it was analyzed that it orders the best route through the LoRaWAN protocol for sending and receiving packets with the notification of the ACK, despite this, the reliability of information transport through the LoRa protocol is reliable in 99 % during the time it was running on the points.

Energy Consumption. The battery consumption at the sensor points despite being used, a peak is observed at the beginning. But, over time this peak stabilizes and only when a request is made and the ACK is received does it return that peak to be displayed, that is, that peak is given by the moment in which it is required for the sending and receipt of the sensors that intervene. A is the current demand in amperes. $Consumption = \frac{A}{h}$ which means the quantity of x Amps per hour. Therefore we can say that $Utilization = Request/Response time$, $\rho = \frac{\lambda}{m\mu}$. It is important to remember that the response time is given by the capacity of the system. That is why despite being a small network, it is observed that the efficiency of the LoRaWAN protocol with this type of algorithm, in attempts to send and receive packages, maintains a high percentage (99%) of ACK, during a prolonged execution of its use, which makes the protocol reliable for this type of communication in this simulation.

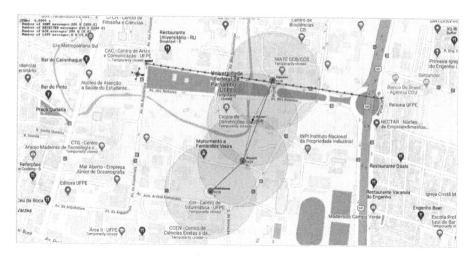

Fig. 12. Simulation 2: Graham algorithm (Color figure online)

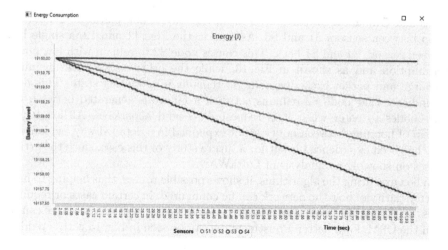

Fig. 13. Battery discharge level

In the same way, the consumption of the battery in the sensor points despite being used, a peak is observed at the beginning, but in the course of time this peak stabilizes and only when a request is made and the ACK is received does it return that peak to be displayed, that is, that peak is given by the moment in which it is required for the sending and receipt of the sensors that intervene. A = Amperage or current demand. Consumption = A/h (a quantity of X Amps per hour) Therefore we can say that $Utilization = (Request/Responsetime)$, $\rho = \frac{\lambda}{m\mu}$, this amount being below 1% in consumption.

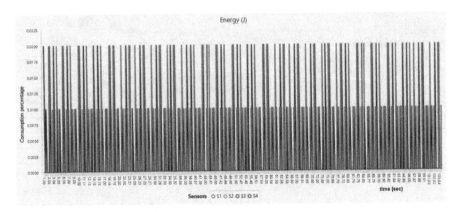

Fig. 14. Percentage of consumption

3.2   Results

Jarvis and Graham algorithms are run on the Cupcarbon platform, generating a hop between sensors S1 and S3. As seen in the Figs. 11 and 12, a single hop between sensors S4 and S1 back. This causes node S2 to remain with low power consumption and as shown in Fig. 13, while the other nodes have an initial discharge and packet exchange node S2 remains in a waiting state. This does not indicate that node S2 remains active if a failure is generated between the other nodes to enter when it is requested to send a package. Although this process of hopping between nodes is not explained in a detailed way, evidence of what has been experienced is left for a future study of this case, since the article focuses on showing an analysis of LoRaWAN.

When executing the algorithms, it shows possible routes, thus helping to have a better clarity of how the network can be configured, in certain cases or required needs. The spectrum level of each node becomes visible and the distances can be set in the OSM, for a better adjustment, as can be seen in Fig. 15 with a reddish tone.

On the other hand, when executing the Graham and Jarvis algorithms, it is observed that a hop is generated in the network between nodes S1 to S4 to reach the destination (S2) as it can be shown in the Figs. 11 and 12. This optimizes communication since the response time decreases due to not doing so.

The two algorithms behave in the same way regarding the consumption, reception and sending of packages which is evidenced in the Figs. 13 and 14, where the values of percentages of consumption over time are shown.

The yellow dots in the center of each node indicate that the information has been received and also show us the route through which the information travels, that is to say, nodes participate in this network, for sending and receiving the information as evidenced in the Figs. 11 and 12.

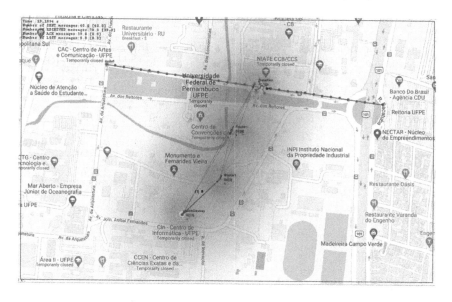

Fig. 15. Spreading (Color figure online)

The relationship time, messages sent and messages received in both algorithms is minimal, no algorithm showed packet loss during the execution period. CupCarbon allows you to visualize what happens when this type of algorithm is executed in a quasi-linear network, thus allowing you to have better control of the events you want to generate for optimization.

During the execution of the two selected routes, route 1 and route 2 established by the algorithms of Graham and Jarvis respectively. The values of the Table 3 show the obtained results.

It is observed that the routes as the execution time increases, the performance of each one also begins to be evident. This is good to be able to get the best option when building the wireless network. When comparing the ACKs with the received messages, it was evident that the difference between this relationship also showed an advantage between routes 2 in the execution interval of 300 s and 700 s.

Additionally, during the execution of the times, the number of messages sent and received began to double, showing good reception of the signal. Moreover, the ACK increased exponentially in each of the routes, but in route 2 an increase in ACK was evident during the timeline in each route. In the sending of messages in the first interval of execution time, route 2 decreases its sending, but in the second and third intervals they increase it with respect to route 1, as it is shown in the Fig. 16.

Table 3. Simulation results

	Execution time [s]	MSG sent	MSG received	ACK	MSG lost	TOTAL MSG SENT+REC
Route 1	100	210	209	209	1	419
Route 2	100	209	208	208	1	417
Route 1	300	596	596	496	0	1192
Route 2	300	598	597	597	1	1195
Route 1	700	1380	1380	1380	0	2760
Route 2	700	1388	1388	1388	0	2776

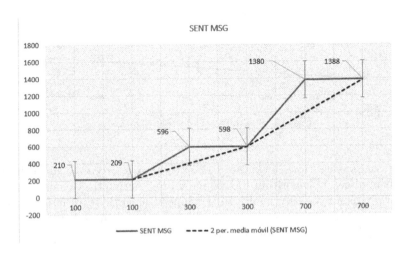

Fig. 16. Sent messages

In the lost messages, the percentages are low, it is evident that in the first interval of time of execution evidences of packet losses, in the second interval, only route two loses a packet and in the third interval of time, neither of the two routes suffers packet loss, This can be seen in the Fig. 17.

It was observed that between routes 1 and 2, route 2 shows a better performance of sending and receiving packets over time than route 1. During the first run time interval, route 1 showed better performance than route 2, but over the course of time, it was losing packet delivery performance. In the first two execution intervals, route 2 presented more packet losses than route 1. Although route 2 lost more packets than route 1, the ability to send packets was better than the one on route 1.

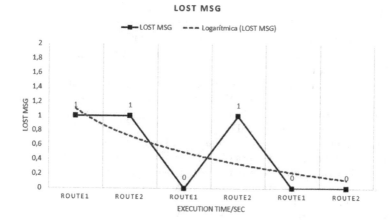

Fig. 17. Lost messages

4   Conclusions

For wireless networks that do not have a high percentage of nodes, this type of algorithm is helpful in finding more effective routes in LPWAN communication. On the other hand, it is analyzed that the S3Router1, remains inactive in both scenarios, this due to the type of algorithms used, therefore this point could be used as a backup and also for new network configuration in a certain case.

It is also concluded that the IoT, LoRa and their LoRaWAN protocol converge in that new universe called UIoT, where things interconnect with each other through the internet to become part of the universe that surrounds us and thus become the universe of the internet of things.

It is concluded that route 2 presents better performance than route 1, being adequate to be used in the project, since in the WSN the performance of both sending and receiving packets is important, this makes communication between the nodes are optimal, making the life of the network prolonged. Also its energy consumption is favored due to the low loss of packages that are presented; This is also considered in the long, medium and short-term economic factor, which is another factor required in WSN networks.

The increase in transmit power is more interesting in terms of the energy consumed per useful bit than the increase in the propagation factor, since a main objective of a sensor network is to preserve it for a long time of its useful life.

For future works, since the Jarvis algorithm shows a triangulation, it would be interesting to verify how much the energy saving could be in more detail with the SX1273 from Semtech Corporation, versus Graham's algorithm, defining the type of battery to be used.

References

1. Vilajosana, X., Tuset-Peiro, P., Martinez, B., Melia-Segui, J., Watteyne, T., Adelantado, F.: Understanding the limits of LoRaWAN. IEEE Commun. Mag. **55**(9), 34–40 (2017)
2. Kieffer, M., Lalam, M., Lestable, T., Bakkali, W.: Kalman filter-based localization for internet of things LoRaWAN^{TM} end points. In: 2017 IEEE 28th Annual International Symposium on Personal, Indoor, and Mobile Radio Communications (PIMRC), pp. 1–6, October 2017
3. Raza, U., Kulkarni, P., Sooriyabandara, M., Pop, A.: Does bidirectional traffic do more harm than good in LoRaWAN based LPWA networks? In: GLOBECOM 2017–2017 IEEE Global Communications Conference, pp. 1–6 (2017)
4. LoRa Alliance®. LoRa Alliance - LoRaWAN (2020)
5. GSMA. Mobile IoT in the 5G future (2018)
6. Hassan, Q.F.: Internet of Things A to Z. Wiley, IEEE Press, New York (2018)
7. Wha Sook, J., Dong Geun, J.: Performance of an exponential backoff scheme for slotted-aloha protocol in local wireless environment. IEEE Trans. Veh. Technol. **44**(3), 470–479 (1995)
8. van Dam, T., van Dam, T., Langendoen, K.: An adaptive Energy-efficient MAC protocol for wireless sensor networks. In: Proceedings of the 1st International Conference on Embedded Networked Sensor Systems, pp. 171–180 (2003)
9. Pathloss. Pathloss Version 5 (2020)
10. Lab-STICC UBO MOCS. CupCarbon Examples & Tutorials (2019)
11. Kutcher, E., et al.: Connected world: An evolution in connectivity beyond the 5G revolution (2020)
12. Ashton, K.: That 'Internet of Things' thing: in the real world, things matter more than ideas. RFiD J. **22**(7), 97–114 (2009)
13. Kundu, T., Kaur, P., Parkash, D.: The RFID technology and ITS applications: a review. Int. J. Electron. Commun. Instrum. Eng. Res. Dev. (IJECIERD) **2**(3), 109–120 (2012)
14. Vangelista, L., Zanella, A., Zorzi, M., Centenaro, M.: Long-range communications in unlicensed bands: the rising stars in the iot and smart city scenarios. IEEE Wirel. Commun. **23**(5), 60–67 (2016)
15. Won, M., Patel, D.: Experimental study on low power wide area networks (LPWAN) for mobile internet of things. In: IEEE Vehicular Technology Conference, vol. 2017, June, May 2017
16. Van den Abeele, F., Moerman, I., Hoebeke Haxhibeqiri, J.: LoRa scalability: a simulation model based on interference measurements. Sensors **17**(6), 1193 (2017)
17. Roedig, U., Voigt, T., Alonso, J., Bor, M.: Do lora low-power wide-area networks scale? In: Proceedings of the 19th ACM International Conference on Modeling, Analysis and Simulation of Wireless and Mobile Systems, MSWiM 2016, New York, NY, USA, pp. 59–67. Association for Computing Machinery (2016)
18. Centenaro, M., Vangelista, L., Magrin, D.: Performance evaluation of LoRa networks in a smart city scenario. In: 2017 IEEE International Conference on Communications (ICC), pp. 1–7 (2017)
19. Magrin, D., Zanella, A., Capuzzo, M.: Confirmed traffic in LoRaWAN: pitfalls and countermeasures. In: 2018 17th Annual Mediterranean Ad Hoc Networking Workshop (Med-Hoc-Net), pp. 1–7 (2018)
20. Kaihnsa, N., Lohne, A., Sturmfels, B., Ciripoi, D.: Computing convex hulls of trajectories. *arXiv: Dynamical Systems* (2018)

21. Kalantari, B.: An $o(1/\epsilon)$-iteration triangle algorithm for a convex hull membership. ArXiv, abs/1810.07346 (2018)
22. Mount, D.: CMSC 754 - Computational Geometry. Lecture Notes (2002). http://www.cs.umd.edu/~mount/754/Lects/754lects.pdf
23. Mai, D.L., Kim, M.K.: Multi-Hop LoRa network protocol with minimized latency. Energies **13**(6), 1–15 (2020)
24. Butun, I., Pereira, N., Gidlund, M.: Security risk analysis of LoRaWAN and future directions. Future Internet **11**(1) (2019)
25. Tomasin, S., Zulian, S., Vangelista, L.: Security analysis of LoRaWAN join procedure for internet of things networks. In: 2017 IEEE Wireless Communications and Networking Conference Workshops (WCNCW), pp. 1–6 (2017)
26. Rahmadhani, A., Kuipers, F.: When LoRaWAN frames collide. In: Proceedings of the 12th International Workshop on Wireless Network Testbeds, Experimental Evaluation & Characterization, WiNTECH 2018, New York, NY, USA, pp. 89–97. Association for Computing Machinery (2018)
27. Lounis, M., Mehdi, K., Bounceur, A.: A CupCarbon tool for simulating destructive insect movements. In: International Conference on Information and Communication Technologies for Disaster Management, USB, Algeria, March 2014
28. Meert, W., Pollin, S., Reynders, B.: Range and coexistence analysis of long range unlicensed communication. In: 2016 23rd International Conference on Telecommunications (ICT), pp. 1–6, May 2016
29. Bounceur, A., Clavier, L., Noreen, U.: A study of LoRa low power and wide area network technology. In: 2017 International Conference on Advanced Technologies for Signal and Image Processing (ATSIP), pp. 1–6, May 2017
30. Baig, S., Noreen, U.: Modified incremental bit allocation algorithm for powerline communication in smart grids. In: 2013 1st International Conference on Communications, Signal Processing, and their Applications (ICCSPA), pp. 1–6, February 2013
31. Semtech Corporation. LoRa Modem Designer's Guide. Technical Report July, 2013
32. Proakis, J.G.: Digital Communications, 4th edn. Mc Graw Hill, London (2000)
33. Kim, P., Thakkar, A., Yeddanapudi, S., Aftab, S., Cheung, O.: Information Theory and the Digital Age (2001)
34. Shannon, C.E.: A mathematical theory of communication. Bell Syst. Tech. J. **27**(4), 623–656 (1948)
35. Semtech Corporation. LoRa Modulation Basics. Technical Report, May 2015
36. Miller, L.E., Lee, J.S.: CDMA Systems Engineering Handbook (1998)
37. Hata, M.: Empirical formula for propagation loss in land mobile radio services. IEEE Trans. Veh. Technol. **29**(3), 317–325 (1980)
38. Okumura, H.: Field strength and its variability in the VHF and UHF land mobile radio service. Rev. Electr. Commun. Lab. **16**, 825–73 (1968)
39. Parsons, J.D.: The Mobile Radio Propagation Channel. Wiley, New York (2001)
40. Kulkarni, P., Sooriyabandara, M., Raza, U.: Low power wide area networks: an overview. IEEE Commun. Surv. Tutor. **19**(2), 855–873 (2017)
41. Fall, K., Varadhan, K.: The ns Manual (formerly ns Notes and Documentation) (2011). https://www.isi.edu/nsnam/ns/doc/
42. Rajaram, M.L., Kougianos, E., Mohanty, S.P., Choppali, U.: Wireless sensor network simulation frameworks: a tutorial review: MATLAB/Simulink bests the rest. IEEE Consum. Electron. Mag. **5**(2), 63–69 (2016)
43. Korkalainen, M., Sallinen, M., Kärkkäinen, N., Tukeva, P.: Survey of wireless sensor networks simulation tools for demanding applications. In: 2009 Fifth International Conference on Networking and Services, pp. 102–106 (2009)

44. ns 3. ns-3 Network Simulator (2011–2020). https://www.nsnam.org/
45. Henderson, T.R., Roy, S., Floyd, S., Riley, G.F.: Ns-3 project goals. In: Proceeding from the 2006 Workshop on Ns-2: The IP Network Simulator, WNS2 2006, New York, NY, USA, 13-es. Association for Computing Machinery (2006)
46. OMNeT. OMNeT++ Discrete Event Simulator (2001–2019). https://omnetpp.org/
47. Chen, F., Dietrich, I., German, R., Dressler, F.: An energy model for simulation studies of wireless sensor networks using OMNeT++. PIK - Praxis der Informationsverarbeitung und Kommunikation **32**(2), 133–138 (2009)
48. TinyOS. TOSSIM (2013). http://tinyos.stanford.edu/tinyos-wiki/index.php/TOSSIM
49. Perla, E., Catháin, Ó.A., Carbajo, S.R., Huggard, M., Goldrick, Mc.C.: Powertossim z: realistic energy modelling for wireless sensor network environments. PM2HW2N, pp. 35–42 (2008)
50. CupCarbon. CupCarbon Simulator (2020). http://www.cupcarbon.com
51. CupCarbon. CupCarbon User Guide (2019). http://labsticc.univ-brest.fr/~bounceur/cupcarbon/doc/cupcarbon_user_guide.pdf

Machine Learning Security Assessment Method Based on Adversary and Attack Methods

Hugo Sebastian Pacheco-Rodríguez[1]([⊠]), Eleazar Aguirre-Anaya[1]([⊠]),
Ricardo Menchaca-Méndez[2], and Manel Medina-Llinàs[3]

[1] Cybersecurity Laboratory, CIC - Instituto Politécnico Nacional, Av. Juan de Dios Bátiz,
Esq. Miguel Othón de Mendizábal S/N, Nueva Industrial Vallejo, 07738 México City, Mexico
b190385@sagitario.cic.ipn.mx, eaguirre@cic.ipn.mx
[2] Network and Data Science Laboratory, CIC - Instituto Politécnico Nacional, Av. Juan de Dios
Bátiz, Esq. Miguel Othón de Mendizábal S/N, Nueva Industrial Vallejo, 07738 México City,
Mexico
ric@cic.ipn.mx
[3] Computer Networks and Distributed System (CNDS), Universitat Politècnica de Catalunya,
Barcelona, Spain
manel@ac.upc.edu

Abstract. Analytical methods for assessing the security of Machine Learning Systems (MLS) that have been proposed in other researches do not provide compatibility with each other and their taxonomies have become incomplete due to the introduction of new properties of adversarial machine learning. In this sense, we have identified carefully relevant concepts of most prevalent researches about the security assessment of MLS. We propose a novel security assessment method based on the modeling of the adversary and the selection of adversarial attack methods for the generation of adversarial examples related to the also proposed taxonomy. This method provides compatibility with other proposed methods as well as practical guidelines and tools for evaluating machine learning systems. We also introduce the concern for efficient metrics capable of measuring the robustness of MLS to adversarial examples. This research is focused on the empirical evaluation of the security of machine learning systems, rather than on classical performance evaluation.

Keywords: Security · Machine learning · Evaluation

1 Introduction

Research on Adversarial Machine Learning (AML) has grown considerably in recent years and the consequences of unsecured Machine Learning Systems (MLS) have been studied in detail [1–10]. Results of these works are of concern to the scientific community, especially in the field of cybersecurity, because machine learning is being used in different applications to assist in decision making where security is paramount: healthcare, autonomous vehicles, power station operation, military operations, computer security, spam and malware detection, etc.

© Springer Nature Switzerland AG 2020
M. F. Mata-Rivera et al. (Eds.): WITCOM 2020, CCIS 1280, pp. 377–389, 2020.
https://doi.org/10.1007/978-3-030-62554-2_27

Due to the growing concern for the security of machine learning systems, methods have been developed for the evaluation of this type of systems [2, 11, 12]. Each of these methods conceptually defined taxonomies, threat models and attack strategies to assess MLS, including the adversarial properties that were known at the time. Due to the accelerated progress in adversarial machine learning, currently none of them contain a complete taxonomy and threat model that includes the adversarial properties found so far, and therefore do not allow benchmarking between MLS security assessments.

This research complements methods presented in [2, 11, 12] proposing a different organization of the threat model, and introducing the concern for effective metrics capable of measuring the robustness of machine learning systems to adverse examples. It is important to emphasize that security of machine learning is a constant concern, as their security properties have not been completely understood.

Although a defense threat model could be defined [13], this research is limited to the definition of an adversarial threat model.

Section 2 summarizes most relevant researches on adversary threat models in order to design the theoretical adversarial threat model and taxonomy of adversarial attacks. Section 3 provides an overview to perform a security assessment of a machine learning system considering a threat model, the different types of adversarial attack methods, metrics and we also recommend software tools for the generation of adversarial samples.

2   Threat Model and Taxonomy

The adversarial threat model is composed of the goals, capabilities, and knowledge of the adversary, that the MLS to be assessed will face. Conceptually defining the threat model is essential, because it describes the adversary against whom the system intends to defend itself, guiding the evaluation of the machine's learning system.

There are researches [2, 4, 11, 12, 14, 15] where threat models and taxonomies are defined, but often are not compatible between them. In [2, 11, 14] methods are proposed to evaluate MLS, the structure of these methods changes in each one, according to their application. Despite the changes, these investigations share the conceptual definition of the threat model, the taxonomy or the attack strategy. In this research, we propose an organization of the threat model and a general taxonomy for attacks that allows the comparison of MLS security assessments.

We have summarized the predominant concepts in the relevant taxonomies and looked for common features to find a description of each concept compatible with previous work [2, 4, 11, 12, 14, 15]. Concepts presented in Sect. 2.1 are based on taxonomies from the most relevant researches in this research field. The taxonomy for the adversary proposed also defines the organization of the analytical threat model.

2.1   Attack Scenario

Attack scenario must be specified in terms of the conceptual model of the adversary. As well as Biggio et al. [11] model, the following scenario is based on the assumption that, the adversary acts rationally to attain a given goal, according to his/her knowledge of the classifier, and his/her capability of manipulating data.

Adversary Knowledge

The adversary can have different levels of knowledge of the targeted system such as the training data, test data, feature set, learning algorithm, model architecture, model methods or trained parameters/hyperparameters.

Biggio et al. [4] characterized the adversarial knowledge of the targeted system in terms of a space:

$$\Theta = (\mathcal{D}, \mathcal{X}, f, w) \tag{1}$$

Where:

- $\mathcal{D}$: Training data.
- $\mathcal{X}$: Feature set.
- f: Machine learning algorithm, along with the objective function $\mathcal{L}$ minimized during training.
- w: Trained parameters/hyper-parameters.

Depending on the adversary knowledge, one can describe three different type of attacks.

- **White-Box Attacks:** the adversary is assumed to know everything about the targeted system. This setting allows to perform a worst-case evaluation of the security of learning algorithms. It can be characterized as follows:

$$\Theta_{WB} = (\mathcal{D}, \mathcal{X}, f, w) \tag{2}$$

- **Grey-Box Attacks:** the adversary has partial information about the model. Two main cases are characterized below:

  - Surrogate-Dataset (adversary is assumed to know the feature representation $\mathcal{X}$ and the kind of learning algorithm f):

$$\Theta_{GB-SD} = \left(\hat{\mathcal{D}}, \mathcal{X}, f, \hat{w}\right) \tag{3}$$

  Where:

  $\hat{\mathcal{D}}$: Surrogate dataset from a similar source.
  $\hat{w}$: Estimated parameters from $\hat{\mathcal{D}}$ (after training a surrogate classifier).

  - Surrogate-Learners (adversary is assumed to know only the feature representation $\mathcal{X}$):

$$\Theta_{GB-SL} = \left(\hat{\mathcal{D}}, \mathcal{X}, \hat{f}, \hat{w}\right) \tag{4}$$

  Where:

  $\hat{\mathcal{D}}$: Surrogate dataset from a similar source.

$\hat{f}$: Surrogate learning algorithm.
$\hat{w}$: Estimated parameters from $\hat{\mathcal{D}}$ (after training a surrogate classifier).

- **Black-Box Attacks:** the adversary has no knowledge about the model except some components that can be obtained externally. Can be characterized as follows:

$$\Theta_{BB} = \left(\hat{\mathcal{D}}, \hat{\mathcal{X}}, \hat{f}, \hat{w} \right) \tag{5}$$

Where:

- $\hat{\mathcal{D}}$: Surrogate dataset from a similar source.
- $\hat{\mathcal{X}}$: Surrogate feature set.
- $\hat{f}$: Surrogate learning algorithm.
- $\hat{w}$: Estimated parameters from $\hat{\mathcal{D}}$ (after training a surrogate classifier).

Table 1 shows the three different types of attacks based on the adversary knowledge and their most known components of an MLS respectively.

Table 1. Adversary knowledge

Known component	White-Box	Gray-Box	Black-Box
Training data	X		
Test data	X		
Parameter values	X		
Training method (loss function)	X	X	
Model architecture	X	X	
Feature set	X	X	
Input-output pairings*	X		X
Input-output samples of training data*	X		X

*Input-output samples and pairings are obtained using the targeted machine learning system as an Oracle. The data obtained can be used to train a substitute machine learning model.

Adversary Goals
Adversary Goals are formulated as the optimization of an objective function. Biggio et al. [11] argue that the adversary goal must be defined on the desired security violation, and on the attack specificity. The attack specificity depends on whether an adversary wants to misclassify a targeted or an indiscriminate set of samples. Table 2 summarizes the attack specificity axis.

In [1] Papernot et al. define targeted or indiscriminate attacks depending on whether the adversary aims to cause-specific or generic errors. Because it can cause confusion

Table 2. Attack specificity axis

Attack specificity	Description	Example attack
Targeted [2, 6, 11, 15, 16]	The focus is on a single or small set of target points	• Targeted misclassification • Source-target misclassification
Indiscriminate [2, 6, 11, 15, 16]	Has a flexible goal, that involves a very general class of points, such as "any false negative". Universal adversarial examples are defined here	• Confidence reduction • Misclassification

with the interpretation of targeted and indiscriminate attack specificity Biggio et al. modify their naming convention. The error specificity can thus be: specific or generic. Error Specificity disambiguates the notion of misclassification in multi-class problems. Table 3 summarizes Error Specificity attacks.

Table 3. Error specificity attacks axis

Error specificity attacks	Description	Intends
Specific [4]	The adversary aims to mislead classification but requires the adversarial samples to be misclassified as a specific class	• Maximizes the confidence assigned to the wrong target class, while minimizing the probability of correct classification
Generic [4]	The adversary is interested in misleading classification, regardless of the output class predicted by the classifiers	• Attack will ensure that adversarial sample will no longer classifies correctly as a sample class, but rather misclassified as a sample of the closest candidate class

Desired end security violation (Table 4) relates to the adversary effort to compromise the system. It is important to emphasize that in the case of MLS, integrity is of paramount importance, because attacks on system integrity and availability are closely related in goal and method.

Adversarial Capabilities

It refers to the control that the adversary has on training and testing data. Table 5 summarizes influence axis.

Table 6 summarizes how each author define the threat model in the literature respectively.

Table 4. Security violation adversary axis

Security violation	Description	Attack examples
Integrity [2, 6, 11, 15, 16]	Result in intrusion points being classified as normal (false negatives)	• Confidence reduction • Misclassification • Targeted misclassification • Source-target misclassification
Availability [2, 6, 11, 15, 16]	Cause so many classification errors, both false negatives and false positives, that the system becomes effectively unusable	• Model corruption • Denial of Service
Confidentiality [11, 16]	The adversary obtains information from the machine learning algorithm, compromising the secrecy or privacy of the system users	• Exposure of the model and training data • Membership test • Training data extraction

Table 5. Adversary influence axis

Influence	Description	Attack examples
Causative [2, 6, 11, 15, 16]	Alter the training process through influence over the training data	• Data manipulation • Label manipulation • Input manipulation • Data injection • Logic corruption • Data access
Exploratory [2, 6, 11, 15, 16]	Do not alter the training process but use other techniques, such as test the classifier, to discover information about it or its training data	• Single step (Gradient-based) • Iterative (Gradient-based) • Gradient-free attacks • Extraction • Inversion • Membership inference

As we can see in Table 6, some authors use the terms 'adversary' or 'adversarial' referring to the 'attacker', we will use the term 'adversary' and 'adversarial' as we consider that it fits better in the context of machine learning security assessment. We also consider the definition of the adversary knowledge involves the definition of the attack surface.

Table 6. Threat model assumptions

Authors	Threat model set assumptions
Barreno et al. [2]	Attacker's goals/incentives Attacker's capabilities
Biggio et al. [11]	Adversarial goals Adversary's knowledge Adversary's capabilities
Carlini and Wagner [14]	Adversary goals Adversary knowledge Adversarial capabilities
Chakraborty and Anirban [15]	Attack surface Adversary capabilities Adversary goals
Papernot et al. [12]	Attack surface Trust model Adversarial capabilities Adversarial goals
Biggio et al. [4]	Attacker's goals Attacker's capabilities

2.2 Attack Strategy

The attack strategy define how the training and test data will be quantitatively modified to optimize the objective function characterizing the adversary goal [11]. Biggio et al. [4] characterized the optimal attack strategy as follows:

$$\mathcal{D}_c^* \in \arg\max_{\mathcal{D}_c' \in \Phi(\mathcal{D}_c)} \mathcal{A}\left(\mathcal{D}_c', \theta\right) \tag{6}$$

Where:

- $\theta \in \Theta$: Adversary knowledge
- $\mathcal{D}_c$: Initial attack samples
- $\Phi\mathcal{D}_c$: Space of possible modifications
- $\mathcal{A}\left(\mathcal{D}_c', \theta\right) \in \mathbb{R}$: Adversary goals objective function
- $\mathcal{D}_c' \in \Phi(\mathcal{D}_c)$: Set of manipulated adversarial examples

3 Security Assessment Method

Most authors proposed security assessments focused on a specific application, classifier, and attack, performing security assessment procedures based on the exploitation of problem knowledge and heuristic techniques. They point to a previously unknown vulnerability or to assess the impact of a known attack on the security of an MLS. Here we propose an analytical method that complements the existing [4, 11] security assessment methods.

As part of the evaluation model, it is necessary to identify the threat model, in order to illustrate necessary concepts to identify it, the organization of the axes mentioned in Sect. 2 are presented in Sect. 3.1.

Threat model could be interpreted as general guidelines for the security assessment of an MLS. Figure 1 illustrates the assumptions of our proposed threat model. Attack scenario must be defined making assumptions about the adversarial knowledge, adversarial goals and adversarial capability. The definition of the attack strategy is a fundamental part of the model since it attempts to optimize the function that characterizes the adversary goals, we will discuss more about this further.

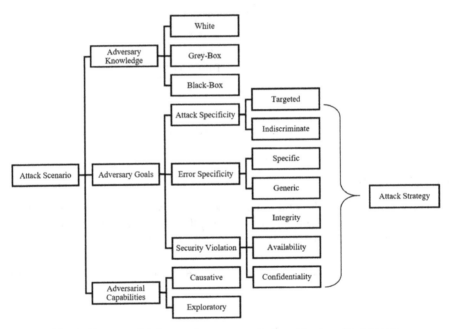

Fig. 1. Threat model for security assessment of machine learning systems.

3.1 Attack Strategy

As we mentioned in Sect. 2.2 the attack strategy must be defined based on the function characterizing the adversary goal. The definition of the attack strategy, the adversary knowledge, and the adversarial capabilities help to define which methods of attack to use. However, it should be mentioned that evaluating MLS with as many methods as possible will provide an even more detailed evaluation.

After defining threat model, attack scenario and attack strategy the adversarial attacks methods must be selected or designed, in Sect. 3.2 we show some state of art methods.

3.2 Adversarial Attacks Methods

Adversarial attack methods should be selected according to the defined threat model to guide the security assessment. Table 7 summarizes the most relevant adversarial attack methods according to our taxonomy proposed in Sect. 2. We consider these attacks as they have shown the best results when vulnering MLS [15], designer/adversary can select state of the art attacks not mentioned in the table that fits their attack scenario.

Table 7. Most relevant adversarial attack methods for generating adversarial examples

Adversarial attack	Adversarial knowledge	Attack specificity	Attack frequency	Metric
L-BFGS Attack [17]	White-Box	Targeted	Iterative	L_2
Fast Gradient Sign Method (FGSM) [3]	White-Box	Indiscriminate	Single-Step	L_∞
Basic Iterative Method and Least-Likely Class [18]	White-Box	Indiscriminate	Iterative	L_∞
Jacobian-based Saliency Map Attack (JSMA) [1]	White-Box	Targeted	Iterative	L_2
DeepFool [8]	White-Box	Indiscriminate	Iterative	L_1, L_∞
C & W Attack [19]	White-Box	Targeted	Iterative	L_1, L_2, L_∞
Zeroth Order Optimization [20]	Black-Box	Targeted and Indiscriminate	Iterative	L_2
Universal Perturbation [21]	White-Box	Indiscriminate	Iterative	L_1, L_∞
One Pixel Attack [9]	White-Box	Targeted and indiscriminate	Iterative	L_0
Feature Adversary [22]	White-Box	Targeted	Iterative	L_2

We recommend that attack methods be used that fit the assumptions about the adversary knowledge, goals and capabilities, as well as consider the computational cost (attack frequency) and whether the model is gradient-free or not.

In Table 7 we categorized adversarial attack methods according to our taxonomy proposed in Sect. 2, also we introduce under which metric each attack is limited. In Sect. 3.3 we go into detail about this metrics.

3.3 Metrics

Throughout the brief history of adversarial attacks, different metrics have been used to measure the change in the original samples from the adverse samples. Goodfellow and others used metrics based on L_p norms, however, these types of metrics are not useful for measuring the robustness of an MLS, which is why Weng et al. [23] introduced CLEVER (Cross Lipschitz Extreme Value for nEtwork Robustness), a metric that provides an agnostic measure of attack to evaluate the robustness of any machine learning classifier trained against adversarial examples. In Table 8, we resume metrics used in adversarial settings.

Table 8. Metrics

Metric		Description
Distance metrics	L_0	Measures the number of coordinates i such that $x_i \neq x'_i$. The L_0 distance corresponds to the number of pixels that have been altered in an image
	L_2	Measures the standard Euclidean (root-mean-square) distance between x and x'. Can remain small when there are many small changes to many pixels
	L_∞	Measured the maximum change to any of the coordinates. $$\lVert x - x' \rVert = \max(\lvert x_1 - x'_1 \rvert, \ldots, \lvert x_n - x'_n \rvert)$$
Accuracy		Most publications use accuracy to argue that attacks are effective or in order to evaluate robustness of machine learning

Weng et al. [23] introduce CLEVER an attack agnostic metric to measure lower bound robustness, based on Lipshitz continuity, however, Goodfellow et al. [24] show that CLEVER fails to correctly estimate lower bound robustness, even in theoretical settings. The question of measuring robustness remains open.

We recommend the use of both distance and accuracy metrics, since attacks that remain below the limits of the corresponding L_p norm and obtain high accuracy could be considered effective, and therefore the adversarial robustness of the MLS is considered low.

Derived from the threat model, we can define two types of evaluation methods; one that is directly related to the designer and other to the adversary. Figure 2 briefly illustrates our method for a designer to perform a security assessment, it is important to emphasize that the order cannot be altered.

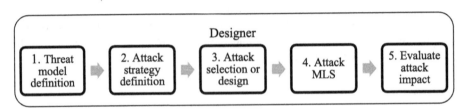

Fig. 2. Designer security assessment method

Figure 3 briefly illustrates our method for an adversary to perform a security assessment, as in designer evaluation method, the order cannot be altered.

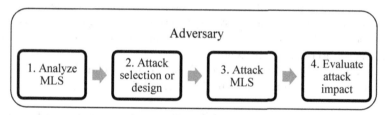

Fig. 3. Adversary security assessment method

4 Discussion

We can observe that the evaluation method proposed is based on modeling the adversary, which allows the designer to anticipate the adversary by identifying threats that the system can face, as well as simulating attacks. The organization of the threat model proposed in Fig. 1 allows us to define the attack scenario and to model the adversary depending on his knowledge, goal, and capability.

On the adversary's side, our threat model will help to analyze the MLS, since he will be able to identify what knowledge, goal and capability he has of the system and then chooses or design an attack method. As a result, we will have a security assessment performed from the adversarial side.

We decided not to include the development of countermeasures as part of the method, as was done in [2, 11] because this research focuses only on the security assessment of MLS. However, we leave open the possibility for the reader to cycle the methods and include the development of countermeasures in order to obtain MLS robust to adversarial attacks.

In Fig. 3.1 we can see in the adversarial goal axis that we include error specificity axis; this is because we find it helpful in evaluating multi-class classifiers. The fact that our method also considers multi-class classifiers makes it a high-level guideline.

5 Conclusions and Future Work

The security assessment method proposed in this paper provides the features necessary to perform security assessments of MLS. Each of the terms used for the conceptual definition of the threat model was compared with its similar, which allowed to choose the organization of the threat model that allows to model the adversary in detail defining assumptions about their goals, knowledge and capabilities. A limitation of the evaluation method for the designer is that it requires a full analysis of the adversary's behavior, which is sometimes difficult and in the case of the evaluation method for the adversary is data-dependent. The unification and update of the previous security assessment methods as well as the introduction of robustness metrics will allow a more detailed security evaluation of the MLS.

However, there are still open problems, such as analyzing the vulnerabilities of the MLS with respect to adversarial attacks and developing metrics capable of quantifying the robustness of a machine learning system to adversarial examples. These issues will need to be addressed soon to help ensure that the implementation of machine learning systems in adversarial settings is secure.

As future work, we will introduce a defense threat model and defense taxonomy, with the purpose of assessing defense methods for MLS.

Acknowledgements. We would like to thank IPN[1] for allowing us to accomplish this work in the CIC[2]. Pacheco-Rodriguez gratefully acknowledges the scholarship from CONACyT[3] to pursue his master studies.

References

1. Papernot, N., et al.: The Limitations of Deep Learning in Adversarial Settings. Institute of Electrical and Electronics Engineers Inc., November 2015
2. Barreno, M., Nelson, B., Joseph, A.D., Tygar, J.D.: The security of machine learning. Mach. Learn. **81**, 121–148 (2010). https://doi.org/10.1007/s10994-010-5188-5
3. Goodfellow, I.J., Shlens, J., Szegedy, C.: Explaining and harnessing adversarial examples. In: 3rd International Conference on Learning Representations, ICLR 2015 - Conference Track Proceedings (2015)
4. Biggio, B., Roli, F.: Wild Patterns: Ten Years After the Rise of Adversarial Machine Learning (2018)
5. Carlini, N., Wagner, D.: Towards evaluating the robustness of neural networks. In: Proceedings - IEEE Symposium on Security and Privacy, pp. 39–57 (2017). https://doi.org/10.1109/sp.2017.49
6. Barreno, M., Nelson, B., Sears, R., Joseph, A.D., Tygar, J.D.: Can machine learning be secure? (Invited Talk). Asiaccs **06**, 16–25 (2006). https://doi.org/10.1145/1128817.1128824
7. Chen, P.-Y., Zhang, H., Sharma, Y., Yi, J., Hsieh, C.-J.: ZOO: zeroth order optimization based black-box attacks to deep neural networks without training substitute models. In: AISec 2017 - Proceedings of 10th ACM Work. Artificial Intelligence and Security co-located with CCS 2017, pp. 15–26, August 2017. https://doi.org/10.1145/3128572.3140448
8. Moosavi-Dezfooli, S.-M., Fawzi, A., Frossard, P.: DeepFool: a simple and accurate method to fool deep neural networks. In: Proceedings of IEEE Computing Society Conference Computer Vision Pattern Recognition, vol. 2016-December, pp. 2574–2582, November 2015
9. Su, J., Vargas, D.V., Sakurai, K.: One Pixel Attack for Fooling Deep Neural Networks (2017)
10. Athalye, A., Engstrom, L., Ilyas, A., Kevin, K.: Synthesizing robust adversarial examples. In: 35th International Conference on Machine Learning, ICML 2018, vol. 1, pp. 449–468 (2018)
11. Biggio, B., Fumera, G., Roli, F.: Security Evaluation of Pattern Classifiers under Attack (2017)
12. Papernot, N., Mcdaniel, P., Sinha, A., Wellman, M.P.: SoK: Security and Privacy in Machine Learning (2018). https://doi.org/10.1109/eurosp.2018.00035

[1] Instituto Politécnico Nacional (https://www.ipn.mx/) .

[2] Centro de Investigación en Computación (https://www.cic.ipn.mx/).

[3] Consejo Nacional de Ciencia y Tecnología (https://www.conacyt.gob.mx/).

13. Serban, A.C., Visser, J.: Adversarial Examples-A Complete Characterisation of the Phenomenon (2019)
14. Carlini, N., et al.: On Evaluating Adversarial Robustness, February 2019
15. Chakraborty, A., Alam, M., Dey, V., Chattopadhyay, A., Mukhopadhyay, D.: Adversarial Attacks and Defences: A Survey, September 2018
16. Huang, L., Joseph, A.D., Nelson, B., Rubinstein, B.I.P., Tygar, J.D.: Adversarial Machine Learning (2011)
17. Szegedy, C., et al.: Intriguing properties of neural networks. In: 2nd International Conference on Learning Representations, ICLR 2014 - Conference Track Proceedings (2014)
18. Kurakin, A., Goodfellow, I.J., Bengio, S., Brain, G., Openai, I.J.G., Bengio, S.: Adversarial examples in the physical world. In: International Conference on Learning Representations, ICLR (2017)
19. Carlini, N., Wagner, D.: Adversarial Examples Are Not Easily Detected: Bypassing Ten Detection Methods, pp. 3–14, May 2017. https://doi.org/10.1145/3128572.3140444
20. Chen, P.-Y., Zhang, H., Sharma, Y., Yi, J., Hsieh, C.-J.: ZOO: Zeroth Order Optimization Based Black-box Attacks to Deep Neural Networks without Training Substitute Models, vol. 17 (2017). https://doi.org/10.1145/3128572.3140448
21. Moosavi-Dezfooli, M., Fawzi, A., Fawzi, O., Frossard, P.: Universal adversarial perturbations, vol. 2017-Janua. Institute of Electrical and Electronics Engineers Inc., pp. 86–94 (2017)
22. Sabour, S., Cao, Y., Faghri, F., Fleet, D.J.: Adversarial manipulation of deep representations. In: 4th International Conference on Learning Representations, ICLR 2016 - Conference Track Proceedings (2016)
23. Weng, T.W., et al.: Evaluating the robustness of neural networks: an extreme value theory approach. In: 6th International Conference on Learning Representations, ICLR 2018 - Conference Track Proceedings (2018)
24. Goodfellow, I.: Gradient Masking Causes CLEVER to Overestimate Adversarial Perturbation Size (2018)

A Novel Approach for Ensemble Feature Selection Using Clustering with Automatic Threshold

Muhammad Shah Jahan[✉] [iD], Anam Amjad, Usman Qamar, Muhammad Talha Riaz, and Kashif Ayub

Department of Computer and Software Engineering, College of Electrical and Mechanical Engineering, National University of Sciences and Technology (NUST), Islamabad, Pakistan
`{shah.jahan18,anam.amjad,talha.riaz18,`
`muhammad.kashif18}@ce.ceme.edu.pk, usmanq@ceme.nust.edu.pk`

Abstract. Feature Selection (FS) is the core part of data processing pipeline. Use of ensemble in FS is a relatively new approach aiming at producing more diversity in feature dataset, which provides better performance as well as more robust and accurate result. An aggregation step combined the output of each FS method and generate the Single feature Subset. In this paper, a novel ensemble method for FS "EFSCAT" is proposed which rank all the features and then cluster the most related features. To reduce the size of ranking an automatic threshold in every ranker is being introduced. This added thresholding step will improve the computational efficiency because it cutoff low-ranking features which were initially ranked by Ranker. Mean-shift clustering is then use to combined the results of each ranker. The process of aggregation will become very time efficient. "EFSCAT" will make the classification more robust and stable.

Keywords: Feature Selection · Ensemble Feature Selection · Clustering · Automatic threshold

1 Introduction

This Current world is facing an exceptional increased in data. This data is growing every year and now come to the stage where processing of large amount of data is difficult. With introduction of Big Data, the data is increasing and only Facebook, Twitter, Genomics and Astronomy is generated a large number of data every year. If social networks and bioinformatics fields considered then this data become even bigger. Storing and processing of this increasing data is not the only problem but a rapid increase in the dimensionality of data is even a bigger problem. The increase in sample size is not as rapid as feature size which make it more difficult to produce effective mathematic models for data analysis. Now we are facing many high and ultra-dimensional dataset cross the domains.

We are facing "curse of dimensionality" due to processing of high dimensional data. Curse of dimensionality causes the inconsistency in data mining algorithm, it overfit the

© Springer Nature Switzerland AG 2020
M. F. Mata-Rivera et al. (Eds.): WITCOM 2020, CCIS 1280, pp. 390–401, 2020.
https://doi.org/10.1007/978-3-030-62554-2_28

model and consume more time and resources. Feature Selection (FS) and dimension-ality reduction methods are used with high dimensional dataset. The main purpose of these methods is to reduce the dimension of dataset with minimum information lost and select only the most relevant features from the dataset. These methods transform the dataset into dimensionally reduce space. This space is not physical that is a drawback of these methods which means original features are presented and cause problems like accidentally correlation between data. FS built models which built upon few but relevant features that are simple and easier to interpret and also required very less storage space. The reduction of feature also reduces the search space which save computational time and storage.

FS method is the most important step of Preprocessing. There are three methods which are used for FS 1) filters, 2) wrapper and 3) embedded. Every method has advan-tages and limitations as well. Filter are computationally cost effective while they work poor in benchmark studies. It is a two-stage process. In first stage, relevancy of fea-ture calculates using fish-score, mutation information and then top-ranked features are selected while low ranked features are discarded. The wrapper method produces most appropriate output but depends upon the classified. Wrapper processed different subjects and choose most optimal. Sequential forward selection and sequential backwards selec-tion is being used in wrapper for search [1, 2]. The embedded is the hybrid approach which has benefits of filters and wrapper but still it depends upon the classifier. There are three types of datasets supervised, semi-supervised and unsupervised. FS has numer-ous benefits like avoid overfitting, control the curse of dimensionality and to remove redundancy [3, 4].

The rational of Ensemble Feature Selection (EFS) is based upon the idea of building set of hypotheses using different techniques and then combined these results, it will be better than single one. In machine learning most of the time only single methods is being use in approaches but now the trend is changing as ensemble prove their worth in many techniques like classification. Josef Kilter and Fabio Rahil are holding workshops on the topic of multiple classifier systems (MCS) since 2000s [5]. There are computational and other benefits of ensemble FS. FS methods are categories on the bases of their output which are (i) Order Ranking (ii) subset of relevant features.

Ensemble FS is relatively new approach. The main concept of ensemble FS is that two heads are better than the one. EFS easily tackle the limitations of individual meth-ods and it has two types (i) Homogenous and (ii) heterogeneous. In homogeneous the dataset is divided in different training data and distributed to several similar nodes but in heterogeneous example the training data is same but the nodes are different. The results of base selectors are combined which called aggregator. There are different algorithms for combining these results [6, 7].

FS is being applied to many Data processing problem with aim of reduced dataset with minimum error. There are different approaches for FS like multivariate, ranking and feature construction. Better results are obtained by ensemble learning which is mostly used in classification but now the use of ensemble for FS getting more and more attention. four search strategies are being used EFS which are generic search, random subset, forward and backward sequential selection [8].

In our novel ensemble FS technique "EFSCAT" will use heterogeneous approach which means there will be different base learners but all will be trained with same training data. Ranking methods used because this approach considered general characteristics of training data like correlation, variance etc. The main cause of using Ranking instead of feature subset is that when features are combined in later technique it could generate subset containing all features when using Union(U) or could produce NULL subset in case of Intersection (^), Also Feature Subset method is very sophisticated and time consuming. On the other hand, the ranking method can combine subsets by Min, Median, Arith-mean and Geom-mean but all these methods are dependent upon the dataset and result of one base learner could affect the whole output. Instead of using these methods will use Clustering methods which called "Mean shift Clustering" and to feed this clustering method will use automatic threshold-cutoff. When threshold is applies then clustering will get only highest-ranking features' "EFSCAT" can use both automatic and fixed threshold and this approach will improve the process of classification and will help in making quick decisions.

Rest of the research paper is organized as follows. In Sect. 2 the literature view is discussed. Section 3 discuss about the purposed methodology and in Sect. 4 discussions and future directions of this research paper will be presented.

2 Literature Review

2.1 Feature Selection

Chormunge et al. [9] solve the problem of irrelevant feature by using k-means clustering algorithm and redundancy by using correlation measure of all clusters. All remaining features are ranked according to their property. This proposed method is applied on microarray using Naïve Bayes classifier which yields better results with high speed. Gao et al. [10] proposed a new FS technique which based on information theory which compose the relevant features. The main advantage of this technique is in minimizing the redundancy and achieve better average and highest accuracy while comparing to other five algorithms.

In this paper Cilia et al. [11] purposed a novel approach for FS which reduces the computational cost and improve the performance of classifier. The author use ranking based FS technique and apply greedy search approach for choosing the feature subset to improve the process of classification in handwriting application by using this novel technique can reduce the features up to 30%.

Bermejo et al. [12] proposed which consist on ensemble of wrapper to automatically select features in fish age classification. A metric based on averaging is being used in ensemble to reduce the instability of subset selection process. This novel technique was tested with SVM and NN on Atlantic COD data search. This novel technique outperforms the results obtained from manual SVM.

Panday et al. [13] FS is used to remove some of the features with minimum information loss. Two novel algorithms for unsupervised FS are proposed witch are minFwfs and max Fwfs. Clustered dependent feature weight is the base of both these algorithms. These methods only choose the relevant features [0,1]. these algorithms could easily select or deselect a given feature. This novel method outperforms FsfW and mcfs.

2.2   Ensemble Feature Selection

Bolón-Canedo et al. [14] perform a systematic literature review on the topic of ensemble FS. On selecting the relevant features and discarding the irrelevant features for a given problem improve the classification accuracy. There are two of ensemble FS heterogeneous and heterogeneous. Filters wrappers and embedded used for FS. Wrappers and depend upon classifier ensemble. FS yields subset of features or ranking of features. In Ranking methods threshold is being applied. Intersection and union are used for subset feature combination and mean, Max and some other used in Ranking method. R, MATLAB, Rapid Miner are used software tools for ensemble FS.

Tüysüzoğlu et al. [15] proposed novel technique for multilayer ensemble which use boostrap as a stopping criterion. Diversity can be achieved by combining results from different rankers which generate robust results, use low, average and high ranking for text classification. Six commonly used filter-based ranker was examined and their use on 17 ensemble of feature ranking techniques. Cao et al. [16] use min, max etc. to advanced complete linear aggregator (CLA), SVM-Rank and robust ensemble FS use for combination of Ranker produced subsets.

Seijo-Pardo et al. [17] Two ensemble FS methods were proposed along with the algorithm. These two methods are homogeneous and heterogeneous. First one will differently be training datasets on same learner on the others side same training data set on different base learners. The later approach minimizes the weaknesses and maximizes the strength of individual base learners.

Seijo-Pardo et al. [18] proposed two novel approaches for automatic threshold in ensemble FS. Both of these techniques are applied on ranking methods. Both techniques are different on the place of Threshold.in first technique the threshold is applied before the combination and in other technique this threshold is applied after the combination. Both of the techniques are tested by fixing the threshold value. These techniques are tested by Support Vector Machine (SVM) classifier in three different datasets where two were from real dataset which yields satisfactory results.

Liu et al. [19] presented a new algorithm which is designed to select features subset from semi-supervised dataset. Rough set base semi-supervised FS is proposed by ensemble. The labeled data would be predicted by label propagation Algorithm (LPA) and then local neighborhood decision error rate is used for fitness functions to evaluate candidate features.

Drotár et al. [6] proposed many ensemble FS method based on voting like STV, boarda count, plurality vote, single transferable and proposed clustered ensemble based on boarda count which yields best results. These ensembles FS are applied on 10 high dimensional datasets and 5 artificial datasets with measurement methods stability, sensitivity and classification performance. E Border, W_{power} B, E-min outperform other FS methods. Still there is need of limit how much top ranked features should be in clusters to generate better results.

Chiew et al. [20] proposed on novel FS framework for phishing detection system which called hybrid ensemble FS. This framework has two phases; In first phase primary features subsets are obtained by applying a novel algorithm which is called commutative distribution function gradient and in second phase secondary features subsets which obtain by yielding primary subset to a perturbation ensemble second phase drives the baseline feature from secondary data. The author proposed that this framework works best which is being used with random forest classifier.

Oskouei et al. [7] proposed novel pruning method which consist upon different combining different pairwise matrix proposed to reduce the number of classifications without worsening the performance. These diversity metrics used to group alike classifiers. A graph coloring method is applied on graphs which are transformed from by combined diversity metrics to generate candidate ensembles. Thus, purposed method is applied upon 21 UCI sets and their results were better than 5 state of the art methods in ensemble pruning.

2.3 Clustering

Manbari et al. [21] A novel hybrid filter based FS algorithm based on a combination of clustering and a new modified binary ant system is proposed. This novel technique reduce the search space and processing of high dimensional data. A new strategy was introduced that avoid falling in local Optima and new redundancy Policy was introduced which improve the above algorithm. This technique has local and global search capability.

Saha et al. [22] Proposed a new FS approach based on clustering. In this technique feature are selected on the basis of intrinsic characteristic following filter approach. To form the final subset each suitable feature is selected from every clustering following the wrapper approach. This novel technique reduces the computational cost. Optimal number of features clusters determined by the quality of feature inside the clusters and define taxonomy of the clusters. Other existing methods use trial and error approach. FS from these clusters can be form by considering relevancy and redundancy of features.

Typically, filters are used for FS due to very less computational consumption but these filters cannot deal with feature redundancy. Clustering and MI methods are time-consuming when applied on very large data set. To deal with issue a novel ensemble FS technique is being purposed which called CCFR. This technique consists of four steps.in first step a preprocess by normalization and discretization operator. In second step two optimal filters are used to obtain two features subset. In third step the features are combined by using union operation based on feature weight. In last step modified HAC algorithm is applied upon that dump subset. The experiments are being done with SVM and KNN classifiers on 10 datasets. CCFR yields better results than CS, PCC and JS [23].

Sahu et al. [24] FS Framework is proposed with ensemble classifier to select general features from the microarray data. This Framework reduce the redundancy of features using k-means clustering, top ranked features selected from each cluster by applying ranking. Selection of topic ranked features are done by applying signal-to-nose ratio, Significance analysis of microarray and T static. the final subset is selected by ensemble classifier. genes subsets selected by Revolutionary wrapper are distinct. In pipeline k-mean and t-test give the 100% accuracy for DLBCL dataset. Breast cancer data, evolution wrapper outperform all orders (Table 1).

Table 1. Literature resume

Author	Year	Technique
Bermejo et al. [12]	2017	EFS using LPA
Cilia et al. [14]	2019	EFS using Greedy Technique
Tüysüzoğlu et al. [15]	2018	Multilayer Ensemble using Bootstrap stopping criteria
Liu et al. [19]	2019	EFS using MINFWFS AND FWFS
Chiew et al. [20]	2019	Hybrid EFS for phishing detection
Saha et al. [22]	2018	EFS using filter and wrapper clustering
Wang et al. [23]	2019	EFS using HAC Algorithm
Sahu et al. [24]	2017	EFS using k-mean
Das et al. [25]	2017	EFS using gene Algorithm

3 Methodology

In this section present our novel approach for ensemble FS using clustering with a threshold cut-off. In this technique employ a heterogenous ensemble with different FS methods. Like could use filters, wrappers or embedded. These all methods use Ranker methods to generate ranking of all features. A threshold is applied to these rankers to generate just highest ranked features and then mean-shift clustering is used to combined these Different rankers to generate a final combined sub set of features which are most relevant and improve the process and results of classification.

3.1 Novel Technique for Ensemble FS "EFSCAT"

Here our novel approach for ensemble FS is being explain. The cause and need of using this technique are to improve classification results, reduction of size of feature subset and produce the most relevant features which used for classification. This technique will reduce the complexity and computational cost. This novel technique starts from the data set and ends with a final combined feature subset. Heterogenous ensemble approach is being used in this technique which requires different base learner trained by sane training dataset. The "EFSCAT" include the following steps (Fig. 1):

1. Collect the Dataset
2. Make a training data set
3. Use different base learners (e.g. Filters)
4. Generate ranking of all features in every base learner (Ranker)
5. Apply threshold on every Ranker (e.g. fixed or automatic)
6. Apply Clustering to combined these features into one Feature Data-set

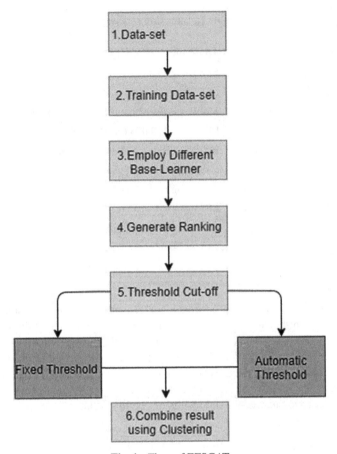

Fig. 1. Flow of EFSCAT

3.2 Construction of "EFSCAT"

Dataset and training Data
A supervised dataset is used which means all the dataset is labeled. Multidimensional data set could be used. A training data set is selected to train the base learners which will distribute over several different nodes.

Base Learner and ranking
As we are proposing a heterogenous approach the base learners will be different. These base learners are different but use ranking not the subset of relevant features. There could be several rankers R1, R2, R3......... Rn which used as base learners. Here the ranking of these rankers is ordinal ranking.

Threshold setting and subset
Ranking in every ranker contains all feature of data in which many are irrelevant or does very little in improving the result of classification.to limit this ranking only select

highest ranked features from every ranker. This threshold could be a fixed value like 10%, 30% etc. [26]. But here we are stressing on automatic threshold which will present with following algorithm

N-Number of Rankers used
F_n-number of features to be selected
For each n from 1 to N do
Use ranker method to produce ranking R_n
F_n = select a threshold cutoff c and apply on every ranker R_n
S-Select then F_n top attribute from each Ranker R_n

With comply with this algorithm will used Complexity Fusion (CF) to apply automatic threshold cut-off. will use combination of three methods which are (I) Value of Overlap Region (F1) (II) Maximum Feature Efficiency (F2) and last (III) Maximum fisher Discriminant Ratio (F3) introduced by Seijo-Pardo.

1. Value of Overlap Region(F1)
   Value of Overlap Region produces the minimum and maximum values of every class.

$$F1 = \prod_l \frac{\max(0, MINMAXi - MAXMINi)}{MAXMAXi - MINMINi} \tag{1}$$

2. Maximum Feature Efficiency (F2)
   It removes unambiguous points fallen outside of the overlapping regions.

$$F2 = \frac{\left|U_{i=1}^d \{x_{ji} \in [MINMAXi, MAXMINi] : x_j \in D\}\right|}{s} \tag{2}$$

Where x_{ji} is the value for feature I,x_j is each of the example in the training set D and S is the total samples in training set. Inverse of Fisher Ratio is being used here.

3. Maximum fisher Discriminant Ratio (F3):'

$$F3 = \frac{\sum_{i=1,j=1,i\neq j}^{c} PiPj(\mu_i - \mu_j)^2}{\sum_{i=1}^{c} Pi\sigma i^2} \tag{3}$$

Inverse Fisher Ratio is being used, the μ_i, σi^2 and P_i are the mean, variant and proportion of the ith class c.

Combined all three methods to set an automatic threshold it means getting average of the formulas as follows:

$$CF = \frac{F1 + \frac{1}{F2} + \frac{1}{F3}}{3} \tag{4}$$

So, the threshold be set by the combination of these Three F1,$\frac{1}{F2}$ and $\frac{1}{F3}$.it will select an optimal number of f features. F1 and $\frac{1}{F2}$ have values in range of [0,1] and $\frac{1}{F3}$ can achieve any positive value.

Now after applying this threshold-cutoff every Ranker will generate its feature sub set means after this step have $S_1, \ldots, S_n$.

Aggregation by Clustering and final combined subset of features. To combined the results of all ranker's purpose mean shift clustering. The main purpose of using mean shift clustering is that it clustered preferences of similar Rankers and does not required priori knowledge of number of clusters and it also provide tradeoff between computational complexity and performance which is the main purpose of it. It is a non-parametric iterative algorithm which is required to locate the modes of density function [27, 28]

$$F(X) = \frac{1}{nh^d} \sum_{i=1}^{n} K\left(\frac{x - x_i}{h}\right) \tag{5}$$

N data-points x_i, i $= 1\ldots\ldots$n in d-dimensionality space, multivariate density estimator with kernel k(x) having window Radius h which means selecting most appeared features in kernel.

Here our focus is only on $k(x) = C_{k,d}K(\| x^2\|)$ with $C_{k,d} > 0$,means featured fall into threshold in every ranker, which ensures that K(x) integrate into one.

$$\nabla f(x) = \frac{2c_{k,d}}{nh^{d+2}} \sum_{i=1}^{n} (x_i - x)g\left(\left\|\frac{x - x_i}{h}\right\|^2\right) \tag{6}$$

$$= \frac{2c_{k,d}}{nh^{d+2}} \left[\sum_{i=1}^{n} g\left(\left\|\frac{x - x_i}{h}\right\|\right)\right] \left[\frac{\sum_{i=1}^{n} x_i g\left(\left\|\frac{x-x_i}{h}\right\|^2\right)}{\sum_{i=1}^{n} g\left(\left\|\frac{x-x_i}{h}\right\|^2\right)} - x\right] \tag{7}$$

The modes are located on zero in ∇ f(x) $= 0$, here assume g(x) $= -$k(x).

The first term is proportional to density estimate at with kernel $G(x) = C_{k,d}g(\| x^2\|)$. the other term is

$$m_{h,g}(x) = \frac{\sum_{i=1}^{n} x_i g\left(\left\|\frac{x-x_i}{h}\right\|^2\right)}{\sum_{i=1}^{n} g\left(\left\|\frac{x-x_i}{h}\right\|^2\right)} - x \tag{8}$$

Is called Mean Shift. It points towards direction of maximum increase in density using above equation one can get mean-shift and translation of kernel G(x) by $m_{h,g(x)}$ which generate uniform kernel.

3.3 EFSCAT

In our novel approach the clustering is being applied to after Ranker block.as using automatic threshold-cutoff which means Rankers will feed clustering with highest and most relevant features Nclu it will definitely reduce the computational cost and also the complexity. If threshold-cutoff not applied then the construction of clustering will become too difficult.

Data sample of dimensionality N_{clu} are the input given to clustering by every Ranker after the input the mean shift clustering identifies the clusters and labeled data sample belongs to same cluster. Mean rank of every feature is used to calculate the centroid.

Now the final subset of features will be generated by using some voting technique like Borda-Count, Weight-Borda account etc.

In Fig. 2 overview of purposed technique is being shown. This technique will make the process of FS more powerful as well as reduce the computational cost as it can be seen in Fig. 2. It is a preprocessing of Classification task which means it will directly improve the process of classification when the classifier only need to search most relevant feature and the time and accuracy of results will increase using our purposed approach. Use of ranking will produce better and fast results then the other methods and by applying fixed or purposed automatic threshold will reduce the size of features which means only highest ranked features will be feed to clustering methods which will then make clusters of similar features and combined them in final subset of feature. Now this feature is only containing most relevant and important features which means the search space is reduced which directly help the process of classification because now the classifier only needs to search this small space which contains no redundant feature.

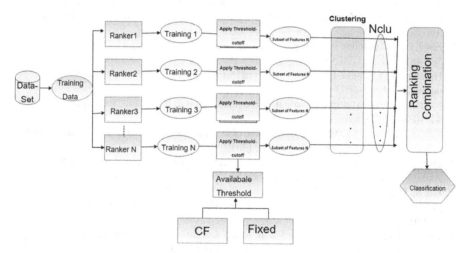

Fig. 2. Overview of the proposed EFSCAT

4   Conclusion and Future Work

In this novel approach "EFSCAT" use a heterogeneous approach so that the results of one base learner do not hijack overall results and dependency of data set reduced. If one base learner is not work fine with training data then there are other base learners. Use Ranking method in our technique to produce ordinal ranking in every ranker. To reduce the dataset, use automatic and also fixed threshold cutoff which is a new concept In Ranking and then to combine the result of these rankers. The use of threshold has 2 basic advantages 1) is selects the best top features from every ranker 2) it reduces the dataset's size which directly improve the classification process. Used Mean shift clustering because it does not require prior knowledge of number of clusters which means the clusters will be develop on spot and depends upon dataset and threshold cut-off. Due to use of Threshold and clustering this technique will produce better and most relevant results which will reduce the computation cost and reduce the chance of error. To take centroid whole dataset is required but, in this technique, take centroid on the base of dataset cutoff by threshold which could change the results.

In future we will test our approach against artificial and real-world datasets and compare results with existed not just ensemble FS technique but also with single FS methods. We will also use different type of base learner which support ranking like Filters, Wrappers and Embedded. Automatic threshold will be testing on different dataset.

References

1. Kozodoi, N., et al.: A multi-objective approach for profit-driven feature selection in credit scoring. Decis. Support Syst. **120**, 106–117 (2019)
2. Sayed, G.I., Hassanien, A.E., Azar, A.T.: Feature selection via a novel chaotic crow search algorithm. Neural Comput. Appl. **31**(1), 171–188 (2017). https://doi.org/10.1007/s00521-017-2988-6
3. Zhou, P., et al.: Online streaming feature selection using adapted neighborhood rough set. Inf. Sci. **481**, 258–279 (2019)
4. Hussain, A., Cambria, E.: Semi-supervised learning for big social data analysis. Neurocomputing **275**, 1662–1673 (2018)
5. Fierrez, J., et al.: Multiple classifiers in biometrics. part 2: trends and challenges. Inf. Fusion **44**, 103–112 (2018)
6. Drotár, P., Gazda, M., Vokorokos, L.: Ensemble feature selection using election methods and ranker clustering. Inf. Sci. **480**, 365–380 (2019)
7. Oskouei, M.D., Razavi, S.N.: An ensemble feature selection method to detect web spam. Asia-Pac. J. Inf. Technol. Multi. **7**(2), 99–133 (2018)
8. Gu, S., Cheng, R., Jin, Y.: Feature selection for high-dimensional classification using a competitive swarm optimizer. Soft. Comput. **22**(3), 811–822 (2016). https://doi.org/10.1007/s00500-016-2385-6
9. Chormunge, S., Jena, S.: Correlation based feature selection with clustering for high dimensional data. J. Electr. Syst. Inf. Technol. **5**(3), 542–549 (2018)
10. Gao, W., et al.: Feature selection considering the composition of feature relevancy. Pattern Recogn. Lett. **112**, 70–74 (2018)
11. Cilia, N.D., et al.: A ranking-based feature selection approach for handwritten character recognition. Pattern Recogn. Lett. **121**, 77–86 (2019)
12. Bermejo, S.: Ensembles of wrappers for automated feature selection in fish age classification. Comput. Electron. Agric. **134**, 27–32 (2017)
13. Panday, D., de Amorim, R.C., Lane, P.: Feature weighting as a tool for unsupervised feature selection. Inf. Process. Lett. **129**, 44–52 (2018)
14. Bolón-Canedo, V., Alonso-Betanzos, A.: Ensembles for feature selection: a review and future trends. Inf. Fusion **52**, 1–12 (2019)
15. Tüysüzoğlu, G., Yaslan, Y.: Sparse coding based classifier ensembles in supervised and active learning scenarios for data classification. Expert Syst. Appl. **91**, 364–373 (2018)
16. Pes, B., Dessì, N., Angioni, M.: Exploiting the ensemble paradigm for stable feature selection: a case study on high-dimensional genomic data. Inf. Fusion **35**, 132–147 (2017)
17. Seijo-Pardo, B., et al.: Ensemble feature selection: homogeneous and heterogeneous approaches. Knowl.-Based Syst. **118**, 124–139 (2017)

18. Seijo-Pardo, B., Bolón-Canedo, V., Alonso-Betanzos, A.: On developing an automatic threshold applied to feature selection ensembles. Inf. Fusion **45**, 227–245 (2019)
19. Liu, K., et al.: Rough set based semi-supervised feature selection via ensemble selector. Knowl.-Based Syst. **165**, 282–296 (2019)
20. Chiew, K.L., et al.: A new hybrid ensemble feature selection framework for machine learning-based phishing detection system. Inf. Sci. **484**, 153–166 (2019)
21. Manbari, Z., AkhlaghianTab, F., Salavati, C.: Hybrid fast unsupervised feature selection for high-dimensional data. Expert Syst. Appl. **124**, 97–118 (2019)
22. Saha, A., Das, S.: Clustering of fuzzy data and simultaneous feature selection: a model selection approach. Fuzzy Sets Syst. **340**, 1–37 (2018)
23. Wang, Y., Feng, L.: Hybrid feature selection using component co-occurrence based feature relevance measurement. Expert Syst. Appl. **102**, 83–99 (2018)
24. Sahu, B., Dehuri, S., Jagadev, A.K.: Feature selection model based on clustering and ranking in pipeline for microarray data. Inform. Med. Unlocked **9**, 107–122 (2017)
25. Das, A.K., Das, S., Ghosh, A.: Ensemble feature selection using bi-objective genetic algorithm. Knowl.-Based Syst. **123**, 116–127 (2017)
26. Yan, Y., et al.: LSTM $^{}$: multi-label ranking for document classification. Neural Process. Lett. **47**(1), 117–138 (2018)
27. Myhre, J.N., et al.: Robust clustering using a kNN mode seeking ensemble. Pattern Recogn. **76**, 491–505 (2018)
28. Xia, X., Lin, T., Chen, Z.: Maximum relevancy maximum complementary based ordered aggregation for ensemble pruning. Appl. Intell. **48**(9), 2568–2579 (2017). https://doi.org/10.1007/s10489-017-1106-x

Fuzzy Logic-Based COVID-19 and Other Respiratory Conditions Pre-clinical Diagnosis System

M. G. Orozco-del-Castillo[1,2], R. A. Novelo-Cruz[1,2],
J. J. Hernández-Gómez[2,3(✉)], P. A. Mena-Zapata[1,2], E. Brito-Borges[1,2],
A. E. Álvarez-Pacheco[1,2], A. E. García-Gutiérrez[4], and G. A. Yáñez-Casas[3,5]

[1] Tecnológico Nacional de México/IT de Mérida,
Departamento de Sistemas y Computación, Mrida, Mexico
[2] AAAI Student Chapter at Yucatán, México (AAAIMX),
Association for the Advancement of Artificial Intelligence, Mérida, Mexico
[3] Instituto Politécnico Nacional, Centro de Desarrollo Aeroespacial,
Mexico City, Mexico
jjhernandezgo@ipn.mx
[4] Instituto Politécnico Nacional,
Unidad Profesional Interdisciplinaria de Ingeniería y Tecnologías Avanzadas,
Mexico City, Mexico
[5] Instituto Politécnico Nacional, Escuela Superior de Ingeniería Mecánica y Eléctrica
Unidad Zacatenco, Sección de Estudios de Posgrado e Investigación,
Mexico City, Mexico

Abstract. The COVID-19 disease, caused by a new coronavirus known
as SARS-CoV-2, has recently emerged and caused the death of thousands
of persons all around the world. One of the main issues with the disease
has been, on one hand, the saturation of the medical personnel, and on
the other, the untimely search of medical attention by patients who could
confuse the symptoms with other common respiratory conditions with
similar symptomatology. Since AI approaches based on machine learning
depend on large training datasets, currently neither easily accessible nor
reliable, a COVID-19 pre-clinical diagnosis system using a fuzzy inference
system is constructed, which is also capable of contrasting it with other
respiratory conditions, particularly allergies, common cold and influenza.
With the use of this fuzzy inference system, complex decisions in the
medical field could be able to be determined more effectively.

Keywords: SARS-CoV-2 · Coronavirus · COVID-19 · Fuzzy logic ·
Artificial intelligence · Diagnostics · Pre-clinic · Fuzzy inference
system · Disease · Infectious · Respiratory · Symptoms · Assessment ·
Alergies · Influenza · Common cold

1 Introduction

Coronaviruses are RNA viruses belonging to the *Coronaviridae* family capable
of causing respiratory diseases of varying severity, from what is known as the

© Springer Nature Switzerland AG 2020
M. F. Mata-Rivera et al. (Eds.): WITCOM 2020, CCIS 1280, pp. 402–419, 2020.
https://doi.org/10.1007/978-3-030-62554-2_29

common cold, to more serious conditions such as fatal pneumonia. Many Coronaviruses cause respiratory, gastrointestinal, liver and neurological diseases in animals, however, so far only seven Coronaviruses capable of causing disease in humans are known. In December 2019, a new Coronavirus known as SARSCoV-2 was identified in the Wuhan province, China, causing the so-called COVID-19 disease [1,2]. Although this disease has a low basic reproduction rate ($R_0 \sim 2.3$) compared to infectious diseases such as measles and chickenpox [3], this human-to-human transmission capacity has been sufficient to spread COVID-19 globally [4]. The World Health Organisation (WHO) recognised it as a global pandemic and has reported, as of August 31st, 2020, 25,118,689 confirmed cases and 844,312 deaths worldwide [5].

Some symptoms associated with COVID-19 include fever, dry cough, sore throat, nasal congestion, malaise, headache, muscle pain and, in more severe cases, shortness of breath [6], which makes them very similar to those presented by other respiratory conditions such as common cold [7], allergies caused by allergens in the air [8] and influenza (flu) [9]. These similarities complicate the correct diagnosis of the disease and consequently the determination of the medical attention necessary for treatment [9,10].

In recent years, medical diagnosis has drawn attention from areas outside of medicine, such as mathematics [11,12] and computer science, including artificial intelligence (AI) [13–16], and in particular machine learning [17,18]. However, AI applications based on machine learning approaches usually require very large datasets to be trained. As of today, there are no datasets of this nature publicly available, and due to the burden imposed by the pandemic on the healthcare institutions, the data related to the symptoms of confirmed cases of COVID-19 is not very reliable. Since the publication of the original fuzzy logic (FL) proposal in 1965 [19], fuzzy set theory has been applied to many fields where uncertainty plays an important role [20]. In this way, FL has proven to be a powerful tool in decision-making systems, such as expert and pattern classification systems [21]. The field of medicine has been one of the best exponents due to the prominent presence of vague concepts and situations, with linguistic uncertainties, of diagnosis, of measurement, prone to subjectivity, etc., being even considered as an area that oscillates between art and science [20]. Within this field, statistical uncertainty can be handled very rigorously, however non-statistical uncertainty remains a challenge [22]. An example of this situation is described in [20], regarding the concept of "high" attributed to the blood pressure of a patient. High pressure varies 1) between patients, (for example, hypotonic and hypertonic), 2) between experts and 3) depending on the medical context (for example, during anesthesia a pressure considered as high may be considered normal in another context). FL is particularly appropriate for medical diagnosis care because it involves a large amount of uncertain and inconsistent information [23], and this has led to the development of various fuzzy expert diagnostic systems [16,23–26].

This paper describes a methodology for the development of a tool that assists in the COVID-19 diagnosis process, particularly supporting situations in which other respiratory conditions could appear instead, particularly allergic rhinitis, common cold and influenza. This tool consists of a Fuzzy Inference System (FIS) based on the Mamdani model [27]. The organization of this article is as follows: Section 2 describes the theoretical foundations of FL, as well as the respiratory conditions under study: COVID-19, allergies, common cold and influenza. In Section 3 the symptoms reported for the mentioned respiratory conditions are presented, as well as the methodology for the development of the FIS. Section 4 shows the results obtained, and finally, Section 5 presents the conclusions of the work.

2   Theoretical Background

In this section, the four respiratory conditions in question are briefly presented, and the theoretical foundations of FL are detailed, as well as some studies that report the use of these concepts in medical diagnosis applications.

2.1   Respiratory Conditions

This section will briefly describe the respiratory conditions studied during this paper in addition to COVID-19: allergies caused by airborne allergens, common cold, and influenza.

Allergies: A large number of aerosols are constantly circulating in the air, of which the most important components are allergens, substances of biological origin that, when entering the human body, promote the induction of the immune response with the subsequent development of an allergic disease [28]. The most common diseases caused by airborne allergens are rhinitis and allergic conjunctivitis [29]. Rhinitis, defined as inflammation of the nasal mucosa, can be caused by allergic, non-allergic, infectious, hormonal, and occupational factors, among others [30]. Allergic rhinitis is a very common condition, affecting between 10 and 25% of the world population, however, in severe cases it has been associated with significant impairments in quality of life, sleep and job performance [31]. Although the term rhinitis implies inflammation of the nasal mucosal membranes, as a clinical term it refers to a heterogeneous group of nasal disorders characterized by one or more of the following symptoms: sneezing, nasal itching, rhinorrhea, and nasal congestion [32], although a chronic cough may be present as well [33]. In what follows, for simplicity, diseases caused by airborne allergens will be considered simply as allergies.

Common Cold: Common cold is the conventional term for an acute viral infection of the upper respiratory tract involving the nose, sinuses, pharynx, and larynx [7]. Although there are a large number of viruses associated with common cold, the most common are rhinoviruses [10]. The virus is spread by direct contact with the secretions of an infected person or by aerosolizing the secretions. In most cases the diagnosis is simple based on symptoms [10], and can be made by adult patients autonomously [34]. The clinical manifestations of common cold include sore throat, runny and stuffy nose, sneezing, cough, headache and malaise [7,10,34,35]. It is not possible to identify the particular virus that causes common cold based on symptoms, because similar symptoms are caused by different viruses [36].

Influenza: Influenza, or flu, is a respiratory infection in mammals and birds caused by an RNA virus divided into three main types (A, B, and C) that has coexisted with humans for more than 400 years [37]. Influenza causes an acute febrile illness associated with myalgia, headache, and cough [9]. Not much is known about the transmission of influenza [37], however it appears to be transmitted by the spread of droplets in the air [9]. It is a very common disease, yet it contributes significantly to global mortality and morbidity [37]. The symptoms of patients with influenza are similar to those of common cold, but the former are generally more serious than the latter [7].

As previously mentioned, the diagnosis of these conditions can be complicated because the symptoms often overlap each other [7]. For example, allergic rhinitis can sometimes mimic common cold [34], common cold can mimic influenza [7,9], influenza can mimic COVID-19 [38], and so on.

2.2   Fuzzy Logic (FL)

FL as a theory was initially developed by Zadeh in 1965 [19] as an alternative to represent and manipulate knowledge that by its nature is inaccurate, imprecise, ambiguous, vague or uncertain. FL arises in response to the demand for approaches to manipulate non-statistical uncertainty. The initial enthusiasm of fuzzy sets was associated with their ability to model linguistic expressions and terms, promising to bring closer automatic reasoning and human thinking, which until then had only been associated with the computation of predicates [20]. At first, fuzzy sets were considered as part of rule-based expert systems with the intention of solving the problem of the lack of flexibility of traditional AI systems [18]. Because most of the areas where the human being intervenes has some or all of these characteristics, FL and its applications have taken on great importance in different areas, such as economic [39], social [40], industrial [41–44], politics [45], among others [46].

The product normally considered final in an FL-based application is the so-called FIS that, from different discrete or fuzzy inputs, infers data and knowledge in a similar way to how humans do, providing at the end an output of that process of inference. The basic structure of a FIS basically consists of three components [47]: a set of rules, a database, and a reasoning mechanism, and they are usually classified as Mamdani, Pedrycs or Takagi-Sugeno [46] FISs. The main difference between these classes is related to the nature of the inputs and outputs of the system. In Mamdani-type FISs, there is an if-then rule base that is used to map the sets of fuzzy inputs to equally fuzzy outputs. Pedrycs-type FISs encode associations between linguistic terms in both domains using fuzzy relationships. Finally, FISs of the Takagi- Sugeno type are commonly used when a discrete output is required, because their output membership functions are linear or constant [43, 48].

Regardless of the used FIS, fuzzy inference is a fundamental stage of development. The purpose of this inference is to interpret the input values and assign output values through a set of fuzzy rules based on the associated membership functions. For the operation of this stage, it is necessary to carry out a process of conversion of the input values into fuzzy values, in a process known as fuzzification. This information is used to combine membership functions with fuzzy rules and get a fuzzy output. Since the outputs of a FIS must normally be discrete, this output is made discrete through a defuzzification process.

2.3 Applications of Fuzzy Logic

In this section some studies related to the application of FL in medical diagnosis are mentioned.

In [26] a method is described to use soft fuzzy sets in the decision process by integrating an analysis of fuzzy preference relationships, which is validated with an application and implementation of medical diagnosis. In [23] Pythagorean fuzzy sets are used as part of an algorithm to solve medical diagnosis problems. This algorithm was tested, based on the symptoms presented, for the diagnosis of two different examples, the first for the possible diagnoses: viral fever, malaria, typhoid, stomach problem and chest problem; the second for: stress, ulcer, vision problem, spinal problem and blood pressure, with favorable results. In [25] a new approach to medical diagnosis with the symptoms of a disease is proposed using intuitionistic fuzzy sets with new operators. In [16] the authors propose new notions of X for intuitionist fuzzy sets and apply them to medical diagnosis to investigate a patient's diseases from their symptoms. The obtained results are better compared to ten other existing methods of medical diagnosis.

Some of the efforts to create diagnostic systems have also focused on respiratory conditions. For example in [24, 49] knowledge-based systems are presented to automate the diagnosis of allergic rhinitis. An application similar to the one presented in the present work is shown in [50], where the authors construct an example of a FL-based system for the pre-clinical diagnosis of severe acute respiratory syndrome (SARS), a disease similar to COVID-19: both caused by Coronavirus, both emerging in Asia and expanded to other continents, and with very similar symptoms between them. Some other efforts to diagnose COVID-19 using AI include diagnosis based on changes in voice sound due to conditions present in the respiratory system [51].

3 Development/Methodology

3.1 The Problem of Fuzzy Medical Diagnosis

The medical diagnosis problem can be formalized as follows. Let $D = \{D_1, D_2, ..., D_N\}$ be a set of N possible diagnoses in the context of a certain medical problem. Let $\mathbf{x}$ be the description of a patient in the form of an n-dimensional vector $\mathbf{x} = [x_1, ..., x_n] \in \mathbb{R}^n$; the components of $\mathbf{x}$ represent the characteristics, that is, the clinical measurements of the patient. A classical classifier C [20] is any mapping

$$C : \mathbb{R}^n \rightarrow D , \tag{1}$$

that is, for each object $\mathbf{x} \in \mathbb{R}^n$, the classifier assigns a class label or medical diagnosis. Diffuse diagnosis is characterized by the fact that classifier C depends not only on discrete sets, but also on fuzzy sets to solve the diagnostic problem [20]. In this sense, a fuzzy classifier $\tilde{C}$ performs the mapping

$$\tilde{C} : \mathbb{R}^n \rightarrow [0, 1]^M , \tag{2}$$

that is to say,

$$\tilde{C}(\mathbf{x}) = [\mu_1(\mathbf{x}), ..., \mu_N(\mathbf{x})] , \tag{3}$$

where $\mu_i(x)$ denotes the degree to which $\mathbf{x}$ belongs to the class, or diagnosis, D_i. This value can be interpreted in various ways [20], such as typicality, severity, support or probability. A more detailed discussion is presented in [52]. When a particular diagnosis is required, the diagnosis with the highest value is commonly used, which is known as the maximum membership rule:

$$\tilde{C}(\mathbf{x}) = D_j \in D \Leftrightarrow \mu_j(\mathbf{x}) = \max_i \mu_i(\mathbf{x}) . \tag{4}$$

In this work, fuzzy sets are used in two different stages of the classifier, both as fuzzy inputs to the system as well as in the fuzzy reasoning process.

3.2 Collection of Symptomatological Data

COVID-19: Due to the recent appearance of COVID-19, there are not many studies that report in detail the existing symptoms, however, there seems to be consistency between the main symptoms of the disease: high fever, cough, and shortness of breath [2,4,38,53–55]. It is important to consider that symptoms may take several days to manifest (between 4 and 5, normally, although it can extend up to 14). The WHO presented statistical data based on 55,924 laboratory-confirmed cases [55], showing that the most important symptoms are fever (87.9%), dry cough (67.7%) and fatigue (38.1%). The compilation of the symptoms reported in these works is presented in Table 1, where the symptoms are reported according to their frequency of appearance as: common (C), unusual (U), present (P). In those cases where statistical data are reported, the percentages are shown in parentheses.

Allergies: The review of the symptoms reported by diseases caused by allergens in the air also shows consistency between the main symptoms: nasal congestion, rhinorrhea, and sneezing [8,30,35,38,56,57]. Less frequently, symptoms such as cough, shortness of breath, sore throat, fatigue, and headache also occur [8,35]. The compilation of the symptoms reported in these works is presented in Table 2, where the same notation of Table 1 is used.

Table 1. Reported symptomatology for COVID-19.

Symptom	Reference					
	[53]	[55]	[4]	[2]	[54]	[38]
Cough	P	P (67.7%)	P (76.0%)	P	C	C
Difficulty breathing	P	P (18.6%)		P		C
Fever (high)	P	P (87.9%)	P (98.0%)	P	C	C
Shaking chills	P	P (11.4%)				
Myalgia	P	P (14.8%)		P	U	C
Sore throat	P	P (13.9%)			U	U
Loss of appetite and smell	P				U	U
Fatigue		P (38.1%)		P	C	
Sputum production		P (33.4%)				
Nasal congestion		P (4.8%)				U
Nasal congestion		P (13.6%)			U	U
Nausea/vomiting		P (5.0%)				
Diarrhea		P (3.7%)	P (3.0%)		U	U
Discomfort			P			
Rhinorrhea						U

Table 2. Reported symptomatology for allergies.

Symptom	Reference					
	[35]	[8]	[56]	[57]	[30]	[38]
Cough	U	P				
Difficulty breathing		P				
Sore throat	U					
Fatigue	U					
Nasal congestion	C		C	P	P	C
Headache	U					
Rhinorrhea	C	P	C	P	P	C
Sneezing	C	P	C	P	P	C

Common Cold: The review of the reported symptoms for common cold shows a greater diversity of symptoms, but particularly cough, sore throat, nasal congestion, rhinorrhea and sneezing, and less frequently fever, myalgia, fatigue, and headache [7,10,34,35,38,58]. One characteristic of common cold is that, when fever is present, it is less intense than in COVID-19 and influenza (Sect. 3.3). In a study of 272 patients with a sore throat associated with upper respiratory diseases, the mean aural temperature was 36.8 °C [10]. The symptomatology reported in these works is presented in Table 3, where the notation from previous tables is used.

Table 3. Reported symptomatology for common cold.

Symptom	Reference					
	[35]	[34]	[7]	[10]	[58]	[38]
Cough	C	C	C	U	C	C
Fever (low)	U	U	U	U	U	U
Myalgia	U	U			U	U
Sore throat	C	C	C	P	P	C
Fatigue	U	U			U	
Nasal congestion	C	C		P	P	C
Headache	U	U		P	U	
Discomfort		U	C		P	
Rhinorrhea	C	C	C	P	P	U
Sneezing	C	C	P	P	P	

Table 4. Reported symptomatology for influenza.

Symptom	Reference					
	[35]	[7]	[10]	[9]	[58]	[38]
Cough	C	P	P (84.9%)	P	P	C
Fever (high)	C	P	P (84.7%)	P	P	C
Myalgia	C	P	P (58.1%)	P	P	C
Sore throat	U		P (49.0%)		P	U
Loss of appetite and smell			P			U
Fatigue	C		P		P	
Nasal congestion	U		P			U
Headache	C	P	P (66.5%)	P	P	U
Diarrhea			P (13.0%)			U
Discomfort		P			P	
Rhinorrhea	U		P (50.1%)		U	U
Sneezing	U				P	

Influenza: Symptoms reported for influenza are similar to those of COVID-19: cough, high fever, and myalgia. Unlike COVID-19, influenza tends to present more commonly with a headache, but does not usually present the difficulty of breathing that is typical of COVID-19. Other symptoms that occur less frequently include loss of appetite or smell, fatigue, nasal congestion, diarrhea, malaise, rhinorrhea, and sneezing [7,9,10,38,53,58]. Symptoms of influenza are similar to those of common cold, but these tend to manifest more intensely [7], and myalgia occurs more commonly in influenza than in common cold [34]. Symptoms for influenza are presented in Table 4, where the notation from previous tables is used.

3.3   Design of the Fuzzy Inference System (FIS)

In accordance with what is described in Sect. 3.1, the set of possible diagnoses is given by the set $D = \{D_C, D_A, D_{CC}, D_I\}$, where D_C represents the diagnosis of COVID-19, D_A that of a disease caused by allergies, D_{CC} for common cold, and D_I for influenza. Based on the symptomatological analysis described in Sect. 3.2, different variables relevant to the diagnosis of respiratory diseases were determined in the study; these variables, together with an identifier for each, are: 1) fever (Fe), 2) headache (H), 3) myalgia (M), 4) fatigue (Fa), 5) nasal congestion (NC), 6) sneezing (S), 7) sore throat (ST), 8) difficulty breathing (DB), and 9) rhinorrhea (R). The symptomatological description of a particular patient is given by a 9-dimensional $\mathbf{x}$ vector with measurements of the intensity of each symptom. The elements of $\mathbf{x}$ are given as:

$$x_i \in \begin{cases} [0, 1] & i \neq 1 \\ [36, 41] & i = 1 \end{cases}, \tag{5}$$

that is, the domain for the linguistic variable "fever" is given by real numbers between 36 and 41 (a range that defines the possible body temperature of a patient in °C), and for all other cases by numbers between 0 and 1 (higher values represent a greater intensity of the symptom, and vice versa). The 9 components of the vector $\mathbf{x}$ represent the inputs of the FIS that acts as the classifier $\tilde{C}(\mathbf{x})$ (Eq. (3)), which has 4 outputs, $\mu_C(\mathbf{x})$, $\mu_A(\mathbf{x})$, $\mu_{CC}(\mathbf{x})$, and $\mu_I(\mathbf{x})$, which denote the degree to which $\mathbf{x}$ belongs to each class, or diagnosis, of the set D, 1) COVID-19, 2) allergies, 3) common cold and 4) influenza, respectively. This design is described in Fig. 1. Although cough is a widely reported symptom for COVID-19, in this work it does not have diagnostic utility since it is also a common symptom in common cold and influenza, and is unnecessary to contrast these conditions with allergies, fever being a more effective discriminator.

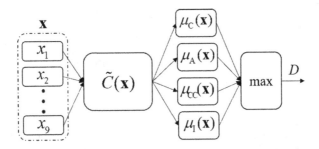

Fig. 1. Structure of the developed FIS. The corresponding values of the 9 symptoms make up the inputs, the vector $\mathbf{x}$, of the FIS that acts as a classifier, $\tilde{C}(\mathbf{x})$. The 4 outputs of the FIS correspond to the different memberships of the potential diagnoses of COVID-19 ($\mu_C(\mathbf{x})$), allergies ($\mu_A(\mathbf{x})$), common cold ($\mu_{CC}(\mathbf{x})$) and influenza ($\mu_I(\mathbf{x})$), respectively. These outputs are evaluated according to the maximum membership rule to determine the resulting diagnosis, D.

The methodology for the design of the FIS consists of three stages:

1. Define linguistic variables that represent inputs and outputs of the FIS.
2. Establish the fuzzy sets that can take these variables, together with the parameters of the membership functions that represent them.
3. Define if-then fuzzy inference rules to relate the input variables (symptoms) to the output variables (possible D_i diagnosis).

The process for defining linguistic variables and values, membership function parameters, and fuzzy inference rules is iterative and non-linear.

Each linguistic variable that represents each of the symptoms has associated different linguistic values according to the symptoms reported in Sect. 3.2. These linguistic values, together with the type of membership function that represents them and their respective parameters, are shown in Table 5. The choice of these functions, as well as the determination of their parameters, was carried out empirically based on the analysis of literature previously reported. The outputs of the system can be understood as the possible "memberships" to each of the four conditions, represented by values between 0 and 1. These output variables were assigned 4 possible linguistic values to each: 1) unlikely (U), possible (Po), probable (Pr) and very probable (VP). The final diagnosis is calculated as the maximum of each of the FIS outputs, according to Eq. (4).

Table 5. FIS Database, including the different variables and linguistic values, the type (S - Sigmoidal and GB - Generalised Bell) and the parameters of the membership functions (MF) for each set.

ID	Linguistic values and parameters of MF		
Fe	No (S)	Mild (CG)	Severe (S)
	[−13.5, 37]	[0.587, 3.28, 38.3]	[11.76, 39.1]
H, M, NC	No (S)		
DB, R, S	[−30, 0.3]		
Fa	No (S) [−64.3, 0.2]		
ST	No (S)	Mild (CG)	Severe (S)
	[−30, 0.3]	[0.24, 3.3, 0.46]	[31.5, 0.67]
Membership	U (S)	Po (CG) Pr (CG)	VP (S)
	[−50, 0.2]	[0.14, 2.5, 0.33] [0.14, 2.5, 0.66]	[50, 0.8]

Table 6. Inference rules (R) used for the FIS.

R	Antecedent	Consequent
1	Fe(No)∧ST(No)	Co(U), Al(VP), CC(U), In(U)
2	Fe(No)∧ST(Mild)	Co(U), CC(U), In(VP)
3	Fe(S)∧DC(¬No)∧M(¬No) ∧Fa(¬No)∧DB(No)	Co(U), Al(U), In(VP)
4	Fe(S)∧DB(¬No)	Co(VP), Al(U), CC(U)
5	Fe(Mild)∧DB(¬No)	Co(Pr)
6	Fe(Leve)∧NC(¬No)∧S(¬No)∧ ST(¬No)∧DB(No)∧R(¬No)	CC(VP)
7	Fe(¬No)∧H(¬No)∧M(¬No) ∧Fa(¬No)∧DB(¬No)	In(VP)
8	Fe(Mild)∧DB(No)	CC(Pr), In(Po)
9	Fe(S)∧H(¬No)∧M(¬No) ∧Fa(¬No)∧DB(¬No)	Co(VP), Al(U), CC(U), In(U)
10	Fe(No)∧ST(S)	Co(U), Al(U), Re(VP), In(U)

The medical diagnosis system uses fuzzy if-then rules designed to classify the different combinations of symptoms for the conditions studied (COVID-19, allergies, common cold, and influenza). The creation of such rules, as well as the selection of the symptoms they represent, was carried out based on the analysis of the respective symptomatology. A total of 10 inference rules were established, which are shown in Table 6.

3.4 Fuzzy Inference System (FIS)

A FIS consists mainly of three components: 1) a set of rules, 2) a database, and 3) a reasoning mechanism. For the developed FIS, the database is shown in Table 5, the set of rules in Table 6, and the reasoning mechanism is described below.

Because the outputs of the FIS are variable with fuzzy values (VP, Pr, Po and U), the natural choice is a Mamdani-type FIS, particularly useful in the design of medical diagnosis systems [59]. For each rule, the data of a patient P_j, given by a vector $\mathbf{x_j}$, are evaluated in the membership functions of the antecedents, which is known as fuzzification. Once all the antecedents of a given rule have been fuzzified, the fuzzy operation defined for the conjunction is applied, in this case the minimum (because the disjunction operator is not used in the rules described in Table 6), the same operator used for fuzzy implication. This process is repeated for the 10 rules and for the 4 outputs, to later calculate the aggregation of each of the results using the operation of adding the areas. The resulting areas are defuzzified based on their respective centroid; these centroids form the output values of the FIS. To determine the final diagnosis, the maximum of these 4 outputs is calculated (Eq. (4)), as shown in Fig. 1. Finally, the reasoning mechanism of the system, under these considerations, is illustrated in Fig. 2.

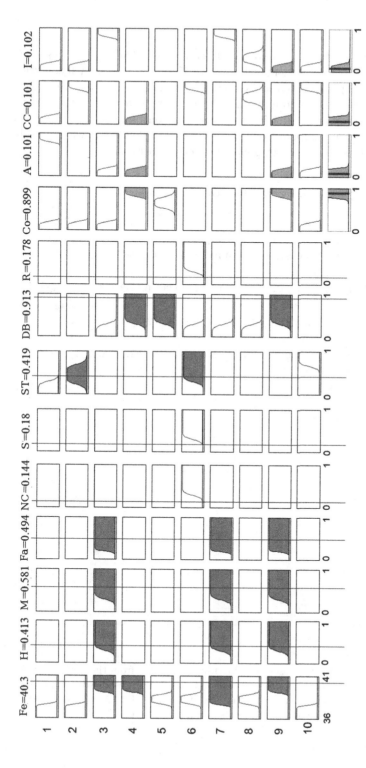

Fig. 2. Diagram illustrating the reasoning mechanism of the system. Each row represents one of the 10 rules of inference on which the system is based. The first 9 columns represent the inputs, or the intensity of the symptoms, while the last 4 represent the outputs, or the possible diagnoses. The case of patient P1 is illustrated, according to the data shown in Table 7, which results in a diagnosis of COVID-19.

4   Results

Table 7 shows the results obtained for five different cases. The first four cases, P_1–P_4, represent hypothetical patients with "typical" symptoms for each condition. The last case corresponds to patients diagnosed with COVID-19. P_5 represents one of the first patients diagnosed with COVID-19, reported in [2], showing the following symptoms consistent with the variables considered for the diagnosis using the system: body temperature of 38.4 °C, with weakness and with difficulty in breathing. These results are graphically observed in Fig. 3.

Table 7. Results obtained from the system.

Patient	D_C	D_A	D_{CC}	D_I	Classif.
P_1	0.899	0.101	0.101	0.102	Dx_1:
$x_1 = [40.28, 0.4128, 0.5805, 0.4942, 0.1437, 0.1802, 0.4195, 0.9128, 0.1782]$					COVID-19
P_2	0.108	0.899	0.219	0.106	Dx_2:
$x_2 = [36.78, 0.1105, 0.08621, 0.1453, 0.8563, 0.8314, 0.1437, 0.5523, 0.6264]$					Allergy
P_3	0.265	0.115	0.783	0.312	Dx_3:
$x_3 = [37.7, 0.3779, 0.3161, 0.1686, 0.9138, 0.8779, 0.8563, 0.2151, 0.9138]$					CC
P_4	0.113	0.102	0.227	0.896	Dx_4:
$x_4 = [40.22, 0.8779, 0.8908, 0.9012, 0.3046, 0.1337, 0.4425, 0.1221, 0.4655]$					Influenza
P_5	0.659	0.269	0.262	0.202	Dx_5:
$x_5 = [38.4, 0, 0, 1, 0, 0, 0, 1, 0]$					COVID-19

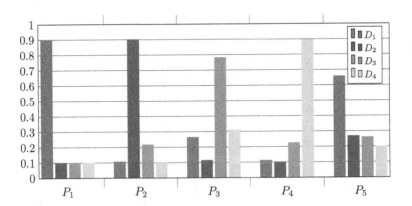

Fig. 3. The results of the diagnoses generated by the system from the data in Table 7. The first four patients ($P_1, \cdots, P_4$) represent hypothetical cases showing typical presentations of the four conditions studied in this study, COVID-19, allergies, cold and influenza, respectively. Patient P_5 represents a real case of COVID-19.

The developed system was initially launched on March 28, 2020 at the URL COVID-19 Assistant for use by patients in Mexico [60], particularly. The main objectives of its launch were 1) to avoid unnecessary care of patients with a low probability of suffering from COVID-19 to health systems in constant saturation, and 2) to avoid the delay in the search for medical care by patients with a high probability of suffering from COVID-19 or some other respiratory infections that could be fatal in high-risk patients. The developed system is hosted on the website of the International Student Chapter of Artificial Intelligence AAAIMX, of the Association for the Advancement of Artificial Intelligence (AAAI). The application consumes an API developed in Python hosted on Heroku, which processes requests for each diagnosis and returns the response corresponding to each type of condition, along with essential prevention and care information for the public about the SARS-CoV-2 virus and COVID-19. Until August 31st, 2020, the system has been used to perform 11,040 diagnoses, of which 630 correspond to COVID-19, 5,130 to allergies, 2,730 to common cold and 2,550 to influenza.

Since there are no reliable datasets at the moment reporting the symptomatology of confirmed COVID-19 cases, and how negative ones could correspond to allergies, influenza or common cold, it is extremely difficult to validate the efficiency of this system, as is the case with other expert systems with no available validation data [61]. Furthermore, at the time of publication of this article, efforts to contact local sanitary authorities to obtain official datasets were unsuccessful. However, this tool could be extremely useful in the screening (pre-diagnosis) process, supporting the healthcare systems to rank cases based on the likelihood of presenting COVID-19. Once the worldwide medical crisis due to the SARS-CoV-2 virus is controlled, and reliable datasets become available, other approaches based on machine learning techniques could prove useful, and expert systems such as the one presented in this work, could be properly validated and refined.

5   Conclusions

This work describes the development of a pre-clinical medical diagnosis system for COVID-19 and other respiratory conditions with similar symptoms: allergies, common cold and influenza; the FIS, based on the Mamdani model, has 9 inputs and 4 outputs, corresponding to the four conditions studied. Symptom data of these four conditions and diagnostic rules reported in the literature were collected to determine both the fuzzy if-then rules, and the set of membership functions necessary to represent the linguistic values of the different linguistic variables associated with each symptom. Based on the collected information, 9 variables were established whose values determine the intensity of each symptom and are the inputs for the FIS. The final diagnosis is obtained through the maximum membership rule (see Eq. (4)).

Carrying out medical diagnosis in an automatic or semi-automatic manner is a task that presents a lot of uncertainty and a high responsibility. However, the results presented in this article reflect the capacity of AI-based systems, particularly in FL, to support medical experts in the diagnosis of different conditions. The proposed system, based on opinion and studies reported by experts, allows measurements of qualitative variables and operations with them, allowing for pre-clinical diagnoses that can help minimise uncertainty at the time of professional medical diagnosis.

It is important to emphasize that this type of system can be very useful for the support, but not the definitive replacement, of a professional medical diagnosis, and that the confirmation of suffering from COVID-19 must be carried out by means of the complete sequencing of the genome and the phylogenetic analysis in the bronchoalveolar lavage fluid [62].

It is worth mentioning that some efforts have already been reported to diagnose COVID-19 based on AI [63], however, they require obtaining computed tomography of the chest for its diagnosis, which implies infrastructure that is difficult to access several regions. As explained before, this system, in comparison with AI applications based on machine learning, does not require a large dataset to be trained, particularly since information about symptoms of confirmed COVID-19 cases is neither widely available nor reliable. In this sense, the present work presents advantages in terms of the number of people potentially benefited.

Finally, this tool aims to be a useful reference in the latin-american region, since some mathematical models expect a second outbreak of the SARS-CoV2 virus located between the end of 2019 and the beginning of 2021, which is potentially dangerous in countries of the northern hemisphere due to at the beginning of the autumn-winter time, parallel to the seasonal influenza season, which will multiply cases of common cold, influenza and COVID-19 simultaneously, so it is essential to have support tools, especially in regions with a strong saturation in their health systems due to the prolonged and intense pandemic during 2020.

Acknowledgements. This work was partially supported by projects 20200378, 20201040, 20200259 and EDI grant, by Secretaría de Investigación y Posgrado, Instituto Politécnico Nacional, as well as by project 8285.20-P from Tecnológico Nacional de México/IT de Mérida.

References

1. Gorbalenya, A.E., et al.: The species severe acute respiratory syndrome-related coronavirus: classifying 2019-nCoV and naming it SARS-CoV-2. Nat. Microbiol. **5**(4), 536–544 (2020)
2. Wu, F., et al.: A new coronavirus associated with human respiratory disease in China. Nature **579**(7798), 265–269 (2020)
3. Bulut, C., Kato, Y.: Epidemiology of covid-19. Turkish J. Med. Sci. **50**(SI-1), 563–570 (2020)
4. Wang, C., et al.: A novel coronavirus outbreak of global health concern. The Lancet **395**(10223), 470–473 (2020)
5. WHO: Coronavirus disease (COVID-19) Situation report - 109. Technical report, May, World Health Organization (2020). https://www.who.int/emergencies/diseases/novel-coronavirus-2019
6. Cascella, M., et al.: Features, evaluation and treatment coronavirus (COVID-19). In: StatPearls, pp. 1–17. StatPearls Publishing (2020)

7. Allan, G.M., Arroll, B.: Prevention and treatment of the common cold: making sense of the evidence. Can. Med. Assoc. J. **186**(3), 190–199 (2014)
8. Molinari, G., Colombo, G., Celenza, C.: Respiratory allergies: a general overview of remedies, delivery systems, and the need to progress. ISRN Allergy 2014, pp. 1–15 (2014)
9. Wiselka, M.: Influenza: diagnosis, management, and prophylaxis. BMJ **308**(6940), 1341 (1994)
10. Eccles, R.: Understanding the symptoms of the common cold and influenza. Lancet Infect. Dis. **5**(11), 718–725 (2005)
11. Ding, W., et al.: A layered-coevolution-based attribute-boosted reduction using adaptive quantum-behavior PSO and its consistent segmentation for neonates brain tissue. IEEE Trans. Fuzzy Syst. **26**(3), 1177–1191 (2018)
12. Fu, C., Liu, W., Chang, W.: Data-driven multiple criteria decision making for diagnosis of thyroid cancer. Ann. Oper. Res. 1–30 (2018)
13. Cao, Z., Lin, C.T.: Inherent fuzzy entropy for the improvement of EEG complexity evaluation. IEEE Trans. Fuzzy Syst. **26**(2), 1032–1035 (2018)
14. De, S.K., Biswas, R., Roy, A.R.: An application of intuitionistic fuzzy sets in medical diagnosis. Fuzzy Sets Syst. **117**(2), 209–213 (2001)
15. Rebouças Filho, P.P., et al.: Automatic histologically-closer classification of skin lesions. Comput. Med. Imaging Graph. **68**, 40–54 (2018)
16. Ngan, R.T., Ali, M., Son, L.H.: δ-equality of intuitionistic fuzzy sets: a new proximity measure and applications in medical diagnosis. Appl. Intell. **48**(2), 499–525 (2018)
17. Afonso, L.C.S., et al.: A recurrence plot-based approach for Parkinson's disease identification. Future Gener. Comput. Syst. **94**, 282–292 (2019)
18. Maiers, J.E.: Fuzzy set theory and medicine: the first twenty years and beyond. In: Proceedings of the Annual Symposium on Computer Application in Medical Care, pp. 325–329 (1985)
19. Zadeh, L.A.: Fuzzy sets. Inf. Control **8**(3), 338–353 (1965)
20. Kuncheva, L.I., Steimann, F.: Fuzzy diagnosis. Math. Sci. Eng. **144**(C), 335–340 (1980)
21. Phuong, N.H., Kreinovich, V.: Fuzzy logic and its applications in medicine. Int. J. Med. Inf. **62**(2–3), 165–173 (2001)
22. Hughes, C.: The representation of uncertainty in medical expert systems. Inf. Health Soc. Care **14**(4), 269–279 (1989)
23. Xiao, F., Ding, W.: Divergence measure of Pythagorean fuzzy sets and its application in medical diagnosis. Appl. Soft Comput. J. **79**(April), 254–267 (2019)
24. Park, K., Chae, Y., Park, M.: Developing a knowledge-based system to automate the diagnosis of allergic rhinitis. Int. J. Biomed. Soft Comput. Hum. Sci. **2**(1), 9–18 (1996)
25. Samuel, A., Kumar, S.: Intuitionistic fuzzy set with new operators in medical diagnosis. Int. J. Math. Trends Technol. **55**(3), 165–169 (2018)
26. Xiao, F.: A hybrid fuzzy soft sets decision making method in medical diagnosis. IEEE Access **6**, 25300–25312 (2018)
27. Cordón, O.: A historical review of evolutionary learning methods for mamdani-type fuzzy rule-based systems: designing interpretable genetic fuzzy systems. Int. J. Approximate Reasoning **52**(6), 894–913 (2011)
28. Ukhanova, O., Bogomolova, E.: Airborne allergens. In: Allergic Diseases - New Insights, chap. 2, pp. 35–67. InTech, April 2015
29. Mehta, R.: Allergy and asthma: allergic rhinitis and allergic conjunctivitis. FP Essentials **472**, 11–15 (2018). http://www.ncbi.nlm.nih.gov/pubmed/30152668

30. Bousquet, J., et al.: Allergic rhinitis and its impact on asthma (ARIA) 2008*. Allergy **63**(s86), 8–160 (2008)
31. Bourdin, A., et al.: Upper airway 1: allergic rhinitis and asthma: united disease through epithelial cells. Thorax **64**(11), 999–1004 (2009)
32. Greiner, A.N., et al.: Allergic rhinitis. The Lancet **378**(9809), 2112–2122 (2011)
33. Guerra, S. et al.: Rhinitis is an independent risk factor for developing cough apart from colds among adults. Allergy: Eur. J. Allergy Clin. Immunol. **60**(3), 343–349 (2005)
34. Heikkinen, T., Järvinen, A.: The common cold. Lancet **361**(9351), 51–59 (2003)
35. NIH: Cold, Flu, or Allergy? NIH News in Health (2014). https://newsinhealth.nih.gov/2014/10/cold-flu-or-allergy. Accessed 12 May 2020
36. Tyrrell, D., Cohen, S., Schilarb, J.: Signs and symptoms in common colds. Epidemiol. Infect. **111**(1), 143–156 (1993)
37. Earn, D.J., Dushoff, J., Levin, S.A.: Ecology and evolution of the flu. Trends Ecol. Evol. **17**(7), 334–340 (2002)
38. American Academy of Allergy Asthma & Immunology: Coronavirus Symptoms, April 2020. https://www.aaaai.org/Aaaai/media/MediaLibrary/Images/Promos/Coronavirus-Symptoms.pdf. Accessed 12 May 2020
39. Goni, I., et al.: Fuzzy logic applied to inflation control in the Nigerian economy. Mach. Learn. Res. **3**(4), 69–72 (2019)
40. Langari, R.K., et al.: Combined fuzzy clustering and firefly algorithm for privacy preserving in social networks. Expert Syst. Appl. **141**, 112968 (2020)
41. Orozco-del-Castillo, M.G., et al.: Fuzzy logic and image processing techniques for the interpretation of seismic data. J. Geophys. Eng. **8**(2), 185–194 (2011)
42. Molina-Puc, J., Orozco-del-Castillo, M.G., Villafaña-Gamboa, D.F., Gómez-Buenfil, R.A., Guzmán-Tolosa, J.M., Sarabia-Osorio, H.: Fuzzy logic controller for automation of an autonomous irrigation system designed for habanero pepper (*Capsicum Chinense* Jacq.). In: Mata-Rivera, M.F., Zagal-Flores, R., Barría-Huidobro, C. (eds.) WITCOM 2019. CCIS, vol. 1053, pp. 284–293. Springer, Cham (2019). https://doi.org/10.1007/978-3-030-33229-7_24
43. Rodríguez-Sánchez, J.E., et al.: A fuzzy inference system applied to estimate the error in the recovery of the Green's function by means of seismic noise correlations. J. Geophys. Eng. **15**(5), 2110–2123 (2018)
44. Ortiz-Alemán, J.C., et al.: Pattern recognition applied to attenuation of multiples in subsalt imaging. Pure Appl. Geophys. **176**(6), 2411–2424 (2019)
45. Andreou, A., Mateou, N., Zombanakis, G.: Soft computing for crisis management and political decision making: the use of genetically evolved fuzzy cognitive maps. Soft Comput. **9**(3), 194–210 (2005)
46. Zapa Perez, E., Cogollo Florez, J.: Fuzzy-BSC methodology for decision making in indemnity area of insurance companies. IEEE Latin Am. Trans. **16**(10), 2539–2546 (2018)
47. Jang, J.S.R., Sun, C.T., Mizutani, E.: Neuro-Fuzzy and Soft Computing: A Computational Approach to Learning and Machine Intelligence. Prentice-Hall, Inc. (1997)
48. Sugeno, M.: Industrial Applications of Fuzzy Control. Elsevier Science Inc., New York (1985)
49. Chung, S.K., et al.: Decision making support system in otolaryngology (part 3) - diagnosis of allergic rhinitis. Korean J. Otorhinolaryngol. **33**(1), 104–110 (1990)
50. Wong, K.W., Gedeon, T., Kóczy, L.: Construction of fuzzy signature from data: an example of SARS pre-clinical diagnosis system. In: IEEE International Conference on Fuzzy Systems, vol. 3, pp. 1649–1654 (2004)

51. Carnegie Mellon University: COVID Voice Detector. https://cvd.lti.cmu.edu/. Accessed 11 May 2020
52. Dubois, D., Prade, H.: The three semantics of fuzzy sets. Fuzzy Sets Syst. **90**(2), 141–150 (1997)
53. Centers for Disease Control and Prevention: Symptoms of Coronavirus (2020). https://www.cdc.gov/coronavirus/2019-ncov/symptoms-testing/symptoms.html. Accessed 12 May 2020
54. WHO: Coronavirus (2020). https://www.who.int/health-topics/coronavirus. Accessed 12 May 2020
55. WHO: Report of the WHO-China Joint Mission on Coronavirus Disease 2019 (COVID-19). Technical report, February, World Health Organization (2020). https://www.who.int/docs/default-source/coronaviruse/who-china-joint-mission-on-covid-19-final-report.pdf
56. Kim, Y.H., Kim, K.S.: Diagnosis and treatment of allergic rhinitis. J. Korean Med. Assoc. **53**(9), 780–790 (2010)
57. Small, P., Kim, H.: Allergic rhinitis. Allergy Asthma Clin. Immunol. **7**(S1), S3 (2011)
58. Rosas, M.R.: Gripe y resfriado. Clínica y tratamiento. Offarm **27**(2), 46–51 (2008)
59. Mamdani, E.H., Assilian, S.: An experiment in linguistic synthesis with a fuzzy logic controller. In: Readings in Fuzzy Sets for Intelligent Systems, pp. 283–289. Elsevier (1993)
60. AAAIMX: AAAIMX — COVID-19 Screening Assistant (2020). https://www.aaaimx.org/covid19-assistant/. Accessed 11 Aug 2020
61. Gilstrap, L.: Validation and verification of expert systems. In: NASA Conference Publication, vol. 3110, p. 241 (1991)
62. Zhu, N., et al.: A novel coronavirus from patients with pneumonia in China, 2019. N. Engl. J. Med. **382**(8), 727–733 (2020)
63. Mei, X., Lee, H., Diao, K., et al.: Artificial intelligence-enabled rapid diagnosis of patients with covid-19. Nat. Med.**26**(August), 1224–1228 (2020)

A Review of the Security Information Controls in Wireless Networks Wi-Fi

Lorena Galeazzi Ávalos[1,2]($\boxtimes$), Cristian Barría Huidobro[1], and Julio Ariel Hurtado[2]

[1] Universidad Mayor, Manuel Montt 367, Santiago, Chile
{lorena.galeazzi,cristian.barria}@umayor.cl,
lorenagaleazzi@unicauca.edu.co
[2] Universidad del Cauca, calle 5#4-70, Cauca, Colombia
ahurtado@unicauca.edu.co

Abstract. Information security is fundamentally based on the components of systems, networks, data and users [15], which are analyzed to manage their vulnerabilities and threats through different international standards that act in a global and adaptive way for several types of organization. Thus, the present research will focus on Wi-Fi wireless networks and ISO 27001, CIS controls and NIST 800-53 standards. All that will be exposed based on a narrative review showing both integration and the most relevant aspects of this component.

Keywords: Standards · Controls · Wireless networks

1 Introduction

Wireless technologies have been maintained in relentless improvement of rapid development, thereby meeting the demand of high-speed data services devices [1], including new security protocols, optimizing their performance, efficiency, and fidelity [2].

All this evolution is being generated from the various service quality requirements of existing applications for new technologies such as vehicle networks, the internet of things, and communications [1].

The organizations behind the standards aim to equalize norms of different governments. They are usually multinational non-profit organizations, formed by members of standards committees from different nations [3].

The IEEE 802.11 standard that corresponds to the Wi-Fi wireless network oversees the technology development and adapts international standards [4].

On the other hand, we have standards focused on information security, such as:

ISO/IEC 27001. It specifies how to establish, implement, and maintain continuous improvements in information security management system of the organization [5].

© Springer Nature Switzerland AG 2020
M. F. Mata-Rivera et al. (Eds.): WITCOM 2020, CCIS 1280, pp. 420–427, 2020.
https://doi.org/10.1007/978-3-030-62554-2_30

NIST 800-53. It is a governmental standard of the United States, which provides security controls and associated assessment procedures defined in it, as a recommendation to federal organizations and information systems [6].

CIS V7.1. It is a non-profit organization targeting the community and creators of the best practice controls to protect IT data systems, thereby providing tools to neutralize threats [7].

The problem statement is that the information security considers many aspects, covering networks, systems, and data. This research focuses on the first of these aspects, i.e., networks and, within all of them, wireless networks. As a product of their growth, it has led to the identification and definition of standards, driven to the distribution and incorporation of updates to keep them current, thus contributing to the development and consolidation of the F/O aspects, which are the focus of this study.

However, these aspects and their extensive and widespread applications have been postponed and, in some cases, overlooked, referring to the security. In other words, wireless networks are beneficial and, at the same time and proportionally, equally insecure.

The following is a proposed taxonomy for the networks development and evolution, facilitating the recognition of threat factors, and contributing to the production of efficient protection systems.

Based on the standards, this study aims to prove that the controls are specific and only related to some concepts. Therefore, it would be possible to argue a future evaluation of the controls associated with wireless networks.

The result is to contribute to engineering, information security management, and standardization.

This study is carried out based on a conceptual review and analysis of the ISO 27001, NIST 800-53 and CIS V7.1 standard, with the objective of defining, clarifying and describing it in a qualitative way, using a narrative review methodology [15].

2   Study Methods

As a concept of analysis and interpretation of the scientific literature, a narrative review methodology [15] will be used as a guide, which synthesizes the search of information, data extraction and analysis. Figure 1 shows research phases.

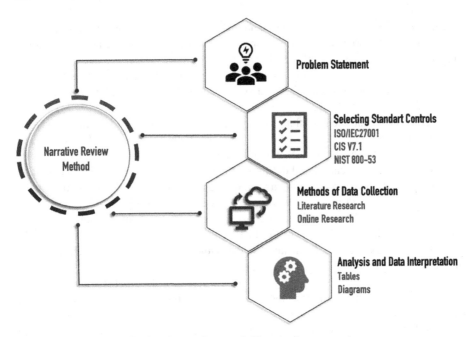

Fig. 1. Phases of research (Source: Own source)

3   Study Results

First, this research was carried out based on the documentation of four standards, the IEEE 802.11, ISO/EIC 27001, NIST - 800-53, and CIS Controls Version 7.1, to verify the number of amendments throughout the time [5, 6, 16].

Secondly, the standards associated with information security were chosen to select only the controls that make references to wireless networks.

The selected controls were compared to show that each standard grants specific approach of security in wireless networks.

3.1   Problem Statement

Standards are necessary for the operational management of an organization; it involves actions that must be taken by IT, providing tools for the control and administration of information security [10, 11].

It is possible to define strategic management to protect data, based on structuring processes and procedures [12].

The standards that impact the organization are a pillar to define the maturity levels of information security [13]. The review, supervision, and management must be constant for data security [14]. Figure 2 shows a diagram that covers topics oriented to impact zones.

Therefore, it is necessary to know what happens to wireless networks if they are adequately considered in the information security standards and if they share the same maturity level compared to the wired network.

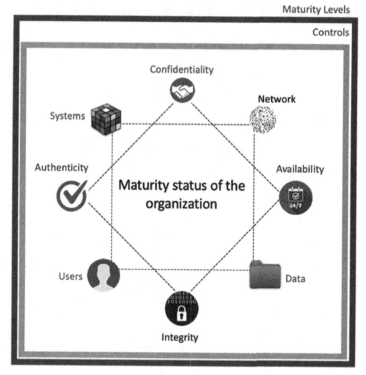

Fig. 2. Diagram impact of controls and maturity levels. (Source: Barría, C, 2020)

3.2 Selecting Standard Controls

The security controls related to the wireless networks were selected from CIS version 7.1, ISO/IEC 27001 and NIST 800-53 standards documentation (Table 1).

The Fig. 3 shows the difference in number of controls referred to the wireless networks among these standards.

3.3 Method of Data Collection

The collected through a narrative review data aims to explore, understand, and describe if the standards have specific controls focused on wireless networks.

Therefore, the method was used to collect data through documents, research literature, and web pages corresponding to the standards' official pages.

3.4 Analysis and Data Interpretation

To carry out the analysis of the controls, we sought to find a relationship within each of them to verify the similarities and differences. Table 2 below shows the selected controls in detail for the association analysis.

Table 1. Selection of controls associated with wireless security.

CIS V 7.1	ISO/IEC 27001	NIST 800-53
1.7	A.8.1.1	PE-18
15.1	A.8.1.3	SC-5
15.2	A.9.1.2	SC-40
15.3	A.9.2.1	SC-40, [1]
15.4	A.10.1.1	SC-40, [2]
15.5	A.13.1.1	SC-40, [3]
15.6	A.13.1.3	SC-40, [4]
15.7		SC-43
15.7		SI-4, [14]
15.8		SI-4, [15]
15.9		SI-10, [4]
15.10		AC-18
20.1		AC-18, [1]
		AC-18, [2]
		AC-18, [3]
		AC-18, [4]
		AC-18, [5]
Total number of controls associated with wireless networks		
13	**07**	**17**

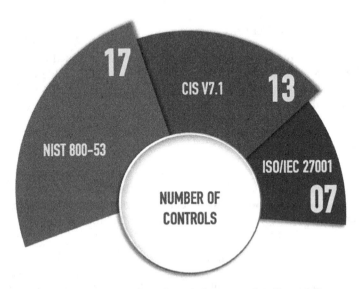

Fig. 3. Comparative controls referred to wireless networks. (Source: Own source)

Table 2. Selection of wireless network controls.

CIS version 7.1		ISO/IEC 27001		NIST 800-53	
1.7	Deploy Port Level Access Control	A.8.1.1	Inventory of assets	P-18	Location of system component
15.1	Maintain an Inventory of Authorized Wireless Access Points	A.8.1.3	Acceptable use of assets	SC-5	Denial of service protection
15.2	Detect Wireless Access Points Connected to the Wired Network	A.9.1.2	Access to networks and network services	SC-40	Wireless Link Protection Control: Protect external and internal
15.3	Use a Wireless Intrusion Detection System	A.9.2.1	User registration and deregistration	SC-40, [1]	1. Electromagnetic Interference
15.4	Disable Wireless Access on Devices if Not Required	A.10.1.1	Policy on the use of cryptographic controls	SC-40, [2]	2. Reduce Detection Potential
15.5	Limit Wireless Access on Client Devices	A.13.1.1	Network Controls	SC-40, [3]	3. Imitative or Manipulative Communications Deception
15.6	Disable Peer-to-Peer Wireless Network abilities on Wireless Clients	A.13.1.3	Segregation in networks	SC-40, [4]	4. Signal Parameter Identification
15.7	Leverage the Advanced Encryption Standard (AES) to Encrypt Wireless Data			SC-43	Usage Restrictions
15.8	Use Wireless Authentication Protocols that Require Mutual, Multi-Factor Authentication			SI-4, [14]	System Monitoring 14. Wireless Intrusion Detection
15.9	Disable Wireless Peripheral Access of Devices			SI-4, [15]	System Monitoring 15. Wireless to Wireline Communications
15.10	Create Separate Wireless Network for Personal and Untrusted Devices			SI-10, [4]	Information Input Validation 4. Timing Interactions
20.1	Establish a Penetration Testing Program			AC-18	Wireless Access
				AC-18, [1]	1. Authentication and Encryption
				AC-18, [2]	2. Monitoring Unauthorized Connections
				AC-18, [3]	3. Disable Wireless Networking
				AC-18, [4]	4. Restrict Configurations By Users
				AC-18, [5]	5. Antennas and Transmission Power Levels

The following diagrams present an estimation done through a narrative review of the relationship between the selected controls.

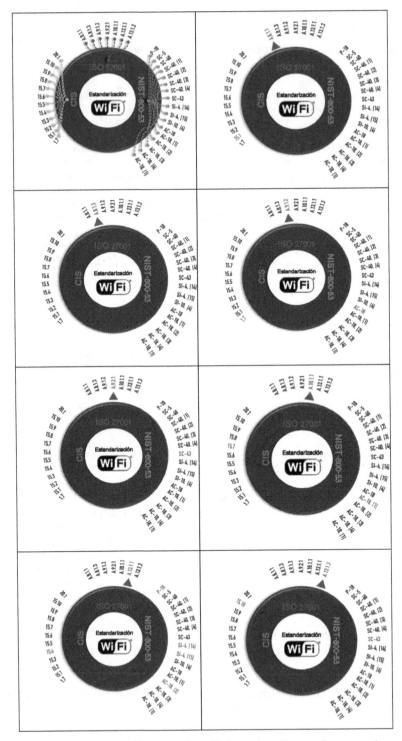

Fig. 4. Analysis and interpretation of information. (Source: Own source)

The analysis was carried out taking into consideration the relationship between the standards, based on the seven selected controls of ISO/IEC 27001, on CIS and NIST 800-53 (see Fig. 4).

4 Conclusions and Future Work

For the future work, it is recommended to do an analysis related to the components and variables that are part of the connectivity in Wi-Fi wireless technology.

This investigation allowed to determine that the controls associated with wireless Wi-Fi networks present different approaches regarding information security.

It is possible to confirm that there is a difference between the specific standards that have been verified, being able to expose that the controls associated with the security of wireless networks differ in their parameters; that is, each standard focuses on controls and audits of different objectives.

On the other hand, it can be seen that the ISO/IEC 27001 standard has a broader approach compared to the other standards, which determines that more aspects of operation, control, safety and monitoring are being covered.

References

1. Yang, H., Alouini, M.: Advanced Wireless Transmission Technologies. University Printing House, Cambridge (2020)
2. WiFi Alliance. https://www.wi-fi.org/who-we-are. Accessed 02 July 2020
3. Goralski, W.: The Illustrate Network, 2nd edn. Elsevier Inc., Cambridge (2017)
4. IEEE. https://standards.ieee.org/. Accessed 02 July 2020
5. ISO. https://www.iso.org/about-us.html. Accessed 02 July 2020
6. NIST, https://www.nist.gov/800-53, last accessed 2020/07/02
7. CIS. https://www.cisecurity.org/about-us/. Accessed 02 July 2020
8. ISO. https://www.iso.org/files/live/sites/isoorg/files/about%20ISO/docs/en/Friendship_a mong_equals.pdf. Accessed 03 Feb 2020
9. Bairagi, V., Munot, M.: Research Methodology: A Practical and Scientific Aproach, 1st edn. CRC Press, New York (2019)
10. Calder, A., Watkins, S.: IT Governance, 6th edn. Kogan Page, London (2015)
11. Williams, L.: Information Security Policy Development for Compliance, 1st edn. CRC Press, Boca Raton (2013)
12. Chopra, A., Chaudhary, M.: Implementing an Information Security Management System. 1st. edn. Apress, New York (2020)
13. Bairagi, V., Munot, M.: Research Methodology A Practical and Scientific Approach, 1st edn. CRC Press, New York (2019)
14. Barria, C., Cordero, D., Galeazzi, L., Acuña, A.: Proposal of a multi-standard model for measuring maturity business levels with reference to information security standards and controls. In: Dzitac, I., Dzitac, S., Filip, F.G., Kacprzyk, J., Manolescu, M.-J., Oros, H. (eds.) ICCCC 2020. AISC, vol. 1243, pp. 121–132. Springer, Cham (2021). https://doi.org/10.1007/978-3-030-53651-0_10
15. Paré, G., Trudel, M., Jaana, M., Kitsiou, S.: Synthesizing information systems knowledge: a typology of literature reviews. Inf. Manag. **52**(2), 183–199 (2015)
16. IEEE802. http://www.ieee802.org/11/Reports/802.11_Timelines.htm. Accessed 02 July 2020

Local Tours Recommendation Applying Machine Learning in Social Networks

Braulio Medina[1], Alejandro Pineda[1], Giovanni Guzmán[2] (iD),
Laura Ivoone Garay Jimenez[1] (iD), and Miguel Félix Mata Rivera[1(✉)] (iD)

[1] Unidad Profesional Interdisciplinaria en Ingeniería y Tecnologías Avanzadas – Instituto Politécnico Nacional, Avenida Instituto Politécnico Nacional No. 2580, Col Barrio la Laguna Ticomán, Gustavo A. Madero, Ciudad de México, C.P. 07340 Mexico City, Mexico
garay@ipn.mx2, mmatar@ipn.mx
[2] Centro de Investigación en Computación – Instituto Politécnico Nacional, Avenida Instituto Politécnico Nacional No. 2580, Col Barrio la Laguna Ticomán, Gustavo A. Madero, Ciudad de México, C.P. 07340 Mexico City, Mexico
jguzmanl@cic.ipn.mx

Abstract. Tourism in Mexico represents a primarily strategic activity for the country's economy. Although the most renowned tourist spots generally have a wide promotion of their attractions, there are local businesses that are not sufficiently linked to this benefit and it is harder for the visitors to find them. Furthermore, social media is rich not only in reactions and opinions, but in experiences, these experiences can be useful to promote and recommend several sites. Web pages also have comments, similar to TripAdvisor, but small businesses are not present in it. In this sense, the techniques of Machine Learning can help to detect businesses with a good experience reflected in comments from web sites, in combination with data from social networks. Therefore, evaluating the quality of the tourist's experience present in comments on social networks, and gathering personal information from apps represent an opportunity to generate not only recommendations, but itineraries based on time, space and experience. In this paper we present a framework to generate itineraries based on experiences of tourists in Mexico city, using machine learning and social mining, the results show similar performance for small-local business compared with the recommendations of popular and larger places.

1 Introduction

Nowadays, the high annual number of tourists to our country gives Mexico the category of being an international tourist power. However, there are some limitations with the promotion of places that could offer the visitor, either useful products or services. This advertising is not developed to the same extent for unfamiliar businesses compared to as it is for well-known ones, which results in many of the unfamiliar businesses being rarely visited. In consequence they have a low amount of visitors or clients.

Another problem that arises is that the tourist does not have enough information about different places that can be visited (even though he knows about them) such as:

© Springer Nature Switzerland AG 2020
M. F. Mata-Rivera et al. (Eds.): WITCOM 2020, CCIS 1280, pp. 428–440, 2020.
https://doi.org/10.1007/978-3-030-62554-2_31

the opening and closing times of the place, its line of operation, the activities that can be carried out, the amount of time it takes to get from one place to another, and so on.

On the other hand, it is well known that people who have Internet access use social networks in order to share their experience either as clients or as consumers of services in various FanPages, which guides other users as to which business to visit, or what services to use while staying in tourist destinations.

Identification and comparative analysis of the functionality of tourism clusters in Eastern Poland. They identified standard features of clusters, differentiation, and identification of strengths in the activities in work [1].

While in [2] authors discuss what kind of deep neural networks is the most appropriate model for tourism flow prediction. and they use Long Short Term Memory Neural Network (LSTM) methods to predict tourism flow, and their experiments had a better performance than Auto-Regressive Integrated Moving Average (ARIMA). For another hand in [4] is treated Recommender systems and Machine Learning is used, in [3] discuss how to choose a suitable machine learning algorithm that is difficult because of the sheer number of algorithms available in the literature. This work presents a systematic review of the literature that analyzes machine learning algorithms in the recommender system. Finally, they showed that Bayesian and decision tree algorithms are widely used in recommender systems because of their low complexity.

Tourism, Recommender, Machine Learning and Big Data are lines that converge and research community have generated different works [5–8]. Nevertheless, in [4] showed a new recommendation meth od based on multi-criteria CF to enhance the predictive accuracy of recommender systems in the tourism domain using clustering, dimensionality reduction, and prediction methods. In [9] The authors present a collaborative filtering approach to Algorithm selection. They mentions a collaborative filtering, popularized by the Netflix challenge, to recommend the items that a user will most probably like, based on the previous items she liked, and the items that have been liked by other users. Finally, Matrix Factorization techniques are the most widely used methods in predicting a user-item rating matrix's missing ratings due to their efficiency and accuracy in prediction. In [10] they proposed Conformal Matrix Factorization and shows different ways of adapting conformal prediction to matrix factorization to be applied in Recommender Systems.

Considering the works mentioned, it can be established in relation to the importance of tourism activity and to the reduced economic spill per capita during the stay in Mexico City, it is feasible to propose an alternative solution to the tourism promotion tools established by the government sector, using mobile apps that implement artificial intelligence in order to increase the interest of the Historic Center of Mexico City as a tourist destination.

Our solution proposed consists of an app for suggesting to users with a list of at least three places he might like to visit, included in an itinerary generated from the semantics found in the posts obtained from social networks and other web pages.

The information collected should be processed in five steps: 1) Data acquisition: Acquirement of information from particular and popular known web sites (coffee shops, bars, pubs, restaurants) and the posts of the fan-pages in social networks and specialized web pages with content from the historic center of Mexico City where people make comments about their experiences and evaluate the place. 2) Pre-processing of the information obtained. Since the information is from different sources, it should be standardized in a recognizable format. 3) Ge-referencing and locate the places on the map to generate the most suitable route. Furthermore, 4) Generates user visit log notifications to suggest places they might like. Finally, 5) Pinpointing analysis: the information of interests and likes is processed to categorize the user's profile in a specific group of people with similar interests and characteristics.

Itinerary management: The compilation of primary data information of users means its profile (which will be a vector) will show a recommended itinerary with the possibility to modify, a confirmed itinerary route, and notifications of the registered visit to a place. It is implementing natural language processing algorithms to recognize the intention and semantics of retrieved posts.

Information is analyzed using a data dictionary and Bayes algorithm in the discovered categories. Execute location algorithms to mark the itinerary's places to offer an efficient route to reach the location. The information considered is related to the reviews and the suggested place's opinions in the last six months (businesses considered: restaurants, coffee shops, clubs, and bars. The rest of the paper is structured as follows: Sect. 2 presents the methodology, Sect. 3 Model generation of machine learning, while Sect. 4 shows testing and results, and finally, the conclusions are outlined.

2 Methodology

The methodology used is composed in three stages: categorization, information extraction from web and social media, route display and machine learning algorithms to cluster the information.

The first stage consists of obtain a list of three categories (functionality [registered or unregistered], intention, schedule). Whole the second stage is performance by a crawler developed in python to extrac of information from touristic websites of Mexico downtown.

Second stage is achieved by extraction of information from sites, opinions and reviews of social networks (Facebook (from 2016) and TripAdvisor). Including the cleaning information and evaluate the classification of the data. Implementing the routing algorithms from the data obtained from the classifier. The last stage is to display the route in a map viewer. The clustering algorithms used is:

K-means: it requires to provide the desired number of clusters. In consequence, the following visual methods are reviewed:
Dendrogram: It is a method that consists of grouping the closest values into pairs, which is done iteratively until everything is combined in a cluster. The suggestion of the number of clusters consists of drawing a horizontal line along the most extended branch, the suggestion being the number of branches cut by the line.
Gap: consists of calculating the most significant distance or difference between the groups. Thus, generating a dendrogram, for which distances between ramifications are considered, and the most significant difference between them is calculated. This algorithm suggests that the maximum point shown in the graph is the optimal number of

clusters to be used. In Fig. 4.8, a result similar to the dendrogram is displayed in the graph. Therefore we take as a suggestion the second-highest point in the graph, resulting in six. Silhouette: This method measures the objects' similarity with the membership cluster that ranges from −1 to 1, with 1 being the high similarity. The graph suggests that where the highest point is the optimal number of clusters. Figure 1 shows the result, concluding in the use of cluster six. By implementing various methods for determining the optimal number of clusters, and given that three of them suggest "6" clusters as the ideal combination, this number is determined as the parameter to provide for the general-purpose clustering algorithm (K-means).

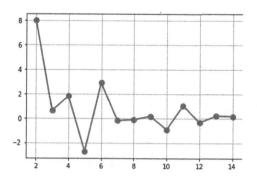

Fig. 1. Silhouette method to calculate the number of clusters.

2.1 K-means Implementation

The axes of the figure are shown that way due to the fact that a characteristic scaling was implemented, which allows the content of the dataset to be contained in a range, thus avoiding a data dispersion. X axis shows the profiles In Fig. 2, the obtained result is shown.

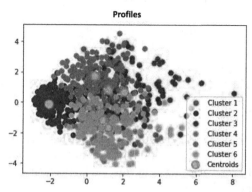

Fig. 2. Visualization of the clustering algorithm of k-means in a two-dimensional graph.

As is shown, grouping data is on 6 clusters, centroids are determined randomly, and the inertia computes data membership to the cluster to its centroid. This process is carried out iteratively up to the point where the inertias' average of the data directed towards a cluster is stable.

The purpose of defining the characteristics of the data groups is to construct a new dataset in which the data provided to the clustering algorithm are combined with the cluster to which each data belongs. Based on the information provided by the new dataset, it is possible to make predictions about tastes according to the profiles; the algorithms "K-NN," "Naive Bayes," and "Random Forest" were chosen for classification purposes. In Fig. 3, the classifiers' confusion matrix is illustrated, which is intended to show the algorithms' performance.

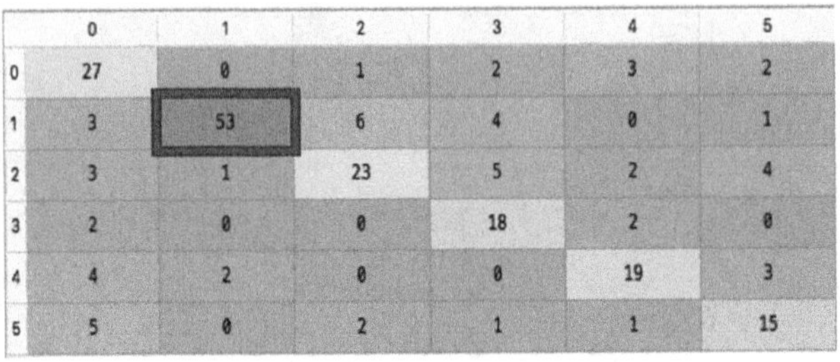

	0	1	2	3	4	5
0	27	0	1	2	3	2
1	3	53	6	4	0	1
2	3	1	23	5	2	4
3	2	0	0	18	2	0
4	4	2	0	0	19	3
5	5	0	2	1	1	15

Fig. 3. Performance confusion matrix of the "Naive bayes" algorithm (Color figure online)

Figure 3 shows the performance (considering, as an example, the value enclosed in a blue box) of the Naive Bayes algorithm with "true positives," which means that 53 values of class 1 (which belong to cluster two) were classified as a correct way, showing a classification performance for that class of 94.64%, leaving the rest as "false positives" which implies that three values belonging to class 1 were classified incorrectly. In Table 1, the performance of each algorithm is described.

Table 1. Obtained performances.

Algorithm	Performance
Naive Bayes	77.10%
K-NN	76.63%
Random Forest	72.42%

Therefore, it is observed that the algorithm with the best performance is the "Naive Bayes" since it presents a 77.10% accuracy in terms of its predictions, so it was decided to use the "Naive Bayes" algorithm. In this work, two types of recommendations (Top 10) are considered, which are:

Global. That is the place that the community is best valued based on the senti-ment/acceptance concept of the comments section that users have expressed on social networks, official store pages, etc.

Personal. This type of recommendation considers tastes, preferences, and even the places previously visited by users to provide a proposal with a greater affinity to their preferences and maximize their personal experience.

Two ways of approaching the problem are considered:

1. Content-based filtering: analyze some or all the characteristics, whether implicit (characteristics of the place) or explicit (e.g., comments) of the objects to be recom-mended, to filter and order n elements according to the corresponding measure of similarity to selected features.
2. Collaborative filtering: This filtering adds, to the previous system, the analysis of the behavior of neighboring objects to a specific object in question. That is, it searches for objects very similar to a given one and later recommends n elements in similar objects that could interest the object being analyzed.

From this analysis, two abstractions emerge:

User-based: It focuses its analysis on users as objects of study. The nature of people represents a high variability in terms of their tastes and behaviors.

Item or item. An item will always be the same item; thus, its behavior is constant. The number of items is stable, and therefore, the recommendations are stable considering the people's characteristics. Regarding the case of global recommendations, as well as far the first personal recommendations (in case, no history allows us to analyze the behavior of users), the implementation of filtering, which is based on the content, represents an optimal solution for the problem considering as a metric reference the following:

1. Average acceptance/sentiment of comments about the place. (Top 10).
2. The previous one (1. Filtering based on content) plus the classification label according to the characteristics, tastes and interests of the user. (Top 10 staff without visit log, new user).

In the case of personal recommendations, with the time, will be there a record of the places that the user has visited, implementing collaborative filtering based on items to learn from the user's visit records. It will generate a precise recommendations, in addition to making the computational resources of the entire system more efficient.

The latter, since there is a constant catalog of places, in addition to isolating the recommendations of the variants of behavior by users, it generates proposals with more excellent stability and affinity, focusing on the following:

1. Places similar to which the user has registered his visit.
2. Average acceptance/sentiment of comments about the place.
3. Random selection of potential options to generate dynamism and variety.
4. Itinerary.

2.2 Sentiment Analysis

Data extraction and preparation. It is in charge of extracting information about the places present, in the catalog of the historic center of Mexico City as well as the homologation of the variant structures in a single one for their subsequent characterization employing a binary vector, which is the basis of the generation of a training dataset for the classifier module, which, along with some filters, provide the first personalized recommendations.

Facebook offers an API for developers in 2016, allowing interaction with the social network and extracting directly from the opinions section. The posts were found on the fan pages (in 2016). The following attributes were used: , , , _, h, , __, , _. you will find 220 places between bars, restaurants, and coffee shops. Nevertheless, as many of them do not have any information, the parameters were reduced to "name," "categorylist," "hours," "location," which is what the vast majority have, so they were reduced to a total of 117 potential sites. The crawler extracts the public information, identified by the HTML tags within the respective web template to the place that had been analyzed.

Homogenization. Both Facebook and the web pages handle their own data structures, which causes disparities to arise when integrating the data from both sources. Therefore, once the data had been structured uniformly, it was saved in the database, MongoDB - The nature of the information that can be mined is highly variable, that is, in some sources, there may be a description of the place, and in others, there is not, or that some places provide their approximate prices and others do not. Due to the above, a document pattern was created to store, although this information is not available.

Sentiment analysis. The first recommendation reflects acceptance and positivity of the comments. This parameter is calculated using indico API (https://indico.io/docs).

Fig. 4. Dictionaries from characterization vector.

Characterization. Machine learning algorithms require numerical information to be processed. Thus, a numerical vector was created to represent a place. Two dictionaries were created using two parameters {key: value}, as is shown inf Fig. 4 (in Spanish). These dictionaries were homologizing the places' mined textual characteristics to the characterization vector.

3 Model Generation

This section shows the process of how the machine learning models were created and their persistence. The first step is Clustering. The K-means clustering algorithm was implemented in order to generate a training data set for the classifier. That is, the K-means algorithm was in charge of grouping the places into six different groups and placing a membership label on them. The number of groups obtained from the system's analysis reflected in the section with the same name in this document. These algorithms were implemented through the Scikit-learn library (1. http://scikit-learn.org/stable/modules/clustering.html#clustering). Upon completion, the algorithm places the attribute named cluster in the database that contains the label generated by this algorithm. Then this label and the characterization vector together represent the training set for the classifier. Recommending systems The goal of this implementation is to create a similarity matrix and an update mechanism for it. This matrix has the direct relationships of the places and their possible recommendation potential. The Jaccard similarity measure requires calculating the number of users who visited both places, dividing the sum of visitors in both of them. With the similarity measure, a square matrix simsMatrix [#Places] was created in which each element α A, B $\in$ [0, 1] represents the similarity of place j concerning place i, which the closer to the unit it is, the more significant recommendation potential is.

As there is a more significant number of records, the matrix, as mentioned above, will update its elements with what it is stated that the system learns from its records. The model, being a Python structural object, was serialized in a binary document. To preserve the previously tested model's structures and relationships to be used through API calls to perform its evaluation exclusively. These modules are responsible for creating the top 10 or the ten better recommendations regarding places users like. The global takes as a metric the sentiment or average acceptance of the attraction sites to generate the list of potentially attractive places. In the case of personal ones, first, the existence of history was taken into account. However, if it does not exist, the history is filtered, taking into account the users' characteristics, analyzing the user's group membership, and later, the order in as for the average acceptance reflected in the comments. Suppose the user already has a history of visits. The registration is used to make recommendations about places of interest, taking at least 80% similarity, so that from the available options, choose one randomly to generate dynamism in as for the recommendations.

Itinerary. This module is in charge of processing itinerary requests, so the update/time management function was created, which enters the start time, the time available for the itinerary, and later records the updated start time (time remaining available for the following proposals). Each time a place is added, the times are updated and taken as a reference for the next activity. These places are stored in an array representing the payload of the response that was sent. See Fig. 5 (in Spanish).

Fig. 5. List of places in spanish.

To display the information corresponding to each button, each one of the "slides" refers to the site data stored in "Firebase", which implies that on this page we obtain the coordinates, the hours or the information of the site. It is shown in Fig. 6.

Fig. 6. Top 10 Map.

Session through social network: Name, email, provider and vector. This last parameter is the vector that contains the user's taste information at the moment of entering the system by means of the login or the creation of a correctly carried out account.

Create an Itinerary. In this section, the goal is to suggest to the user an itinerary according to the parameters of available time, type of departure, and whether or not he wishes to register visits. When the user confirms the parameters and is correct, the necessary data is executed and calculated for the generation of the itinerary: a) Hour and minute of the start of the itinerary. b) Hour and minute of completion of the itinerary. c) Day the request is made. d) Type of output. e) Email of the requesting user. These parameters are of vital importance because the system makes recommendations in the Historic Center of the City. However, users can be either inside or outside the area, then travel time (using public transport) to the City's Historic Center.

The user is shown an itinerary suggestion on this page, allowing him to do two actions: delete sites along with their respective restriction and reorder the list at will. This page is in charge of displaying the map and the directions to follow to start the tour. The Google Maps API services are once again used to display the map on the screen, for the generation of "markers" at the points where the sites are located and for displaying the instructions panel of the route to follow.

4 Testings and Results

In this section, the tests that were applied and the obtained results are described. The app starts with two options:

- First option: Top 10 here the apps display the Global Top 10 places without creating an account or logging in.
- Second option: Login the apps display not only top 10 places using their email account or preferred social network (Google or Facebook). Upon entering Top 10, the user views a screen containing the ten sites' list best evaluated by users in the mined comments. Similarly, for each of the sites, Top 10 allows the display of a menu of three options:

1. Map: Allows to locate the position of the site on a map.
2. Hours: Displays the opening and closing information of the site on the day it is consulted.
3. Shows a brief description of the site (if the information is available).

When a user want to have personalized recommendations, it is necessary to create a profile, for which their basic information is collected using both social networks and their email. Subsequently, give the information of tastes and interests regarding the categories of sites contemplated in the system. An the itinerary generation, it is shown in Fig. 7.

This was achieved by providing the user with two aspects of personalized use of the system, which are:

- Top 10 Staff: Recommending the top 10 rated sites along with collaborative item-based filtering.

Fig. 7. Global Top 10 without login.

With two different sources of information led to an analysis and a restructuring for a standard format using dictionaries that would allow the information to be coupled to the needs of the system. Using an item-based recommender system allows users to suggest sites that have already been visited by other users who share characteristics based on their tastes and likes, in order to suggest sites of similar interest. Separating the storage into two parts was of great help since Firebase was used to maintain a persistence of data that must be displayed in the application. However, this procedure avoids storing information that will not be used directly by the user, which avoids a service charge by Google. Using Mongo DB allows to streamline queries locally that, although they are not presented to the user directly, they are processed and filtered to show a response to the various requests. Making use of a framework for mobile development was not the best option because, although they allow the construction of hybrid applications, you are subject to versions of plugins and specific operating systems causing an execution failure. The verification of a user's stay on a site in order to make a visit registration depends on whether the user is within a radius of 35 m around the site's location; however, there are places in which the surface is greater. It is illustrated in Fig. 8.

The Top 10 Personal list consists of the ten best-evaluated sites of the group to which the user belongs. The application allows the modification of tastes at the user's request, which allows the user to modify information on tastes and interests provided when creating an account or when making previous modifications. It implies that the Top 10 Personal list will be readapted to the new information that we have about the user. For creating an itinerary, three mandatory parameters are required: a) Available time ranging from 3 to 8 h with a step of 0.5. b)Type of departure that has three options (Personal, Family, and Friends), c) Check-in that aims to activate the registration service whether or not to visit.

Once the user confirms the request, the application is in charge of building a structure that facilitates the system's query by providing an object that contains well-defined information, which is: • Start time: Contains the hour and minute at which the itinerary will begin. • horaFin: Contains hour and minute when the itinerary ends. • day: Contains

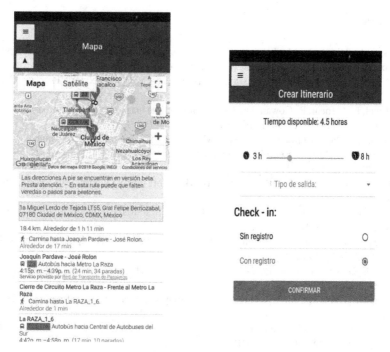

Fig. 8. Itinerary generation.

an integer parameter which indicates the day on which the request is made, starting with Sunday - 0 and Saturday - 6. • departure: Contains a string parameter that indicates the type of departure that the user wants on his itinerary. • email: Identifies the user to be able to carry out the processing according to their tastes and interests.

5   Conclusions and Future Work

We show a recommender system capable of collecting, categorizing and processing the information provided by a user and give recommendations regarding to itinerary of sites in the Historic Center of Mexico City, considering the diffusion of places that are affected by different problems of tourism, and the use of Data Mining techniques and classifiers of machine learning with a line where social media and machine learning converge.

Finally, as future work, is considering add other datasets to include other parameters in the itinerary generation and Restructure the recommender system matrix by adding a user satisfaction measurement column.

Acknowledgments. The authors want to thank God, CONACYT, SIP (Secretaría de Investigación y Posgrado), IPN (Instituto Politécnico Nacional), COFAA (Comisión de Operación y Fomento a las Actividades Académicas del IPN), UPIITA-IPN and CIC-IPN for their support, and the SIP Project 20200612 and 20200331. CONACyT Project 2016/2110 and SECTEI 289/2019.

References

1. Borkowska-Niszczota, M.: Tourism clusters in Eastern Poland-analysis of selected aspects of the operation. Procedia Soc. Behav. Sci. **213**, 957–964 (2015)
2. Li, Y., Cao, H.: Prediction for tourism flow based on LSTM neural network. Procedia Comput. Sci. **129**, 277–283 (2018)
3. Portugal, I., Alencar, P., Cowan, D.: The use of machine learning algorithms in recommender systems: a systematic review. Expert Syst. Appl. (2017)
4. Nilashi, M., Bagherifard, K., Rahmani, M., Rafe, V.: A recommender system for tourism industry using cluster ensemble and prediction machine learning techniques. Comput. Ind. Eng. **109**, 357–368 (2017)
5. Peng, S., Yu, S., Mueller, P.: Social networking big data: Opportunities, solutions, and challenges (2018)
6. Li, J., Xu, L., Tang, L., Wang, S., Li, L.: Big data in tourism research: a literature review. Tour. Manag. **68**, 301–323 (2018)
7. Fundeanu, D.D.: Innovative regional cluster, model of tourism development. Procedia Econ. Financ. **23**, 744–749 (2015)
8. Richards, G.: Cultural tourism: a review of recent research and trends. J. Hosp. Tour. Manag. **36**, 12–21 (2018)
9. Mısır, M., Sebag, M.: Alors: an algorithm recommender system. Artif. Intell. **244**, 291–314 (2017)
10. Himabindu, T.V., Padmanabhan, V., Pujari, A.K.: Conformal matrix factorization based recommender system. Inf. Sci. (2018)

Author Index

Aguilar-Fernandez, Mario   116
Aguirre-Anaya, Eleazar   333, 377
Alvarado Escoto, Luis Arturo   268
Alvarez-Cedillo, Jesus   116
Álvarez-Pacheco, A. E.   402
Alvarez-Sanchez, Teodoro   116
Amjad, Anam   390
Arenas, Victoria Eugenia Patiño   140
Ávalos, Lorena Galeazzi   420
Avelar-Barragán, José Ángel   281
Ayub, Kashif   390

Becerra, Emanuel   244
Beltrán-García, Pamela   333
Bolaños, Thalia Alejandra Hoyos   140
Brito-Borges, E.   402
Burbano G., Diana C.   128

Corona-Bermudez, Uriel   83
Couder-Castañeda, C.   97

de Alba González, Luis   155
de Oca, Eduardo Yudho Montes   297
de-la-Rosa-Rabago, R.   97

Efren, Gorrostieta   185
Emilio, Vargas-Soto   185
Escamilla-Ambrosio, Ponciano Jorge   309, 333
Eslava, René Tolentino   297
Esquivel-García, Saúl   61

Garay Jimenez, Laura Ivoone   428
García Ortega, Víctor Hugo   48
García, Blanca   319
García, Nayeli Vega   319
García-Gutiérrez, A. E.   402
García-Mendoza, Consuelo Varinia   169
González González, Oscar Arturo   48
Gorrostieta Hurtado, Efren   268
Guzmán, Giovanni   428

Hernández, Viridiana   30
Hernández-Gómez, J. J.   97, 402

Hernández-Uribe, Óscar   61, 155, 256
Huidobro, Cristian Barría   215, 420
Hurtado, Julio Ariel   420

Ibarra, R. Roman   30

Jahan, Muhammad Shah   390
Jorge, Espinosa   185

Kinani, Jean Marie Vianney   1

León, Jacobo Gerardo González   202
López, Roberto   244

Manuel, Ramos-Arreguín Juan   185
Manzano, Julio Eduardo Mejía   140
Márquez, Moisés V.   30
Martínez, Gerardo   30
Matuz-Cruz, Manuel   1
Medina, Braulio   428
Medina, I.   97
Medina-Llinàs, Manel   377
Mena-Zapata, P. A.   402
Menchaca-Méndez, Ricardo   83, 225, 244, 377
Menchaca-Méndez, Rolando   83, 225, 244, 281
Meneses González, Salvador Ricardo   18
Molina-Lozano, Herón   225
Montenegro, Mauro   244
Mújica-Vargas, Dante   1
Muñoz, Miguel Ángel Ortega   140

Novelo-Cruz, R. A.   402

Orozco, Helmer Paz   140
Orozco-del-Castillo, M. G.   97, 402
Ortega, Jesús Carlos Pedraza   268

Pacheco-Rodríguez, Hugo Sebastian   377
Pérez Soberanes, Alina Mariana   48
Pérez, Jaime Vega   319
Pineda, Alejandro   428

Qamar, Usman   390

Ramírez-Cortés, Juan M.   309
Ramos Arreguin, Juan Manuel   268
Ramos-Díaz, Eduardo   1
Rangel, Héctor Rodríguez   297
Riaz, Muhammad Talha   390
Rivera, Miguel Félix Mata   202, 428
Rivero-Ángeles, Mario Eduardo   225
Rodríguez Márquez, Rita Trinidad   18
Rodríguez, Mario Cesar Maya   297
Rodríguez-Molina, Alejandro   169
Rodríguez-Mota, Abraham   309, 333
Rojas-López, Alam Gabriel   169
Romo-Montiel, Edgar   225

Sadok, Djamel Fawzi Hadj   352
Sanchez, Esau Bermudez   352
Soler, Jaime Alvarez   128
Solórzano-Espíndola, Carlos Emiliano   281
Sosa Savedra, Julio César   48

Tovar Arriaga, Saúl   268

Valencia, Margarita Dorado   73
Vázquez, Anna Lucía Díaz   256
Vázquez, José Francisco Uribe   297
Vidal, David Cordero   215
Villarreal-Calva, Ricardo C.   309
Villarreal-Cervantes, Miguel Gabriel   169

Yáñez-Casas, G. A.   97, 402

Printed in the United States
By Bookmasters